PHI[...] ESSENTIAL

ATLAS

GEORGE
PHILIP

World

8-9 World: Northern part
10-11 World: Southern part
12-13 Arctic
14-15 Antarctic

Europe

16-17 Europe: Physical
18-19 Europe: Political

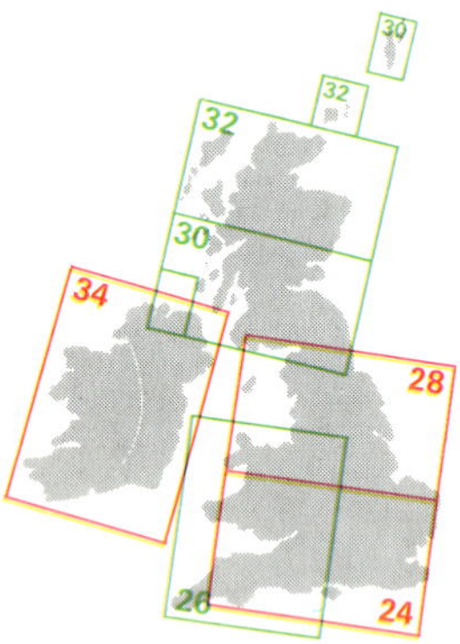

20-21 British Isles: South
22-23 British Isles: North
24-25 Southern England
26-27 Wales and South West England
28-29 Northern England
30-31 Southern Scotland
32-33 Northern Scotland
34-35 Ireland

Edited by
B. M. Willett, Cartographic Editor
David Gaylard
Lilla Prince-Smith
George Philip and Son Ltd., London

Maps prepared by
Cox Cartographic Ltd., and
George Philip Cartographic Services Ltd.,
London under the direction of Alan Poynter.

ISBN 0-540-05582-4

Printed in Italy.

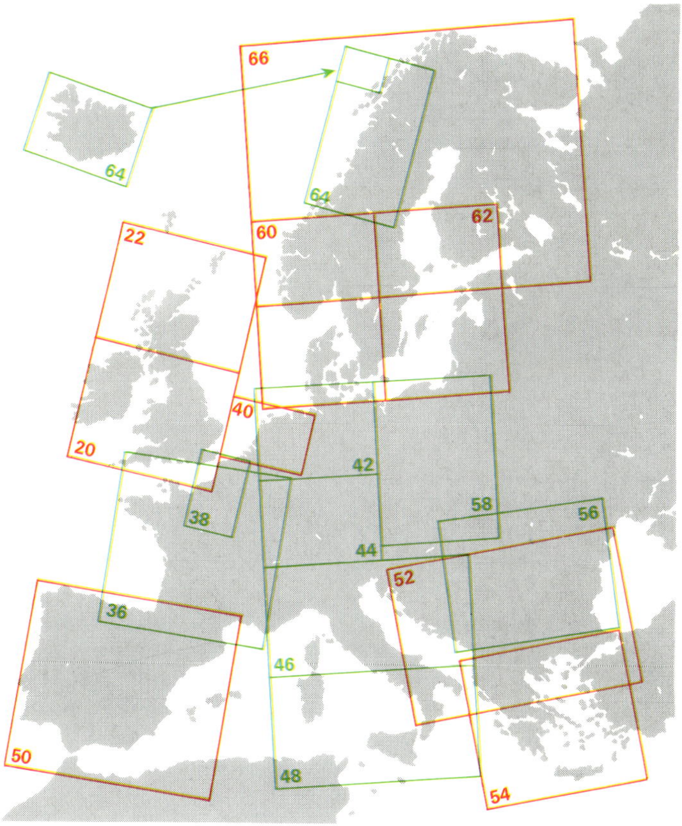
64
66
64
62
60
22
20
40
42
38
58
56
44
52
36
46
50
48
54

36-37 France
38-39 Northern France
40-41 Netherlands
42-43 Germany and the Low Countries
44-45 Alpine Lands
46-47 Northern Italy and Corsica
48-49 Southern Italy and Sardinia
50-51 Spain and Portugal
52-53 Danube Lands
54-55 Greece and Albania
56-57 Romania
58-59 Central Europe
60-61 Southern Scandinavia
62-63 Baltic Lands
64-65 North West Scandinavia and Iceland
66-67 Northern Scandinavia

Asia

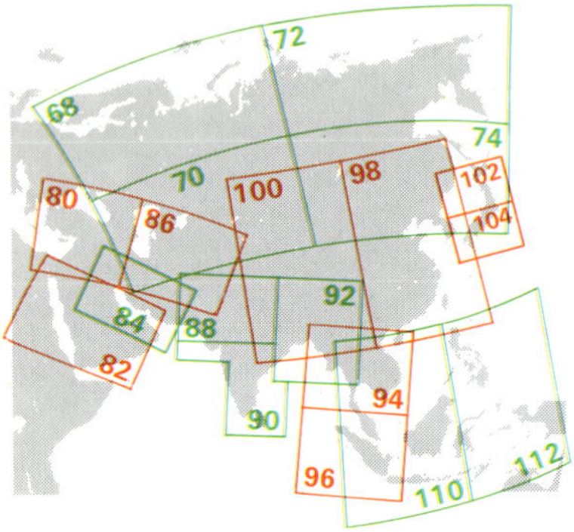
68
70
72
74
80
82
84
86
88
90
92
94
96
98
100
102
104
110
112

68-75 U.S.S.R.
68-69 West
70-71 South West
72-73 North East
74-75 South East and Mongolia

76-77 Asia: Physical
78-79 Asia: Political
80-81 Turkey and the Middle East
82-83 Arabian Peninsula
84-85 The Gulf
86-87 Central Asia and Afghanistan
88-89 Pakistan and North West India
90-91 Central and Southern India, Sri Lanka
92-93 Eastern India, Bangladesh and Burma
94-95 Mainland South East Asia
96-97 The Malay Peninsula
98-99 China: East
100-101 China: West

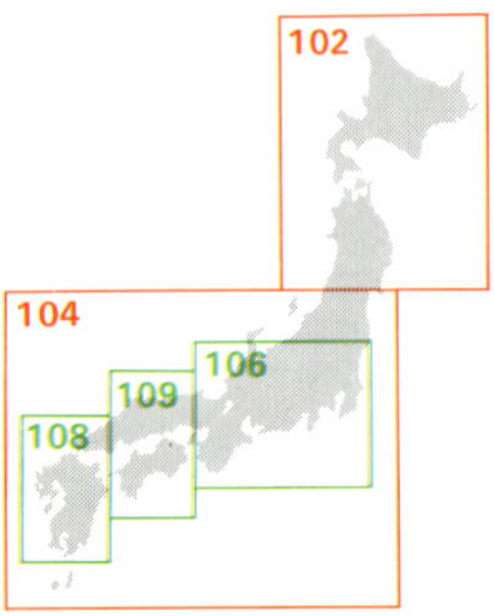
102
104
106
108
109

102-109 Japan
102-103 North
104-105 South
106-107 Tokyo, Kyoto, Osaka
108 Kyushu
109 West Honshu and Shikoku

110-111 Indonesia: West
112-113 Indonesia: East

Australasia

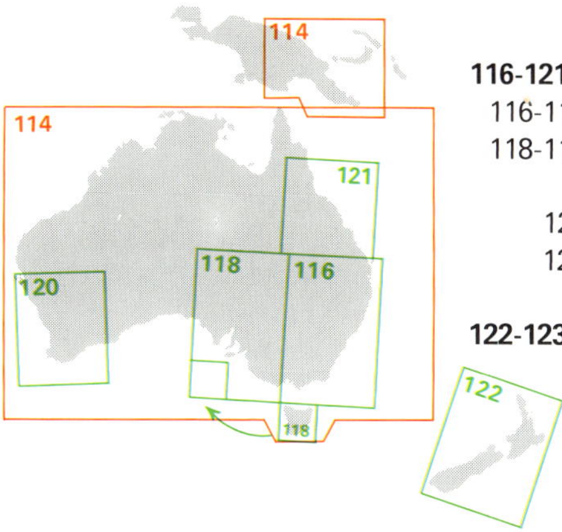

114-115 **Australia, New Zealand and Papua New Guinea**

116-121 **Australia**
116-117 Brisbane, Sydney, Melbourne
118-119 Adelaide, Melbourne, Tasmania
120 Perth
121 North East Queensland

122-123 **New Zealand, Central and South West Pacific**

Africa

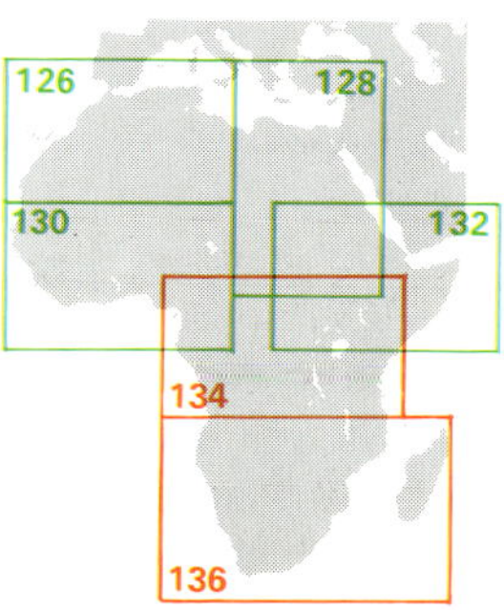

124-137 **Africa**
124 Physical
125 Political
126-127 North West
128-129 North East
130-131 West
132-133 East
134-135 Central
136-137 South

North America

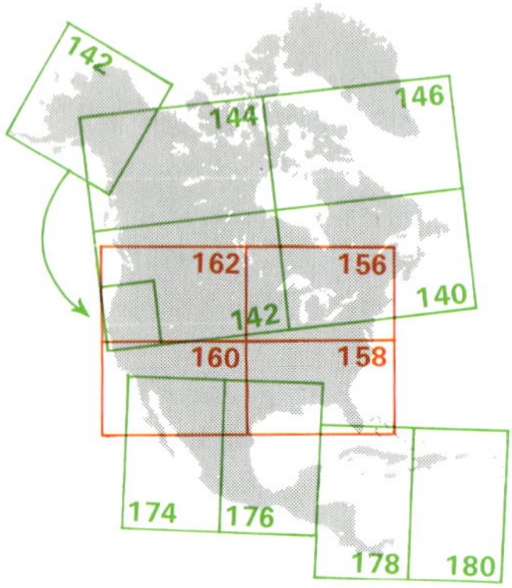

138 **North America: Physical**
139 **North America: Political**

140-155 **Canada**
140-141 South East
142-143 South West and Alaska
144-145 North West
146-147 North East
148-149 Saint Lawrence Estuary
150-151 The Great Lakes
152-153 Southern Saskatchewan and Manitoba
154-155 Southern British Columbia and Alberta

156-173 **U.S.A.**
156-157 North East
158-159 South East
160-161 South West
162-163 North West
164 Boston, New York, Washington
165 Washington, Atlanta
166-167 Upper Mississippi
168-169 Lower Mississippi and Gulf Coast
170 Florida
171 Columbia Basin
172-173 California

174-175 **Mexico: West**
176-177 **Mexico: East**
178-179 **Caribbean: West**
180-181 **Caribbean: East**

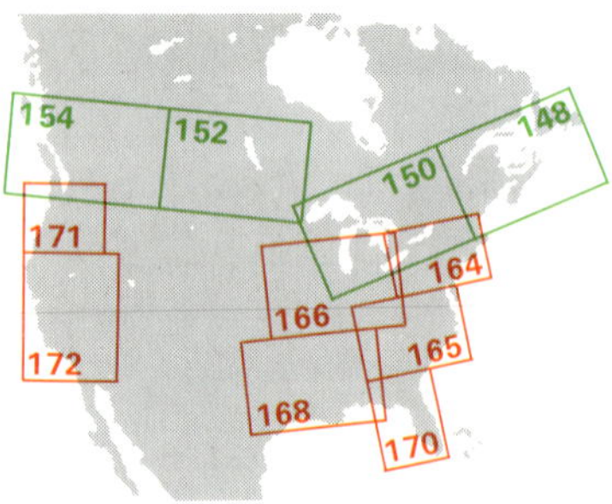

South America

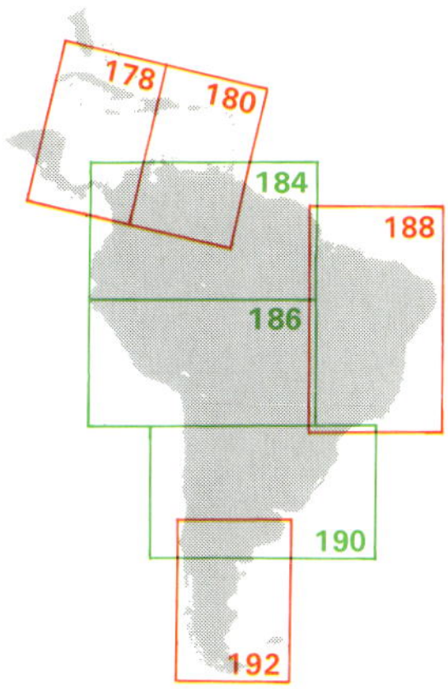

182-192	**South America**
182	Physical
183	Political
184-185	North West
186-187	West
188-189	East
190-191	Central
192	South

Index

Map Symbols

Settlement symbols in order of size

- International boundary
- Internal boundary
- Principal railway
- Principal road
- Canal
- Principal airport
- Tunnel
- Permanent river
- Intermittent river
- Permanent lake
- Intermittent lake
- Marsh
- ▲ 8 848 Altitude above sea level
- ▼ 10 497 Depth below sea level
- *263* Level of lake
- (18) Indicates the adjoining map

As far as possible the de facto situation of international boundaries is shown

Scale note
To the right of each map title there is a number representing the scale of the map for example, 1 : 2 000 000. This means that one centimetre on the map represents 2 million centimetres or 20 kilometres on the ground. Or, if the number is 1 : 40 000 000, one centimetre represents 40 million centimetres or 400 kilometres.

Height and depth colours

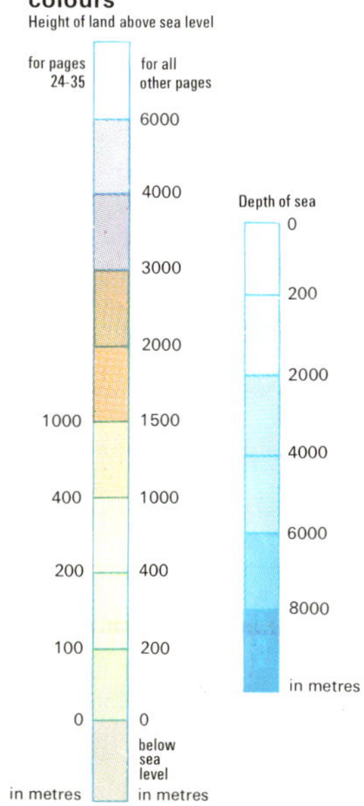

World: Northern Part

Map 8

1:120 000 000

Map 9

World: Southern Part

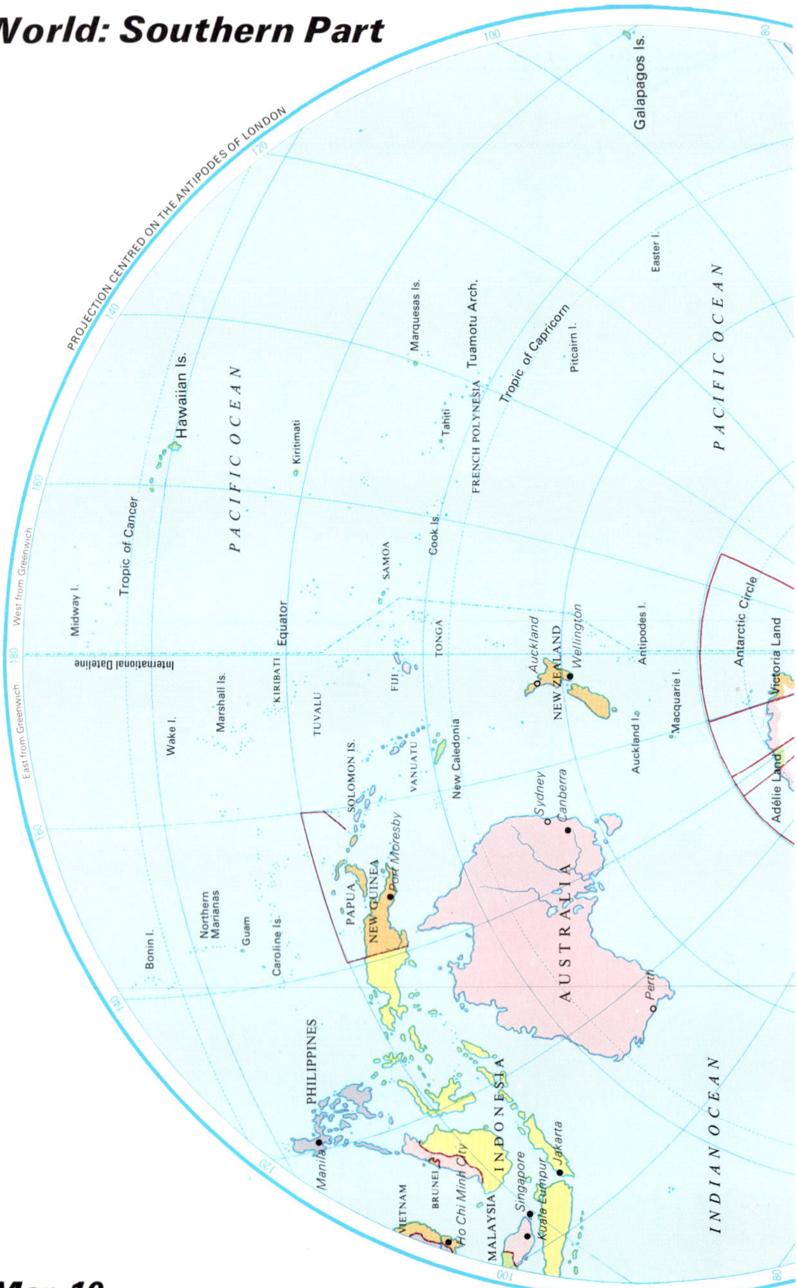

Map 10

Ross Sea
Wilkes Land
Byrd Land
Amundsen Sea
Antarctica
Ellsworth Land
South Pole
Kerguelen
Heard I.
Enderby Land
Weddell Sea
Queen Maud Land
Falkland Is.
Crozet I.
Pr. Edward I.
South Sandwich Is.
South Georgia
Bouvet I.
ATLANTIC OCEAN
Lima
PERU
CHILE
Santiago
BOLIVIA
ARGENTINA
PARAGUAY
Buenos Aires
URUGUAY
Montevideo
BRAZIL
PROJECTION CENTRED ON CAIRO
PROJECTION CENTRED ON SHANGHAI
North Pole
Greenwich
International Dateline
Equator
PACIFIC OCEAN
INDIAN OCEAN
West from Greenwich
East from Greenwich
Capital Cities
TIME ZONES
9.00 6.00
Time zone in hours fast (+) or slow (−) of Greenwich Mean Time
Standard Time not the Zone hour
No Official Time
1:120 000 000

Map 11

Arctic

Map 12

1:42 000 000
Arctic Explorers
Cook 1778
Franklin 1826-47
McClure 1850-53
Nansen ("Fram") 1893-96
Sverdrup 1902
Peary 1892-1906
Amundsen 1903-6 & 1926
Bernier 1906-1913
Peary 1908-9
Knud Rasmussen 1912
Stefansson 1914-15
Byrd 1926 (by air)
Wilkins 1928 (by air)
Lindsay 1934
Papanin (Drift of Soviet Expedition) 1937-8
Sedov 1937-40
Knuth (Danish Pearyland Expedition) 1948 49
Skate (Nuclear submarine) 1959
Manhattan (Tanker) 1969
Seas open all year
Extreme limits of drift-ice
Seas covered by pack-ice in Spring
Seas permanently covered by pack-ice
Ice-caps and permanent ice shelf
Progress of Exploration
Coasts explored before 1800
between 1800 & 1850
between 1850 & 1900
since 1900
Highest latitudes reached by explorers with date
Byrd 1926
GREENLAND
(To Denmark)
Greenland Sea
Norwegian Sea
Barents Sea
Kara Sea
Baffin Bay
Davis Str.
Denmark Strait
North Sea
Baltic Sea
Gulf of Bothnia
White Sea
ATLANTIC OCEAN
BRITISH ISLES
ICELAND
Svalbard
Franz Joseph Land
Novaya Zemlya
Ellesmere I.
Devon I.
Baffin I.
FINLAND
SWEDEN
NORWAY
POLAND
GERMANY
EUROPE
USSR
Leningrad
Moscow
London
Berlin
Arctic Circle
POLE

Map 13

Antarctic

Map 14

Map 15

1:42 000 000

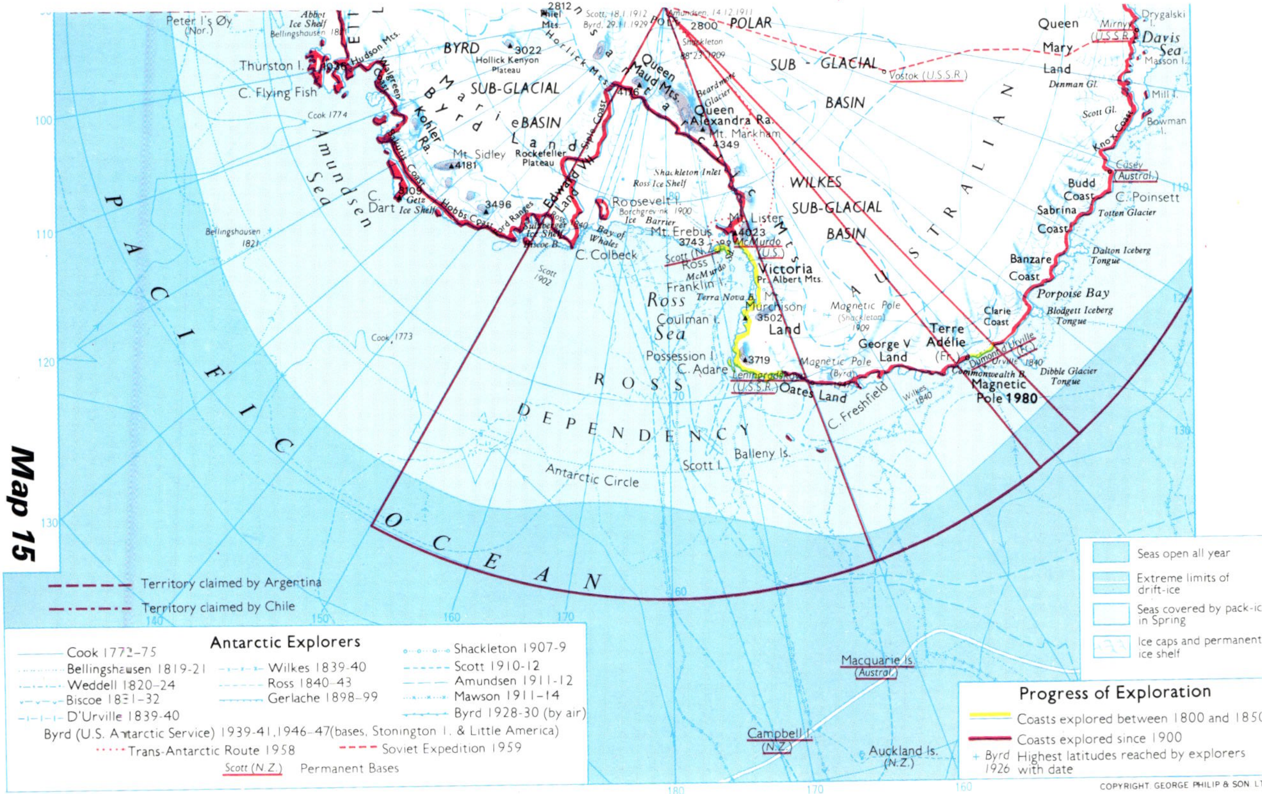

Europe: Physical

Map 16

1:24 000 000
North Cape
Nordkinn
L. Inari
Mts.
Lapland
Torne
Kola Peninsula
White Sea
Mezen
Ural Mountains
Bothnia
Onega
N. Dvina
Finland
L. Onega
L. Ladoga
Svir
European Plain
Kama
G. of Finland
Neva
Rybinsk Res.
L. Chudskoye
Volga
SEA
G. of Riga
Central Russian Uplands
Volga Uplands
Obshchi Syrt
W. Dvina
Oka
Niemen
Don
Pripyat Marshes
Pripyat (Pripet)
Ural
Tsimlyansk Res.
Ukraine
Dnepr (Dnieper)
CASPIAN SEA
-28
2655
Tatra
Carpathians
Dnestr (Dniester)
Bug
Manych
Prut
Sea of Azov
Plain of Hungary
Kuban
Terek
Mures
Crimea
Tisza
Transylvanian Alps
Danube
Str. of Kerch
Caucasus
Elbrus 5633
Wallachia
Kura
Morava
BLACK SEA
2211
Rion
Balkans
Araks
Rhodope
Balkan Peninsula
Bosporus
5165
Ararat
L. Van
L. Urmia
S. of Marmara
Ida 1766
Kizil Irmak
Tigris
Pindus
Aegean Sea
L. Tuz
Anatolia
Erciyas 3770
Taurus
Euphrates
Morea
Is.
5121
C. Matapan
Crete
Cyprus
1951
COPYRIGHT GEORGE PHILIP & SON LTD

Map 17

Europe: Political

Map 18

1:24 000 000

Map 19

C. Malin
I. Tory
Portrush
North Channel
22
Aran I.
Derryveagh Mts.
Letterkenny
Lifford
Londonderry
Coleraine
Antrim Mts.
Ballymena
Larne
Stranraer
Wigtown
Donegal
NORTHERN IRELAND
Antrim
Bangor
Belfast
L. Neagh
Mull of Galloway
Donegal Bay
Killala Bay
Bundoran
L. Erne
Omagh
Blackwater
Lisburn
Erris Hd.
Sligo
Enniskillen
Armagh
Downpatrick
Dundrum
ISLE OF MAN
Douglas
Ballina
Upper L. Erne
Monaghan
Clones
Newry
Mourne Mts.
L. Conn
Achill I.
Clare I.
Castlebar
Leitrim
Carrick-on-Shannon
Cavan
Dundalk
Greenore
Westport
Longford
L. Mask
Ceanannus Mor
An Uaimh
Drogheda
IRISH S
Roscommon
Connemara
L. Corrib
Ree
Mullingar
Boyne
Balbriggan
Athlone
IRELAND
Galway
Athenry
Galway Bay
Dublin
Tullamore
(Baile Atha Cliath)
Dun Laoghaire
Anglesey
Holyhead
Liffey
Birr
Naas
Bray
Llangefni
Kildare
Port Laoise
Athy
Caernarfon Bay
L. Derg
Wicklow Mts.
Wicklow
Ennis
Nenagh
Carlow
Pwllheli
Loop Hd.
Kilrush
Limerick
Thurles
Kilkenny
Arklow
Shannon
Golden Vale
Listowel
Tipperary
Enniscorthy
Cardigan Bay
Rath Luirc
Carrick-on-Suir
Clonmel
Tralee
New Ross
Wexford
Mallow
Blackwater
Fermoy
Waterford
Rosslare
Macgillycuddy's Reeks
Cahirciveen
1040
Killarney
Dungarvan
Youghal
Carnsore Pt.
St. George's Channel
Fishguard
Cardigan
Blarney
Cork
Lee
Cobh
St. David's Hd.
Tywi
Bandon
Kinsale
Cork Harbour
Haverfordwest
Carmarthen
Bantry
Castletown Bere
Llanelli
Milford Haven
Pembroke
C. Clear
Bristol C
Lundy I.
Hartland Point
Bude
St. Austell
Devonport
Truro
Camborne
Penzance
Falmouth
Land's End
Scilly Is.
Lizard
10
8
50

Map 20

British Isles: South

1:4 000 000

23

36

British Isles: North

Map 22

1:4 000 000

Map 23

Southern England

26 28 26 27

1:2 000 000

29

Map 25

Wales and South West England

28

35

Map 26

1:2 000 000

Map 27

Northern England

Map 28

1:2 000 000

NORTH SEA
Peterlee
Hartlepool
Stockton
Billingham
Tees Bay
CLEVELAND
Redcar
(Teeside)
Middlesbrough
Thornaby on Tees
Cleveland
Esk
Whitby
N. York Moors
Scarborough
Pickering
Thirsk
Filey
Rye
Malton
York Wolds
Flamborough Hd.
Bridlington
Driffield
York
Wharfe
Derwent
Hull
Hornsea
Beverley
Holderness
Selby
Ouse
HUMBERSIDE
Hull
Withernsea
Aire
Castleford
Barton-upon-Humber
Pontefract
Goole
Immingham
Humber
Spurn Hd.
Don
Greater Grimsby
Scunthorpe
Cleethorpes
Doncaster
Brigg
Trent
Lincoln Wolds
Rotherham
Gainsborough
Louth
Mablethorpe
Market Rasen
Alford
Worksop
East Retford
Lincoln
Horncastle
NOTTS
LINCOLN
Mansfield
Sherwood
Skegness
Sutton-in-Ashfield
Newark
Witham
Alfreton
Heanor
Forest
Ilkeston
Sleaford
Boston
The Wash
Cromer
Hunstanton
Wells
Nottingham
Grantham
Beeston
Long Eaton
The Fens
Sandringham
North Walsham
Fakenham
Bourne
Spalding
Loughborough
Nene
Gt. Ouse
Kings Lynn
Bure
The Broads
Great Yarmouth
Melton Mowbray
Coalville
Oakham
Welland
Wisbech
NORFOLK
Norwich
LEICESTER
Leicester
Stamford
Peterborough
Downham Market
Wymondham
Yare
Lowestoft
Hinckley
Fletton
March
Breckland
Beccles
Little Ouse
Corby
Rugby
East from Greenwich
55
54
53
0
1
25

29

Southern Scotland

Map 30

1:2 000 000

33

28

Northern Scotland

30

Map 32

1:2 000 000

30

31

Ireland

ATLANTIC
OCEAN
NORTHERN IRELAND
IRELAND
Londonderry
Belfast
Lisburn
Bangor
Newtownards
Antrim
Ballymena
Larne
Carrickfergus
Coleraine
Portrush
Ballycastle
Ballymoney
Limavady
Strabane
Omagh
Cookstown
Magherafelt
Dungannon
Armagh
Portadown
Banbridge
Downpatrick
Newry
Newcastle
Enniskillen
Dundalk
Drogheda
Dublin
Sligo
Donegal
Letterkenny
Killybegs
Bundoran
Ballina
Westport
Castlebar
Athlone
Mullingar
Longford
Roscommon
Tuam
Clifden
Lough Neagh
Mourne Mts.
Sperrin Mts.
DONEGAL
LEITRIM
SLIGO
CAVAN
MONAGHAN
LOUTH
MEATH
WESTMEATH
LONGFORD
ROSCOMMON
MAYO
GALWAY
CONNACHT
Donegal Bay
Lough Swilly
Rathlin I.
Giant's Causeway
Malin Hd.
Tory I.
Aran I.
Achill I.
Clew Bay
Dundalk Bay

1:2 000 000

Map 35

France

Map 36

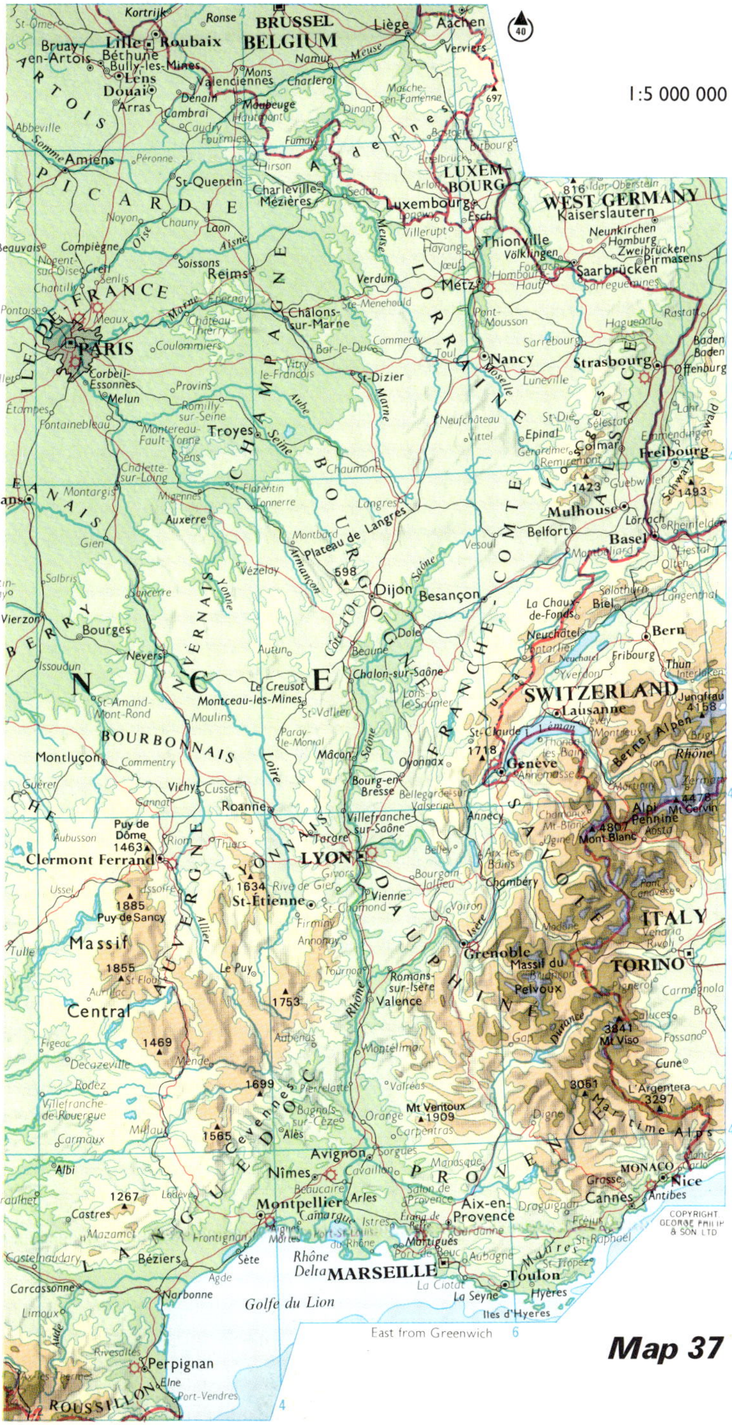
1:5 000 000
BRUSSEL
BELGIUM
Kortrijk
Ronse
Liège
Aachen
Verviers
Lille
Roubaix
Bruay-en-Artois
Béthune
Bully-les-Mines
Lens
Douai
Arras
ARTOIS
Valenciennes
Mons
Namur
Charleroi
Meuse
Denain
Cambrai
Maubeuge
Dinant
Marche-en-Famenne
Abbeville
Somme
Amiens
Péronne
St-Quentin
Hirson
Ardennes
Bastogne
LUXEMBOURG
Luxembourg
Esch
Charleville-Mézières
Sedan
PICARDIE
Noyon
Chauny
Laon
Aisne
Oise
Beauvais
Compiègne
Soissons
Reims
Verdun
Thionville
Völklingen
WEST GERMANY
Kaiserslautern
Neunkirchen
Homburg
Zweibrücken
Pirmasens
Saarbrücken
Sarreguemines
Metz
LORRAINE
Chantilly
Senlis
Creil
ÎLE DE FRANCE
Pontoise
Meaux
Marne
Épernay
Château-Thierry
Châlons-sur-Marne
Ste-Menehould
Pont-à-Mousson
Haguenau
Rastatt
Baden-Baden
PARIS
Coulommiers
CHAMPAGNE
Bar-le-Duc
Commercy
Toul
Nancy
Sarrebourg
Strasbourg
Offenburg
Corbeil-Essonnes
Melun
Provins
Vitry-le-François
St-Dizier
Lunéville
Moselle
ALSACE
Étampes
Fontainebleau
Romilly-sur-Seine
Aube
Montereau-Fault-Yonne
Troyes
Seine
Sens
Neufchâteau
Vittel
Épinal
St-Dié
Sélestat
Colmar
Emmendingen
Freibourg
Schwarzwald
Gérardmer
Remiremont
Chaumont
1423
Guebwiller
1493
Châlette-sur-Loing
Montargis
Orléans
Migennes
St-Florentin
Tonnerre
Langres
Mulhouse
Lörrach
Rheinfelden
Basel
Belfort
Auxerre
Montbard
Plateau de Langres
Vesoul
Montbéliard
Liestal
Olten
Gien
Armançon
598
Vézelay
Yonne
Dijon
Saône
Besançon
Solothurn
Langenthal
Biel
La Chaux-de-Fonds
Neuchâtel
Bern
Vierzon
BERRY
Bourges
Sancerre
NIVERNAIS
Côte d'Or
Dole
Nevers
Autun
Beaune
BOURGOGNE
FRANCHE-COMTÉ
Pontarlier
Fribourg
Thun
Interlaken
Issoudun
Chalon-sur-Saône
Le Creusot
Montceau-les-Mines
Lons-le-Saunier
Jura
Yverdon
SWITZERLAND
Lausanne
Jungfrau
4158
Vevey
Montreux
Berner Alpen
Brig
Rhône
St-Amand-Mont-Rond
Moulins
Paray-le-Monial
Mâcon
St-Claude
L. Léman
1718
Genève
Thonon-les-Bains
Annemasse
Sion
Zermatt
BOURBONNAIS
Montluçon
Commentry
Vichy
Cusset
Loire
Oyonnax
Bourg-en-Bresse
Bellegarde-sur-Valserine
Guéret
Gannat
Roanne
Villefranche-sur-Saône
Tarare
Annecy
SAVOIE
Chamonix
Mt-Blanc
Ugine
4807
Mont Blanc
Alpi Pennine
4478
Mt Cervin
Aosta
Aubusson
Puy de Dôme
1463
Clermont Ferrand
Riom
Thiers
LYONNAIS
LYON
Givors
Rive de Gier
1634
St-Étienne
St-Chamond
Vienne
Bourgoin-Jallieu
Belley
Aix-les-Bains
Chambéry
Ussel
Issoire
1885
Puy de Sancy
AUVERGNE
Allier
Firminy
Annonay
DAUPHINÉ
Voiron
Isère
Grenoble
Modane
ITALY
Venaria
Rivoli
TORINO
Tulle
Massif
Central
1855
St Flour
Aurillac
Le Puy
1753
Tournon
Romans-sur-Isère
Valence
Rhône
Massif du Pelvoux
Briançon
Pinerolo
Carmagnola
Durance
3841
Mt Viso
Saluzzo
Bra
Fossano
Cuneo
1469
Figeac
Decazeville
Mende
Aubenas
Montélimar
Gap
Rodez
1699
Pierrelatte
Valréas
3051
L'Argentera
3297
Villefranche-de-Rouergue
Cévennes
Bagnols-sur-Cèze
Orange
Mt Ventoux
1909
Carpentras
Digne
Maritime Alps
Millau
1565
Alès
LANGUEDOC
Carmaux
Avignon
Sorgues
PROVENCE
Manosque
Albi
Nîmes
Cavaillon
MONACO
Monte Carlo
Nice
Grasse
Cannes
Antibes
Graulhet
1267
Lodève
Beaucaire
Arles
Salon-de-Provence
Aix-en-Provence
Draguignan
Castres
Montpellier
Camargue
Istres
Étang de Berre
Gardanne
Fréjus
St-Raphaël
Mazamet
Frontignan
Aigues-Mortes
Port-St-Louis-du-Rhône
Martigues
Castelnaudary
Béziers
Sète
Rhône Delta
MARSEILLE
Port-de-Bouc
Aubagne
Maures
St-Tropez
Agde
Toulon
Carcassonne
Narbonne
La Ciotat
La Seyne
Hyères
Limoux
Golfe du Lion
Îles d'Hyères
Aude
Rivesaltes
Perpignan
Elne
Port-Vendres
ROUSSILLON
East from Greenwich
COPYRIGHT GEORGE PHILIP & SON LTD

Map 37

Northern France

Map 38

1:2 000 000

42
37
36

Netherlands

1:2 000 000

61

42

Map 41

Germany and the Low Countries

1:5 000 000

Map 43

Alpine Lands

42

37

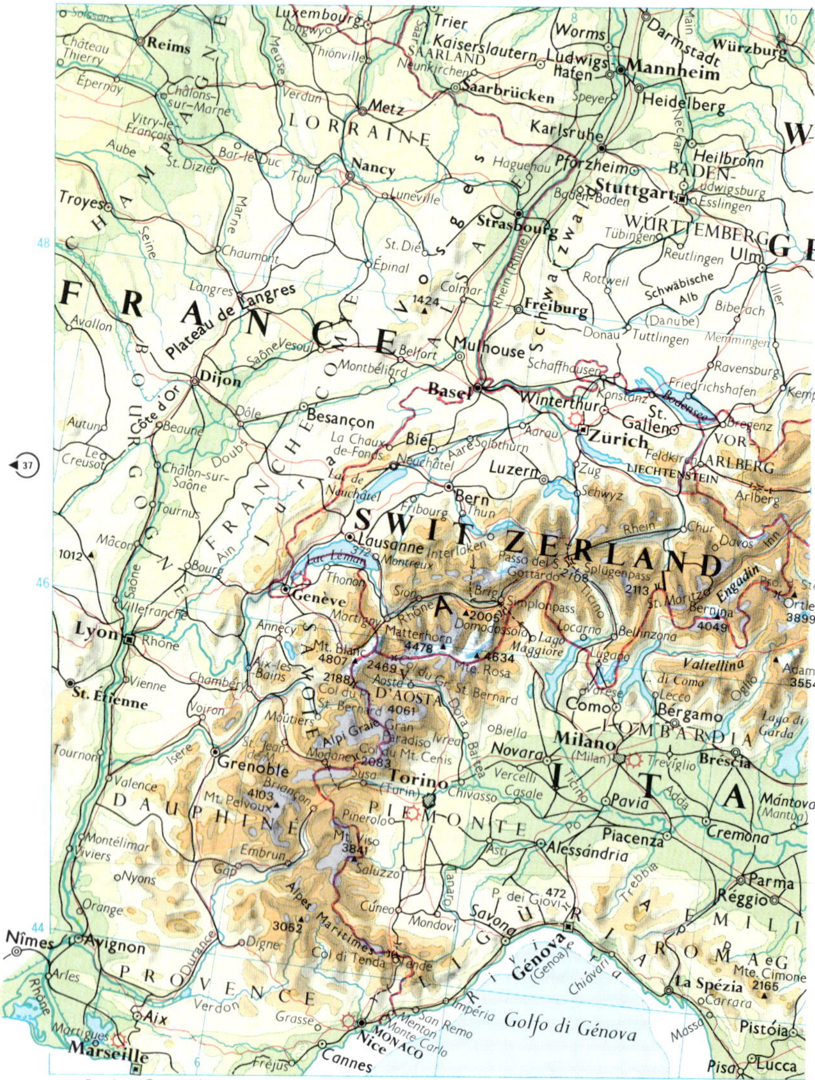

46

Map 44

1:5 000 000

43

59

52

Northern Italy and Corsica

Map 46

1:5 000 000

AUSTRIA
HUNGARY
YUGOSLAVIA
HRVATSKA
BOSNA I HERCEGOVINA
SLOVENIJA
ADRIATIC SEA
Golfo di Venézia
45
52
49
Drave
Villach
Carniche
Triglav
2863
FRIULI VENEZIA GIULIA
Kobarid (Caporetto)
Klagenfurt
Karawanken
Bleiburg
Maribor
Drava
Varaždin
Celje
Údine
Tagliamento
Ljubljana
Sava
Isonzo
Gorizia
Trieste
Kras
Cerknica
Postojna
Kočevje
Koper
Istra
Rijeka (Fiume)
Kupa
Karlovac
Zagreb
Bjelovar
Sisak
Sava
Novska
Nagykanizsa
Kaposvár
Kapos
Szekszárd
Pécs
Mohács
Drava
Osijek
Vinkovci
Brod
Bosanska Gradiška
Odžak
Bosna
Brčko
Tuzla
Tešanj
Una
Banja Luka
Bihać
Sana
Vrbas
Rovinj
Pula (Pola)
Rt. Kamenjak
Krk
Kvarner
Cres
Lošinj
Kvarnerić
Senj
Kapela
Velebit Planina
Gospić
Kremen
1591
Pag
Gračac
Unac
Sanica
Travnik
Dugi Otok
Zadar
Dinara Planina
1913
Troglav
Dalmacija
Šibenik
Split
Sarajevo
Konjic
Neretva
Mostar
Brač
Hvar
Vis
Stolac
Korčula
Lastovo
Dubrovnik
Trebinje
Hercegnovi
Palagruža (Yugoslavia)
1224
Pésaro
Fano
Senigállia
Ancona
Loreto
MARCHE
Macerata
Fabriano
Civitanova
San Benedetto
Monti Vettore
2478
Ascoli Piceno
Téramo
Gran Sasso
2914
Pescara
Chieti
L'Aquila
Salto
ABRUZZI
Ortona
Lanciano
Mt. Amaro
2795
Vasto
Appennini
Térmoli
Sannicandro
Monte Gargano
1056
Monte S. Ángelo
MOLISE
S. Severo
Campobasso
Frosinone
Fóggia
G. di Manfredónia
Latina
Fondi
Sabáudia
Terracina
Gaeta
Garigliano
Volturno
Cerignola
Barletta
Trani
Molfetta
Ofanto
Andria
Corato
Bari
Benevento
Caserta
Aversa
CAMPANIA
Ischia
Vesuvio
1277
Avellino
Nocera
Spinazzola
Monopoli
Putignano
PUGLIA
Matera
Napoli (Naples)
Torre Annunziata
Capri
Sorrento
Castellammare
Salerno
Sele
Éboli
Potenza
BASILICATA
Taranto
Francavilla
Bríndisi
Lecce
14
16
18
42
44
46
COPYRIGHT GEORGE PHILIP & SON. LTD

Southern Italy and Sardinia

46

127

Map 48

1:5 000 000

Map 49

Spain and Portugal

Map 50

1:6 000 000

36

127

Danube Lands

Map 52

1:6 000 000

57

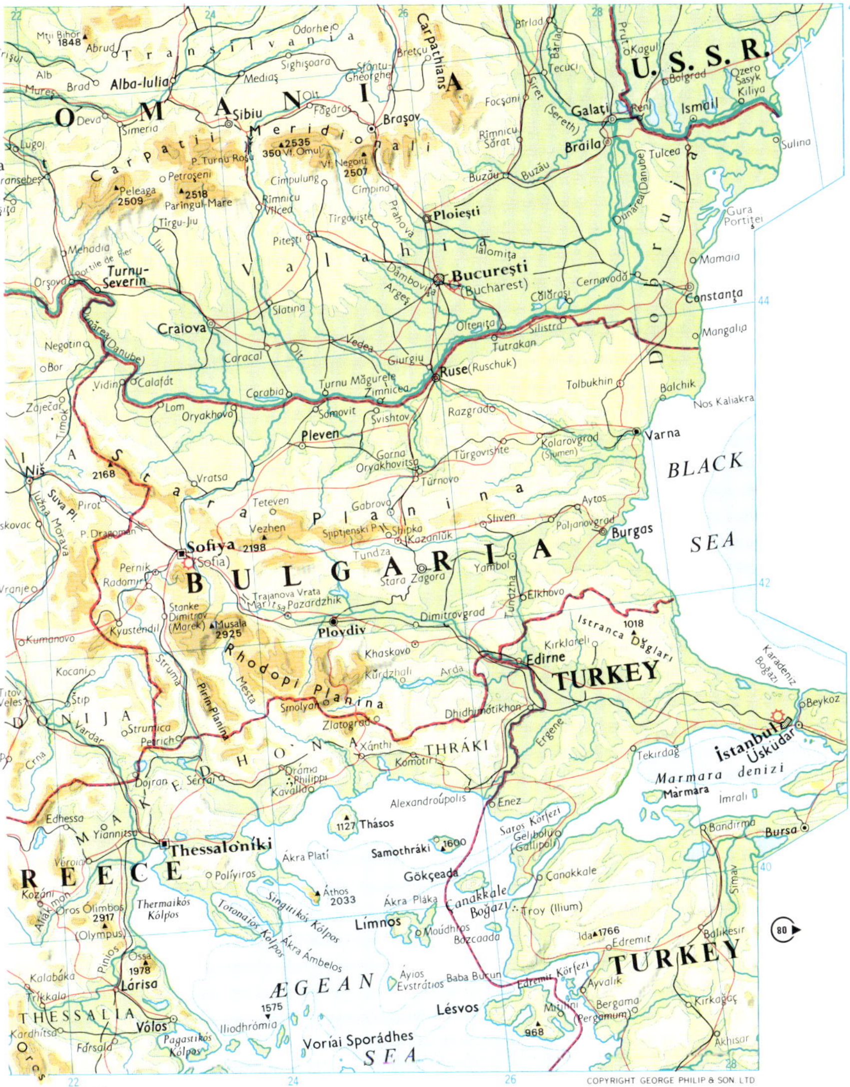

80

54

Map 53

Greece and Albania

Map 54

1:5 000 000

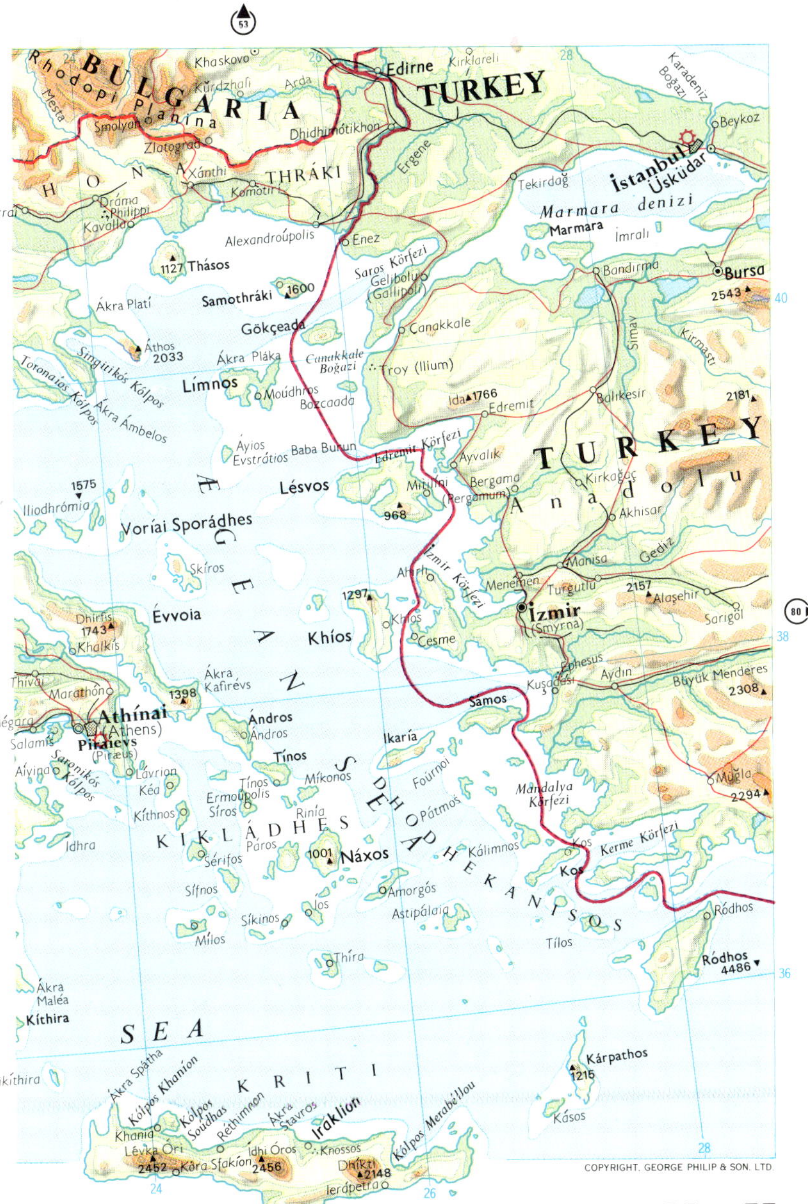

Map 55

Romania

58

59

52

Map 56

1:5 000 000

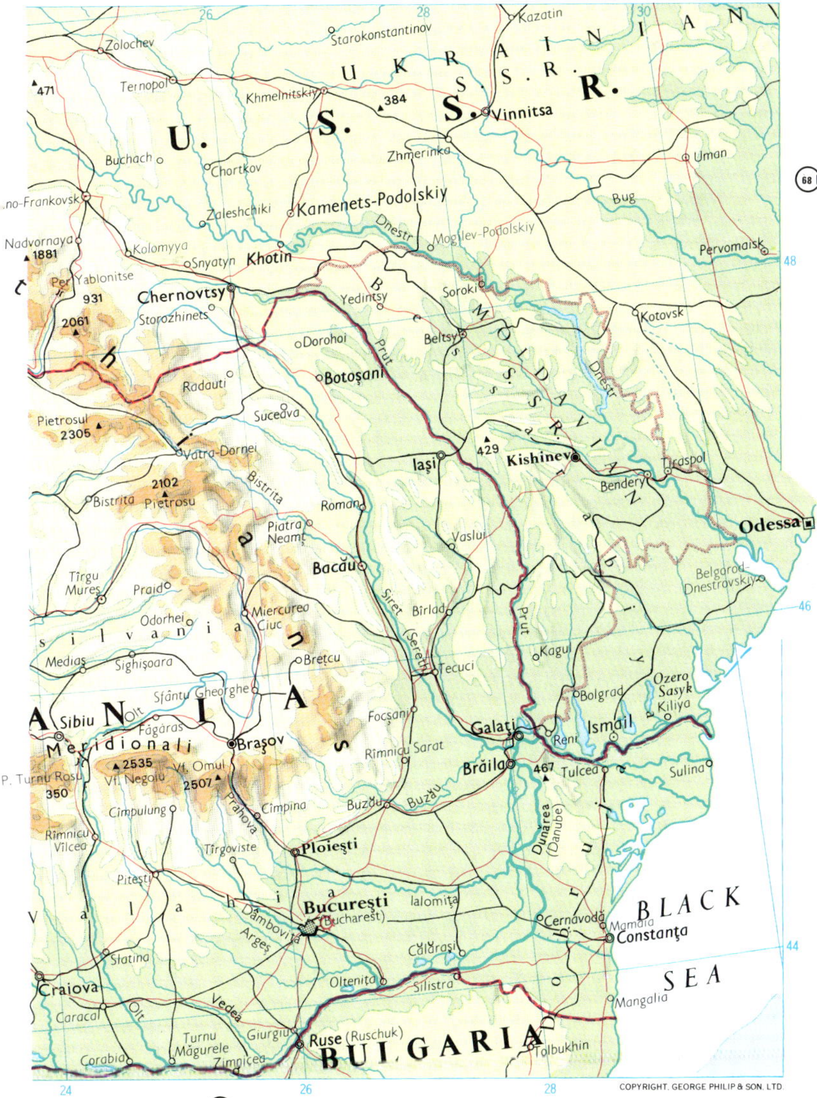

68

53

Central Europe

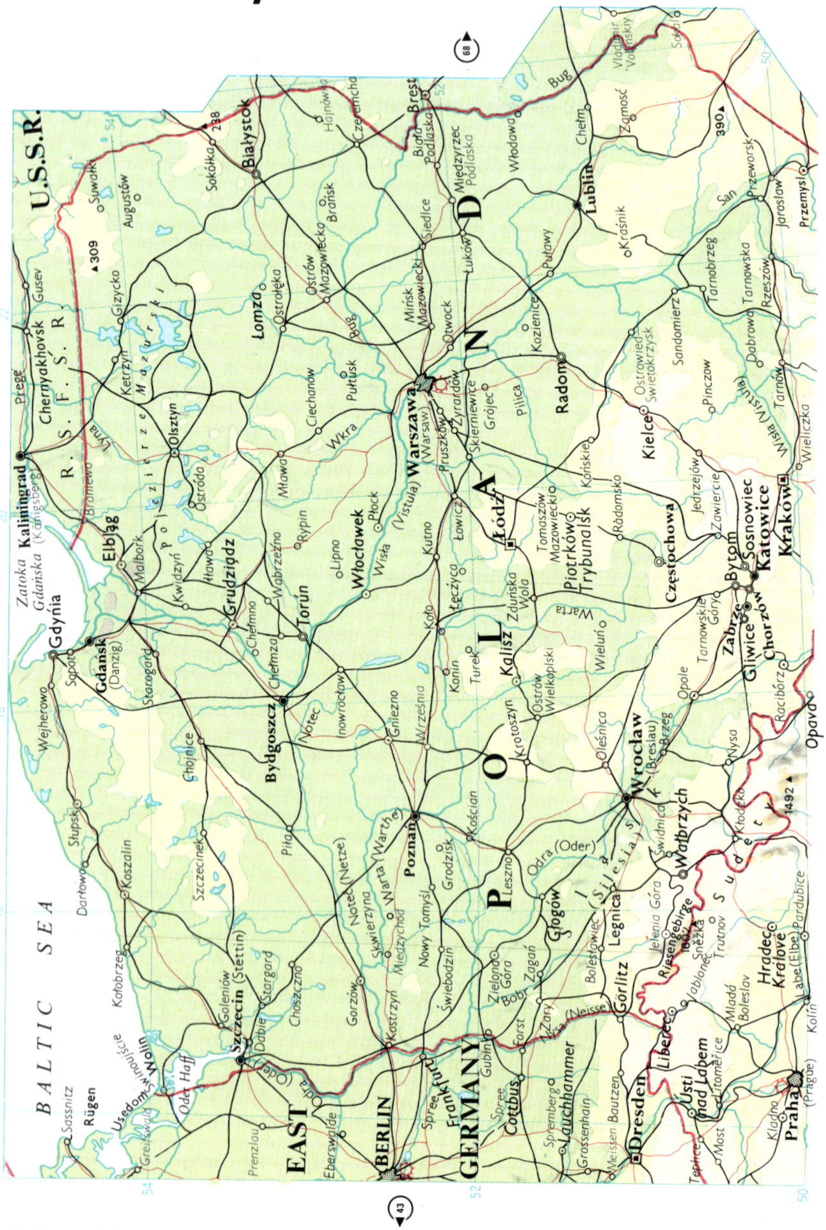

Map 58

1:5 000 000

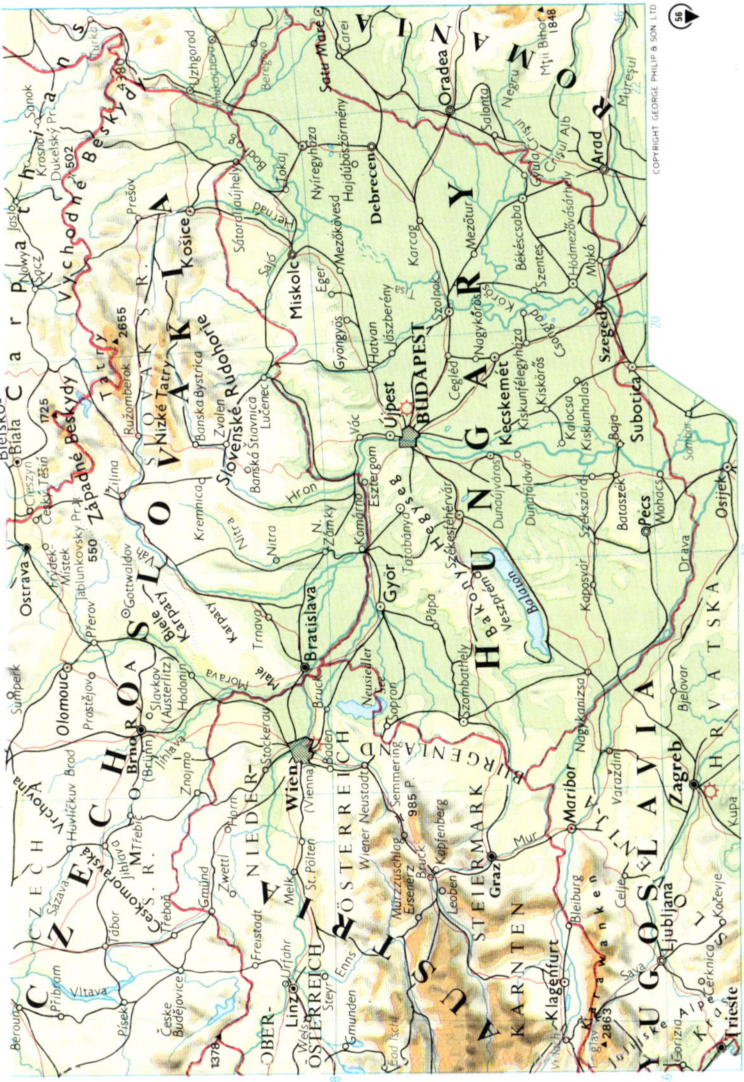

56
52
45

Map 59

Southern Scandinavia

Map 60

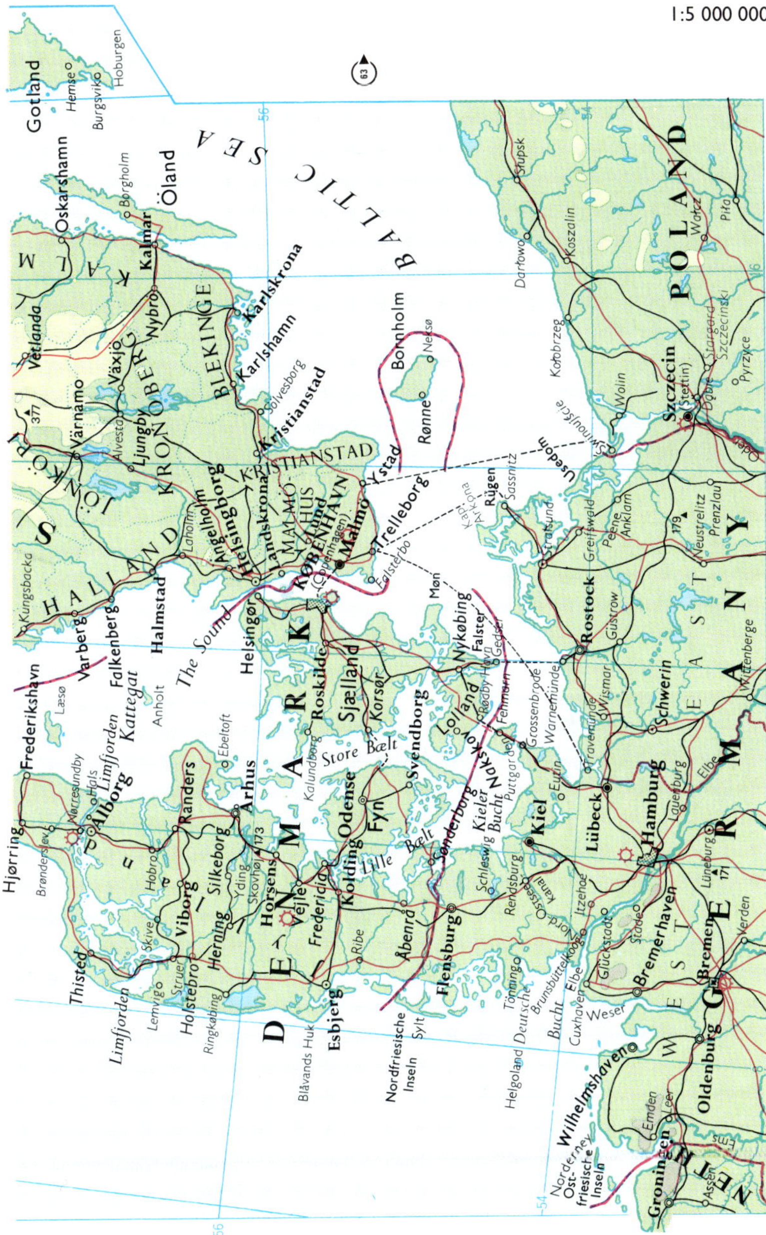
1:5 000 000
BALTIC SEA
DENMARK
GERMANY
POLAND
SWEDEN
HALLAND
KRONOBERG
BLEKINGE
KALMAR
JÖNKÖPING
KRISTIANSTAD
MALMÖHUS
Gotland
Öland
Bornholm
Rügen
Usedom
Fyn
Sjælland
Lolland
Falster
Møn
Kattegat
The Sound
Store Bælt
Lille Bælt
Limfjorden
Kieler Bucht
Deutsche Bucht
Nordfriesische Inseln
Ostfriesische Inseln
København (Copenhagen)
Malmö
Helsingborg
Helsingør
Lund
Landskrona
Trelleborg
Ystad
Kristianstad
Karlshamn
Karlskrona
Kalmar
Växjö
Ljungby
Halmstad
Falkenberg
Varberg
Kungsbacka
Oskarshamn
Vetlanda
Värnamo
Rønne
Frederikshavn
Hjørring
Ålborg
Randers
Århus
Viborg
Silkeborg
Herning
Holstebro
Thisted
Horsens
Vejle
Fredericia
Kolding
Esbjerg
Ribe
Odense
Svendborg
Nykøbing
Korsør
Roskilde
Sønderborg
Åbenrå
Flensburg
Schleswig
Rendsburg
Kiel
Lübeck
Hamburg
Bremerhaven
Bremen
Oldenburg
Wilhelmshaven
Emden
Groningen
Cuxhaven
Rostock
Wismar
Schwerin
Stralsund
Greifswald
Szczecin (Stettin)
Świnoujście
Koszalin
Słupsk
Neubrandenburg
East from Greenwich
COPYRIGHT GEORGE PHILIP & SON LTD

Map 61

Baltic Lands

1:5 000 000

68

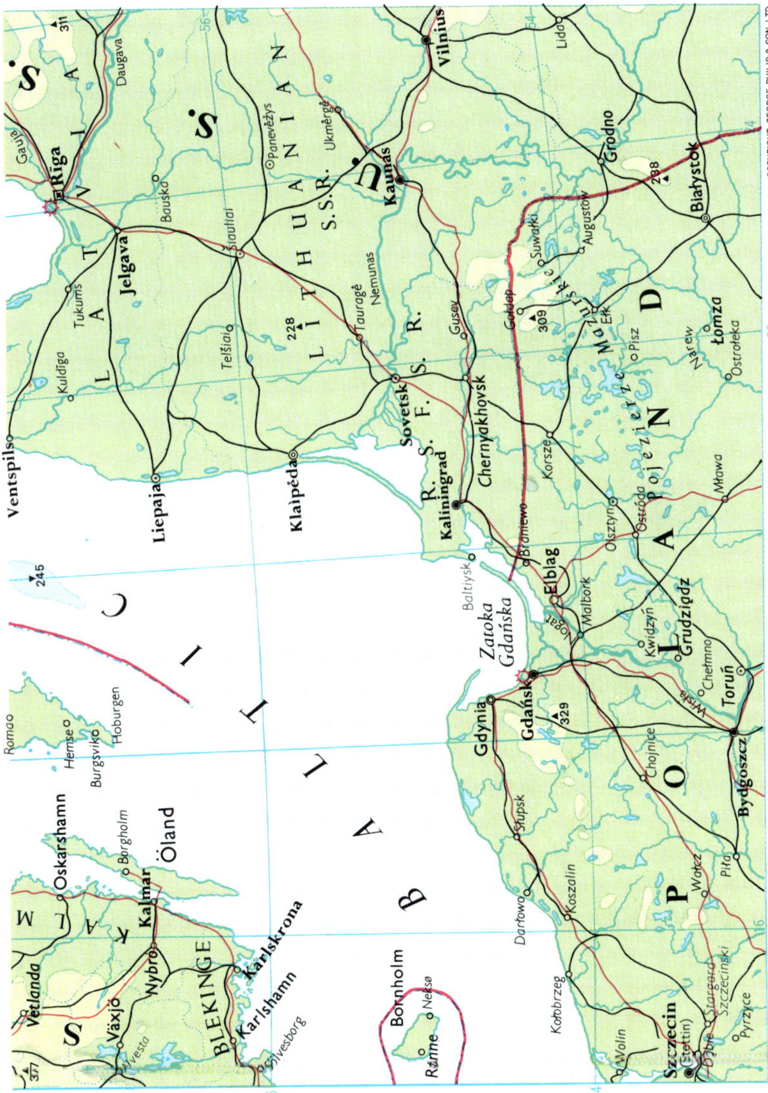

61

58

Map 63

North West Scandinavia and Iceland

Map 64

1:5 000 000

66

60

Map 65

Northern Scandinavia

Map 66

1:10 000 000

Map 67

U.S.S.R.: West

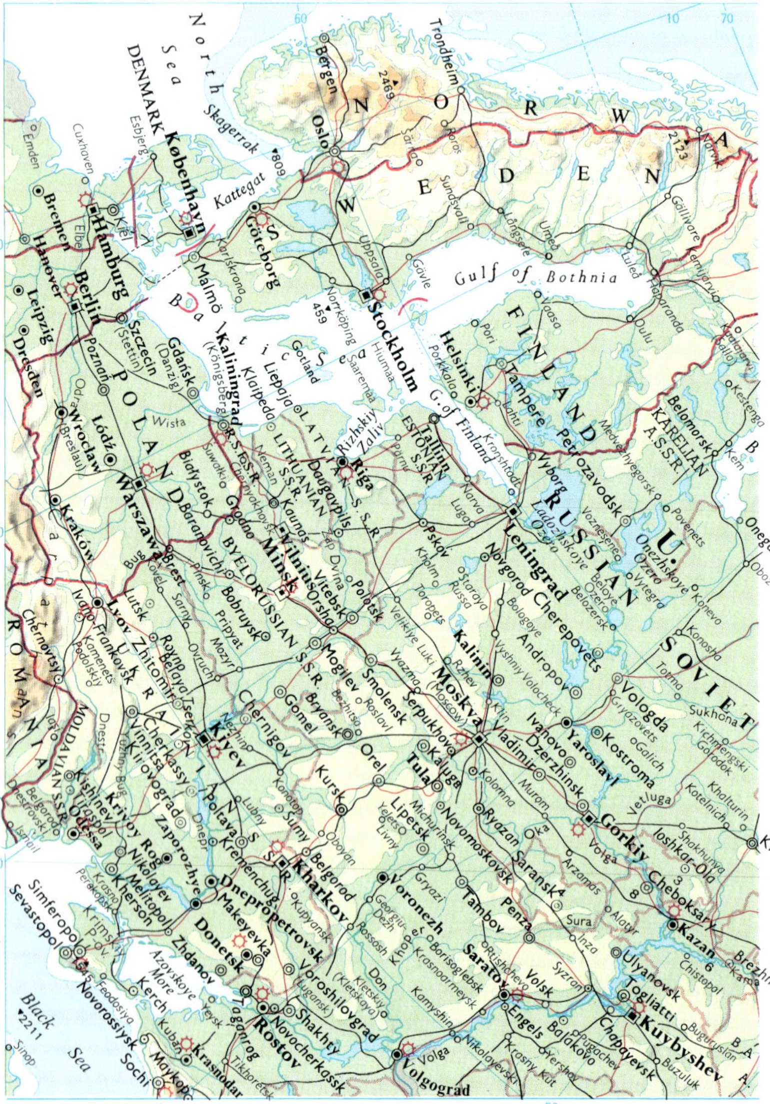

58
57
70

Map 68

1:20 000 000

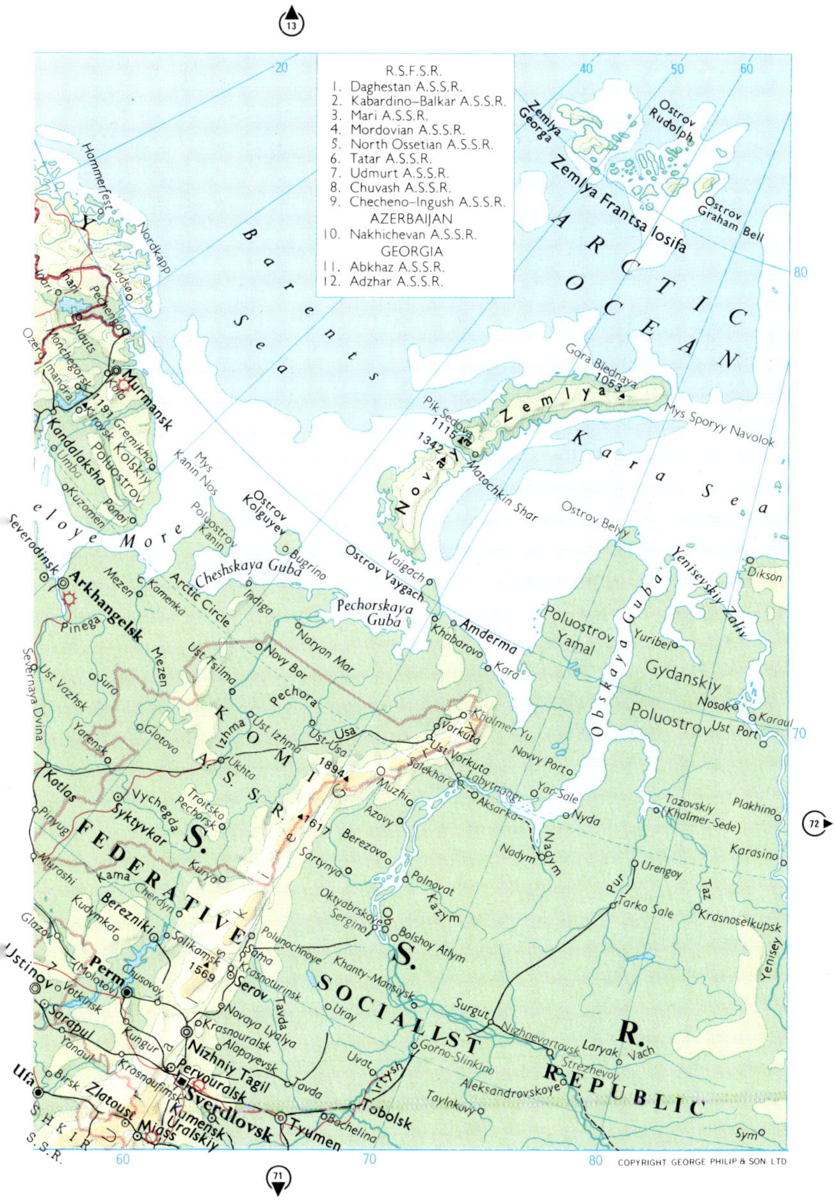

Map 69

U.S.S.R.: South West

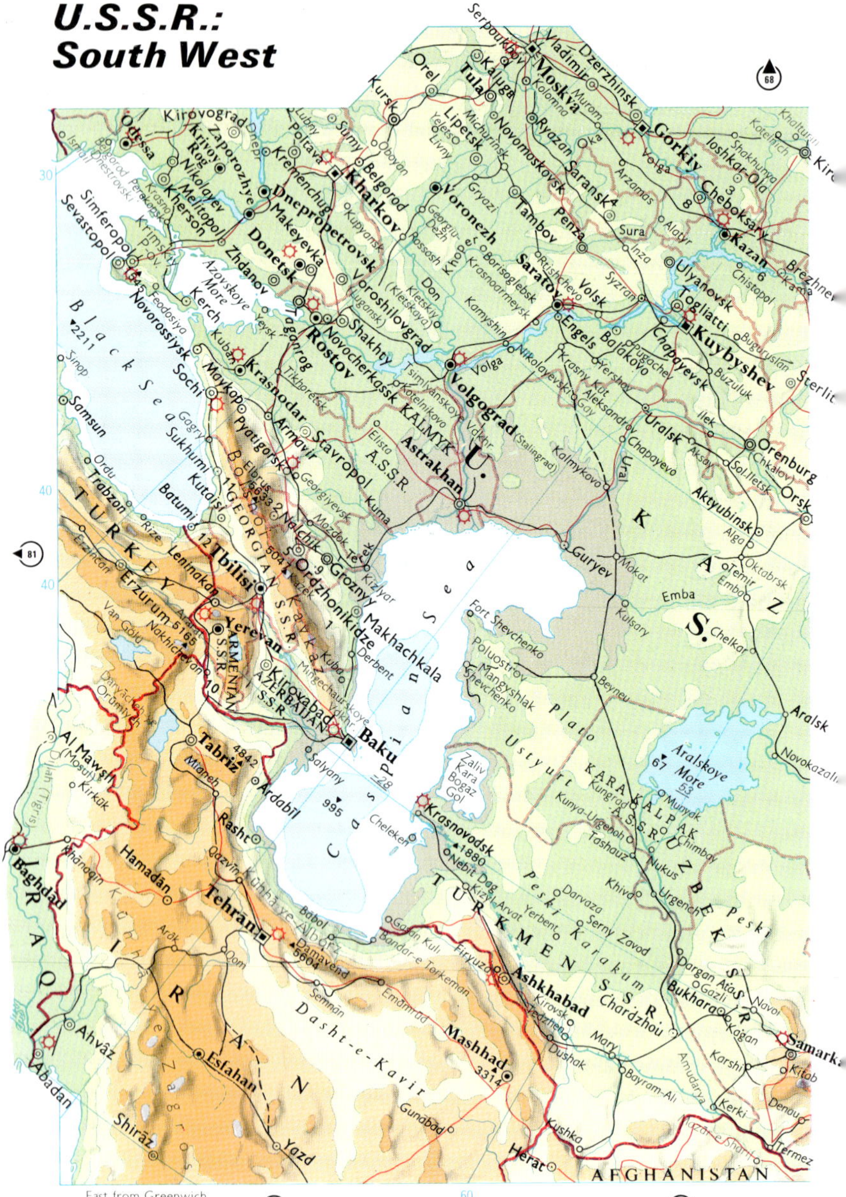

Map 70

1:20 000 000

69

74

89

Map 71

U.S.S.R.: North East

12

69

74

Map 72

1:20 000 000
Mys Dezhneva
(East C.)
Uelen
Lavrentiya
Provideniya
St. Lawrence I.
(U.S.A.)
Chukotskoye More
Vankarem
Amen
1843
Rene
Egvekinot
Anadyrskiy Zaliv
Beringovskiy
Chukotskiy Khrebet
Ostrov Vrangelya
East Siberian Sea
Pevek
Ust-Chaun
Ostrov Ayon
Ostrova Medvezhi
Ambarchik
Cherskiy
1853
Bilibino
Anadyr
Koryakskiy Khrebet
Khatyrka
2562
Penzhino
Markovo
Yeropol
1742
Bolshoy Anyuy
Nizhne Kolymsk
Oloy
Omolon
Kamenskoye
Meynypilgyno
Korf
Kondakova
Chokurdakh
Ercha
Indigirka
Srednekolymsk
Paren
Penzhinskaya Guba
Gizhiga
Rekinniki
Tilichiki
Ostrov Karaginskiy
Bering Sea
Kichiga
Ossora
Uyandi
(Otur-Kyuyel)
Druzhina
Stolbovaya
Ambarchik
Evensk
Nayakhan
Zyryanka
Kolyma
Balygychan
Seymchan
Omsukchan
Okhotsko Kolymskoye
Viliga
Gizhiginskaya Guba
Srediniy Khrebet
Palana
Uka
Ust-Kamchatsk
Komandorskiye Ostrova
Nikolskoye
Zashiversk
Khonu
Pobeda
3147
S.
Taskan
Orotukan
Gora Chen
2682
Ust-Nera
Khrebet Cherskogo
Yagodnoye
Iret
Zaliv Shelikhova
Tigil
Poluostrov Kamchatka
4750
Mt. Klyuchevskaya
Alyaskitovyy
Susuman
Sanga-Tolon
Atka
Palatka
Magadan
Kyulyunken
Oymyakon
2959
Loshkalakh
Ust-Omchug
Staryy Kheydzhan
Ust-Khayryuzovo
Icha
3621
Pushchino
Zhupanovo
3456
Petropavlovsk-Kamchatskiy
Sobolevo
Aldan
Khandyga
Okhotskiy Perevoz
Okhotsk
Vorovskoye
Kirovskiy
Opala
Borogontsy
Ytyk-Kel
Allakh-Yun
Arka
Ulya
Ust Bolsheretsk
Severo-Kurilsk
Yakutsk
Maya
Amga
Ust Maya
Ynykchanskiy
Yur
Dzhugdzur
Sea of Okhotsk
Ostrov Paramushir
Ostrov Onekotan
Ust-Mil
Aim
Nelkan
1780
Ostrova
Chagda
Uchur
Chasovnya-Uchurskaya
Khrebet
Ayan
Ostrov Bolshoy Shantar
Sakhalinskiy Zaliv
Okha
Sakhalin
Kurilskiy Ostrov Simushir
2246
Kununskiy
2482
Nomuy
Chumikan
Tugur
Nikolayevsk-na-Amur
Susanino
Bogorodskoye
Katangli
Aleksandrovsk-Sakhalinskiy
G. Lopatina
1609
170
60
180
170
160
50
130
140
COPYRIGHT GEORGE PHILIP & SON LTD.

75

U.S.S.R.: South East and Mongolia

72

71

Map 74

1:20 000 000

73

104

98

Map 75

Asia: Physical

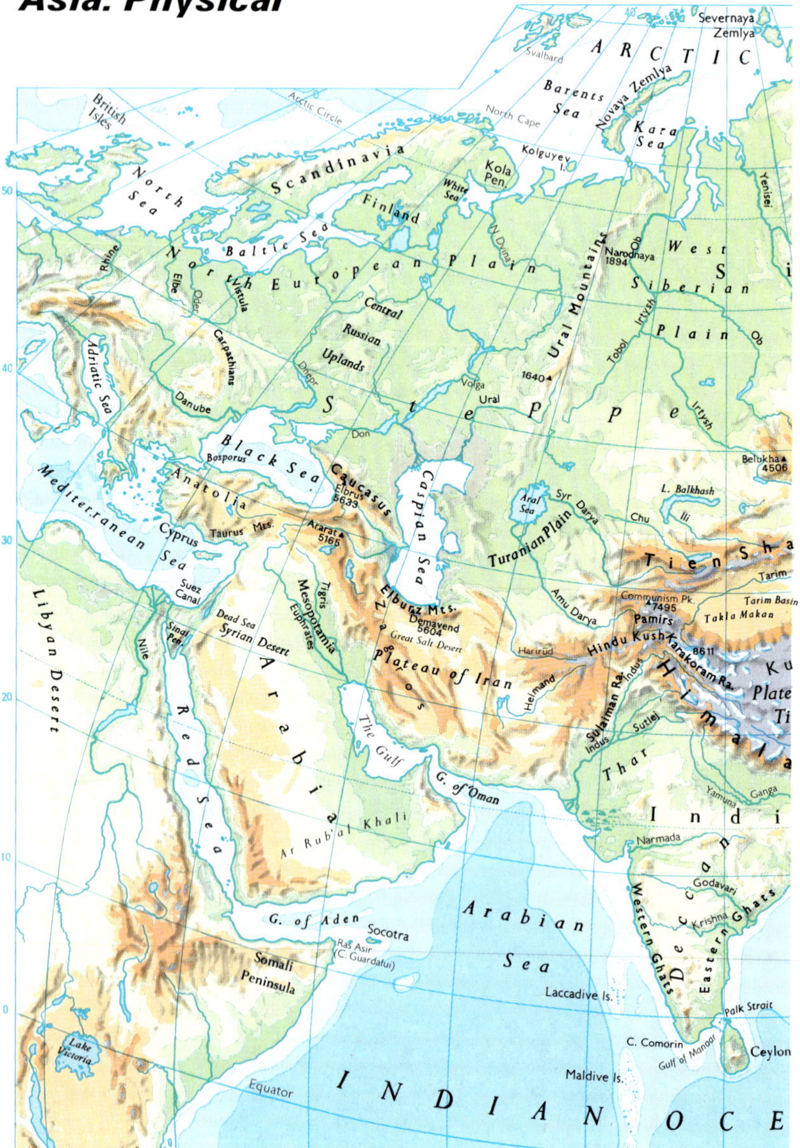

1:60 000 000

Map 77

Asia: Political

1:60 000 000

Map 79

Turkey and the Middle East

Map 80

1:10 000 000

70

86

82

Arabian Peninsula

Map 82

1:15 000 000

Map 83

The Gulf

81

82

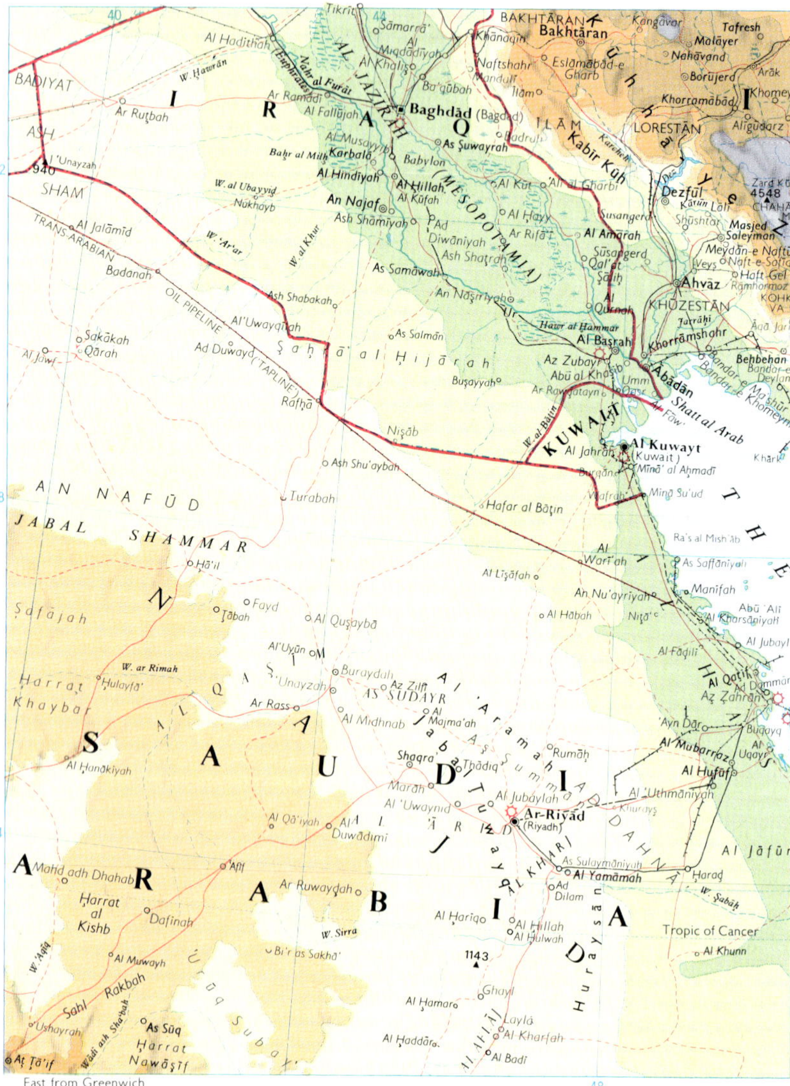

East from Greenwich

82

Map 84

1:10 000 000

86

88

83

Map 85

Central Asia and Afghanistan

Map 86

1:10 000 000

70

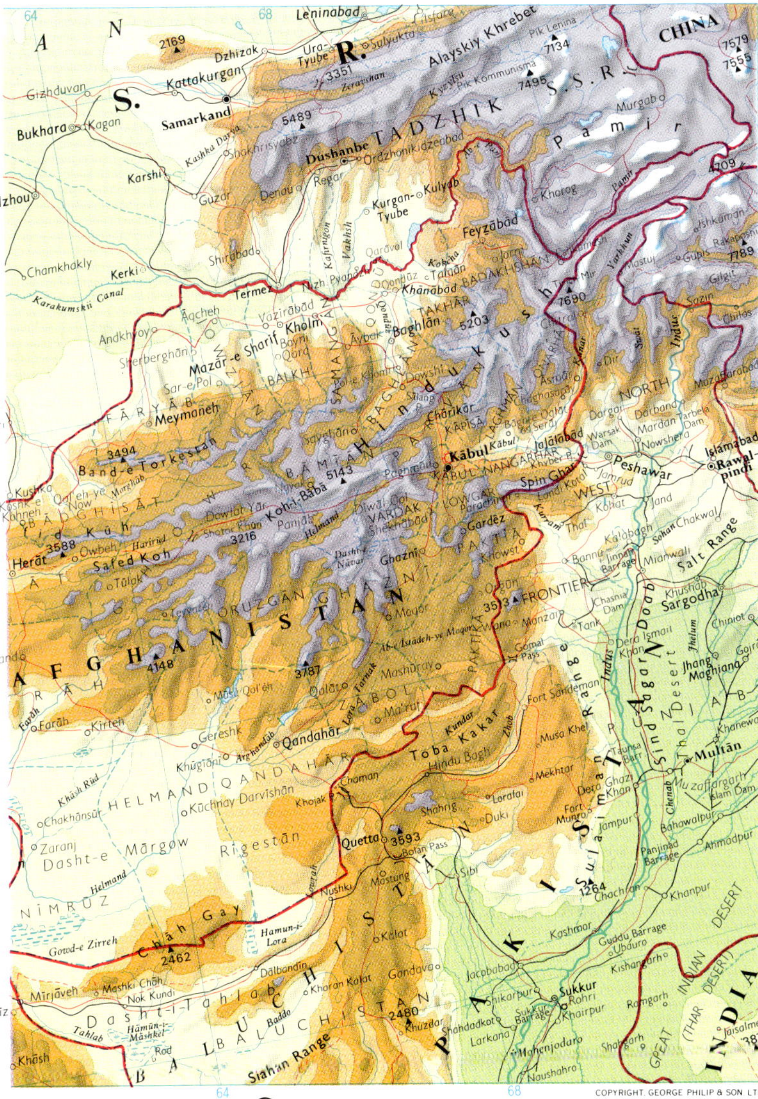

88

89

Map 87

Pakistan and North West India

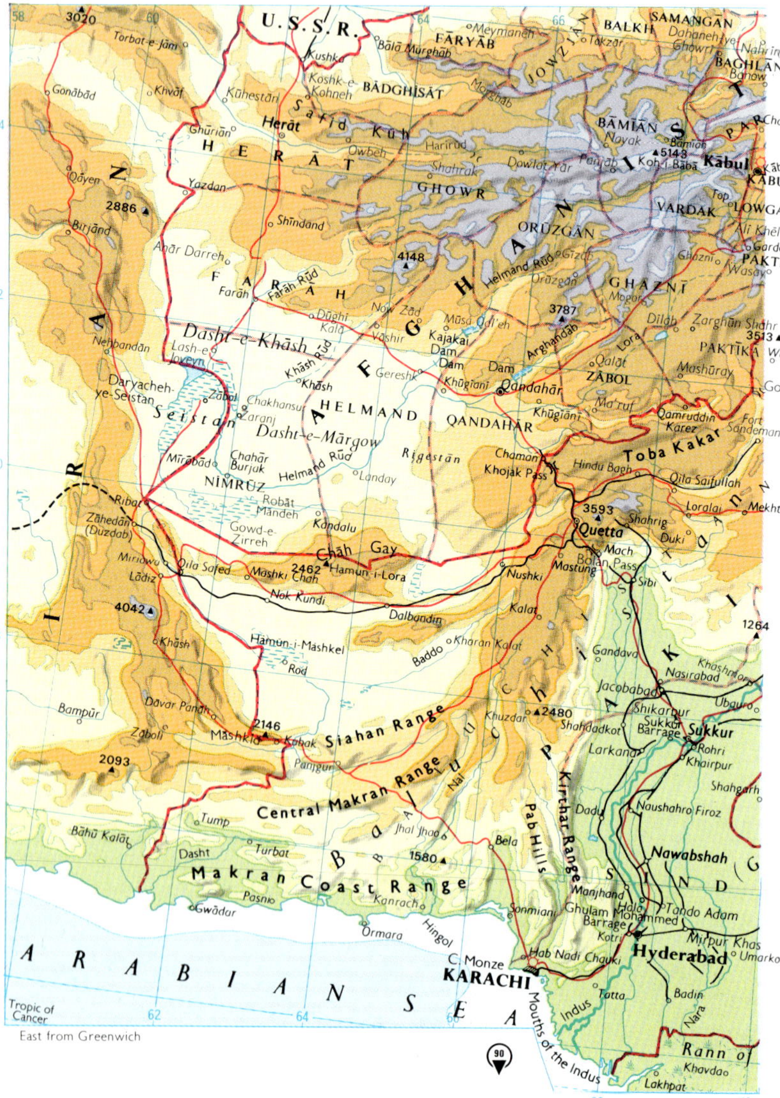

Map 88

1:10 000 000

CHINA
JAMMU AND KASHMIR
INDIA
RAJASTHAN
PUNJAB
HARYANA
UTTAR PRADESH
HIMACHAL PRADESH
NORTH WEST FRONTIER
BADAKHSHAN
TAKHAR
KAPISA
LAGHMAN
KONARHA
NANGARHAR
Hindu Kush
Karakoram
Aghil Mountains
Ladakh Range
Zaskar Mountains
Himalaya
Deosai Mountains
Sulaiman Range
Thar or Great Indian Desert
Sind Sagar Doab
Thal Desert
Bari Doab
Rechna Doab
CEASE FIRE LINE 1949
Mintaka P
4709
Ishkuman
Disteghil Sar
7885
Aghil Pass
4779
K 2
8611
Rakaposhi
7788
Tirich Mir
7690
Yarkhun
Mastuj
Gupis
Gilgit
Chitral
Sazin
Bunji
Indus
Skardu
Shyok
Karakoram Pass
5575
Haji Langar
Aksai Chin
Chilas
8126
Nanga Parbat
Dir
Saidu
Malakand
Dargai
Warsak Dam
Sorubi
Konar-e Khas
Jalalabad
Landi Kotal
Khyber Pass
Peshawar
Mardan
Tarbela Dam
Naushahra
Attock
Darband
Muzaffarabad
Baramula
Abbottabad
Murree
Srinagar
Kargil
Saser
7672
Lanak P.
5486
Leh
Nunkun 7135
Shyok
Pangong Tso
Pal
Chushul
Rudok
Punch
Anantnag
Kishtwar
Rawalpindi
Islamabad
Thal
Kohat
Khowst
Jand
Miram Shah
Bannu
Kalabagh
Jinnah Barrage
Mangla Dam
Jhelum
Riasi
Chakwal
Rasul Dam
Chenab
Udhampur
Jammu
Chamba
Brahmaur
Hanle
Demchok
Mianwali
Manzai
Gujrat
Wazirabad
Sialkot
Gujranwala
Pathankot
Gurdaspur
Palampur
Kulu
Dankhar Gompa
7026
Gar Dzong
Khushab
Sargodha
Hafizabad
Dera Ismail Khan
Chiniot
Shekhupura
Amritsar
Mandi
Shipki La
Gartok
Langchen Khambab
Musa Khel
Jhang Maghiana
Trimmu Dam
Lahore
Faisalabad
Hoshiarpur
Bhakra Dam
Jullundur
Nangal Dam
Phagwara
Simla
Gojra
Ravi
Kasur
Ludhiana
Kandaghat
Kamet
7756
Chakrata
Badrinath
Sahiwal
(Montgomery)
Firozpur
Jagraon
Mussoorie
Chandigarh
Ambala
Dehra Dun
7817
Nanda Devi
Dera Ghazi Khan
Multan
Khanewal
Fazilka
Muktsar
Bhatinda
Patiala
Pauri
Haridwar Dam
Jagadhri
Munro
Jampur
Musaffargarh
Sutlej
Abohar
Ganganagar
Saharanpur
Haridwar
Almora
Lodhran
Alipur
Roorkee
Karnal
Muzaffarnagar
Najibabad
Panjinad Barrage
Sirsa
Haldwani
Bahawalpur
Suratgarh
Bijnor
Chachran
Ahmadpur
Anupgarh
Hisar
Hansi
Sonipat
Meerut
Amroha
Moradabad
Rampur
Bhiwani
New Delhi
Rohtak
Hapur
Guddu Barrage
DELHI
Ghaziabad
Sambhal
Pilibhit
Sardarshahr
Churu
Gurgaon
Bulandshahr
Bareilly
Rajasthan Canal
Bikaner
Ratangarh
Jhunjhunu
Rewari
Kishangarh
Kolayat
Fatehpur
Aligarh
Budaun
Nawalgarh
Ramgarh
Sikar
1052
Alwar
Hathras
Fatehgarh
Phalodi
Nagaur
Mathura
Bharatpur
Mainpuri
Hardoi
Kannauj
Pokaran
Sambhar
Jaipur
Agra
Firozabad
387
Ajmer
Daulpur
Etawah
Ganga
Jodhpur
Luni
Bilara
Malpura
Tonk
Chambal
Bhind
Kanpur
Nasirabad
Gwalior
Munabao
Pachpadra
Beawar
Kekri
Sawai Madhopur
Orai
Pali
Kunch
Hamirpur
Barmer
Marwar
Bundi
Sheopur Kalan
Datia
Jalor
Bhilwara
Mau Ranipur
Banda
Shivpuri
Jhansi
Sirohi
Nathdwara
Kota
Baran
521
Raniwara
Chhatarpur
1722
Nagar Parkar
Tharad
Chittaurgarh
Gandhi Sagar
Kachchh
72
74
76
78
80
36
34
32
30
28
26
101
92
91
COPYRIGHT GEORGE PHILIP & SON LTD

Central and Southern India, Sri Lanka

88

Map 90

1:10 000 000

89

92

Eastern India, Bangladesh and Burma

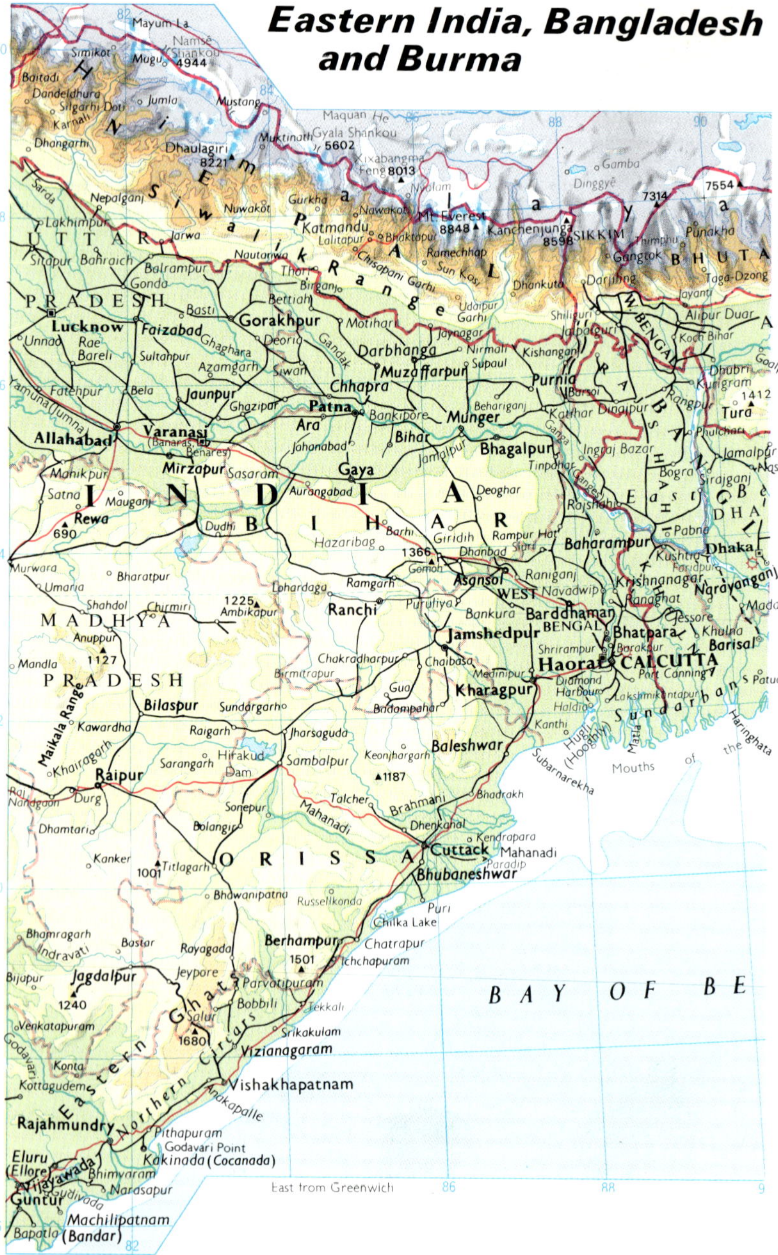

Map 92

1:10 000 000

Map 93

Mainland South East Asia

93

96

Map 94

1:10 000 000

Map 95

The Malay Peninsula

94

Map 96

1:10 000 000

95

111

China: East

74

100

Map 98

1:20 000 000

104

112

97

101

Map 99

China: West

98

71

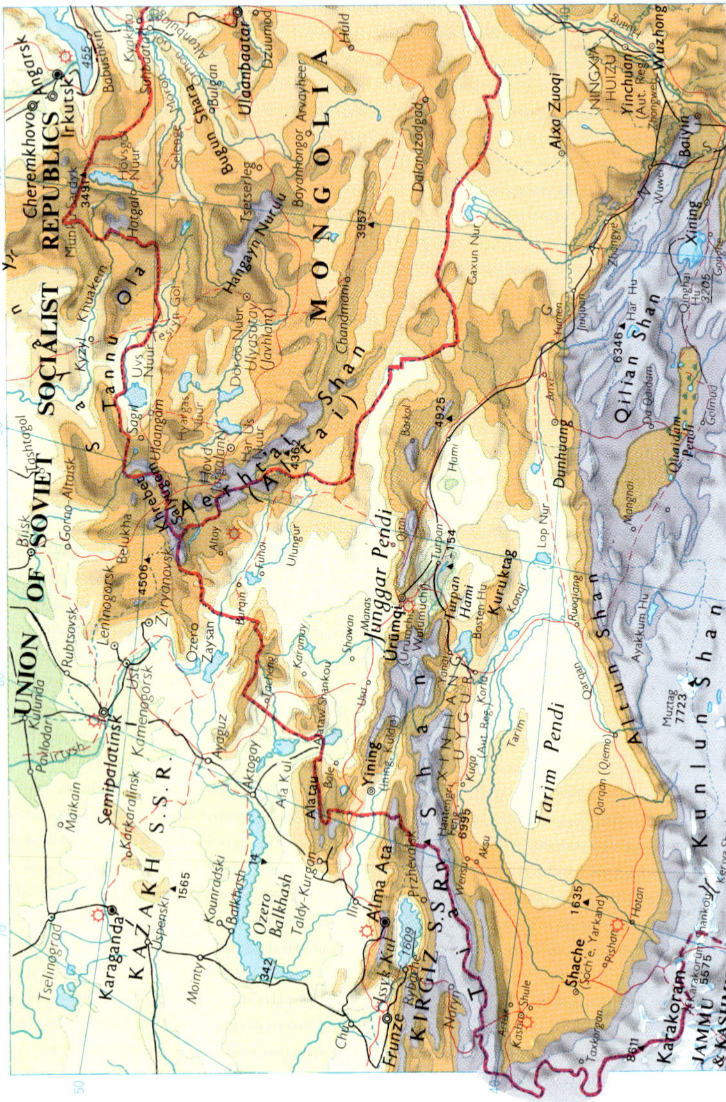

1:20 000 000

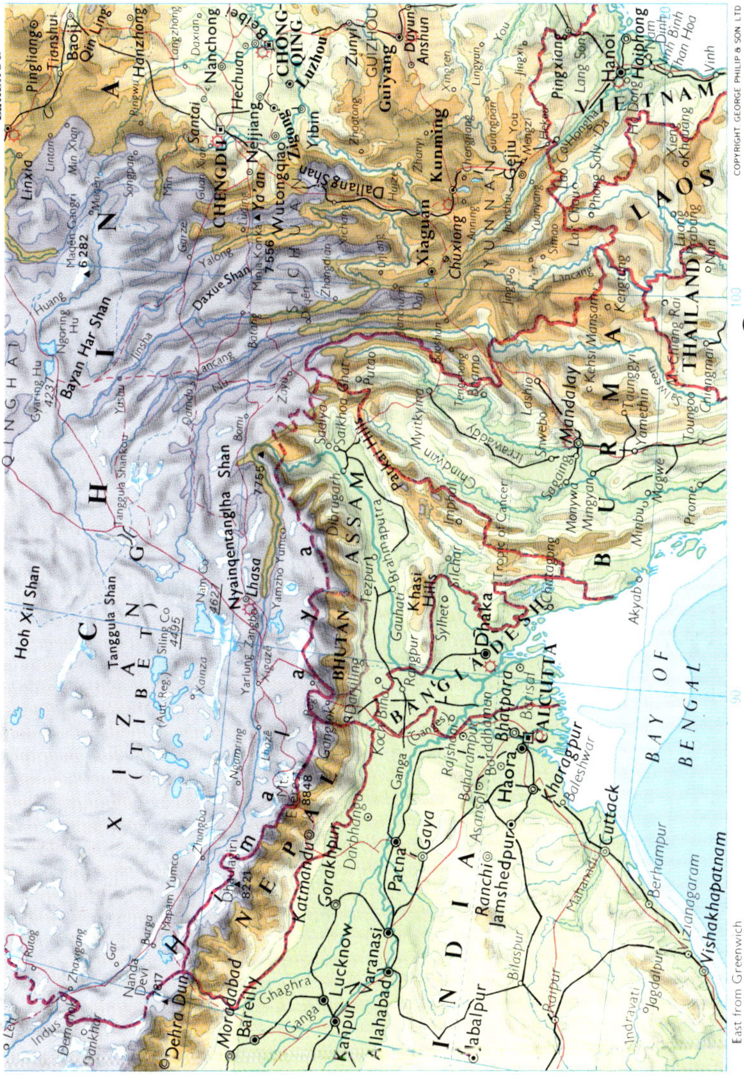

Map 101

Japan: North

75

98

East from Greenwich

The numbers refer to prefectures which are listed on page 105.

Map 102

1:7 500 000

Sea of Okhotsk
Rebun-Tō
Rishiri-Tō
Wakkanai
Teshio
Teshio
Otoineppu
Enbetsu
HOKKAIDŌ
Monbetsu
Yūbetsu
Abashiri-Wan
Nemuro-Kaikyō
Shibetsu
Kitami
Abashiri
Rumoi
Ishikari-Wan
(Otaru-Wan)
Daisetsu-Zan
2290
Asahikawa
Atsuta
HOKKAIDŌ
1
Kushiro
Nemuro
Kamui-Misaki
Bibai
Honbetsu
Iwamisawa
Obihiro
Otaru
Iwanai
Yūbari
Tokachi
Kushiro
Sapporo
Tomakomai
2052
Poroshiri Dake
Shiraoi
Mombetsu
Setana
Uchiura-Wan
Muroran
Urakawa
Samani
Okushiri-Tō
Erimo-Misaki
Esashi
Hakodate
Esan-Misaki
Tsugaru-Kaikyō
Shiriya-Zaki
Matsumae
Mutsu
Mutsu-Wan
Habomai, Shikotan,
Kunashiri and Etorofu,
occupied by the U.S.S.R.
since 1945, are claimed
by Japan pending a final
peace treaty.
Aomori
2
Hirosaki
Towada-Ko
Hachinohe
F
Odate
Kuji
Noshiro
Yoneshiro
40
Oga-Hantō
Iwate San
2041
Akita
3
Omono
Morioka
4
Miyako
Hanamaki
Kamaishi
Honjō
Yokote
Kitakami
Ichinoseki
Sakata
Tsuruoka
Mogami
Shinjō
TŌHOKU
N
Kogota
5
Ishinomaki
Shiogama
Yamagata
6
Sendai
Iwanuma
Sado
Niigata
Shibata
Yonezawa
Agano
Fukushima
Bandai San
1819
Suzu-Misaki
8
Nagaoka
Wajima
Aizuwakamatsu
Kashiwazaki
Koriyama
7
Naoetsu
Tajima
Toyama-Wan
Takada
Iwaki
Nanao
Himi
Shinano
18
Nikkō
Takaoka
Toyama
Nagano
Hitachi
Maebashi
Kiryū
Utsunomiya
10
Ueda
17
Nakaminato
Tochigi
Matsumoto
13
Takasaki
20
Mito
Gyoda
Chichibu
19
Tsuchiura
Takayama
Suwa
Kawagoe
Omiya
KANTŌ
Shin Tone
Urawa
Sawara
Kawaguchi
Ichikawa
TOKYO
Chōshi
140
145
45
105

Japan: South

98

East from Greenwich

Map 104

1:7 500 000

103

Japan: Tokyo, Kyoto, Osaka

Map 106

1:2 500 000

105

105

Map 107

Japan: Kyushu

1:2 500 000

Map 108

West Honshu and Shikoku

1:2 500 000

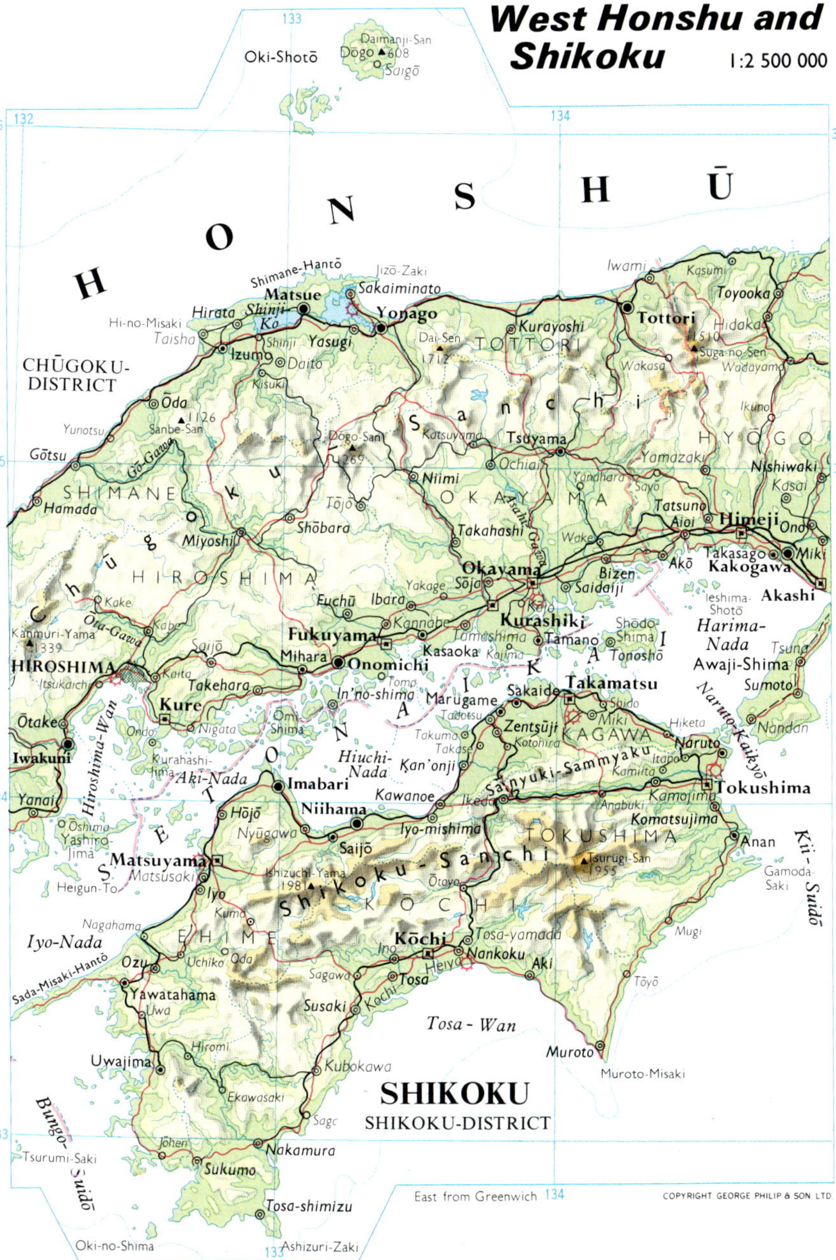

Indonesia: West

112

99

93

Map 110

Map 111

1:20 000 000

113

Indonesia: East

1:20 000 000

Map 113

Australia, New Zealand and Papua New Guinea

Map 114

113

1:24 000 000

Map 115

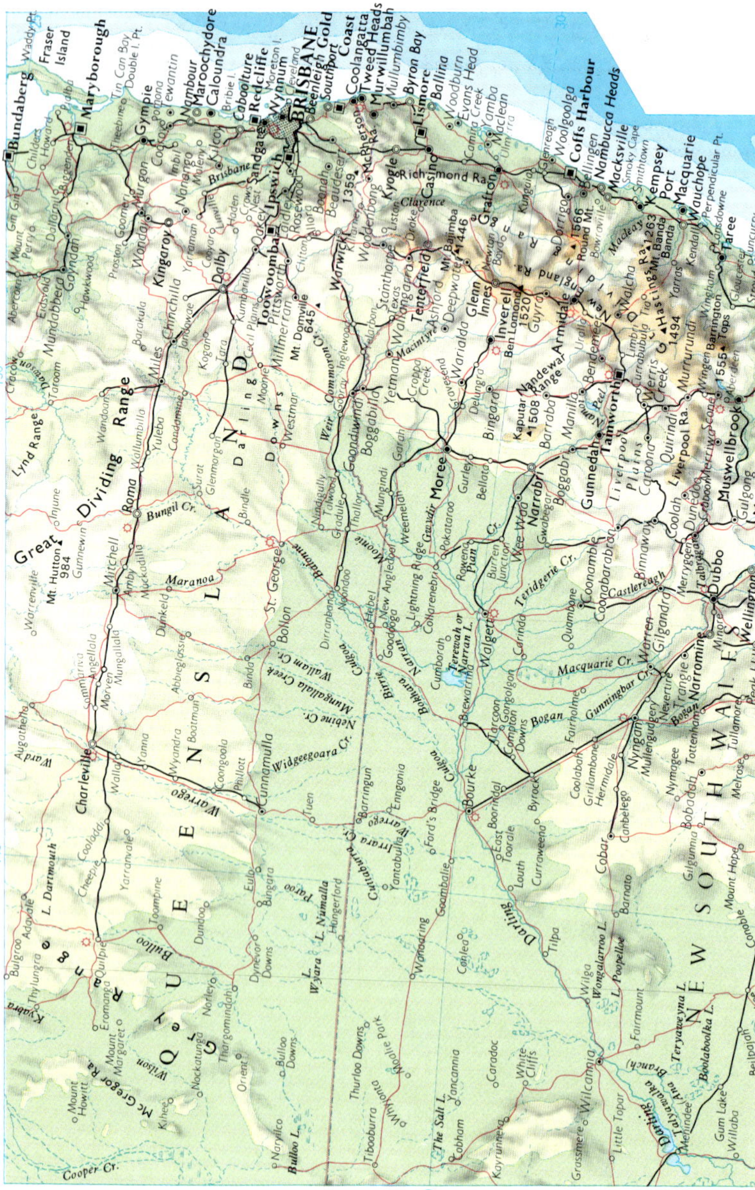
QUEENSLAND
NEW SOUTH WALES
Great Dividing Range
Darling Downs
Grey Range
Brisbane
Bundaberg
Maryborough
Fraser Island
Gympie
Nambour
Maroochydore
Caloundra
Redcliffe
Gold Coast
Southport
Coolangatta
Tweed Heads
Murwillumbah
Byron Bay
Lismore
Ballina
Casino
Grafton
Coffs Harbour
Nambucca Heads
Macksville
Kempsey
Port Macquarie
Wauchope
Taree
Toowoomba
Ipswich
Dalby
Kingaroy
Warwick
Goondiwindi
Tenterfield
Glenn Innes
Inverell
Armidale
Tamworth
Gunnedah
Narrabri
Moree
Walgett
Dubbo
Wellington
Mudgee
Muswellbrook
Roma
Mitchell
Charleville
Cunnamulla
St. George
Bourke
Cobar
Nyngan
Narromine
Wilcannia
Darling
Warrego
Condamine
Balonne
Macquarie
Bogan
Castlereagh
Namoi
Gwydir
Paroo
Bulloo
Cooper Cr.
Wilson
McGregor Ra.
Lynd Range
Liverpool Ra.
Liverpool Plains
Mt. Hutton 984
Mt. Domville 645
Kaputar 1508
Ben Lomond 1520
Round Mt. 1566
Barrington Tops 1555
145
150
30
121
118

Map 116

Australia: Brisbane, Sydney, Melbourne

1:8 000 000

122

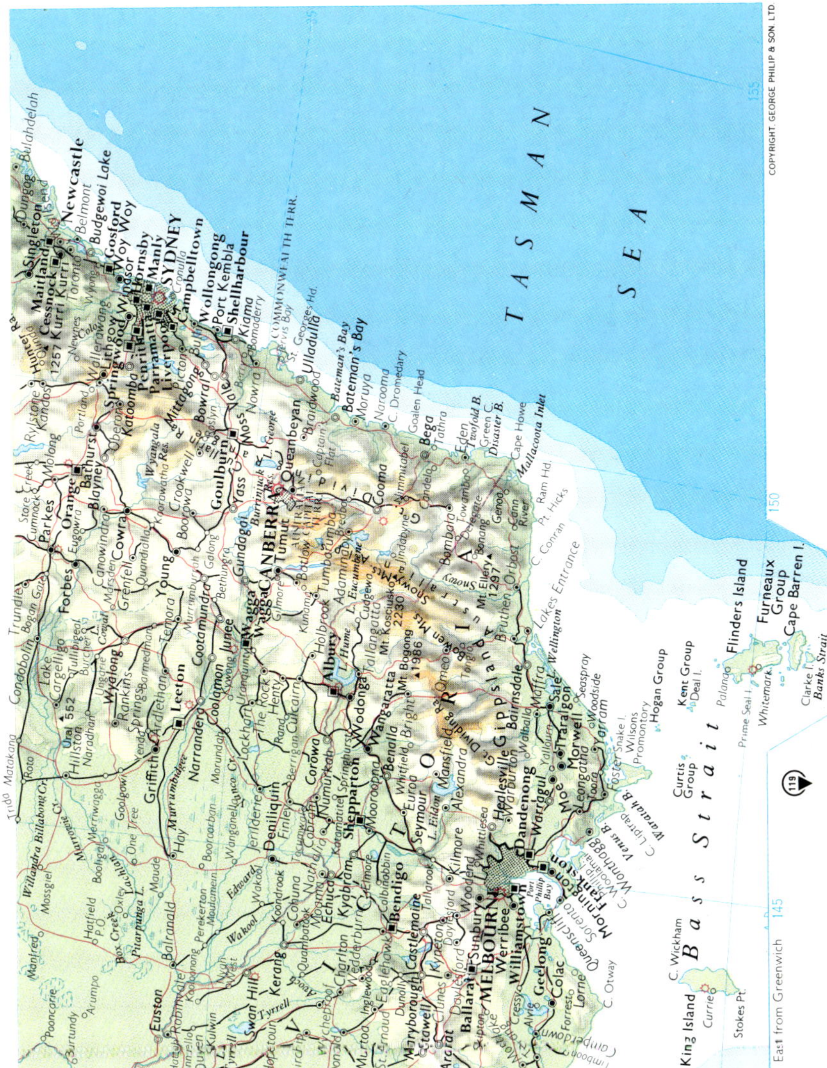

119

119

Australia: Adelaide, Melbourne, Tasmania

116

115

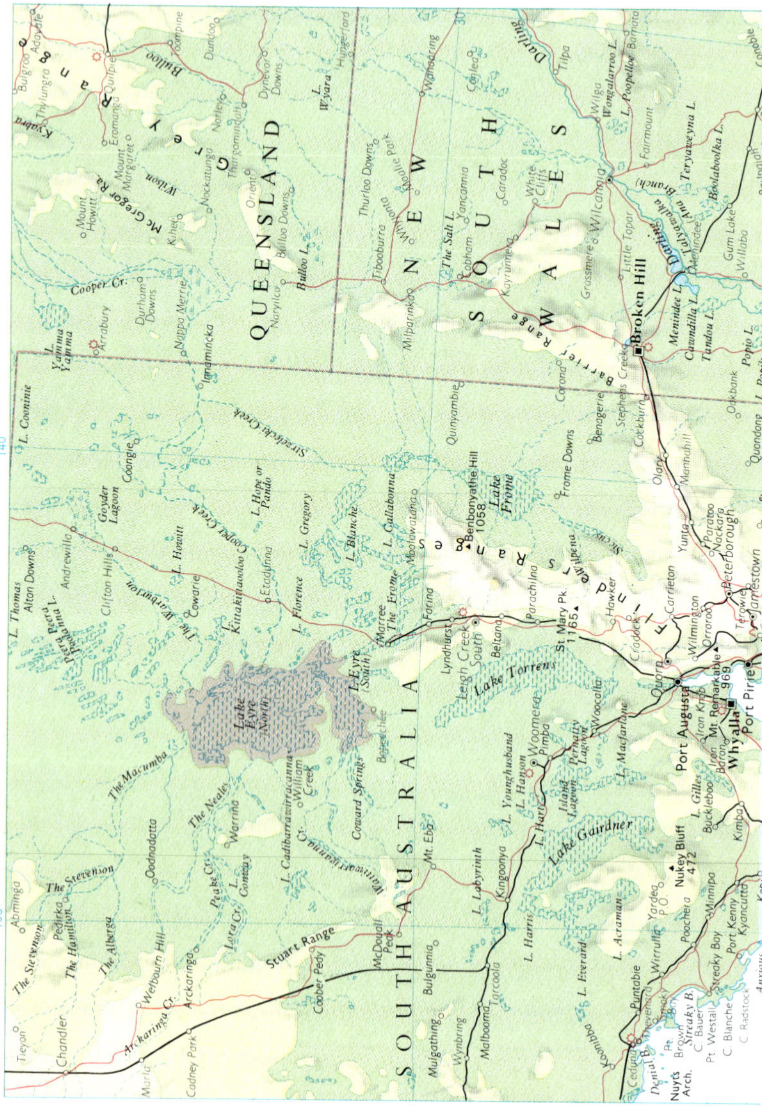

114

Map 118

1:8 000 000

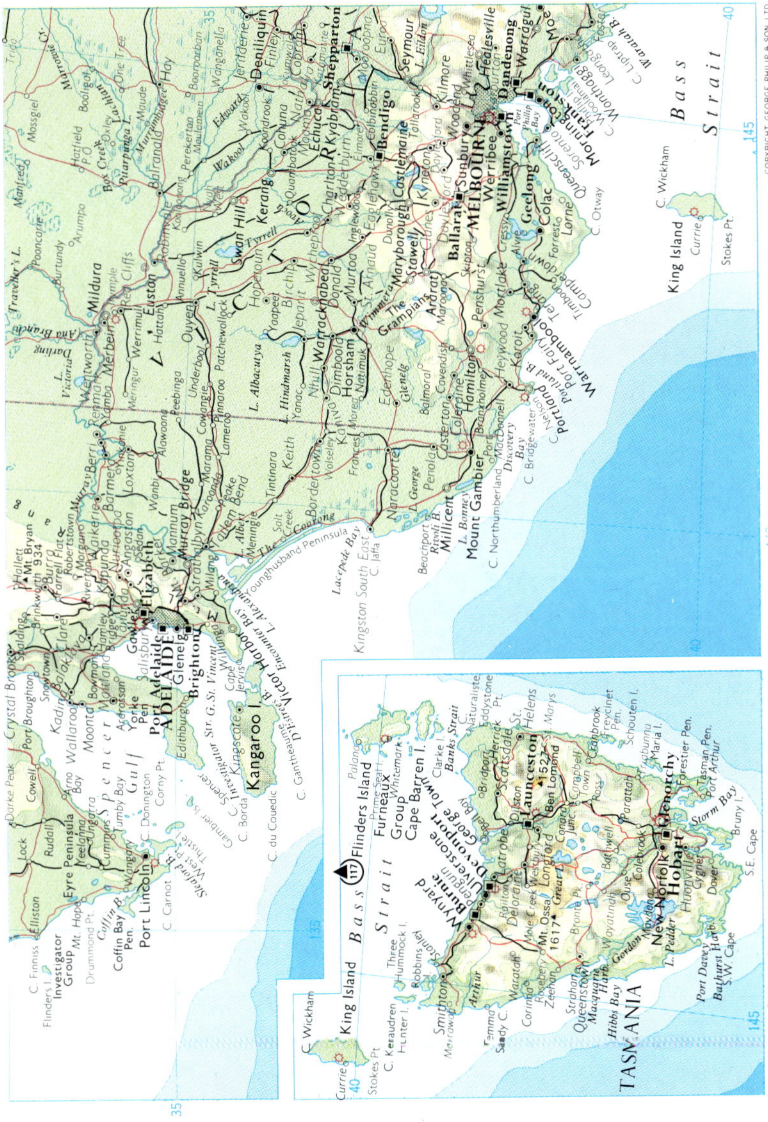

Map 119

Australia: Perth

1:8 000 000

114

East from Greenwich

115

Map 120

Australia: North East Queensland

1:8 000 000

115

15

116

New Zealand, Central and South West Pacific

Map 122

1:7 000 000

◄115

Africa: Physical

1:70 000 000

Map 124

Africa: Political

1:70 000 000

Africa: North West

1:20 000 000

Map 127

Africa: North East

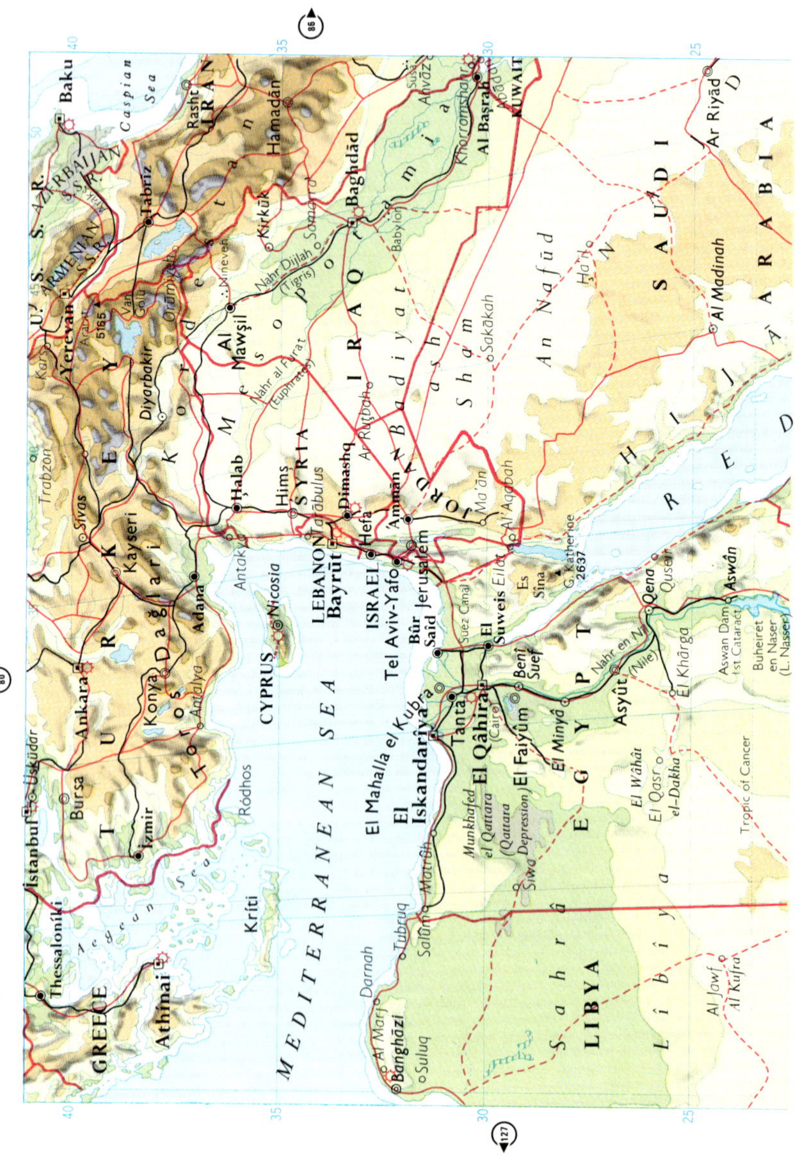

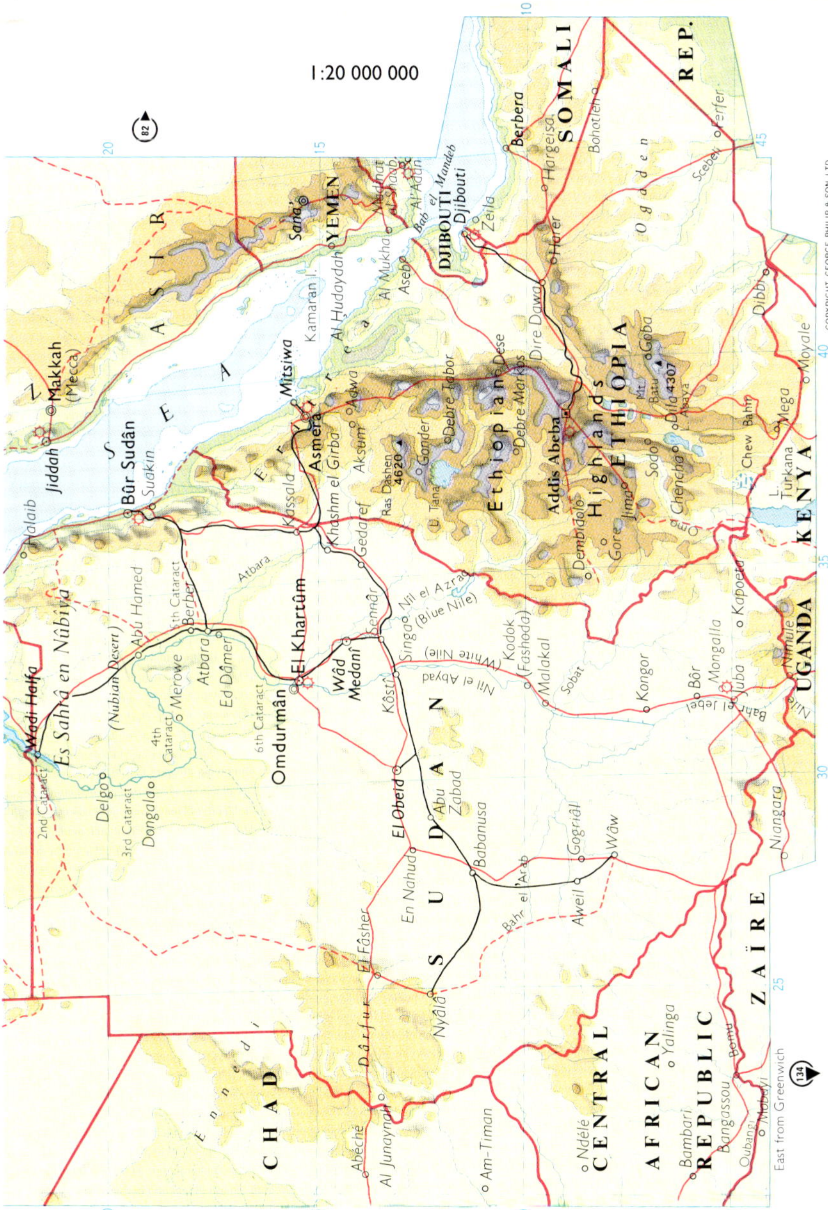
1:20 000 000
82
131
134
135
SUDAN
CHAD
CENTRAL AFRICAN REPUBLIC
ZAÏRE
UGANDA
KENYA
ETHIOPIA
SOMALI REP.
DJIBOUTI
YEMEN
ASIA
RED SEA
Ethiopian Highlands
Es Sahrâ en Nûbîya
(Nubian Desert)
Darfur
Ennedi
Ogaden
El Khartûm
Omdurmân
Bûr Sudân
Suakin
Wadi Halfa
Abu Hamed
Atbara
Ed Dâmer
Berber
Merowe
Dongola
Delgo
Wâd Medanî
Sennâr
Kôstî
Singa
Kassala
Khashm el Girba
Gedaref
El Obeid
Abu Zabad
En Nahud
El Fâsher
Nyâlâ
Babanusa
Aweil
Gogriâl
Wâw
Malakal
Kodok (Fashoda)
Kongor
Bôr
Mongalla
Juba
Kapoeta
Nimule
Nîl el Azraq (Blue Nile)
Nîl el Abyad (White Nile)
Bahr el Jebel
Bahr el 'Arab
Sobat
Atbara
2nd Cataract
3rd Cataract
4th Cataract
5th Cataract
6th Cataract
Halaib
Jiddah
Makkah (Mecca)
Sana'
Al Hudaydah
Al Mukha
Kamaran I.
Mitsiwa
Asmera
Aksum
Adwa
Aseb
Bab el Mandeb
Djibouti
Zeila
Berbera
Hargeisa
Harer
Dire Dawa
Addis Abeba
Dese
Debre Markos
Debre Tabor
Gonder
Ras Dashen 4620
L. Tana
Gore
Jima
Dembidolo
Sodo
Chencha
Dila
Goba
Mt. Batu 4307
L. Abaya
Moyale
Mega
Dibbi
Chew Bahir
L. Turkana
Omo
Bohotleh
Scebeli
Ferfer
Abéché
Al Junaynah
Am-Timan
Ndélé
Bambari
Bangassou
Yalinga
Bomu
Oubangi
Mobayi
Niangara
East from Greenwich
COPYRIGHT GEORGE PHILIP & SON LTD

Map 129

Africa: West

126

Map 130

1:20 000 000

127

132

134

Africa: East

128

131

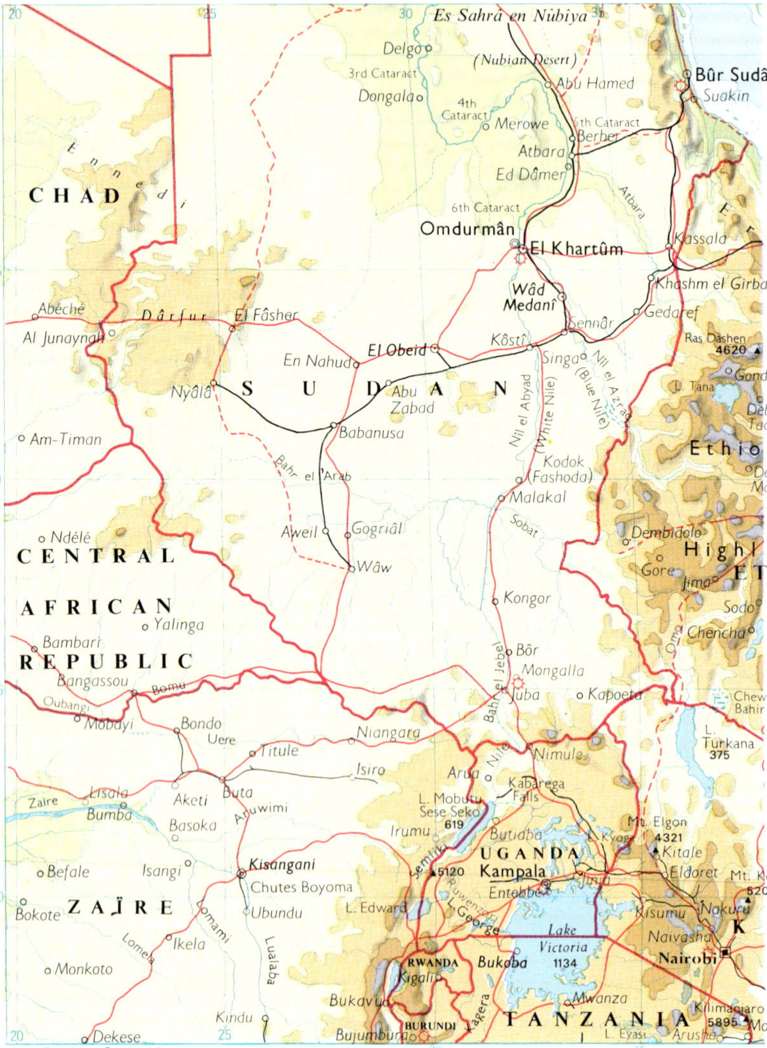

135

Map 132

1:20 000 000

82
SAUDI ARABIA
ASIR
Rub 'al Khali
OMAN
RED SEA
SOUTH YEMEN
Hadramawt
Mitsiwa
Kamaran I.
Sana'
YEMEN
Al Hudaydah
Adwa
Al Mukha
Madinat ash Sha'b
Al 'Adan (Aden)
Al Mukalla
Aseb
Socotra
(South Yemen)
Bab el Mandeb
Gulf of Aden
DJIBOUTI
Djibouti
Candala
Ras Asir
(C. Guardafui)
Zeila
Dese
Berbera
Dire Dawa
Bender Beila
Addis Abeba
Harer
Hargeisa
Bohotleh
SOMALI
HIOPIA
Eil
Mt. Batu
Goba
Ogaden
Dila
4307
L. Abaya
REPUBLIC
Scebeli
Ferfer
Obbia
Dibbi
Mega
Moyale
El Dere
INDIAN
Bardera
Marsabit
Giuba
Merca
Muqdisho
(Mogadishu)
Wajir
Brava
Equator
NYA
Chisimaio
Tana
OCEAN
Lamu
Malindi
Voi
40
45
50
55
20
15
10
5
0

Africa: Central

131

136

Map 134

1:20 000 000

132

133

137

Map 135

Africa: South

134

Map 136

1:20 000 000

137

North America: Physical

1:60 000 000

Map 138

North America: Political

1:60 000 000

Canada: South East

146

143

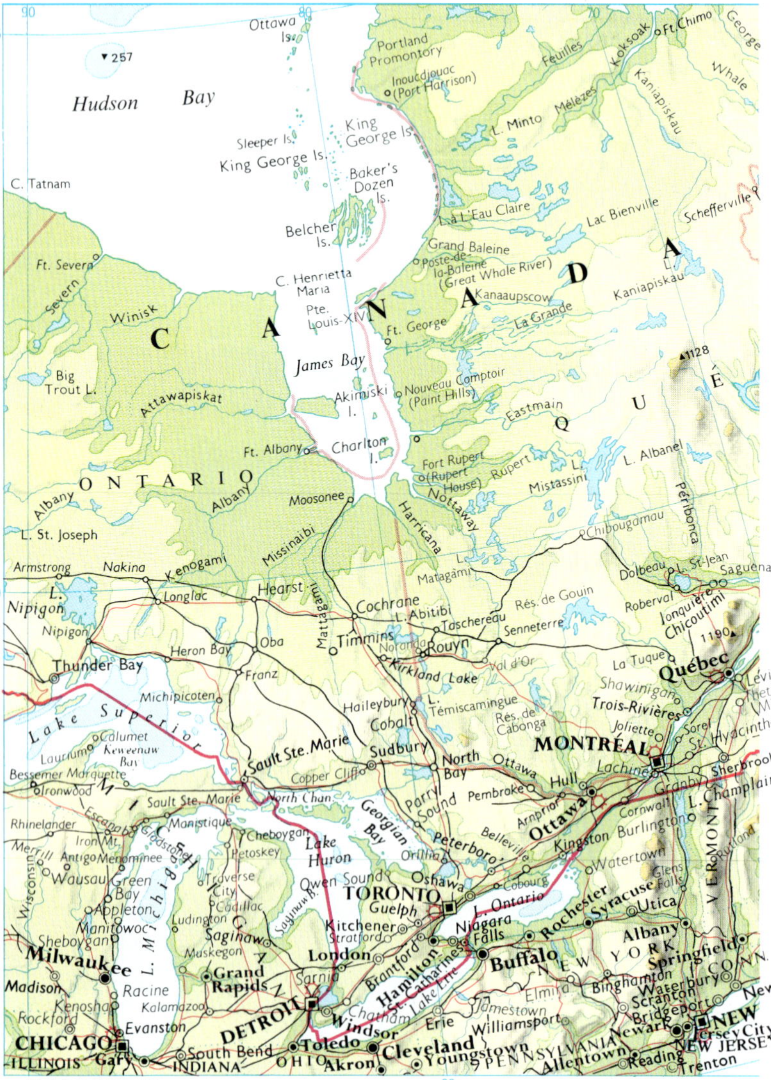

West from Greenwich
80

157

1:15 000 000

147

Canada: South West and Alaska

144

1:15 000 000

145

140

163

Canada: North West

142

142

Map 144

1:15 000 000

12

146

143

Canada: North East

12

145

West from Greenwich

140

Map 146

1:15 000 000

Map 147

Canada: Saint Lawrence Estuary

140

151

164

1:7 000 000

141

Map 149

Canada: The Great Lakes

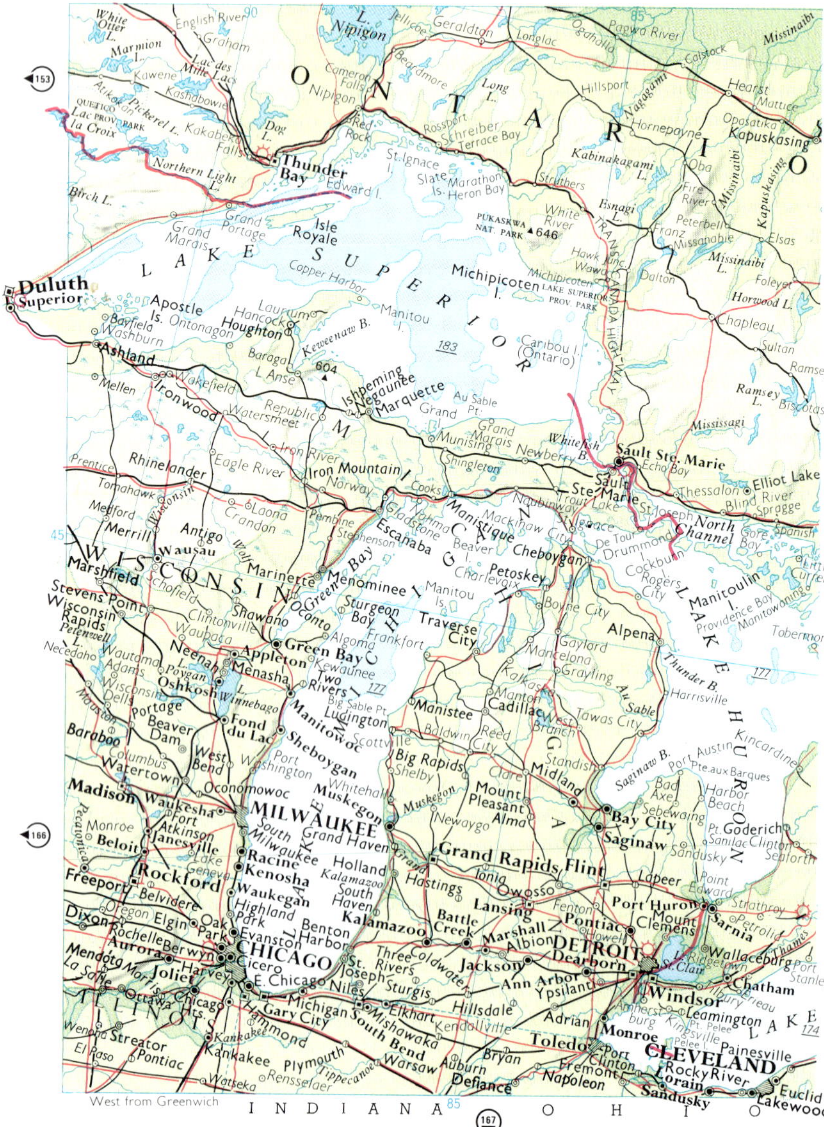

1:7 000 000

140

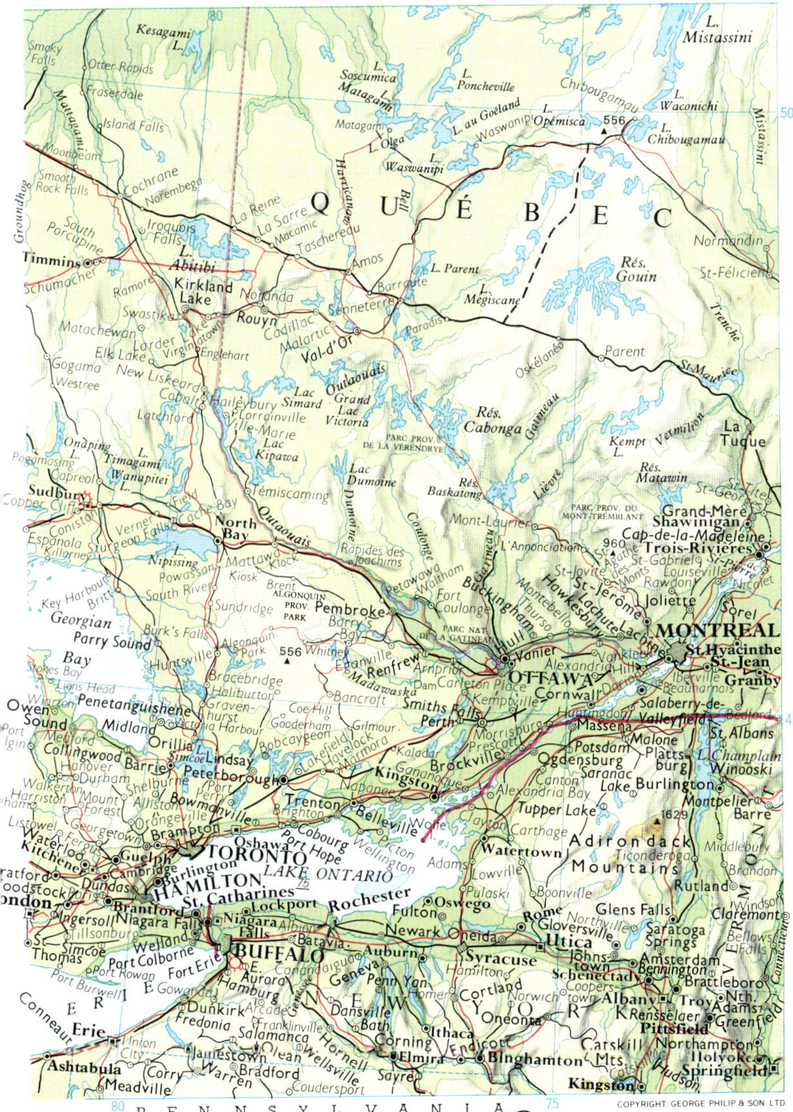

148

164

Map 151

Canada: Southern Saskatchewan and Manitoba

145

155

163

Map 152

1:7 000 000

140

150

156

Canada: Southern British Columbia and Alberta

144

171

Map 154

1:7 000 000

145

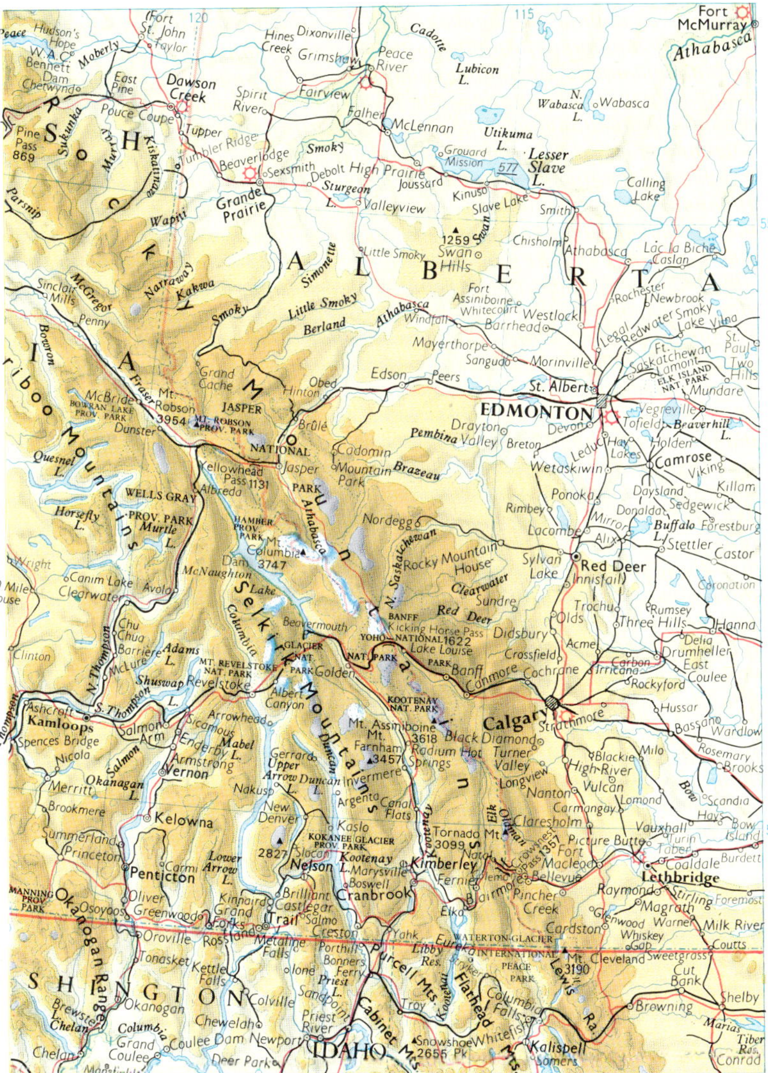

152

162

Map 155

U.S.A.: North East

140

163

158

1:12 000 000

141

COPYRIGHT GEORGE PHILIP & SON. LTD

159

U.S.A.: South East

156

161

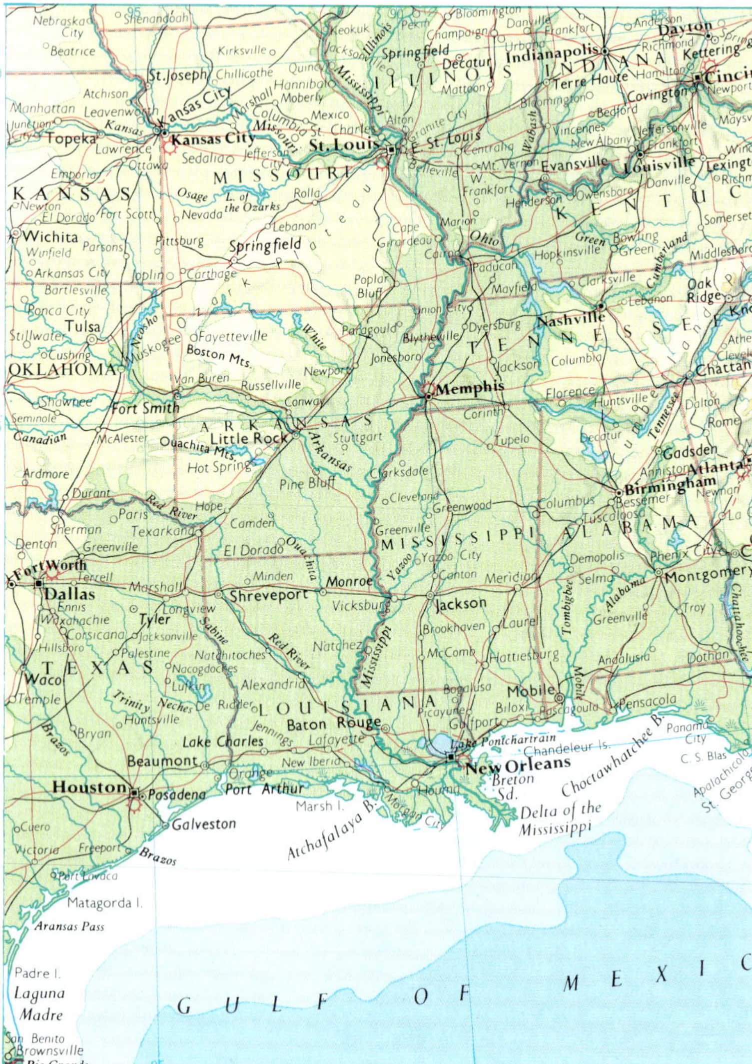

1:12 000 000

157

178

Map 159

U.S.A.: South West and Hawaii

162

Map 160

1:12 000 000

163

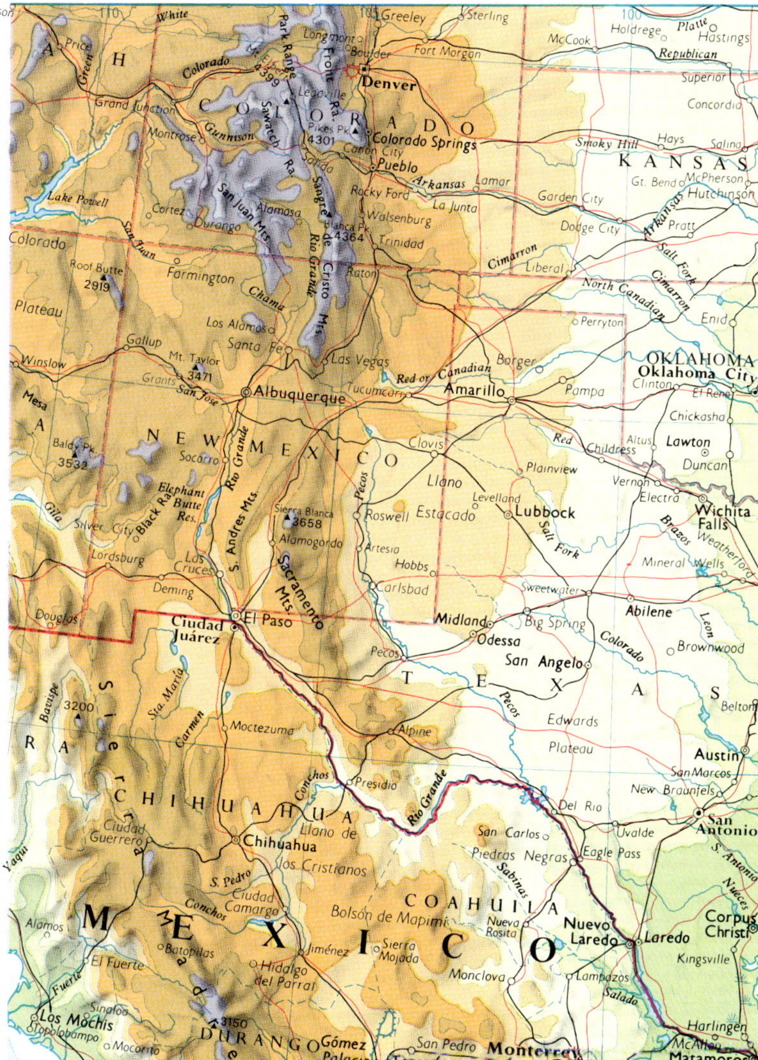

West from Greenwich

158

174

Map 161

U.S.A.: North West

142

160

1:12 000 000

143

156

161

U.S.A.: Boston, New York, Washington

1:6 000 000

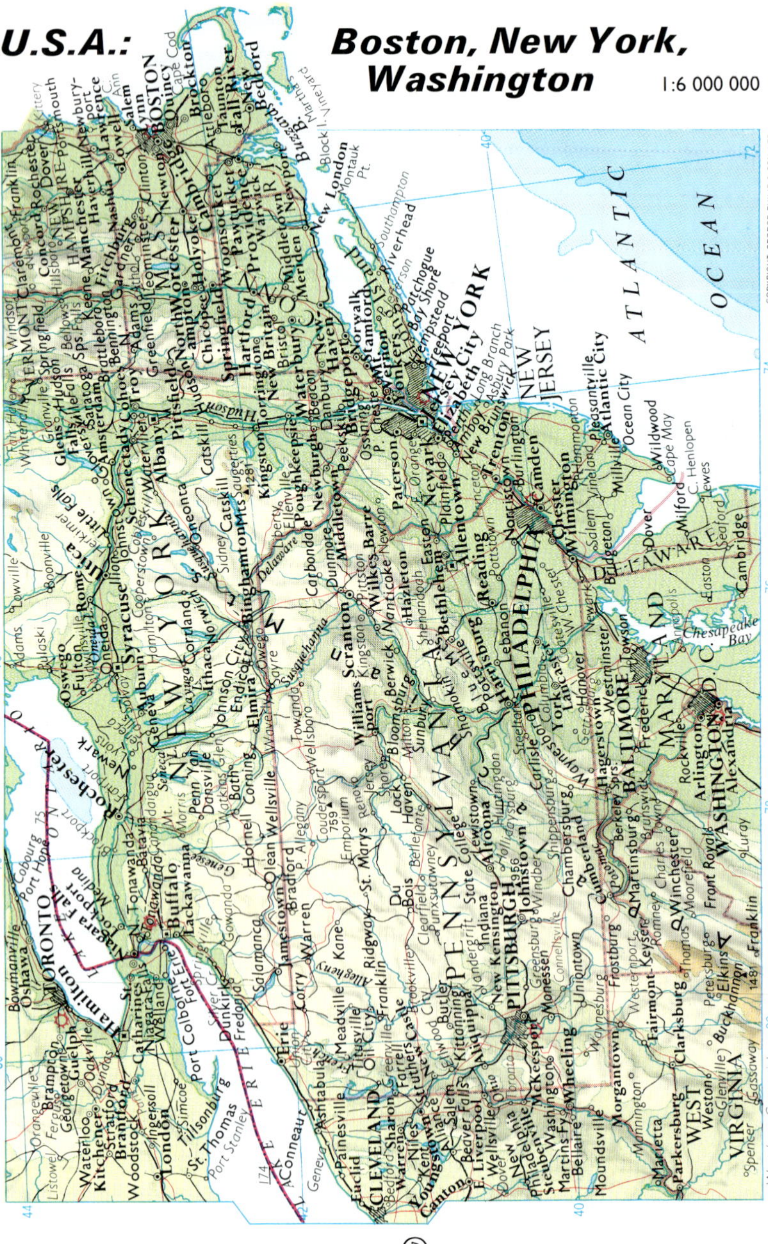

U.S.A.: Washington, Atlanta

1:6 000 000

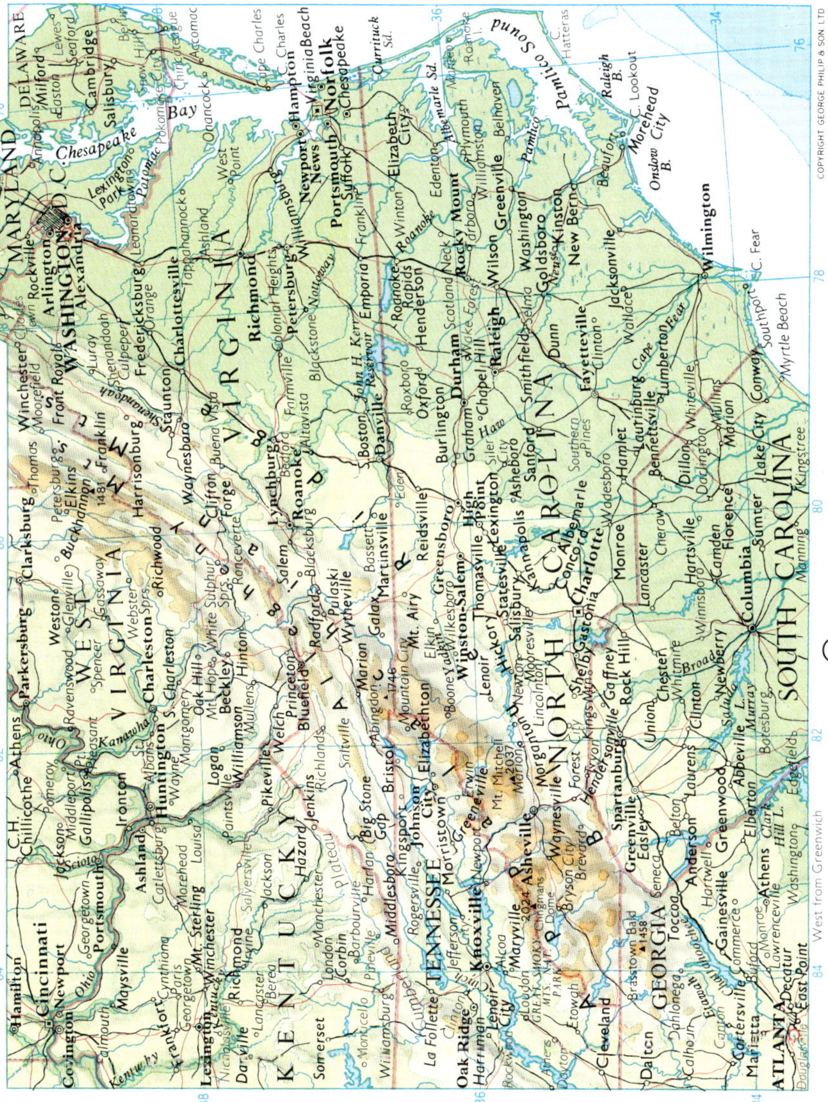

U.S.A.: Upper Mississippi

156

163

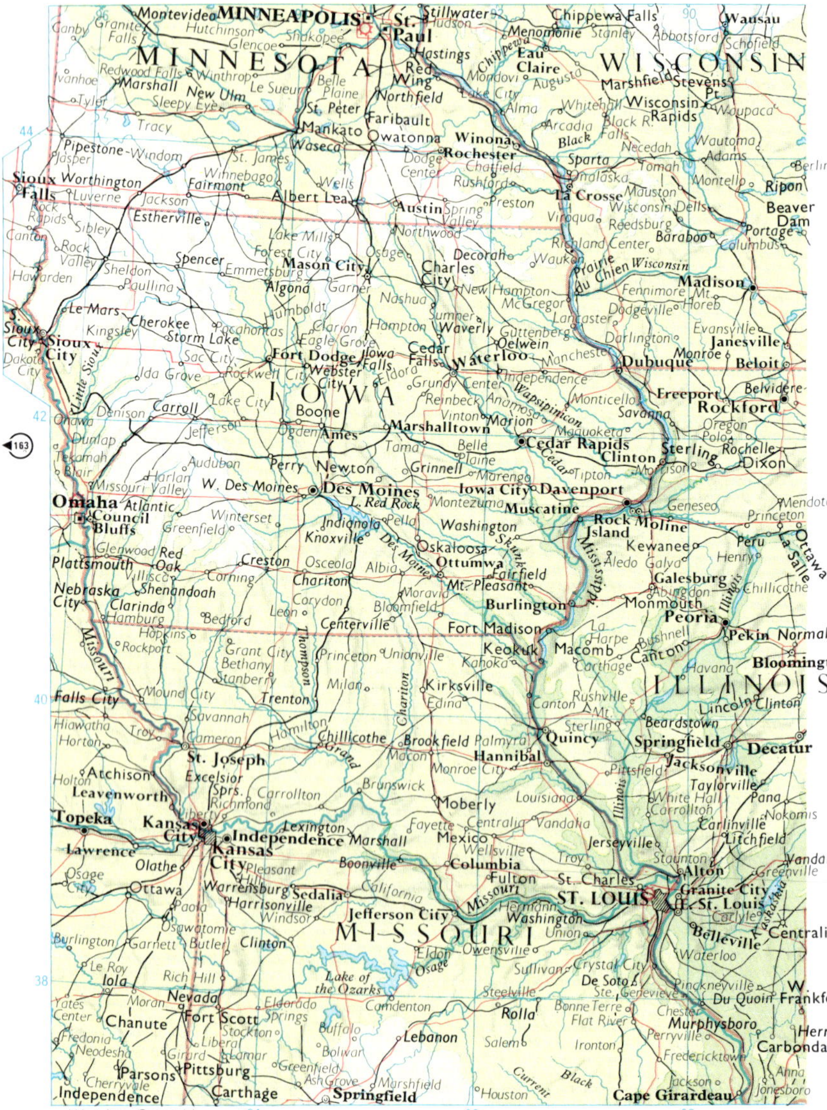

168

1:6 000 000

150

164

165

169

Map 167

U.S.A.: Lower Mississippi and Gulf Coast

166

161

176

Map 168

1:6 000 000

167

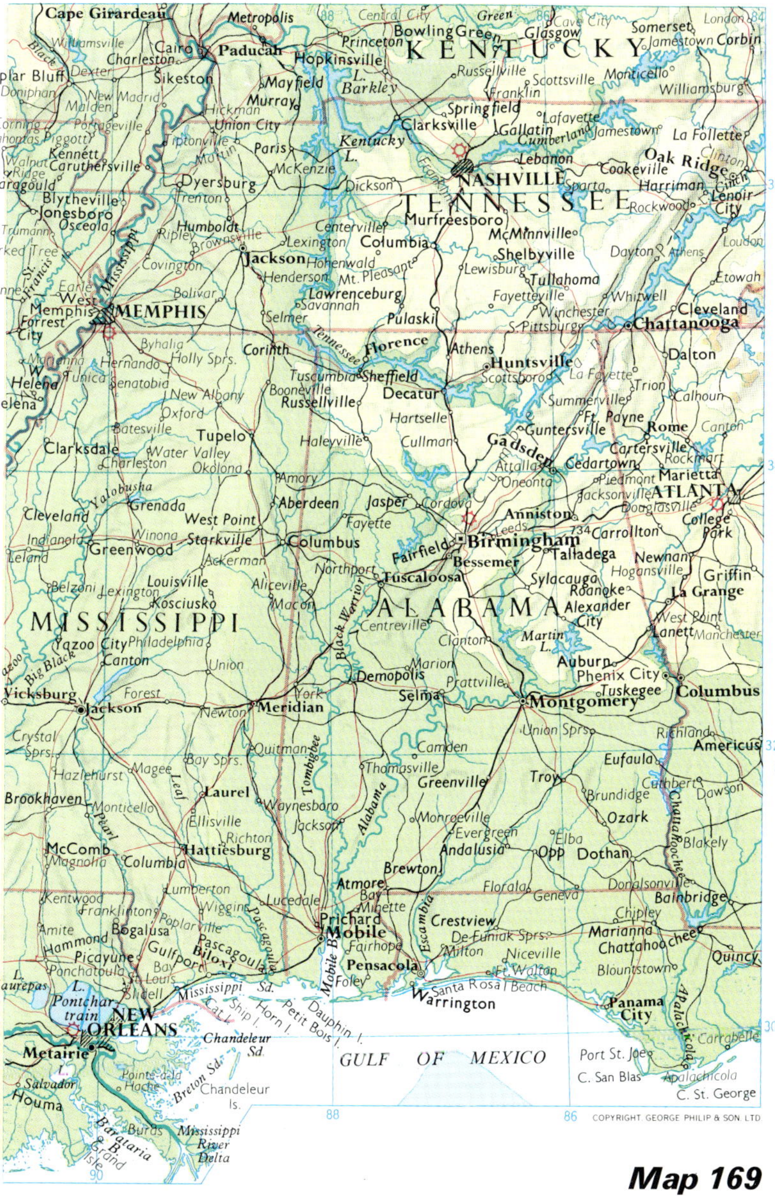

165

170

U.S.A.: Florida

1:6 000 000

U.S.A.: Columbia Basin

1:6 000 000

U.S.A.: California

163

171

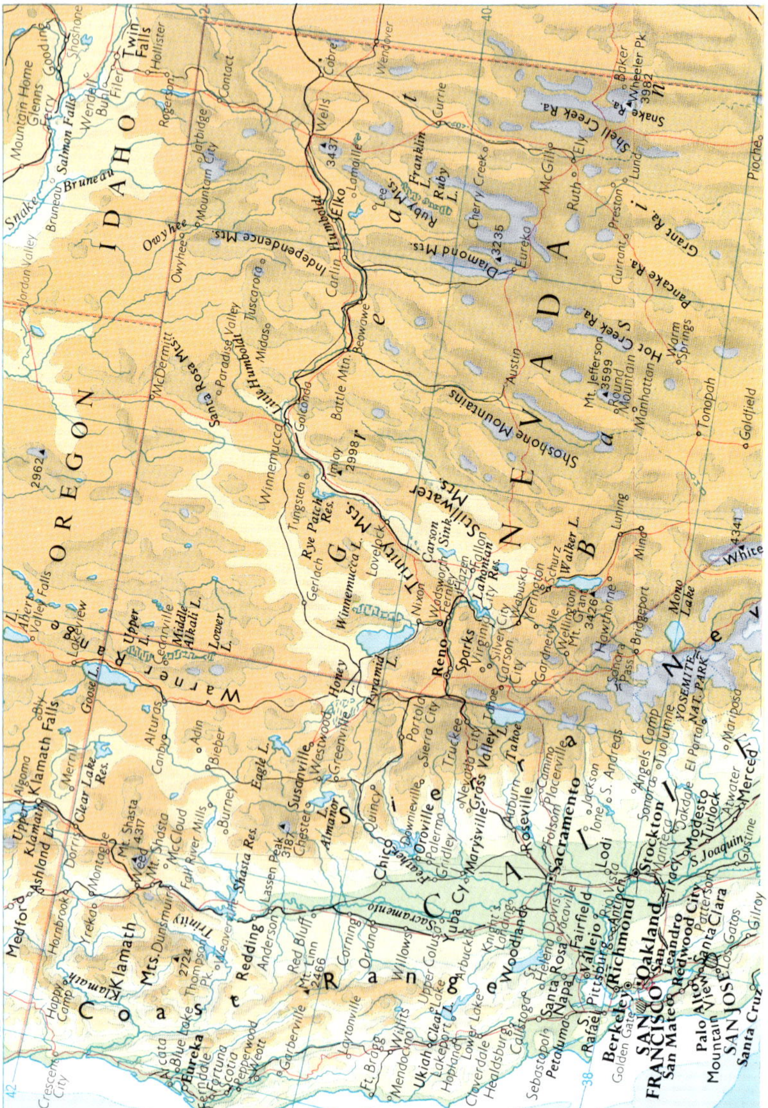

Map 172

1:6 000 000

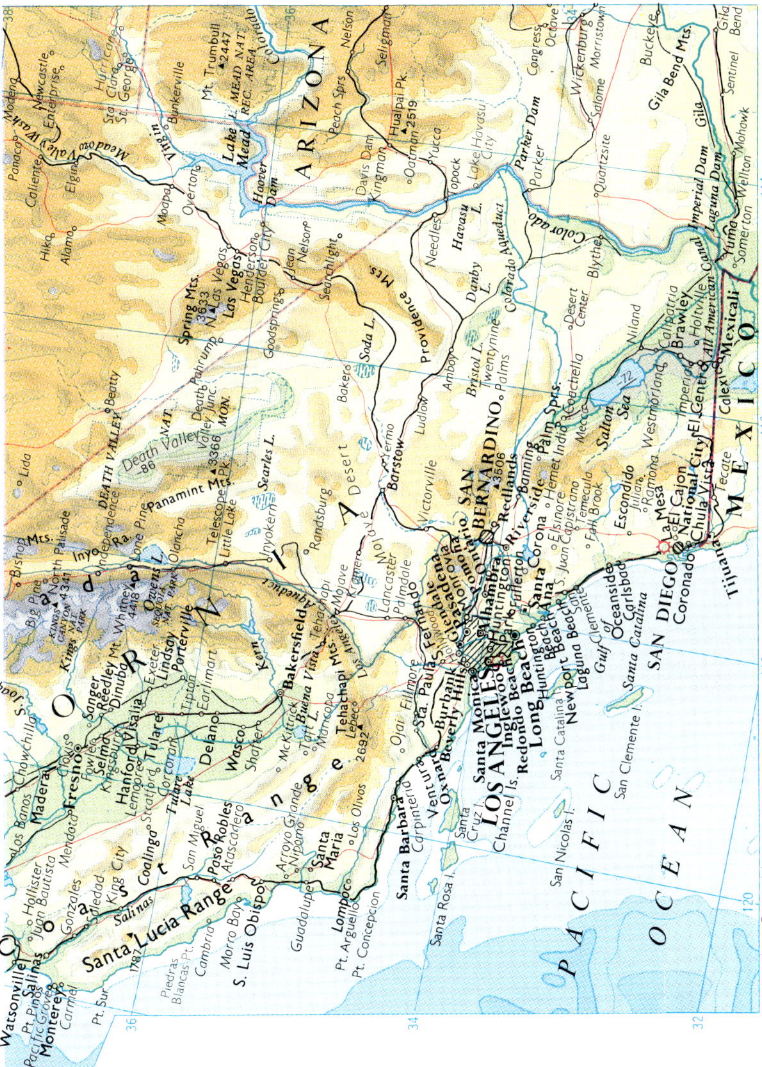

Map 173

Mexico: West

176

181

1:12 000 000

Map 175

Mexico: East

UNITED STATES
GULF OF MEXICO
MEXICO
TEXAS
LOUISIANA
MISSISSIPPI
ALABAMA
ARKANSAS
COAHUILA
NUEVO LEÓN
TAMAULIPAS
HOUSTON
DALLAS
FORT WORTH
SAN ANTONIO
NEW ORLEANS
MONTERREY
BIRMINGHAM
Austin
Jackson
Baton Rouge
Little Rock
Shreveport
Corpus Christi
Galveston
Port Arthur
Beaumont
Lake Charles
Lafayette
Alexandria
Mobile
Pensacola
Panama City
Montgomery
Gulfport
Biloxi
Hattiesburg
Meridian
Tuscaloosa
Vicksburg
Natchez
Monroe
Texarkana
Tyler
Waco
Temple
Abilene
San Angelo
Lubbock
Wichita Falls
Laredo
Nuevo Laredo
Brownsville
Matamoros
Reynosa
McAllen
Harlingen
Saltillo
Torreón
Monclova
Piedras Negras
Del Rio
Sabinas
Linares
Montemorelos
Rio Grande
Mississippi
Red
Brazos
Colorado
Trinity
Sabine
Pecos
Nueces
Guadalupe
Mississippi Delta
Atchafalaya Bay
Terrebonne B.
Mobile B.
Laguna Madre
Serranías del Burro
5203
2896
884
85
90
95
100
30
25
158
174

1:12 000 000

Map 177

Caribbean: West

159

180

177

1:12 000 000

Map 179

Caribbean: East

178

Map 180

1:12 000 000

Map 181

South America: Physical

1:50 000 000

Map 182

South America: Political

1:50 000 000

Map 183

South America: North West

181

179

186

Map 184

1:16 000 000

Map 185

South America: West

184

1:16 000 000

185

188

190

Map 187

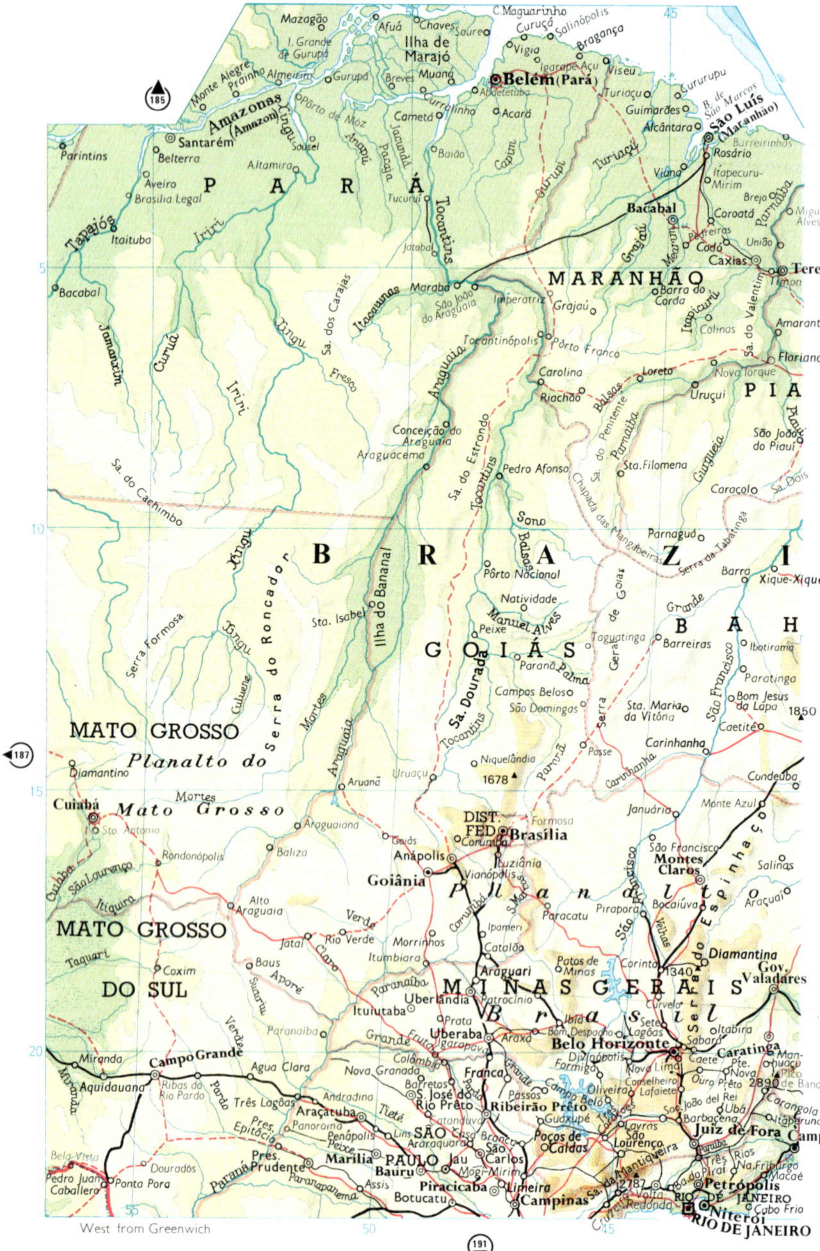
185
187
191
West from Greenwich
50
45
55
5
10
15
20
C. Maguarinho
Mazagão
Afuá
Chaves
Soure
Curuçá
Salinópolis
Bragança
I. Grande de Gurupá
Ilha de Marajó
Vigia
Igarapé Açu
Viseu
Monte Alegre
Prainha
Almeirim
Gurupá
Breves
Muaná
Belém (Pará)
Abaetetuba
Cururupu
Amazonas (Amazon)
Xingu
Pôrto de Móz
Curralinho
Cametá
Acará
Turiaçu
Guimarães
B. de São Marcos
São Luís (Maranhão)
Alcântara
Parintins
Santarém
Belterra
Sousel
Anapú
Pacajá
Jacundá
Baião
Capim
Gurupi
Turiaçu
Barreirinhas
Rosário
Altamira
Aveiro
Brasília Legal
P A R Á
Tucuruí
Tocantins
Viana
Itapecuru-Mirim
Brejo
Parnaíba
Bacabal
Coroatá
Pedreiras
Codó
União
Tapajós
Itaituba
Iriri
Jatobal
Grajaú
Mearim
Caxias
Teresina
Timon
Bacabal
MARANHÃO
Barra do Corda
Marabá
Itacaiunas
São João do Araguaia
Imperatriz
Grajaú
Itapicuru
Colinas
Sa. do Valentim
Amarante
Jamanxim
Curuá
Xingu
Sa. dos Carajás
Tocantinópolis
Pôrto Franco
Floriano
Fresco
Araguaia
Carolina
Loreto
Nova Iorque
Iriri
Riachão
Balsas
Uruçuí
PIAUÍ
Sa. do Penitente
Parnaíba
Piauí
São João do Piauí
Conceição do Araguaia
Araguacema
Sa. do Estrondo
Pedro Afonso
Sta. Filomena
Gurguéia
Sa. do Cachimbo
Chapada das Mangabeiras
Caracolo
Sa. Dois
Tocantins
Sono
Balsas
Parnaguá
Serra da Tabatinga
Xingu
B R A Z I L
Serra do Roncador
Ilha do Bananal
Pôrto Nacional
Barra
Xique-Xique
Natividade
Serra Geral de Goiás
Grande
Sta. Isabel
Manuel Alves
Peixe
Taguatinga
Barreiras
BAHIA
Serra Formosa
Xingu
GOIÁS
Ibotirama
Paraná
Palma
São Francisco
Paratinga
Culuene
Campos Belos
São Domingos
Bom Jesus da Lapa
Sa. Dourada
Sta. Maria da Vitória
1850
Mortes
Caetité
MATO GROSSO
Tocantins
Serra
Carinhanha
Planalto do
Niquelândia
Paranã
Posse
Carinhanha
Diamantino
Araguaia
Uruaçu
1678
Condeúba
Aruanã
Cuiabá
Mato Grosso
Mortes
DIST. FED.
Formosa
Monte Azul
Januária
Sto. Antonio
Araguaiana
Goiás
Corumbá
Brasília
São Francisco
Rondonópolis
Baliza
Anápolis
Luziânia
Montes Claros
Salinas
Cuiabá
São Lourenço
Goiânia
Vianópolis
S. Marcos
Planalto Brasil
Serra do Espinhaço
Itiquira
Alto Araguaia
Corumbá
Paracatu
Pirapora
Bocaiúva
Araçuaí
Verde
Ipameri
São Francisco
Velhas
MATO GROSSO
Jataí
Rio Verde
Morrinhos
Catalão
Claro
Itumbiara
Patos de Minas
Corinto
Diamantina
Taquari
1340
Gov. Valadares
Coxim
Baus
Aporé
Araguari
Paranaíba
MINAS GERAIS
DO SUL
Sucuriú
Ituiutaba
Uberlândia
Patrocínio
Curvelo
Verde
Prata
Ibiá
Sete Lagoas
Itabira
Paranaíba
Grande
Uberaba
Araxá
Bom Despacho
Belo Horizonte
Sabará
Caratinga
Frutal
Igarapava
Divinópolis
Formiga
Nova Lima
Caeté
Pte. Nova
Manhuaçu
Pico da Bandeira
2890
Miranda
Campo Grande
Colômbia
Conselheiro Lafaiete
Ouro Prêto
Miranda
Aquidauana
Ribas do Rio Pardo
Pardo
Agua Clara
Nova Granada
Barretos
França
Grande
Passos
Campo Belo
Oliveira
São João del Rei
Ubá
Carangola
Itaperuna
Três Lagoas
Andradina
S. José do Rio Prêto
Ribeirão Prêto
Barbacena
Juiz de Fora
Campos
Araçatuba
Tietê
Catanduva
Guaxupé
Lavras
Pres. Epitácio
Panorama
Penápolis
Lins
SÃO PAULO
Araraquara
Casa Branca
Poços de Caldas
São Lourenço
Paraíba
Três Rios
Na. Friburgo
Bela Vista
Dourados
Pres. Prudente
Marília
Bauru
Jau
São Carlos
Mogi-Mirim
Sa. da Mantiqueira
2787
Macaé
Paraná
Paranapanema
Assis
Piracicaba
Limeira
Volta Redonda
Barra do Piraí
Petrópolis
Pedro Juan Caballero
Ponta Pora
Botucatu
Campinas
RIO DE JANEIRO
Niterói
Cabo Frio
RIO DE JANEIRO

Map 188

South America: East

1:16 000 000

South America: Central

187

192

1:16 000 000

188

South America: South

1:16 000 000

190

Index

Introduction to Index

The number printed in bold type against each entry indicates the map page where the feature can be found. This is followed by its geographical coordinates. The first coordinate indicates latitude, i.e. distance north or south of the Equator. The second coordinate indicates longitude, i.e. distance east or west of the meridian of Greenwich in England (shown as 0° longitude). Both latitude and longitude are measured in degrees and minutes (with 60 minutes in a degree), and appear on the map as horizontal and vertical gridlines respectively. Thus the entry for Paris in France reads.

Paris, France........**39** 48 50N 2 20E

This entry indicates that Paris is on page **39,** at latitude 48 degrees 50 minutes north (approximately five-sixths of the distance between horizontal gridlines 48 and 49 , marked on either side of the page) and at longitude 2 degrees 20 minutes east (approximately one-third of the distance between vertical gridlines 2 and 3, marked at top and bottom of the page). Paris can be found where lines extended from these two points cross on the page. The geographical coordinates are sometimes only approximate but are close enough for the place to be located. Rivers have been indexed to their mouth or confluence.

An open square □ signifies that the name refers to an administrative subdivision of a country while a solid square ■ follows the name of a country. An arrow → follows the name of a river.

The alphabetical order of names composed of two or more words is governed primarily by the first word and then by the second. This rule applies even if the second word is a description or its abbreviation, R., L., I. for example.

North Walsham
Northallerton
Northampton
Northern Circars
Northumberland Is.
Northumberland Str.

Names composed of a proper name (Gibraltar) and a description (Strait of) are positioned alphabetically by the proper name. This is the case where the definite article follows a proper name (Mans, Le). If the same word occurs in the name of a town and a geographical feature, the town name is listed first followed by the name or names of the geographical features.

Names beginning with M', Mc are all indexed as if they were spelled Mac. All names beginning St. are alphabetised under Saint, but Sankt, Sint, Santa and San are all spelt in full and are alphabetised accordingly.

If the same place name occurs twice or more times in the index and all are in the same country, each is followed by the name of the administrative subdivision in which it is located. The names are placed in the alphabetical order of the subdivisions. If the same place name occurs twice or more in the index and the places are in different countries they will be followed by their country names, the latter governing the alphabetical order. In a mixture of these situations the primary order is fixed by the alphabetical sequence of the countries and the secondary order by that of the country subdivisions.

Abbreviations used

A.S.S.R. – *Autonomous Soviet Socialist Republic*
Ala. – *Alabama*
Arch. – *Archipelago*
Ark. – *Arkansas*
Austral. – *Australia*
B. – *Baie, Bahia, Bay, Boca, Bucht, Bugt*
B.C. – *British Columbia*
Bangla. – *Bangladesh*
Br. – *British*
C. – *Cabo, Cap, Cape, Coast, Costa*
C. Rica – *Costa Rica*
Calif. – *California*
Cap. Terr. – *Capital Territory*
Cat. – *Cataract*
Cent. – *Central*
Chan. – *Channel*
Colo. – *Colorado*
Conn. – *Connecticut*
Cord. – *Cordillera*
D.C. – *District of Columbia*
Del. – *Delaware*
Dét. – *Détroit*
Dom. Rep. – *Dominican Republic*
Domin. – *Dominica*
E. – *East, Eastern*
Est. – *Estrecho*
Falk. Is. – *Falkland Is.*
Fla. – *Florida*
Fr. Gui. – *French Guiana*
G. – *Golfe, Golfo, Gulf, Guba, Gebel*
Ga. – *Georgia*
Gt. – *Great*
Guat. – *Guatemala*
Hants. – *Hampshire*
Hd. – *Head*
Hond. – *Honduras*
Hts. – *Heights*
I.(s) – *Ile, Ilha, Insel, Isla, Island(s)*
I. of W. – *Isle of Wight*
Ill. – *Illinois*
Ind. – *Indiana*
Ind. Oc. – *Indian Ocean*
J. – *Jabal, Jazira*
K. – *Kap. Kapp*
Kans. – *Kansas*
Ky. – *Kentucky*
L. – *Lac, Lacul, Lago, Lagoa, Lake, Limni, Loch, Lough*
La. – *Louisiana*
Lag. – *Laguna*
Lancs. – *Lancashire*
Man. – *Manitoba*
Mass. – *Massachusetts*
Md. – *Maryland*
Mich. – *Michigan*
Minn. – *Minnesota*
Miss. – *Mississippi*
Mo. – *Missouri*
Mont. – *Montana*
Mt.(s) – *Mont, Monta, Monti, Muntii, Montaña, Mount, Mountain(s)*
N. – *North, Northern*
N.B. – *New Brunswick*
N.C. – *North Carolina*
N. Dak. – *North Dakota*
N.H. – *New Hampshire*
N.J. – *New Jersey*
N. Mex. – *New Mexico*
N.S.W. – *New South Wales*
N.W.T. – *North West Territories*
N.Y. – *New York*
N.Z. – *New Zealand*
Nebr. – *Nebraska*
Neth. – *Netherlands*
Nev. – *Nevada*
Nfld. – *Newfoundland*
Nic. – *Nicaragua*
Okla. – *Oklahoma*
Ont. – *Ontario*
Oreg. – *Oregon*
Os. – *Ostrov*
Oz. – *Ozero*
P. – *Pass, Passo, Pasul, Pulau*
P.E.I. – *Prince Edward Island*
Pa. – *Pennsylvania*
Pac. Oc. – *Pacific Ocean*
Papua N.G. – *Papua New Guinea*
Pen. – *Peninsula*
Pk. – *Peak*
Plat. – *Plateau*
P-ov. – *Poluostrov*
Pt. – *Point*
Pta. – *Ponta, Punta*
Queens. – *Queensland*
R. – *Rio, River, Rivière*
R.I. – *Rhode Island*
R.S.F.S.R. – *Russian Soviet Federative Socialist Republic*
Ra.(s) – *Range(s)*
Raj. – *Rajasthan*
Rep. – *Republic*
Res. – *Reserve, Reservoir*
S. – *South, Southern, Sea, Sur*
S.C. – *South Carolina*
S.S.R. – *Soviet Socialist Republic*
S. Africa – *South Africa*
S. Dak. – *South Dakota*
Sa. – *Serra, Sierra*
Salop. – *Shropshire*
Sard. – *Sardinia*
Sask. – *Saskatchewan*
Sd. – *Sound*
Sev. – *Severnaya*
Si. Arabia – *Saudi Arabia*
St. – *Saint*
Sta. – *Santa*
Ste. – *Sainte*
Str. – *Strait, Stretto*
Switz. – *Switzerland*
Tas. – *Tasmania*
Tenn. – *Tennessee*
Terr. – *Territory*
Tex. – *Texas*
Tipp. – *Tipperary*
Trin. & Tob. – *Trinidad and Tobago*
U.K. – *United Kingdom*
U.S.A. – *United States of America*
U.S.S.R. – *Union of Soviet Socialist Republics*
Ut. P. – *Uttar Pradesh*
Va. – *Virginia*
Vic. – *Victoria*
Vol. – *Volcano*
Vt. – *Vermont*
Wash. – *Washington*
W. – *West, Western, Wadi*
W. Va. – *West Virginia*
Wis. – *Wisconsin*
Worcs. – *Worcestershire*
Yorks. – *Yorkshire*

Aachen	**42**	50 47N	6 4 E
Aalborg = Ålborg	**61**	57 2N	9 54 E
Aalsmeer	**40**	52 17N	4 43 E
Aalst	**42**	50 56N	4 2 E
Aalten	**41**	51 56N	6 35 E
Aarhus = Århus	**61**	56 8N	10 11 E
Aba	**131**	5 10N	7 19 E
Ābādān	**84**	30 22N	48 20 E
Ābādeh	**85**	31 8N	52 40 E
Abadla	**126**	31 2N	2 45W
Abai	**191**	25 58S	55 54W
Abakan	**74**	53 40N	91 10 E
Abancay	**186**	13 35S	72 55W
Abariringa I.	**122**	2 50S	171 40W
Abashiri	**103**	44 0N	144 15 E
Abashiri-Wan	**103**	44 0N	144 30 E
Abaya, L.	**133**	6 30N	37 50 E
Abbay = Nîl el Azraq →	**129**	15 38N	32 31 E
Abbeville, France	**38**	50 6N	1 49 E
Abbeville, U.S.A.	**165**	34 12N	82 21W
Abéché	**129**	13 50N	20 35 E
Abeokuta	**131**	7 3N	3 19 E
Aberaeron	**26**	52 15N	4 16W
Aberayron = Aberaeron	**26**	52 15N	4 16W
Aberdare	**27**	51 43N	3 27W
Aberdeen, U.K.	**33**	57 9N	2 6W
Aberdeen, S. Dak., U.S.A.	**163**	45 30N	98 30W
Aberdeen, Wash., U.S.A.	**171**	47 0N	123 50W
Aberdovey	**26**	52 33N	4 3W
Aberfeldy	**33**	56 37N	3 50W
Abergavenny	**26**	51 49N	3 1W
Aberystwyth	**26**	52 25N	4 6W
Abha	**82**	18 0N	42 34 E
Abidjan	**130**	5 26N	3 58W
Abilene	**161**	32 22N	99 40W
Abington	**25**	55 30N	3 42W
Abkhaz A.S.S.R. □	**70**	43 0N	41 0 E
Abohar	**89**	30 10N	74 10 E
Abomey	**131**	7 10N	2 5 E
Abong-Mbang	**131**	4 0N	13 8 E
Abrud	**56**	46 19N	23 5 E
Abruzzi □	**47**	42 15N	14 0 E
Absaroka Ra.	**163**	44 40N	110 0W
Abū al Khaşīb	**84**	30 25N	48 0 E
Abū 'Alī	**84**	27 20N	49 27 E
Abū 'Arīsh	**82**	16 58N	45 20 E
Abu Dhabi = Abū Ẓāby	**85**	24 28N	54 22 E
Abu Hamed	**129**	19 32N	33 13 E
Abū Ẓāby	**85**	24 28N	54 22 E
Abunã	**187**	9 40S	65 20W
Abunã →	**187**	9 41S	65 20W
Abut Hd.	**123**	43 7S	170 15 E
Acámbaro	**177**	20 2N	100 44W
Acaponeta	**175**	22 30N	105 22W
Acapulco	**177**	16 51N	99 56W
Acatlán	**177**	18 10N	98 3W
Acayucan	**177**	17 57N	94 55W
Accra	**130**	5 35N	0 6W
Accrington	**28**	53 46N	2 22W
Achill I.	**34**	53 58N	10 5W
Achinsk	**74**	56 20N	90 20 E
Aconcagua, Cerro	**190**	32 39S	70 0W
Aconquija, Mt.	**190**	27 0S	66 0W
Açores, Is. dos = Azores	**126**	38 44N	29 0W
Acre = 'Akko	**80**	32 55N	35 4 E
Acre □	**187**	9 1S	71 0W
Ad Dawhah	**85**	25 15N	51 35 E
Ada	**168**	34 50N	96 45W
Adamaoua, Massif de l'	**131**	7 20N	12 20 E
Adamawa Highlands = Adamaoua, Massif de l'	**131**	7 20N	12 20 E
Adaminaby	**117**	36 0S	148 45 E
Adams, Mt.	**171**	46 10N	121 28W
Adam's Bridge	**90**	9 15N	79 40 E
Adana	**80**	37 0N	35 16 E
Adapazarı	**80**	40 48N	30 25 E
Adare, C.	**15**	71 0S	171 0 E
Addis Ababa = Addis Abeba	**133**	9 2N	38 42 E
Addis Abeba	**133**	9 2N	38 42 E
Adelaide	**119**	34 52S	138 30 E
Adelaide Pen.	**145**	68 15N	97 30W
Adélie, Terre	**15**	68 0S	140 0 E
Aden = Al 'Adan	**83**	12 45N	45 0 E
Aden, G. of	**133**	13 0N	50 0 E
Adige →	**47**	45 9N	12 20 E
Adirondack Mts.	**151**	44 0N	74 15W
Admiralty Is.	**115**	2 0S	147 0 E
Adoni	**90**	15 33N	77 18W
Adrian	**167**	41 55N	84 0W
Adriatic Sea	**52**	43 0N	16 0 E
Adwa	**132**	14 15N	38 52 E
Adzhar A.S.S.R. □	**70**	42 0N	42 0 E
Ægean Sea	**55**	37 0N	25 0 E
Æolian Is. = Eólie, I.	**49**	38 30N	14 50 E
Aerht'ai Shan	**100**	46 40N	92 45 E
Afars & Issas, Terr. of = Djibouti ■	**133**	12 0N	43 0 E
Afghanistan ■	**87**	33 0N	65 0 E
Afuá	**188**	0 15S	50 20W
Afyonkarahisar	**80**	38 45N	30 33 E
Agadir	**126**	30 28N	9 35W
Agano →	**103**	37 57N	139 8 E
Agartala	**93**	23 50N	91 23 E
Agen	**36**	44 12N	0 38 E
Ageo	**107**	35 58N	139 36 E
Aghil Pass	**89**	36 15N	76 35 E
Agra	**89**	27 17N	77 58 E
Ağri Daği	**81**	39 50N	44 15 E
Água Clara	**188**	20 25S	52 45W
Agua Prieta	**174**	31 18N	109 34W
Aguadas	**184**	5 40N	75 38W
Aguadilla	**180**	18 27N	67 10W
Aguas Blancas	**190**	24 15S	69 55W
Aguascalientes	**175**	21 53N	102 18W
Aguascalientes □	**175**	22 0N	102 30W
Agulhas, Kaap	**136**	34 52S	20 0 E
Ahaggar	**127**	23 0N	6 30 E
Ahaura →	**123**	42 21S	171 34 E
Ahmadabad	**91**	23 0N	72 40 E
Ahmadnagar	**91**	19 7N	74 46 E
Ahmedabad = Ahmadabad	**91**	23 0N	72 40 E
Ahmednagar = Ahmadnagar	**91**	19 7N	74 46 E
Ahvāz	**84**	31 20N	48 40 E
Ahvenanmaa = Åland	**66**	60 15N	20 0 E
Ahwar	**83**	13 30N	46 40 E
Aigle, L'	**39**	48 46N	0 38 E
Aigues-Mortes	**37**	43 35N	4 12 E
Aiken	**170**	33 34N	81 50W
Ailsa Craig	**30**	55 15N	5 7W
Aimorés	**189**	19 30S	41 4W
Aïn Ben Tili	**126**	25 59N	9 27W
Aioi	**109**	34 48N	134 28 E
Aïr	**127**	18 30N	8 0 E
Airdrie	**31**	55 53N	3 57W
Aire →	**29**	53 42N	0 55W
Airlie Beach	**121**	20 16S	148 43 E
Aisne →	**37**	49 26N	2 50 E
Aix-en-Provence	**37**	43 32N	5 27 E
Aix-la-Chapelle = Aachen	**42**	50 47N	6 4 E
Aix-les-Bains	**37**	45 41N	5 53 E
Aizuwakamatsu	**105**	37 30N	139 56 E
Ajaccio	**36**	41 55N	8 40 E
Ajanta Ra.	**91**	20 28N	75 50 E
Ajmer	**91**	26 28N	74 37 E
Akaishi-Dake	**107**	35 27N	138 9 E
Akaishi-Sammyaku	**107**	35 25N	138 10 E
Akashi	**109**	34 45N	135 0 E
Akershus fylke □	**60**	60 0N	11 10 E
Akhelóös →	**54**	38 36N	21 14 E
Akhisar	**80**	38 56N	27 48 E
Aki	**109**	33 30N	133 54 E
Aki-Nada	**109**	34 5N	132 40 E
Akita	**103**	39 45N	140 7 E
'Akko	**80**	32 55N	35 4 E
Aklavik	**144**	68 12N	135 0W
Akō	**109**	34 45N	134 24 E
Akola	**91**	20 42N	77 2 E
Akranes	**64**	64 19N	21 58W
Akron	**167**	41 7N	81 31W
Aksaray	**80**	38 25N	34 2 E
Aksarka	**69**	66 31N	67 50 E
Akşehir	**80**	38 18N	31 30 E

Aksum	**132**	14 5N	38 40 E
Aktyubinsk	**70**	50 17N	57 10 E
Akune	**108**	32 1N	130 12 E
Akureyri	**64**	65 40N	18 6W
Al 'Adan	**83**	12 45N	45 0 E
Al Amādīyah	**81**	37 5N	43 30 E
Al Amārah	**84**	31 55N	47 15 E
Al 'Aqabah	**80**	29 31N	35 0 E
Al Başrah	**84**	30 30N	47 50 E
Al Ḥadīthah	**81**	31 28N	37 8 E
Al Hāmad	**80**	31 30N	39 30 E
Al Ḥasakah	**81**	36 35N	40 45 E
Al Ḥawrah	**83**	13 50N	47 35 E
Al Ḥayy	**84**	32 5N	46 5 E
Al Ḥillah, Iraq	**84**	32 30N	44 25 E
Al Ḥillah, Si. Arabia	**83**	23 35N	46 50 E
Al Hindīyah	**84**	32 30N	44 10 E
Al Ḥudaydah	**82**	14 50N	43 0 E
Al Hūfuf	**84**	25 25N	49 45 E
Al Jāfūrah	**84**	25 0N	50 15 E
Al Jawf, Libya	**128**	24 10N	23 24 E
Al Jawf, Si. Arabia	**82**	29 55N	39 40 E
Al Jazirah	**81**	33 30N	44 0 E
Al Khalīl	**80**	31 32N	35 6 E
Al Kūt	**84**	32 30N	46 0 E
Al Kuwayt	**84**	29 30N	47 30 E
Al Lādhiqīyah	**80**	35 30N	35 45 E
Al Lidām	**82**	20 33N	44 45 E
Al Luḥayyah	**82**	15 45N	42 40 E
Al Madīnah	**82**	24 35N	39 52 E
Al Manāmāh	**85**	26 10N	50 30 E
Al Marj	**128**	32 25N	20 30 E
Al Mawşil	**81**	36 15N	43 5 E
Al Mubarraz	**84**	25 30N	49 40 E
Al Muḥarraq	**85**	26 15N	50 40 E
Al Mukallā	**83**	14 33N	49 2 E
Al Qaţīf	**84**	26 35N	50 0 E
Al Quds = Jerusalem	**80**	31 47N	35 10 E
Al Qunfudhah	**82**	19 3N	41 4 E
Al Qurnah	**84**	31 1N	47 25 E
Al 'Ubaylah	**83**	21 59N	50 57 E
Al 'Uthmānīyah	**84**	25 5N	49 22 E
Al Wajh	**82**	26 10N	36 30 E
Alabama □	**169**	33 0N	87 0W
Alabama →	**169**	31 8N	87 57W
Alagoas □	**189**	9 0S	36 0W
Alagoinhas	**189**	12 7S	38 20W
Alajuela	**179**	10 2N	84 8W
Alamogordo	**161**	32 59N	106 0W
Álamos	**174**	27 1N	108 56W
Alamosa	**163**	37 30N	106 0W
Åland	**66**	60 15N	20 0 E
Alaska □	**142**	65 0N	150 0W
Alaska, G. of	**142**	58 0N	145 0W
Alaska Pen.	**142**	56 0N	160 0W
Alaska Range	**142**	62 50N	151 0W
Alba Iulia	**56**	46 8N	23 39 E
Albacete	**51**	39 0N	1 50W
Albania ■	**52**	41 0N	20 0 E
Albany, Australia	**120**	35 1S	117 58 E
Albany, Ga., U.S.A.	**170**	31 40N	84 10W
Albany, N.Y., U.S.A.	**164**	42 35N	73 47W
Albany, Oreg., U.S.A.	**171**	44 41N	123 0W
Albany →	**140**	52 17N	81 31W
Albemarle	**165**	35 27N	80 15W
Albemarle Sd.	**165**	36 0N	76 30W
Albert	**38**	50 0N	2 38 E
Albert, L. = Mobutu Sese Seko, L.	**132**	1 30N	31 0 E
Albert Lea	**166**	43 32N	93 20W
Alberta □	**155**	54 40N	115 0W
Albertville = Kalemie	**135**	5 55S	29 9 E
Albi	**37**	43 56N	2 9 E
Albion	**167**	42 15N	84 45W
Ålborg	**61**	57 2N	9 54 E
Alborz, Reshteh-ye Kūhhā-ye	**86**	36 0N	52 0 E
Albuquerque	**161**	35 5N	106 47W
Alburquerque	**50**	39 15N	6 59W
Albury	**117**	36 3S	146 56 E
Alcântara	**188**	2 20S	44 30W
Alcázar de San Juan	**50**	39 24N	3 12W
Alcira	**51**	39 9N	0 30W
Aldan →	**75**	63 28N	129 35 E
Aldeburgh	**25**	52 9N	1 35 E
Alderney	**36**	49 42N	2 12W
Aldershot	**25**	51 15N	0 43W
Alençon	**39**	48 27N	0 4 E
Aleppo = Ḥalab	**80**	36 10N	37 15 E
Alès	**37**	44 9N	4 5 E
Alessándria	**46**	44 54N	8 37 E
Ålesund	**65**	62 28N	6 12 E
Aleutian Is.	**142**	52 0N	175 0W
Alexander Arch.	**143**	57 0N	135 0W
Alexander City	**169**	32 58N	85 57W
Alexandra, Australia	**117**	37 8S	145 40 E
Alexandra, N.Z.	**123**	45 14S	169 25 E
Alexandretta = İskenderun	**80**	36 32N	36 10 E
Alexandria = El Iskandarîya	**128**	31 0N	30 0 E
Alexandria, La., U.S.A.	**168**	31 20N	92 30W
Alexandria, Va., U.S.A.	**164**	38 47N	77 1W
Alexandrina, L.	**119**	35 25S	139 10 E
Alexandroúpolis	**55**	40 50N	25 54 E
Alexis Creek	**154**	52 10N	123 20W
Alfreton	**29**	53 6N	1 22W
Algarve	**50**	36 58N	8 20W
Alger	**127**	36 42N	3 8 E
Algeria ■	**127**	35 10N	3 11 E
Algiers = Alger	**127**	36 42N	3 8 E
Algoa B.	**136**	33 50S	25 45 E
Alhambra	**173**	34 2N	118 10W
Alicante	**51**	38 23N	0 30W
Alice Springs	**114**	23 40S	133 50 E
Aligarh	**89**	27 55N	78 10 E
Alipur Duar	**92**	26 30N	89 35 E
Aliquippa	**164**	40 38N	80 18W
Alkmaar	**40**	52 37N	4 45 E
Allahabad	**92**	25 25N	81 58 E
Allegheny Mts.	**165**	38 0N	80 0W
Allen, Bog of	**35**	53 15N	7 0W
Allende	**174**	28 20N	100 51W
Allentown	**164**	40 36N	75 30W
Alleppey	**90**	9 30N	76 28 E
Aller →	**42**	52 57N	9 10 E
Allier →	**37**	46 57N	3 4 E
Alloa	**31**	56 7N	3 49W
Alma, Canada	**148**	48 35N	71 40W
Alma, U.S.A.	**167**	43 25N	84 40W
Alma Ata	**71**	43 15N	76 57 E
Almada	**50**	38 40N	9 9W
Almelo	**41**	52 22N	6 42 E
Almería	**51**	36 52N	2 27W
Almirante	**179**	9 10N	82 30W
Alor	**113**	8 15S	124 30 E
Alor Setar	**96**	6 7N	100 22 E
Alpena	**150**	45 6N	83 24W
Alphen	**40**	51 29N	4 58 E
Alpine	**161**	30 25N	103 35W
Alps	**16**	47 0N	8 0 E
Alsace	**37**	48 15N	7 25 E
Alsask	**152**	51 21N	109 59W
Alston	**28**	54 48N	2 26W
Alta Gracia	**190**	31 40S	64 30W
Altagracia	**184**	10 45N	71 30W
Altai = Aerht'ai Shan	**100**	46 40N	92 45 E
Altamaha →	**170**	31 19N	81 17W
Altamira	**188**	3 12S	52 10W
Alto Adige = Trentino-Alto Adige □	**47**	46 30N	11 0 E
Alton	**166**	38 55N	90 5W
Altona	**43**	53 32N	9 56 E
Altoona	**164**	40 32N	78 24W
Altun Shan	**100**	38 30N	88 0 E
Alvarado	**177**	18 46N	95 46W
Älvsborgs län □	**60**	58 30N	12 30 E
Alwar	**89**	27 38N	76 34 E
Alxa Zuoqi	**98**	38 50N	105 40 E
Am-Timan	**129**	11 0N	20 10 E
Amadjuak	**146**	64 0N	72 39W
Amadjuak L.	**146**	65 0N	71 8W
Amagasaki	**106**	34 42N	135 20 E
Amagi	**108**	33 25N	130 39 E
Amakusa-Nada	**108**	32 35N	130 5 E

Amalner	**91**	21 5N	75 5E
Amapá	**185**	2 5N	50 50W
Amapá □	**185**	1 40N	52 0W
Amarillo	**161**	35 14N	101 46W
Amasya	**80**	40 40N	35 50E
Amatitlán	**177**	14 29N	90 38W
Amazon = Amazonas →	**185**	0 5S	50 0W
Amazonas □	**185**	4 0S	62 0W
Amazonas →	**185**	0 5S	50 0W
Ambala	**89**	30 23N	76 56E
Ambato	**184**	1 5S	78 42W
Ambikapur	**92**	23 15N	83 15E
Ambleside	**28**	54 26N	2 58W
Ambo	**186**	10 5S	76 10W
Ambon	**113**	3 35S	128 20E
Amboyna I.	**112**	7 50N	112 50E
Amderma	**69**	69 45N	61 30E
Ameca	**175**	20 33N	104 2W
Ameca, R. →	**175**	20 41N	105 18W
Ameland	**41**	53 27N	5 45E
American Highland	**14**	73 0S	75 0E
American Samoa ■	**123**	14 20S	170 40W
Americus	**170**	32 0N	84 10W
Amersfoort	**40**	52 9N	5 23E
Amery	**143**	56 34N	94 3W
Ames	**166**	42 0N	93 40W
Amga →	**75**	62 38N	134 32E
Amgu	**75**	45 45N	137 15E
Amgun →	**75**	52 56N	139 38E
Amherst	**148**	45 48N	64 8W
Amherstburg	**150**	42 6N	83 6W
Amiens	**38**	49 54N	2 16E
Amlwch	**26**	53 24N	4 21W
'Ammān	**80**	31 57N	35 52E
Amorgós	**55**	36 50N	25 57E
Amos	**151**	48 35N	78 5W
Amoy = Xiamen	**99**	24 25N	118 4E
Amravati	**91**	20 55N	77 45E
Amreli	**91**	21 35N	71 17E
Amritsar	**89**	31 35N	74 57E
Amsterdam, Neth.	**40**	52 23N	4 54E
Amsterdam, U.S.A.	**164**	42 58N	74 10W
Amudarya →	**70**	43 40N	59 0E
Amundsen Gulf	**145**	71 0N	124 0W
Amundsen Sea	**15**	72 0S	115 0W
Amur →	**75**	52 56N	141 10E
An Nafūd	**82**	28 15N	41 0E
An Najaf	**84**	32 3N	44 15E
An Nāşirīyah	**84**	31 0N	46 15E
An Nhon	**95**	13 55N	109 7E
An Nu'ayrīyah	**84**	27 30N	48 30E
An Uaimh	**34**	53 39N	6 40W
Anabar →	**72**	73 8N	113 36E
Anaconda	**163**	46 7N	113 0W
Anacortes	**171**	48 30N	122 40W
Anadolu	**80**	38 0N	30 0E
Anadyr →	**73**	64 55N	176 5E
Anadyrskiy Zaliv	**73**	64 0N	180 0E
Anaheim	**173**	33 50N	118 0W
Anambas Is.	**111**	3 20N	106 30E
Anamur	**80**	36 8N	32 58E
Anan	**109**	33 54N	134 40E
Anápolis	**188**	16 15S	48 50W
Anārak	**85**	33 25N	53 40E
Anatolia = Anadolu	**80**	38 0N	30 0E
Añatuya	**190**	28 20S	62 50W
Anchorage	**142**	61 10N	149 50W
Ancohuma, Nevada	**187**	16 0S	68 50W
Ancona	**47**	43 37N	13 30E
Ancud	**192**	42 0S	73 50W
Ancud, G. de	**192**	42 0S	73 0W
Åndalsnes	**65**	62 35N	7 43E
Andalucía □	**50**	37 35N	5 0W
Andalusia	**169**	31 19N	86 30W
Andalusia □ = Andalucía □	**50**	37 35N	5 0W
Andaman Is.	**94**	12 30N	92 30E
Andaman Sea	**94**	13 0N	96 0E
Andaman Str.	**94**	12 15N	92 20E
Andelys, Les	**39**	49 15N	1 25E
Anderson, Ind., U.S.A.	**167**	40 5N	85 40W
Anderson, S.C., U.S.A.	**165**	34 32N	82 40W
Andes, Cord. de los	**182**	20 0S	68 0W
Andhra Pradesh □	**91**	16 0N	79 0E
Andikíthira	**55**	35 52N	23 15E
Andizhan	**71**	41 10N	72 0E
Andorra ■	**36**	42 30N	1 30E
Andover	**24**	51 13N	1 29W
Andreanof Is.	**142**	52 0N	178 0W
Andrewilla	**118**	26 31S	139 17E
Ándria	**49**	41 13N	16 17E
Andropov	**68**	58 5N	38 50E
Ándros	**55**	37 50N	24 57E
Andros I.	**178**	24 30N	78 0W
Angara →	**74**	58 30N	97 0E
Angarsk	**74**	52 30N	104 0E
Angaston	**119**	34 30S	139 8E
Ånge	**66**	62 31N	15 35E
Ängelholm	**61**	56 15N	12 58E
Angels Camp	**172**	38 8N	120 30W
Ångerman →	**66**	64 0N	17 20E
Angers	**36**	47 30N	0 35W
Angkor	**95**	13 22N	103 50E
Anglesey	**26**	53 17N	4 20W
Angmagssalik	**147**	65 40N	37 20W
Angol	**190**	37 56S	72 45W
Angola ■	**134**	12 0S	18 0E
Angoulême	**36**	45 39N	0 10E
Angoumois	**36**	45 50N	0 25E
Anguilla	**180**	18 14N	63 5W
Angus, Braes of	**33**	56 51N	3 10W
Anhui □	**99**	32 0N	117 0E
Anhwei □ = Anhui □	**99**	32 0N	117 0E
Anin	**94**	15 36N	97 50E
Anjō	**106**	34 57N	137 5E
Anjou	**36**	47 20N	0 15W
Anju	**98**	39 36N	125 40E
Ankang	**99**	32 40N	109 1E
Ankara	**80**	40 0N	32 54E
Ann Arbor	**167**	42 17N	83 45W
Annaba	**127**	36 50N	7 46E
Annam = Trung-Phan	**95**	16 0N	108 0E
Annamitique, Chaîne	**95**	17 0N	106 0E
Annan	**31**	55 0N	3 17W
Annapolis	**164**	39 0N	76 30W
Annecy	**37**	45 55N	6 8E
Anniston	**169**	33 45N	85 50W
Annobón	**131**	1 25S	5 36E
Annonay	**37**	45 15N	4 40E
Annotto Bay	**180**	18 17N	77 3W
Anqing	**99**	30 30N	117 3E
Anse, L'	**150**	46 47N	88 28W
Anshan	**98**	41 3N	122 58E
Anshun	**99**	26 18N	105 57E
Anstruther	**31**	56 14N	2 40W
Antabamba	**186**	14 40S	73 0W
Antakya	**80**	36 14N	36 10E
Antalya	**80**	36 52N	30 45E
Antalya Körfezi	**80**	36 15N	31 30E
Antananarivo	**137**	18 55S	47 31E
Antarctic Pen.	**14**	67 0S	60 0W
Antarctica	**14**	90 0S	0 0E
Anti Atlas	**126**	30 0N	8 30W
Antibes	**37**	43 34N	7 6E
Anticosti, Î. d'	**148**	49 30N	63 0W
Antigo	**150**	45 8N	89 5W
Antigua, Guat.	**177**	14 34N	90 41W
Antigua, W. Indies	**180**	17 0N	61 50W
Antigua and Barbuda ■	**180**	17 20N	61 48W
Antilla	**178**	20 40N	75 50W
Antioch	**172**	38 7N	121 45W
Antioquia	**184**	6 40N	75 55W
Antipodes Is.	**11**	49 45S	178 40E
Antofagasta	**190**	23 50S	70 30W
Antrim	**34**	54 43N	6 13W
Antrim, Mts. of	**34**	54 57N	6 8W
Antsiranana	**137**	12 25S	49 20E
Antwerp = Antwerpen	**42**	51 13N	4 25E
Antwerpen	**42**	51 13N	4 25E
Anvers = Antwerpen	**42**	51 13N	4 25E
Anvik	**142**	62 37N	160 20W
Anxious B.	**119**	33 24S	134 45E
Anyang	**98**	36 5N	114 21E

Anzhero-Sudzhensk	**71**	56 10N	86 0 E
Ánzio	**46**	41 28N	12 37 E
Aoga-Shima	**105**	32 28N	139 46 E
Aomori	**103**	40 45N	140 45 E
Apalachee B.	**170**	30 0N	84 0W
Apalachicola	**170**	29 40N	85 0W
Apalachicola →	**170**	29 40N	85 0W
Aparri	**112**	18 22N	121 38 E
Apatzingan	**175**	19 5N	102 21W
Apeldoorn	**41**	52 13N	5 57 E
Apennines	**16**	44 20N	10 20 E
Apizaco	**177**	19 25N	98 9W
Aplao	**186**	16 0S	72 40W
Apolo	**187**	14 30S	68 30W
Apostle Is.	**150**	47 0N	90 30W
Apostolos Andreas, C.	**80**	35 42N	34 35 E
Appalachian Mts.	**138**	38 0N	80 0W
Appingedam	**41**	53 19N	6 51 E
Appleby	**28**	54 35N	2 29W
Appleton	**167**	44 17N	88 25W
Apulia = Púglia □	**49**	41 0N	16 30 E
Apure →	**184**	7 37N	66 25W
Aqabah = Al 'Aqabah	**80**	29 31N	35 0 E
Aquidauana	**188**	20 30S	55 50W
Áquila, L'	**47**	42 21N	13 24 E
Aquiles Serdán	**174**	28 36N	105 53W
Ar Riyāḑ	**83**	24 41N	46 42 E
Ar Ruţbah	**81**	33 0N	40 15 E
Ara	**92**	25 35N	84 32 E
Arab, Bahr el →	**129**	9 50N	29 0 E
Arab, Shatt al	**84**	30 0N	48 31 E
Arabia	**76**	25 0N	45 0 E
Arabian Gulf = Gulf, The	**85**	27 0N	50 0 E
Arabian Sea	**76**	16 0N	65 0 E
Aracaju	**189**	10 55S	37 4W
Aracati	**189**	4 30S	37 44W
Araçatuba	**188**	21 10S	50 30W
Arad	**56**	46 10N	21 20 E
Arafura Sea	**113**	9 0S	135 0 E
Aragón □	**51**	41 25N	1 0W
Araguacema	**188**	8 50S	49 20W
Araguaia →	**188**	5 21S	48 41W
Araguari	**188**	18 38S	48 11W
Arāk	**84**	34 0N	49 40 E
Arakan Coast	**93**	19 0N	94 0 E
Arakan Yoma	**93**	20 0N	94 40 E
Araks = Aras, Rūd-e →	**81**	39 10N	47 10 E
Aral Sea = Aralskoye More	**70**	44 30N	60 0 E
Aralsk	**70**	46 50N	61 20 E
Aralskoye More	**70**	44 30N	60 0 E
Aran I.	**34**	55 0N	8 30W
Aran Is.	**35**	53 5N	9 42W
Aranjuez	**50**	40 1N	3 40W
Aransas Pass	**158**	27 55N	97 9W
Arao	**108**	32 59N	130 25 E
Araraquara	**188**	21 50S	48 0W
Ararat	**119**	37 16S	143 0 E
Ararat, Mt. = Ağri Daği	**81**	39 50N	44 15 E
Aras, Rūd-e →	**81**	39 10N	47 10 E
Araya, Pen. de	**185**	10 40N	64 0W
Arbīl	**81**	36 15N	44 5 E
Arbroath	**31**	56 34N	2 35W
Arcachon	**36**	44 40N	1 10W
Arcadia	**170**	27 20N	81 50W
Archangel = Arkhangelsk	**69**	64 40N	41 0 E
Arcot	**90**	12 53N	79 20 E
Arctic Bay	**146**	73 1N	85 7W
Arctic Ocean	**12**	78 0N	160 0W
Arctic Red River	**144**	67 15N	134 0W
Ardabīl	**81**	38 15N	48 18 E
Ardennes	**42**	50 0N	5 10 E
Ardgour	**32**	56 45N	5 25W
Ardlethan	**117**	34 22S	146 53 E
Ardmore	**168**	34 10N	97 5W
Ardnacrusha	**35**	52 43N	8 38W
Ardnamurchan, Pt. of	**32**	56 44N	6 14W
Ards Pen.	**34**	54 30N	5 25W
Arecibo	**180**	18 29N	66 42W
Arequipa	**187**	16 20S	71 30W
Arezzo	**46**	43 28N	11 50 E
Argentan	**39**	48 45N	0 1W
Argentário, Mte.	**46**	42 23N	11 11 E
Argentina ■	**190**	35 0S	66 0W
Argentino, L.	**192**	50 10S	73 0W
Árgos	**54**	37 40N	22 43 E
Argostólion	**54**	38 12N	20 33 E
Argun →	**74**	53 20N	121 28 E
Århus	**61**	56 8N	10 11 E
Arica, Chile	**187**	18 32S	70 20W
Arica, Colombia	**184**	2 0S	71 50W
Arida	**106**	34 5N	135 8 E
Arima	**180**	10 38N	61 17W
Ario de Rosales	**175**	19 12N	101 43W
Aripuanã	**187**	9 25S	60 30W
Aripuanã →	**187**	5 7S	60 25W
Ariquemes	**187**	9 55S	63 6W
Arisaig	**32**	56 55N	5 50W
Aristazabal I.	**154**	52 40N	129 10W
Arizona □	**160**	34 20N	111 30W
Arjona	**184**	10 14N	75 22W
Arkadelphia	**168**	34 5N	93 0W
Arkansas □	**168**	35 0N	92 30W
Arkansas →	**168**	33 48N	91 4W
Arkansas City	**158**	37 4N	97 3W
Arkhangelsk	**69**	64 40N	41 0 E
Arklow	**35**	52 48N	6 10W
Arkticheskiy, Mys	**72**	81 10N	95 0 E
Arles	**37**	43 41N	4 40 E
Arlington	**164**	38 52N	77 5W
Armagh	**34**	54 22N	6 40W
Armavir	**70**	45 2N	41 7 E
Armenia	**184**	4 35N	75 45W
Armenia S.S.R. □	**70**	40 0N	41 0 E
Armentières	**38**	50 40N	2 50 E
Armidale	**116**	30 30S	151 40 E
Armstrong	**155**	50 25N	119 10W
Arnaouti, C.	**80**	35 6N	32 17 E
Arnaud →	**146**	59 59N	69 46W
Arnhem	**41**	51 58N	5 55 E
Arnhem, C.	**115**	12 20S	137 30 E
Arnhem Land	**114**	13 10S	134 30 E
Arnprior	**151**	45 26N	76 21W
Arran	**30**	55 34N	5 12W
Arras	**38**	50 17N	2 46 E
Arriaga	**177**	16 14N	93 54W
Árta	**54**	39 8N	21 2 E
Artigas	**191**	30 20S	56 30W
Artois	**38**	50 20N	2 30 E
Aru, Kepulauan	**113**	6 0S	134 30 E
Arua	**132**	3 1N	30 58 E
Aruanã	**188**	14 54S	51 10W
Aruba	**181**	12 30N	70 0W
Arusha	**135**	3 20S	36 40 E
Arvida	**148**	48 25N	71 14W
Arys	**71**	42 26N	68 48 E
'As Saffānīyah	**84**	28 5N	48 50 E
As Samāwah	**84**	31 15N	45 15 E
As Sulaymānīyah	**83**	24 9N	47 18 E
As Sumaymānīyah	**81**	35 35N	45 29 E
As Suwaydā'	**80**	32 40N	36 30 E
As Şuwayrah	**84**	32 55N	45 0 E
Asahi	**107**	35 43N	140 39 E
Asahi-Gawa →	**109**	34 36N	133 58 E
Asahigawa	**103**	43 46N	142 22 E
Asama-Yama	**107**	36 24N	138 31 E
Asamankese	**130**	5 50N	0 40W
Asansol	**92**	23 40N	87 1 E
Asbestos	**148**	45 47N	71 58W
Ascension I.	**125**	8 0S	14 15W
Áscoli Piceno	**47**	42 51N	13 34 E
Aseb	**133**	13 0N	42 40 E
Ash Shām, Bādiyat	**80**	32 0N	40 0 E
Ash Shāmīyah	**84**	31 55N	44 35 E
Ash Shāriqah	**85**	25 23N	55 26 E
Ash Shaţrah	**84**	31 30N	46 10 E
Ashburton	**123**	43 53S	171 48 E
Ashby-de-la-Zouch	**28**	52 45N	1 29W
Ashcroft	**155**	50 40N	121 20W
Asheboro	**165**	35 43N	79 46W
Asheville	**165**	35 39N	82 30W
Ashford, Australia	**116**	29 15S	151 3 E
Ashford, U.K.	**25**	51 8N	0 53 E

Ashikaga	**107**	36 28N	139 29 E
Ashizuri-Zaki	**109**	32 44N	133 0 E
Ashkhabad	**70**	38 0N	57 50 E
Ashland, Kans., U.S.A.	**156**	37 13N	99 43W
Ashland, Ky., U.S.A.	**165**	38 25N	82 40W
Ashland, Oreg., U.S.A.	**171**	42 10N	122 38W
Ashland, Wis., U.S.A.	**150**	46 40N	90 52W
Ashq'elon	**80**	31 42N	34 35 E
Ashtabula	**164**	41 52N	80 50W
Ashton-under-Lyne	**28**	53 30N	2 8W
Ashuanipi, L.	**147**	52 45N	66 15W
Asinara I.	**48**	41 5N	8 15 E
'Asīr □	**82**	18 40N	42 30 E
Asir, Ras	**133**	11 55N	51 10 E
Asmara = Asmera	**132**	15 19N	38 55 E
Asmera	**132**	15 19N	38 55 E
Aso	**108**	33 0N	131 5 E
Aso-Zan	**108**	32 53N	131 6 E
Aspiring, Mt.	**123**	44 23S	168 46 E
Assam □	**93**	26 0N	93 0 E
Assen	**41**	53 0N	6 35 E
Assiniboia	**152**	49 40N	105 59W
Assiniboine →	**153**	49 53N	97 8W
Assisi	**46**	43 4N	12 36 E
Asti	**46**	44 54N	8 11 E
Astipálaia	**55**	36 32N	26 22 E
Astoria	**171**	46 16N	123 50W
Astrakhan	**70**	46 25N	48 5 E
Asturias □	**50**	43 15N	6 0W
Asunción	**191**	25 10S	57 30W
Aswân	**128**	24 4N	32 57 E
Asyût	**128**	27 11N	31 4 E
At Ṭafīlah	**80**	30 45N	35 30 E
At Ta'if	**82**	21 5N	40 27 E
Atacama, Desierto de	**190**	24 0S	69 20W
Atacama, Salar de	**190**	23 30S	68 20W
Atalaya	**186**	10 45S	73 50W
Atami	**107**	35 5N	139 4 E
Atbara	**129**	17 42N	33 59 E
'Atbara →	**129**	17 40N	33 56 E
Atchafalaya B.	**168**	29 30N	91 20W
Atchison	**166**	39 40N	95 10W
Athabasca	**155**	54 45N	113 20W
Athabasca →	**145**	58 40N	110 50W
Athabasca, L.	**145**	59 15N	109 15W
Athenry	**35**	53 18N	8 45W
Athens = Athínai	**55**	37 58N	23 46 E
Athens, Ala., U.S.A.	**169**	34 49N	86 58W
Athens, Ga., U.S.A.	**165**	33 56N	83 24W
Athens, Ohio, U.S.A.	**167**	39 25N	82 6W
Athens, Tenn., U.S.A.	**169**	35 45N	84 38W
Athens, Tex., U.S.A.	**168**	32 11N	95 48W
Atherton	**121**	17 17S	145 30 E
Athínai	**55**	37 58N	23 46 E
Athlone	**34**	53 26N	7 57W
Atholl, Forest of	**33**	56 51N	3 50W
Áthos	**55**	40 9N	24 22 E
Athy	**35**	53 0N	7 0W
Atico	**186**	16 14S	73 40W
Atlanta	**170**	33 50N	84 24W
Atlantic	**166**	41 25N	95 0W
Atlantic City	**164**	39 25N	74 25W
Atlantic Ocean	**9**	0 0	20 0W
Atlas Mts. = Haut Atlas	**126**	32 30N	5 0W
Atmore	**169**	31 2N	87 30W
Atsugi	**107**	35 25N	139 21 E
Atsumi	**106**	34 35N	137 4 E
Atsumi-Wan	**106**	34 44N	137 13 E
Attawapiskat →	**140**	52 57N	82 18W
Attleboro	**164**	41 56N	71 18W
Aubagne	**37**	43 17N	5 37 E
Aube →	**37**	48 34N	3 43 E
Aubenas	**37**	44 37N	4 24 E
Auburn, Ala., U.S.A.	**169**	32 37N	85 30W
Auburn, N.Y., U.S.A.	**164**	42 57N	76 39W
Auckland	**122**	36 52S	174 46 E
Auckland Is.	**15**	50 40S	166 5 E
Aude →	**37**	43 13N	3 14 E
Augsburg	**43**	48 22N	10 54 E
Augusta, Ga., U.S.A.	**170**	33 29N	81 59W
Augusta, Maine, U.S.A.	**148**	44 20N	69 46W
Aunis	**36**	46 5N	0 50W
Aurangabad	**91**	19 50N	75 23 E
Aurillac	**37**	44 55N	2 26 E
Aurora	**167**	41 42N	88 12W
Aust-Agder fylke □	**60**	58 55N	7 40 E
Austin, Minn., U.S.A.	**166**	43 37N	92 59W
Austin, Tex., U.S.A.	**161**	30 20N	97 45W
Austral Is. = Tubuai Is.	**123**	25 0S	150 0W
Australia ■	**114**	23 0S	135 0 E
Australian Alps	**117**	36 30S	148 30 E
Australian Cap. Terr. □	**117**	35 30S	149 0 E
Austria ■	**45**	47 0N	14 0 E
Autlán	**175**	19 40N	104 30W
Auvergne	**37**	45 20N	3 15 E
Auxerre	**39**	47 48N	3 32 E
Avalon Pen.	**149**	47 30N	53 20W
Aveiro	**185**	3 10S	55 5W
Avellaneda	**190**	34 50S	58 10W
Aves, I. de	**181**	15 45N	63 55W
Avesnes-sur-Helpe	**38**	50 8N	3 55 E
Aveyron →	**36**	44 7N	1 5 E
Aviemore	**33**	57 11N	3 50W
Avignon	**37**	43 57N	4 50 E
Ávila	**50**	40 39N	4 43W
Avon □	**27**	51 30N	2 40W
Avon →, Avon, U.K.	**24**	51 30N	2 43W
Avon →, Hants., U.K.	**24**	50 44N	1 45W
Avonmouth	**27**	51 30N	2 42W
Avranches	**36**	48 40N	1 20W
Awaji-Shima	**109**	34 30N	134 50 E
Aweil	**129**	8 42N	27 20 E
Axel Heiberg I.	**12**	80 0N	90 0W
Axminster	**27**	50 47N	3 1W
Ayabe	**106**	35 20N	135 20 E
Ayacucho	**186**	13 0S	74 0W
Aylos Evstrátios	**55**	39 34N	24 58 E
Ayon, Ostrov	**73**	69 50N	169 0 E
Ayr, Australia	**121**	19 35S	147 25 E
Ayr, U.K.	**31**	55 28N	4 37W
Ayre, Pt. of	**28**	54 27N	4 21W
Aytos	**53**	42 42N	27 16 E
Ayutla	**177**	16 58N	99 17W
Az Ẓahrān	**84**	26 10N	50 7 E
Az Zubayr	**84**	30 20N	47 50 E
Azamgarh	**92**	26 5N	83 13 E
Azbine = Aïr	**127**	18 30N	8 0 E
Azerbaijan S.S.R. □	**70**	40 20N	48 0 E
Azores	**126**	38 44N	29 0W
Azov Sea = Azovskoye More	**68**	46 0N	36 30 E
Azovskoye More	**68**	46 0N	36 30 E
Azúa de Compostela	**180**	18 25N	70 44W
Azuero, Pen. de	**179**	7 30N	80 30W
Azul	**190**	36 42S	59 43W
Ba Ngoi = Cam Lam	**95**	11 54N	109 10 E
Baarn	**40**	52 12N	5 17 E
Bāb el Māndeb	**133**	12 35N	43 25 E
Babahoyo	**184**	1 40S	79 30W
Babinda	**121**	17 20S	145 56 E
Babine L.	**154**	54 48N	126 0W
Bābol	**86**	36 40N	52 50 E
Babuyan Is.	**112**	19 10N	121 40 E
Babylon	**84**	32 40N	44 30 E
Bac Ninh	**95**	21 13N	106 4 E
Bac Phan	**95**	22 0N	105 0 E
Bac Quang	**95**	22 30N	104 48 E
Bacabal	**188**	4 15S	44 45W
Bacău	**57**	46 35N	26 55 E
Back →	**145**	65 10N	104 0W
Bacolod	**112**	10 40N	122 57 E
Bad Lands	**163**	43 40N	102 10W
Badajoz	**50**	38 50N	6 59W
Badakhshān □	**87**	36 30N	71 0 E
Badalona	**51**	41 26N	2 15 E
Badanah	**82**	30 58N	41 30 E
Baden-Baden	**42**	48 45N	8 15 E
Baden-Württemberg □	**42**	48 40N	9 0 E
Bādghīsāt □	**87**	35 0N	63 0 E
Badin	**88**	24 38N	68 54 E

Baffin □	**146**	70 0N	80 0W
Baffin B.	**13**	72 0N	64 0W
Baffin I.	**146**	68 0N	75 0W
Bafra	**80**	41 34N	35 54 E
Bāft	**85**	29 15N	56 38 E
Bagé	**191**	31 20S	54 15W
Baghdād	**84**	33 20N	44 30 E
Baghlān	**87**	36 12N	69 0 E
Baghlān □	**87**	36 0N	68 30 E
Bahamas ■	**178**	24 0N	75 0W
Baharampur	**92**	24 2N	88 27 E
Bahawalpur	**89**	29 24N	71 40 E
Bahía = Salvador	**189**	13 0S	38 30W
Bahía □	**189**	12 0S	42 0W
Bahía Blanca	**190**	38 35S	62 13W
Bahr el Jebel →	**129**	7 30N	30 30 E
Bahraich	**92**	27 38N	81 37 E
Bahrain ■	**85**	26 0N	50 35 E
Baia Mare	**56**	47 40N	23 35 E
Baie Comeau	**148**	49 12N	68 10W
Baie-St-Paul	**148**	47 28N	70 32W
Ba'ījī	**81**	35 0N	43 30 E
Baikal, L. = Baykal, Oz.	**74**	53 0N	108 0 E
Baile Atha Cliath = Dublin	**35**	53 20N	6 18W
Bailleul	**38**	50 44N	2 41 E
Bainbridge	**170**	30 53N	84 34W
Baird Mts.	**142**	67 10N	160 15W
Bairnsdale	**117**	37 48S	147 36 E
Baiyin	**98**	36 45N	104 14 E
Baja	**59**	46 12N	18 59 E
Baja California	**174**	31 10N	115 12W
Baja California Norte □	**174**	30 0N	115 0W
Baja California Sur □	**174**	25 50N	111 50W
Bajimba, Mt.	**116**	29 17S	152 6 E
Baker	**171**	44 50N	117 55W
Baker I.	**122**	0 10N	176 35W
Baker Lake	**145**	64 20N	96 3W
Bakersfield	**173**	35 25N	119 0W
Bākhtarān	**84**	34 23N	47 0 E
Bakony Forest = Bakony Hegység	**59**	47 10N	17 30 E
Bakony Hegység	**59**	47 10N	17 30 E
Baku	**70**	40 25N	49 45 E
Bala	**26**	52 54N	3 36W
Balabac, Str.	**112**	7 53N	117 5 E
Balabakk	**80**	34 0N	36 10 E
Balaghat	**91**	21 49N	80 12 E
Balaghat Ra.	**91**	18 50N	76 30 E
Balaklava	**119**	34 7S	138 22 E
Balakovo	**68**	52 4N	47 55 E
Balaton	**59**	46 50N	17 40 E
Balboa	**179**	9 0N	79 30W
Balbriggan	**34**	53 35N	6 10W
Balcarce	**190**	38 0S	58 10W
Balclutha	**123**	46 15S	169 45 E
Baldy Peak	**161**	33 50N	109 30W
Baleares, Islas	**51**	39 30N	3 0 E
Balearic Is. = Baleares, Islas	**51**	39 30N	3 0 E
Bali	**111**	8 20S	115 0 E
Balikesir	**80**	39 35N	27 58 E
Balikpapan	**111**	1 10S	116 55 E
Balkan Mts. = Stara Planina	**53**	43 15N	23 0 E
Balkan Pen.	**17**	42 0N	22 0 E
Balkh □	**87**	36 30N	67 0 E
Balkhash	**71**	46 50N	74 50 E
Balkhash, Ozero	**71**	46 0N	74 50 E
Ballachulish	**32**	56 40N	5 10W
Ballarat	**117**	37 33S	143 50 E
Ballard, L.	**120**	29 20S	120 10 E
Ballater	**33**	57 2N	3 2W
Ballina, Australia	**116**	28 50S	153 31 E
Ballina, Mayo, Ireland	**34**	54 7N	9 10W
Ballina, Tipp., Ireland	**35**	52 49N	8 27W
Ballinasloe	**35**	53 20N	8 12W
Ballinrobe	**34**	53 36N	9 13W
Ballycastle	**34**	55 12N	6 15W
Ballymena	**34**	54 53N	6 18W
Ballymoney	**34**	55 5N	6 30W
Ballyshannon	**34**	54 30N	8 10W
Balmaceda	**192**	46 0S	71 50W
Balmoral	**33**	57 3N	3 13W
Balrampur	**92**	27 30N	82 20 E
Balranald	**117**	34 38S	143 33 E
Balsas, R. →	**177**	17 55N	102 10W
Baltic Sea	**16**	56 0N	20 0 E
Baltimore	**164**	39 18N	76 37W
Baluchistan □	**88**	27 30N	65 0 E
Bamako	**130**	12 34N	7 55W
Bambari	**129**	5 40N	20 35 E
Bamberg	**43**	49 54N	10 53 E
Bāmīān □	**87**	35 0N	67 0 E
Ban Aranyaprathet	**95**	13 41N	102 30 E
Ban Don = Surat Thani	**96**	9 6N	99 20 E
Ban Houei Sai	**95**	20 22N	100 32 E
Ban Khe Bo	**95**	19 10N	104 39 E
Ban Khun Yuam	**94**	18 49N	97 57 E
Ban Nong Pling	**94**	15 40N	100 10 E
Ban Phai	**95**	16 4N	102 44 E
Banaras = Varanasi	**92**	25 22N	83 0 E
Banbridge	**34**	54 21N	6 17W
Banbury	**25**	52 4N	1 21W
Bancroft	**151**	45 3N	77 51W
Banda	**91**	25 30N	80 26 E
Banda, Kepulauan	**113**	4 37S	129 50 E
Banda Aceh	**111**	5 35N	95 20 E
Banda Banda, Mt.	**116**	31 10S	152 28 E
Banda Sea	**113**	6 0S	130 0 E
Bandar = Machilipatnam	**92**	16 12N	81 8 E
Bandār 'Abbās	**85**	27 15N	56 15 E
Bandar-e Anzalī	**81**	37 30N	49 30 E
Bandar-e Khomeyni	**84**	30 30N	49 5 E
Bandar-e Lengeh	**85**	26 35N	54 58 E
Bandar-e Nakhīlū	**85**	26 58N	53 30 E
Bandar-e Torkeman	**86**	37 0N	54 10 E
Bandar Seri Begawan	**112**	4 52N	115 0 E
Bandeira, Pico da	**188**	20 26S	41 47W
Bandırma	**80**	40 20N	28 0 E
Bandon	**35**	51 44N	8 45W
Bandung	**111**	6 54S	107 36 E
Banes	**178**	21 0N	75 42W
Banff, Canada	**155**	51 10N	115 34W
Banff, U.K.	**33**	57 40N	2 32W
Bangalore	**90**	12 59N	77 40 E
Bangassou	**129**	4 55N	23 7 E
Banggai	**113**	1 40S	123 30 E
Banghāzī	**128**	32 11N	20 3 E
Bangka, Selat	**111**	2 30S	105 30 E
Bangkok	**94**	13 45N	100 35 E
Bangladesh ■	**92**	24 0N	90 0 E
Bangor, N. Ireland, U.K.	**34**	54 40N	5 40W
Bangor, Wales, U.K.	**26**	53 13N	4 9W
Bangor, U.S.A.	**148**	44 48N	68 42W
Bangui	**131**	4 23N	18 35 E
Bangweulu, L.	**135**	11 0S	30 0 E
Bani	**180**	18 16N	70 22W
Banja Luka	**52**	44 49N	17 11 E
Banjarmasin	**111**	3 20S	114 35 E
Banjul	**130**	13 28N	16 40W
Bankipore	**92**	25 35N	85 10 E
Banks I., B.C., Canada	**154**	53 20N	130 0W
Banks I., N.W.T., Canada	**145**	73 15N	121 30W
Banks Pen.	**123**	43 45S	173 15 E
Banks Str.	**119**	40 40S	148 10 E
Bann →	**34**	54 30N	6 31W
Banning	**173**	33 58N	116 52W
Bannockburn	**31**	56 5N	3 55W
Bannu	**89**	33 0N	70 18 E
Bantry	**35**	51 40N	9 28W
Baoding	**98**	38 50N	115 28 E
Baoji	**99**	34 20N	107 5 E
Baotou	**98**	40 32N	110 2 E
Ba'qūbah	**81**	33 45N	44 50 E
Bar	**52**	42 8N	19 8 E
Bar Harbor	**148**	44 15N	68 20W
Baraboo	**166**	43 28N	89 46W
Baracoa	**178**	20 20N	74 30W
Barahona	**180**	18 13N	71 7W
Barail Range	**93**	25 15N	93 20 E
Baramula	**89**	34 15N	74 20 E
Baran	**91**	25 9N	76 40 E
Baranof I.	**143**	57 0N	135 10W
Baranovichi	**68**	53 10N	26 0 E

Barbacoas	**184**	1 45N	78 0W
Barbados ■	**180**	13 0N	59 30W
Barbuda I.	**180**	17 30N	61 40W
Barca, La	**175**	20 17N	102 34W
Barcaldine	**121**	23 43S	145 6E
Barcelona, Spain	**51**	41 21N	2 10E
Barcelona, Venezuela	**185**	10 10N	64 40W
Barcelos	**185**	1 0S	63 0W
Barddhaman	**92**	23 14N	87 39E
Bardera	**133**	2 20N	42 27E
Bardsey I.	**26**	52 46N	4 47W
Bareilly	**89**	28 22N	79 27E
Barentin	**38**	49 33N	0 58E
Barents Sea	**13**	73 0N	39 0E
Bargara	**121**	24 50S	152 25E
Bari	**49**	41 6N	16 52E
Bari Doab	**89**	30 20N	73 0E
Barīm	**82**	12 39N	43 25E
Barinas	**184**	8 36N	70 15W
Barisal	**92**	22 45N	90 20E
Barito →	**111**	4 0S	114 50E
Barlee, L.	**120**	29 15S	119 30E
Barletta	**49**	41 20N	16 17E
Barmer	**91**	25 45N	71 20E
Barmera	**119**	34 15S	140 28E
Barmouth	**26**	52 44N	4 3W
Barnard Castle	**28**	54 33N	1 55W
Barnaul	**71**	53 20N	83 40E
Barneveld	**41**	52 7N	5 36E
Barnsley	**28**	53 33N	1 29W
Barnstaple	**27**	51 5N	4 3W
Baro	**131**	8 35N	6 18E
Baroda = Vadodara	**91**	22 20N	73 10E
Barpeta	**93**	26 20N	91 10E
Barquísimeto	**184**	10 4N	69 19W
Barra	**32**	57 0N	7 30W
Barra Hd.	**32**	56 47N	7 40W
Barraba	**116**	30 21S	150 35E
Barranca	**186**	10 45S	77 50W
Barrancabermeja	**184**	7 0N	73 50W
Barrancas	**185**	8 55N	62 5W
Barranqueras	**190**	27 30S	59 0W
Barranquilla	**184**	11 0N	74 50W
Barre	**151**	44 15N	72 30W
Barreiros	**188**	8 49S	35 12W
Barrhead	**155**	54 10N	114 24W
Barrie	**151**	44 24N	79 40W
Barrier Ra.	**118**	31 0S	141 30E
Barrington Tops	**116**	32 6S	151 28E
Barrow →	**35**	52 10N	6 57W
Barrow, Pt.	**138**	71 22N	156 30W
Barrow-in-Furness	**28**	54 8N	3 15W
Barry	**27**	51 23N	3 19W
Barry's Bay	**151**	45 29N	77 41W
Barsi	**91**	18 10N	75 50E
Barstow	**173**	34 58N	117 2W
Bartica	**185**	6 25N	58 40W
Bartow	**170**	27 53N	81 49W
Basel	**44**	47 35N	7 35E
Bashi Channel	**99**	21 15N	122 0E
Bashkir A.S.S.R. □	**69**	54 0N	57 0E
Basilan	**112**	6 35N	122 0E
Basildon	**25**	51 34N	0 29E
Basilicata □	**49**	40 30N	16 0E
Basim = Washim	**91**	20 3N	77 0E
Basle = Basel	**44**	47 35N	7 35E
Basoka	**134**	1 16N	23 40E
Basque Provinces = Vascongadas	**50**	42 50N	2 45W
Basra = Al Başrah	**84**	30 30N	47 50E
Bass Rock	**31**	56 5N	2 40W
Bass Str.	**117**	39 15S	146 30E
Bassano	**155**	50 48N	112 20W
Basse-Terre	**180**	16 0N	61 40W
Bassein	**93**	16 45N	94 30E
Basseterre	**180**	17 17N	62 43W
Basti	**92**	26 52N	82 55E
Bastia	**36**	42 40N	9 30E
Batabanó	**178**	22 40N	82 20W
Batamay	**74**	63 30N	129 15E
Batan Is.	**112**	20 25N	121 59E
Batang	**101**	30 1N	99 0E
Batavia	**164**	43 0N	78 10W
Batemans Bay	**117**	35 44S	150 11E
Batesville	**168**	35 48N	91 40W
Bath, U.K.	**27**	51 22N	2 22W
Bath, Maine, U.S.A.	**148**	43 50N	69 49W
Bath, N.Y., U.S.A.	**164**	42 20N	77 17W
Bathurst = Banjul	**130**	13 28N	16 40W
Bathurst, Australia	**117**	33 25S	149 31E
Bathurst, Canada	**148**	47 37N	65 43W
Bathurst, C.	**145**	70 34N	128 0W
Bathurst Inlet	**145**	66 50N	108 1W
Batlow	**117**	35 31S	148 9E
Batman	**81**	37 55N	41 5E
Batna	**127**	35 34N	6 15E
Baton Rouge	**168**	30 30N	91 5W
Batopilas	**174**	27 1N	107 44W
Battambang	**95**	13 7N	103 12E
Batticaloa	**90**	7 43N	81 45E
Battle	**25**	50 55N	0 30E
Battle Creek	**167**	42 20N	85 6W
Battle Harbour	**147**	52 16N	55 35W
Battleford	**152**	52 45N	108 15W
Batu Gajah	**96**	4 28N	101 3E
Batu Is.	**111**	0 30S	98 25E
Batumi	**70**	41 30N	41 30E
Bauchi	**131**	10 22N	9 48E
Bauru	**188**	22 10S	49 0W
Bavaria = Bayern □	**43**	49 7N	11 30E
Bawdwin	**93**	23 5N	97 20E
Bawean	**111**	5 46S	112 35E
Bawku	**130**	11 3N	0 19W
Bay City	**167**	43 35N	83 51W
Bay Shore	**164**	40 44N	73 15W
Bayamo	**178**	20 20N	76 40W
Bayamón	**180**	18 24N	66 10W
Bayan Har Shan	**101**	34 0N	98 0E
Bayan Hot = Alxa Zuoqi	**98**	38 50N	105 40E
Bayern □	**43**	49 7N	11 30E
Bayeux	**36**	49 17N	0 42W
Bayfield	**150**	43 34N	81 42W
Baykal, Oz.	**74**	53 0N	108 0E
Baykonur	**71**	47 48N	65 50E
Bayonne	**36**	43 30N	1 28W
Bayreuth	**43**	49 56N	11 35E
Bayrūt	**80**	33 53N	35 31E
Baytown	**168**	29 42N	94 57W
Beachy Head	**25**	50 44N	0 16E
Beagle, Canal	**192**	55 0S	68 30W
Béarn	**36**	43 8N	0 36W
Beauce, Plaine de la	**37**	48 10N	1 45E
Beaudesert	**116**	27 59S	153 0E
Beaufort	**170**	32 25N	80 40W
Beaufort Sea	**12**	72 0N	140 0W
Beaugency	**39**	47 47N	1 38E
Beauharnois	**151**	45 20N	73 52W
Beauly	**33**	57 29N	4 27W
Beaumaris	**26**	53 16N	4 7W
Beaumont	**168**	30 5N	94 8W
Beaumont-sur-Oise	**39**	49 9N	2 17E
Beauséjour	**153**	50 5N	96 35W
Beauvais	**38**	49 25N	2 8E
Beauval	**152**	55 9N	107 37W
Beaver	**142**	66 20N	147 30W
Beaver →	**152**	55 26N	107 45W
Beaver Falls	**164**	40 44N	80 20W
Beaverlodge	**155**	55 11N	119 29W
Beawar	**91**	26 3N	74 18E
Bečej	**52**	45 36N	20 3E
Béchar	**127**	31 38N	2 18W
Beckley	**165**	37 50N	81 8W
Bedford, U.K.	**25**	52 8N	0 29W
Bedford, U.S.A.	**167**	38 50N	86 30W
Bedford □	**25**	52 4N	0 28W
Beenleigh	**116**	27 43S	153 10E
Be'er Sheva'	**80**	31 15N	34 48E
Beersheba = Be'er Sheva'	**80**	31 15N	34 48E
Beeston	**29**	52 55N	1 11W
Bega	**117**	36 41S	149 51E
Behbehān	**84**	30 30N	50 15E
Beibei	**99**	29 47N	106 22E

Beihai	**99**	21 28N	109 6 E
Beijing	**98**	39 55N	116 20 E
Beira	**137**	19 50S	34 52 E
Beira-Alta	**50**	40 35N	7 35W
Beira-Baixa	**50**	40 2N	7 30W
Beira-Litoral	**50**	40 5N	8 30W
Beirut = Bayrūt	**80**	33 53N	35 31 E
Bejaia	**127**	36 42N	5 2 E
Békéscsaba	**59**	46 40N	21 5 E
Bela	**92**	25 50N	82 0 E
Bela Crkva	**52**	44 55N	21 27 E
Belaya Tserkov	**68**	49 45N	30 10 E
Belcher Is.	**140**	56 15N	78 45W
Belém	**188**	1 20S	48 30W
Belfast, U.K.	**34**	54 35N	5 56W
Belfast, U.S.A.	**148**	44 30N	69 0W
Belfort	**37**	47 38N	6 50 E
Belgaum	**91**	15 55N	74 35 E
Belgium ■	**42**	50 30N	5 0 E
Belgorod	**68**	50 35N	36 35 E
Belgrade = Beograd	**52**	44 50N	20 37 E
Belitung	**111**	3 10S	107 50 E
Belize ■	**177**	17 0N	88 30W
Belize City	**177**	17 25N	88 0W
Bell Peninsula	**146**	63 50N	82 0W
Bell Ville	**190**	32 40S	62 40W
Bella Coola	**154**	52 25N	126 40W
Bellaire	**164**	40 1N	80 46W
Bellary	**90**	15 10N	76 56 E
Belle Fourche →	**163**	44 25N	102 19W
Belle Glade	**170**	26 43N	80 38W
Belle Isle	**147**	51 57N	55 25W
Belle Isle, Str. of	**141**	51 30N	56 30W
Bellefontaine	**167**	40 20N	83 45W
Belleville, Canada	**151**	44 10N	77 23W
Belleville, U.S.A.	**166**	38 30N	90 0W
Bellevue	**155**	49 35N	114 22W
Bellin	**146**	60 0N	70 0W
Bellingham	**171**	48 45N	122 27W
Bellingshausen Sea	**14**	66 0S	80 0W
Belmont	**117**	33 4S	151 42 E
Belmopan	**177**	17 18N	88 30W
Belo Horizonte	**188**	19 55S	43 56W
Belogorsk	**75**	51 0N	128 20 E
Beloit	**166**	42 35N	89 0W
Belomorsk	**68**	64 35N	34 30 E
Belovo	**71**	54 30N	86 0 E
Beloye More	**69**	66 30N	38 0 E
Beloye Ozero	**68**	45 15N	46 50 E
Belper	**28**	53 2N	1 29W
Belukha	**71**	49 50N	86 50 E
Belyy, Ostrov	**69**	73 30N	71 0 E
Bemidji	**156**	47 30N	94 50W
Ben Lomond, N.S.W., Australia	**116**	30 1S	151 40 E
Ben Lomond, Tas., Australia	**119**	41 38S	147 42 E
Ben Macdhui	**33**	57 4N	3 40W
Ben More, Central, U.K.	**32**	56 23N	4 31W
Ben More, Strathclyde, U.K.	**30**	56 26N	6 2W
Ben More Assynt	**32**	58 7N	4 51W
Ben Nevis	**32**	56 48N	5 0W
Benalla	**117**	36 30S	146 0 E
Benares = Varanasi	**92**	25 22N	83 0 E
Benbecula	**32**	57 26N	7 21W
Benbonyathe, Mt.	**118**	30 25S	139 11 E
Bencubbin	**120**	30 48S	117 52 E
Bend	**171**	44 2N	121 15W
Bendemeer	**116**	30 53S	151 8 E
Bender Beila	**133**	9 30N	50 48 E
Bendigo	**117**	36 40S	144 15 E
Benevento	**49**	41 7N	14 45 E
Bengal, Bay of	**92**	15 0N	90 0 E
Bengbu	**99**	32 58N	117 20 E
Benghazi = Banghāzī	**128**	32 11N	20 3 E
Benguela	**134**	12 37S	13 25 E
Beni →	**187**	10 23S	65 24W
Beni Suef	**128**	29 5N	31 6 E
Benidorm	**51**	38 33N	0 9W
Benin ■	**131**	10 0N	2 0 E
Benin, Bight of	**131**	5 0N	3 0 E
Benin City	**131**	6 20N	5 31 E
Benjamin Constant	**187**	4 40S	70 15W
Bennett	**144**	59 56N	134 53W
Bennettsville	**165**	34 38N	79 39W
Benton	**168**	34 30N	92 35W
Benue →	**131**	7 48N	6 46 E
Benxi	**98**	41 20N	123 48 E
Beograd	**52**	44 50N	20 37 E
Beppu	**108**	33 15N	131 30 E
Berau, Teluk	**113**	2 30S	132 30 E
Berber	**129**	18 0N	34 0 E
Berbera	**133**	10 30N	45 2 E
Berck-sur-Mer	**38**	50 25N	1 36 E
Berezniki	**69**	59 24N	56 46 E
Bérgamo	**46**	45 42N	9 40 E
Bergen, Neth.	**40**	52 40N	4 43 E
Bergen, Norway	**60**	60 23N	5 20 E
Bergen-op-Zoom	**40**	51 30N	4 18 E
Bergerac	**36**	44 51N	0 30 E
Berhala, Selat	**111**	1 0S	104 15 E
Berhampore = Baharampur	**92**	24 2N	88 27 E
Berhampur	**92**	19 15N	84 54 E
Bering Sea	**142**	58 0N	167 0 E
Bering Str.	**142**	66 0N	170 0W
Berkeley	**172**	37 52N	122 20W
Berkshire □	**25**	51 30N	1 20W
Berkshire Downs	**24**	51 30N	1 30W
Berlin, Germany	**43**	52 32N	13 24 E
Berlin, U.S.A.	**148**	44 29N	71 10W
Bermuda ■	**180**	32 45N	65 0W
Bern	**44**	46 57N	7 28 E
Bernay	**39**	49 5N	0 35 E
Berne = Bern	**44**	46 57N	7 28 E
Berri	**119**	34 14S	140 35 E
Berry	**37**	47 0N	2 0 E
Bertoua	**131**	4 30N	13 45 E
Berwick-upon-Tweed	**31**	55 47N	2 0W
Berwyn Mts.	**26**	52 54N	3 26W
Besançon	**37**	47 15N	6 0 E
Bessemer, Ala., U.S.A.	**169**	33 25N	86 57W
Bessemer, Mich., U.S.A.	**156**	46 27N	90 0W
Bethel	**142**	60 50N	161 50W
Bethlehem	**164**	40 39N	75 24W
Béthune	**38**	50 30N	2 38 E
Betsiboka →	**137**	16 3S	46 36 E
Beverley	**29**	53 52N	0 26W
Beverly Hills	**173**	34 4N	118 29W
Beverwijk	**40**	52 28N	4 38 E
Bexhill	**24**	50 51N	0 29 E
Beyneu	**70**	45 10N	55 3 E
Beyşehir Gölü	**80**	37 40N	31 45 E
Béziers	**37**	43 20N	3 12 E
Bezwada = Vijayawada	**92**	16 31N	80 39 E
Bhadravati	**90**	13 49N	75 40 E
Bhagalpur	**92**	25 10N	87 0 E
Bhakra Dam	**89**	31 30N	76 45 E
Bhandara	**91**	21 5N	79 42 E
Bhanrer Ra.	**91**	23 40N	79 45 E
Bharat = India ■	**78**	20 0N	78 0 E
Bharatpur	**89**	27 15N	77 30 E
Bharuch	**91**	21 47N	73 0 E
Bhatpara	**92**	22 50N	88 25 E
Bhaunagar = Bhavnagar	**91**	21 45N	72 10 E
Bhavnagar	**91**	21 45N	72 10 E
Bhilwara	**91**	25 25N	74 38 E
Bhima →	**91**	16 25N	77 17 E
Bhiwandi	**91**	19 20N	73 0 E
Bhiwani	**89**	28 50N	76 9 E
Bhopal	**91**	23 20N	77 30 E
Bhubaneshwar	**92**	20 15N	85 50 E
Bhusaval	**91**	21 3N	75 46 E
Bhutan ■	**92**	27 25N	90 30 E
Biafra, B. of = Bonny, Bight of	**131**	3 30N	9 20 E
Biała Podlaska	**58**	52 4N	23 6 E
Białystok	**58**	53 10N	23 10 E
Biarritz	**36**	43 29N	1 33W
Bibai	**103**	43 19N	141 52 E
Bicester	**25**	51 53N	1 9W
Biche, L. la	**155**	54 50N	112 3W
Bidar	**91**	17 55N	77 35 E
Biddeford	**148**	43 30N	70 28W

Bideford	**27**	51 1N	4 13W
Bié, Planalto de	**136**	12 0S	16 0 E
Bieber	**172**	41 4N	121 6W
Biel	**44**	47 8N	7 14 E
Bielé Karpaty	**59**	49 5N	18 0 E
Bielefeld	**42**	52 2N	8 31 E
Bielsko-Biała	**59**	49 50N	19 2 E
Bien Hoa	**95**	10 57N	106 49 E
Bienne = Biel	**44**	47 8N	7 14 E
Bienville, L.	**146**	55 5N	72 40W
Big Belt Mts.	**163**	46 50N	111 30W
Big Cypress Swamp	**170**	26 12N	81 10W
Big Horn Mts. = Bighorn Mts.	**163**	44 30N	107 30W
Big Rapids	**167**	43 42N	85 27W
Big Sioux →	**156**	42 30N	96 25W
Big Spring	**161**	32 10N	101 25W
Big Stone Gap	**165**	36 52N	82 45W
Big Trout L.	**153**	53 40N	90 0W
Biggar, Canada	**152**	52 4N	108 0W
Biggar, U.K.	**31**	55 38N	3 31W
Bighorn →	**163**	46 9N	107 28W
Bighorn Mts.	**163**	44 30N	107 30W
Bihar	**92**	25 5N	85 40 E
Bihar □	**92**	25 0N	86 0 E
Bijagós, Arquipélago dos	**130**	11 15N	16 10W
Bijapur	**91**	16 50N	75 55 E
Bijeljina	**52**	44 46N	19 17 E
Bikaner	**89**	28 2N	73 18 E
Bikin	**75**	46 50N	134 20 E
Bilaspur	**92**	22 2N	82 15 E
Bilauk Taungdan	**94**	13 0N	99 0 E
Bilbao	**50**	43 16N	2 56W
Billingham	**29**	54 36N	1 18W
Billings	**163**	45 43N	108 29W
Billiton Is. = Belitung	**111**	3 10S	107 50 E
Bilma	**127**	18 50N	13 30 E
Biloela	**121**	24 24S	150 31 E
Biloxi	**169**	30 24N	88 53W
Bina-Etawah	**91**	24 13N	78 14 E
Bīnālūd, Kūh-e	**86**	36 30N	58 30 E
Bindi Bindi	**120**	30 37S	116 22 E
Bingara	**116**	29 52S	150 36 E
Bingerville	**130**	5 18N	3 49W
Bingham	**148**	45 5N	69 50W
Binghamton	**164**	42 9N	75 54W
Binh Dinh = An Nhon	**95**	13 55N	109 7 E
Binnaway	**116**	31 28S	149 24 E
Binzert = Bizerte	**127**	37 15N	9 50 E
Bioko	**131**	3 30N	8 40 E
Bir Mogrein	**126**	25 10N	11 25W
Birchip	**119**	35 56S	142 55 E
Bird I. = Aves, I. de	**181**	15 45N	63 55W
Birdum	**114**	15 39S	133 13 E
Birkenhead	**28**	53 24N	3 1W
Birmingham, U.K.	**24**	52 30N	1 55W
Birmingham, U.S.A.	**169**	33 31N	86 50W
Birobidzhan	**75**	48 50N	132 50 E
Birr	**35**	53 7N	7 55W
Bisai	**106**	35 16N	136 44 E
Biscay, B. of	**36**	45 0N	2 0W
Biscostasing	**150**	47 18N	82 9W
Bishop Auckland	**28**	54 40N	1 40W
Bishop's Stortford	**25**	51 52N	0 11 E
Bismarck	**163**	46 49N	100 49W
Bismarck Arch.	**115**	2 30S	150 0 E
Bissagos = Bijagós, Arquipélago dos	**130**	11 15N	16 10W
Bissau	**130**	11 45N	15 45W
Bitola	**52**	41 5N	21 10 E
Bitolj = Bitola	**52**	41 5N	21 10 E
Bitterroot Range	**162**	46 0N	114 20W
Biu	**131**	10 40N	12 3 E
Biwa-Ko	**106**	35 15N	136 10 E
Biysk	**71**	52 40N	85 0 E
Bizen	**109**	34 43N	134 8 E
Bizerte	**127**	37 15N	9 50 E
Bjørnøya	**13**	74 30N	19 0 E
Black → = Da →	**95**	21 15N	105 20 E
Black Diamond	**155**	50 45N	114 14W
Black Forest = Schwarzwald	**42**	48 0N	8 0 E
Black Hills	**163**	44 0N	103 50W
Black Mts.	**26**	51 52N	3 5W
Black Sea	**17**	43 30N	35 0 E
Blackall	**121**	24 25S	145 45 E
Blackburn	**28**	53 44N	2 30W
Blackpool	**28**	53 48N	3 3W
Blackwater	**121**	23 35S	148 53 E
Blackwater →, Meath, Ireland	**34**	53 46N	7 0W
Blackwater →, Munster, Ireland	**35**	51 55N	7 50W
Blackwater →, U.K.	**34**	54 31N	6 35W
Blackwell	**168**	36 55N	97 20W
Blaenau Ffestiniog	**26**	53 0N	3 57W
Blagoveshchensk	**75**	50 20N	127 30 E
Blair Atholl	**33**	56 46N	3 50W
Blairmore	**155**	49 40N	114 25W
Blanc, Mont	**37**	45 48N	6 50 E
Blanca Peak	**163**	37 35N	105 29W
Blanche L.	**118**	29 15S	139 40 E
Blanco, C.	**171**	42 50N	124 40W
Blandford Forum	**24**	50 52N	2 10W
Blantyre	**137**	15 45S	35 0 E
Blarney	**35**	51 57N	8 35W
Blaydon	**28**	54 56N	1 47W
Blayney	**117**	33 32S	149 14 E
Blekinge län □	**61**	56 20N	15 20 E
Blenheim	**123**	41 38S	173 57 E
Bletchley	**25**	51 59N	0 44W
Blida	**127**	36 30N	2 49 E
Blind River	**150**	46 10N	82 58W
Blitar	**111**	8 5S	112 11 E
Bloemfontein	**137**	29 6S	26 14 E
Blois	**36**	47 35N	1 20 E
Bloody Foreland	**34**	55 10N	8 18W
Bloomington, Ill., U.S.A.	**166**	40 27N	89 0W
Bloomington, Ind., U.S.A.	**167**	39 10N	86 30W
Bloomsburg	**164**	41 0N	76 30W
Blue Mts., Oreg., U.S.A.	**171**	45 15N	119 0W
Blue Mts., Pa., U.S.A.	**164**	40 30N	76 30W
Blue Nile = Nîl el Azraq →	**129**	15 38N	32 31 E
Blue Ridge Mts.	**165**	36 30N	80 15W
Bluefield	**165**	37 18N	81 14W
Bluefields	**179**	12 20N	83 50W
Bluestack, mt.	**34**	54 46N	8 5W
Bluff	**123**	46 37S	168 20 E
Blumenau	**191**	27 0S	49 0W
Blyth	**28**	55 8N	1 32W
Bo	**130**	7 55N	11 50W
Bo Hai	**98**	39 0N	120 0 E
Boa Vista	**185**	2 48N	60 30W
Boaco	**179**	12 29N	85 35W
Bobadah	**116**	32 19S	146 41 E
Bobcaygeon	**151**	44 33N	78 33W
Bobo-Dioulasso	**130**	11 8N	4 13W
Bobraomby, Tanjon' i	**137**	12 40S	49 10 E
Bobruysk	**68**	53 10N	29 15 E
Bôca do Acre	**187**	8 50S	67 27W
Boca Raton	**170**	26 21N	80 5W
Bocas del Toro	**179**	9 15N	82 20W
Bocholt	**42**	51 50N	6 35 E
Bochum	**42**	51 28N	7 12 E
Boden	**67**	65 50N	21 42 E
Bodensee	**44**	47 35N	9 25 E
Bodhan	**91**	18 40N	77 44 E
Bodmin	**27**	50 28N	4 44W
Bodmin Moor	**27**	50 33N	4 36W
Bodø	**64**	67 17N	14 24 E
Bogalusa	**169**	30 50N	89 55W
Boggabilla	**116**	28 36S	150 24 E
Boggabri	**116**	30 45S	150 0 E
Boggeragh Mts.	**35**	52 2N	8 55W
Bognor Regis	**25**	50 47N	0 40W
Bogong, Mt.	**117**	36 47S	147 17 E
Bogor	**111**	6 36S	106 48 E
Bogota	**184**	4 34N	74 0W
Boguchany	**74**	58 40N	97 30 E
Bohain	**38**	49 59N	3 28 E
Bohemian Forest = Böhmerwald	**43**	49 30N	12 40 E
Böhmerwald	**43**	49 30N	12 40 E
Bohol	**112**	9 50N	124 10 E

Bohol Sea	**112**	9 0N	124 0 E
Bohotleh	**133**	8 20N	46 25 E
Boise	**162**	43 43N	116 9W
Boissevain	**153**	49 15N	100 5W
Boké	**130**	10 56N	14 17W
Bolan Pass	**88**	29 50N	67 20 E
Bolaños, R. →	**175**	21 12N	104 5W
Bolbec	**38**	49 30N	0 30 E
Bolgatanga	**130**	10 44N	0 53W
Bolívar	**190**	36 15S	60 53W
Bolivia ■	**187**	17 6S	64 0W
Bollnäs	**60**	61 21N	16 24 E
Bollon	**116**	28 2S	147 29 E
Bologna	**47**	44 30N	11 20 E
Boloven, Cao Nguyen	**95**	15 10N	106 30 E
Bolsena, L. di	**46**	42 35N	11 55 E
Bolshevik, Ostrov	**72**	78 30N	102 0 E
Bolshoi Kavkas	**70**	42 50N	44 0 E
Bolshoy Begichev, Ostrov	**72**	74 20N	112 30 E
Bolsward	**41**	53 3N	5 32 E
Bolton	**28**	53 35N	2 26W
Bolzano	**47**	46 30N	11 20 E
Boma	**134**	5 50S	13 4 E
Bombala	**117**	36 56S	149 15 E
Bombay	**91**	18 55N	72 50 E
Bomu →	**129**	4 40N	23 30 E
Bon, C.	**127**	37 1N	11 2 E
Bonaire	**181**	12 10N	68 15W
Bonavista	**149**	48 40N	53 5W
Bonifacio, Bouches de	**48**	41 12N	9 15 E
Bonn	**42**	50 43N	7 6 E
Bonneval	**39**	48 11N	1 24 E
Bonnie Rock	**120**	30 29S	118 22 E
Bonny, Bight of	**131**	3 30N	9 20 E
Bonnyville	**152**	54 20N	110 45W
Bonthe	**130**	7 30N	12 33W
Boonah	**116**	27 58S	152 41 E
Boone	**166**	42 5N	93 53W
Boonville	**167**	38 3N	87 13W
Boorowa	**117**	34 28S	148 44 E
Boothia, Gulf of	**146**	71 0N	90 0W
Boothia Pen.	**145**	71 0N	94 0W
Bootle	**28**	53 28N	3 1W
Bôr	**129**	6 10N	31 40 E
Borås	**60**	57 43N	12 56 E
Borāzjān	**85**	29 22N	51 10 E
Bordeaux	**36**	44 50N	0 36W
Borders □	**31**	55 35N	2 50W
Bordertown	**119**	36 19S	140 45 E
Bordj Omar Driss	**127**	28 10N	6 40 E
Borger	**161**	35 40N	101 20W
Borja	**186**	4 20S	77 40W
Borlänge	**60**	60 29N	15 26 E
Borneo	**111**	1 0N	115 0 E
Bornholm	**61**	55 10N	15 0 E
Borujerd	**84**	33 55N	48 50 E
Borzya	**74**	50 24N	116 31 E
Boscastle	**27**	50 42N	4 42W
Boshan	**98**	36 28N	117 49 E
Bosna →	**52**	45 4N	18 29 E
Bosna i Hercegovina □	**52**	44 0N	18 0 E
Bosnia = Bosna i Hercegovina □	**52**	44 0N	18 0 E
Bōsō-Hantō	**107**	35 20N	140 20 E
Bosporus = Karadeniz Boğazı	**80**	41 10N	29 10 E
Bossangoa	**131**	6 35N	17 30 E
Bossembélé	**131**	5 25N	17 40 E
Bossier City	**168**	32 28N	93 48W
Bosten Hu	**100**	41 55N	87 40 E
Boston, U.K.	**29**	52 59N	0 2W
Boston, U.S.A.	**164**	42 20N	71 0W
Bothnia, G. of	**67**	63 0N	20 0 E
Botletle →	**136**	20 10S	23 15 E
Botoşani	**57**	47 42N	26 41 E
Botswana ■	**136**	22 0S	24 0 E
Botucatu	**188**	22 55S	48 30W
Bou Djébéha	**126**	18 25N	2 45W
Bouaké	**130**	7 40N	5 2W
Bougie = Bejaia	**127**	36 42N	5 2 E
Boulogne-sur-Mer	**38**	50 42N	1 36 E
Bourbonnais	**37**	46 28N	3 0 E
Bourem	**130**	17 0N	0 24W
Bourg-en-Bresse	**37**	46 13N	5 12 E
Bourges	**37**	47 9N	2 25 E
Bourgogne	**37**	47 0N	4 30 E
Bourke	**116**	30 8S	145 55 E
Bournemouth	**24**	50 43N	1 53W
Bousso	**131**	10 34N	16 52 E
Bouvet I. = Bouvetøya	**14**	54 26S	3 24 E
Bouvetøya	**14**	54 26S	3 24 E
Bowen	**121**	20 0S	148 16 E
Bowland, Forest of	**28**	54 0N	2 30W
Bowling Green, Ky., U.S.A.	**169**	37 0N	86 25W
Bowling Green, Ohio, U.S.A.	**167**	41 22N	83 40W
Bowling Green, C.	**121**	19 19S	147 25 E
Bowmanville	**151**	43 55N	78 41W
Bowral	**117**	34 26S	150 27 E
Boyle	**34**	53 58N	8 19W
Boyne →	**34**	53 43N	6 15W
Boyne City	**150**	45 13N	85 1W
Boyup Brook	**120**	33 50S	116 23 E
Bozeman	**163**	45 40N	111 0W
Bozen = Bolzano	**47**	46 30N	11 20 E
Brač	**52**	43 20N	16 40 E
Bracciano, L. di	**46**	42 8N	12 11 E
Bracebridge	**151**	45 2N	79 19W
Bräcke	**66**	62 45N	15 26 E
Brad	**56**	46 10N	22 50 E
Bradenton	**170**	27 25N	82 35W
Bradford, U.K.	**28**	53 47N	1 45W
Bradford, U.S.A.	**164**	41 58N	78 41W
Braemar	**33**	57 2N	3 20W
Braga	**50**	41 35N	8 25W
Bragança, Brazil	**188**	1 0S	47 2W
Bragança, Portugal	**50**	41 48N	6 50W
Brahmanbaria	**93**	23 58N	91 15 E
Brahmani →	**92**	20 39N	86 46 E
Brahmaputra →	**93**	24 2N	90 59 E
Braidwood	**117**	35 27S	149 49 E
Brăila	**57**	45 19N	27 59 E
Brainerd	**156**	46 20N	94 10W
Braintree	**25**	51 53N	0 34 E
Brampton	**151**	43 45N	79 45W
Branco →	**185**	1 20S	61 50W
Branco, Cabo	**182**	7 9S	34 47W
Brandenburg	**43**	52 24N	12 33 E
Brandon	**153**	49 50N	99 57W
Brantford	**151**	43 10N	80 15W
Brasil, Planalto	**188**	18 0S	46 30W
Brasília	**188**	15 47S	47 55 E
Braşov	**57**	45 38N	25 35 E
Brassey, Banjaran	**111**	5 0N	117 15 E
Brasstown Bald, Mt.	**165**	34 54N	83 45W
Bratislava	**59**	48 10N	17 7 E
Bratsk	**74**	56 10N	101 30 E
Brattleboro	**164**	42 53N	72 37W
Braunschweig	**43**	52 17N	10 28 E
Brava	**133**	1 20N	44 8 E
Bravo del Norte →	**174**	25 57N	97 9W
Brawley	**173**	32 58N	115 30W
Bray	**35**	53 12N	6 6W
Brazil	**167**	39 32N	87 8W
Brazil ■	**188**	10 0S	50 0W
Brazilian Highlands = Brasil, Planalto	**188**	18 0S	46 30W
Brazos →	**168**	28 53N	95 23W
Brazzaville	**134**	4 9S	15 12 E
Brčko	**52**	44 54N	18 46 E
Breadalbane	**31**	56 30N	4 15W
Bream Bay	**122**	35 56S	174 28 E
Brecon	**26**	51 57N	3 23W
Brecon Beacons	**26**	51 53N	3 27W
Breda	**40**	51 35N	4 45 E
Breiðafjörður	**64**	65 15N	23 15W
Bremen	**42**	53 4N	8 47 E
Bremerhaven	**42**	53 34N	8 35 E
Bremerton	**171**	47 30N	122 38W
Brenham	**168**	30 5N	96 27W
Brentwood	**25**	51 37N	0 19 E
Bréscia	**46**	45 33N	10 13 E
Breslau = Wrocław	**58**	51 5N	17 5 E

Brest, France	**36**	48 24N	4 31W
Brest, U.S.S.R.	**68**	52 10N	23 40 E
Bretagne	**36**	48 0N	3 0W
Bretçu	**57**	46 7N	26 18 E
Breton Sd.	**169**	29 40N	89 12W
Brett, C.	**122**	35 10S	174 20 E
Brewer	**148**	44 43N	68 50W
Brewster	**171**	48 10N	119 51W
Brewton	**169**	31 9N	87 2W
Brezhnev	**68**	55 42N	52 19 E
Briançon	**37**	44 54N	6 39 E
Bridgend	**27**	51 30N	3 35W
Bridgeport	**164**	41 12N	73 12W
Bridgeton	**164**	39 29N	75 10W
Bridgetown, Australia	**120**	33 58S	116 7 E
Bridgetown, Barbados	**180**	13 0N	59 30W
Bridgnorth	**24**	52 33N	2 25W
Bridgwater	**27**	51 7N	3 0W
Bridlington	**29**	54 6N	0 11W
Bridport	**27**	50 43N	2 45W
Brigham City	**163**	41 30N	112 1W
Bright	**117**	36 42S	146 56 E
Brighton, Australia	**119**	42 42S	147 16 E
Brighton, U.K.	**25**	50 50N	0 9W
Brindisi	**49**	40 39N	17 55 E
Brisbane	**116**	27 25S	153 2 E
Bristol, U.K.	**27**	51 26N	2 35W
Bristol, Conn., U.S.A.	**164**	41 44N	72 57W
Bristol, Tenn., U.S.A.	**165**	36 36N	82 11W
Bristol B.	**142**	58 0N	160 0W
Bristol Channel	**27**	51 18N	4 30W
Bristow	**168**	35 55N	96 28W
British Columbia □	**154**	55 0N	125 15W
British Guiana = Guyana ■	**185**	5 0N	59 0W
British Honduras = Belize ■	**177**	17 0N	88 30W
British Isles	**18**	55 0N	4 0W
Brittany = Bretagne	**36**	48 0N	3 0W
Brive-la-Gaillarde	**36**	45 10N	1 32 E
Brlik	**71**	44 0N	74 5 E
Brno	**59**	49 10N	16 35 E
Broach = Bharuch	**91**	21 47N	73 0 E
Broad Law	**31**	55 30N	3 22W
Broad Sd.	**121**	22 0S	149 45 E
Broads, The	**29**	52 45N	1 30 E
Brochet	**145**	57 53N	101 40W
Brockton	**164**	42 8N	71 2W
Brockville	**151**	44 35N	75 41W
Brod	**52**	41 35N	21 17 E
Brodeur Pen.	**146**	72 30N	88 10W
Broken Hill = Kabwe	**135**	14 30S	28 29 E
Broken Hill	**118**	31 58S	141 29 E
Bromley	**25**	51 20N	0 5 E
Brookhaven	**169**	31 40N	90 25W
Brooks	**155**	50 35N	111 55W
Brooks Ra.	**142**	68 40N	147 0W
Brosna →	**35**	53 8N	8 0W
Brough	**28**	54 32N	2 19W
Broughty Ferry	**31**	56 29N	2 50W
Brouwershaven	**40**	51 45N	3 55 E
Brownsville	**158**	25 56N	97 25W
Brownwood	**161**	31 45N	99 0W
Bruay-en-Artois	**38**	50 29N	2 33 E
Bruce, Mt.	**114**	22 37S	118 8 E
Bruce Rock	**120**	31 52S	118 8 E
Bruck an der Leitha	**45**	48 1N	16 47 E
Bruges = Brugge	**42**	51 13N	3 13 E
Brugge	**42**	51 13N	3 13 E
Brunei = Bandar Seri Begawan	**112**	4 52N	115 0 E
Brunei ■	**111**	4 50N	115 0 E
Bruno	**152**	52 20N	105 30W
Brunswick = Braunschweig	**43**	52 17N	10 28 E
Brunswick, Ga., U.S.A.	**170**	31 10N	81 30W
Brunswick, Maine, U.S.A.	**148**	43 53N	69 50W
Bruny I.	**119**	43 20S	147 15 E
Brussel	**42**	50 51N	4 21 E
Bruthen	**117**	37 42S	147 50 E
Bruton	**27**	51 6N	2 28W
Bryan, Ohio, U.S.A.	**167**	41 30N	84 30W
Bryan, Tex., U.S.A.	**168**	30 40N	96 27W
Bryan, Mt.	**119**	33 30S	139 0 E
Bryansk	**68**	53 13N	34 25 E
Brzeg	**58**	50 52N	17 30 E
Bucaramanga	**184**	7 0N	73 0W
Buchan	**33**	57 32N	2 8W
Buchan Ness	**33**	57 29N	1 48W
Buchanan	**130**	5 57N	10 2W
Buchans	**149**	48 50N	56 52W
Bucharest = Bucureşti	**57**	44 27N	26 10 E
Buckhannon	**165**	39 2N	80 10W
Buckhaven	**31**	56 10N	3 2W
Buckingham, Canada	**151**	45 37N	75 24W
Buckingham, U.K.	**25**	52 0N	0 59W
Buckingham □	**25**	51 50N	0 55W
Buckleboo	**118**	32 54S	136 12 E
Bucureşti	**57**	44 27N	26 10 E
Bucyrus	**167**	40 48N	83 0W
Budalin	**93**	22 20N	95 10 E
Budapest	**59**	47 29N	19 5 E
Budaun	**89**	28 5N	79 10 E
Bude	**27**	50 49N	4 33W
Budgewoi Lake	**117**	33 13S	151 34 E
Buenaventura, Colombia	**184**	3 53N	77 4W
Buenaventura, Mexico	**174**	29 51N	107 29W
Buenos Aires	**190**	34 30S	58 20W
Buffalo	**164**	42 55N	78 50W
Bug →	**58**	52 31N	21 5 E
Buga	**184**	4 0N	76 15W
Bugun Shara	**100**	49 0N	104 0 E
Builth Wells	**26**	52 10N	3 26W
Buir Nur	**98**	47 50N	117 42 E
Bujumbura	**135**	3 16S	29 18 E
Bukachacha	**74**	52 55N	116 50 E
Bukavu	**23**	2 20S	28 52 E
Bukhara	**70**	39 48N	64 25 E
Bukit Mertajam	**96**	5 22N	100 28 E
Bukittinggi	**111**	0 20S	100 20 E
Bukoba	**135**	1 20S	31 49 E
Bukuru	**131**	9 42N	8 48 E
Bulahdelah	**117**	32 23S	152 13 E
Bulandshahr	**89**	28 28N	77 51 E
Bulawayo	**137**	20 7S	28 32 E
Bulgaria ■	**53**	42 35N	25 30 E
Bull Shoals L.	**168**	36 40N	93 5W
Bully-les-Mines	**38**	50 27N	2 44 E
Bulsar = Valsad	**91**	20 40N	72 58 E
Bulun	**72**	70 37N	127 30 E
Bunbury	**120**	33 20S	115 35 E
Buncrana	**34**	55 8N	7 28W
Bundaberg	**116**	24 54S	152 22 E
Bundi	**91**	25 30N	75 35 E
Bundoran	**34**	54 24N	8 17W
Bungo-Suidō	**109**	33 0N	132 15 E
Buorkhaya, Mys	**72**	71 50N	132 40 E
Bûr Sa'îd	**128**	31 16N	32 18 E
Bûr Sûdân	**129**	19 32N	37 9 E
Buraymī, Al Wāhāt al	**83**	24 10N	55 43 E
Burbank	**173**	34 9N	118 23W
Burdur	**80**	37 45N	30 22 E
Burdwan = Barddhaman	**92**	23 14N	87 39 E
Burgas	**53**	42 33N	27 29 E
Burgenland □	**45**	47 20N	16 20 E
Burgos	**50**	42 21N	3 41W
Burgundy = Bourgogne	**37**	47 0N	4 30 E
Burin	**149**	47 1N	55 14W
Burkina Faso ■	**130**	12 0N	1 0W
Burlington, Canada	**151**	43 18N	79 45W
Burlington, Iowa, U.S.A.	**166**	40 50N	91 5W
Burlington, N.C., U.S.A.	**165**	36 7N	79 27W
Burlington, N.J., U.S.A.	**164**	40 5N	74 50W
Burlington, Vt., U.S.A.	**151**	44 27N	73 14W
Burma ■	**93**	21 0N	96 30 E
Burnie	**119**	41 4S	145 56 E
Burnley	**28**	53 47N	2 15W
Burns	**171**	43 40N	119 4W
Burns Lake	**154**	54 20N	125 45W
Burra	**119**	33 40S	138 55 E
Bursa	**80**	40 15N	29 5 E
Burton-upon-Trent	**28**	52 48N	1 39W
Buru	**113**	3 30S	126 30 E
Burundi ■	**135**	3 15S	30 0 E
Bury	**28**	53 36N	2 19W

Bury St. Edmunds	**25**	52 15N	0 42 E
Buryat A.S.S.R. □	**74**	53 0N	110 0 E
Buskerud fylke □	**60**	60 13N	9 0 E
Busselton	**120**	33 42S	115 15 E
Bussum	**40**	52 16N	5 10 E
Bute	**30**	55 48N	5 2W
Butiaba	**132**	1 50N	31 20 E
Butler	**164**	40 52N	79 52W
Butte	**163**	46 0N	112 31W
Butterworth	**96**	5 24N	100 23 E
Butuan	**112**	8 57N	125 33 E
Butung	**113**	5 0S	122 45 E
Buxton	**28**	53 16N	1 54W
Buyaga	**74**	59 50N	127 0 E
Buzău	**57**	45 10N	26 50 E
Buzen	**108**	33 35N	131 5 E
Buzzards Bay	**164**	41 45N	70 38W
Bydgoszcz	**58**	53 10N	18 0 E
Byelorussian S.S.R. □	**68**	53 30N	27 0 E
Bylot I.	**146**	73 13N	78 34W
Byrd Land	**15**	79 30S	125 0W
Byron Bay	**116**	28 43S	153 37 E
Byrranga, Gory	**72**	75 0N	100 0 E
Bytom	**58**	50 25N	18 54 E
Cabimas	**184**	10 23N	71 25W
Cabinda	**134**	5 33S	12 11 E
Cabinda □	**134**	5 0S	12 30 E
Cabo Pantoja	**184**	1 0S	75 10W
Cabonga, Réservoir	**151**	47 20N	76 40W
Caboolture	**116**	27 5S	152 58 E
Cabora Bassa Dam	**137**	15 20S	32 50 E
Caborca	**174**	30 40N	112 10W
Cabot Strait	**149**	47 15N	59 40W
Cabrera, I.	**51**	39 8N	2 57 E
Cabri	**152**	50 35N	108 25W
Cačak	**52**	43 54N	20 20 E
Cáceres	**50**	39 26N	6 23W
Cache Bay	**151**	46 22N	80 0W
Cachoeira	**189**	12 30S	39 0W
Cachoeira de Itapemirim	**189**	20 51S	41 7W
Cachoeira do Sul	**191**	30 3S	52 53W
Cader Idris	**26**	52 43N	3 56W
Cadibarrawirracanna, L.	**118**	28 52S	135 27 E
Cadillac, Canada	**151**	48 14N	78 23W
Cadillac, U.S.A.	**167**	44 16N	85 25W
Cádiz	**50**	36 30N	6 20W
Cádiz, G. de	**50**	36 40N	7 0W
Caen	**36**	49 10N	0 22W
Caernarfon	**26**	53 8N	4 17W
Caernarfon B.	**26**	53 4N	4 40W
Caernarvon = Caernarfon	**26**	53 8N	4 17W
Caerphilly	**27**	51 34N	3 13W
Cagayan de Oro	**112**	8 30N	124 40 E
Cágliari	**48**	39 15N	9 6 E
Caguas	**180**	18 14N	66 4W
Caha Mts.	**35**	51 45N	9 40W
Caher	**35**	52 23N	7 56W
Cahors	**36**	44 27N	1 27 E
Cahuapanas	**186**	5 15S	77 0W
Caibarién	**178**	22 30N	79 30W
Caicos Is.	**180**	21 40N	71 40W
Cairngorm Mts.	**33**	57 6N	3 42W
Cairns	**121**	16 57S	145 45 E
Cairo = El Qâhira	**128**	30 1N	31 14 E
Cairo	**169**	37 0N	89 10W
Cajamarca	**186**	7 5S	78 28W
Calabar	**131**	4 57N	8 20 E
Calabozo	**184**	9 0N	67 28W
Calábria □	**49**	39 24N	16 30 E
Calais, France	**38**	50 57N	1 50 E
Calais, U.S.A.	**148**	45 11N	67 20W
Calama, Brazil	**187**	8 0S	62 50W
Calama, Chile	**190**	22 30S	68 55W
Calamar	**184**	10 15N	74 55W
Calamian Group	**112**	11 50N	119 55 E
Calca	**187**	13 22S	72 0W
Calcutta	**92**	22 36N	88 24 E
Caldwell	**171**	43 45N	116 42W
Calgary	**155**	51 0N	114 10W
Cali	**184**	3 25N	76 35W
Calicut	**90**	11 15N	75 43 E
California □	**172**	37 25N	120 0W
California, Golfo de	**174**	28 0N	112 0W
Callander	**31**	56 15N	4 14W
Callao	**186**	12 0S	77 0W
Caloundra	**116**	26 45S	153 10 E
Caltanissetta	**49**	37 30N	14 3 E
Cam Lam	**95**	11 54N	109 10 E
Cam Ranh	**95**	11 54N	109 12 E
Camagüey	**178**	21 20N	78 0W
Camaná	**186**	16 30S	72 50W
Camargue	**37**	43 34N	4 34 E
Camarones	**192**	44 50S	65 40W
Cambay = Khambhat	**91**	22 23N	72 33 E
Cambodia ■	**95**	12 15N	105 0 E
Camborne	**27**	50 13N	5 18W
Cambrai	**38**	50 11N	3 14 E
Cambrian Mts.	**26**	52 25N	3 52W
Cambridge, Canada	**151**	43 23N	80 15W
Cambridge, N.Z.	**122**	37 54S	175 29 E
Cambridge, U.K.	**25**	52 13N	0 8 E
Cambridge, Mass., U.S.A.	**164**	42 20N	71 8W
Cambridge, Md., U.S.A.	**164**	38 33N	76 2W
Cambridge, Ohio, U.S.A.	**167**	40 1N	81 35W
Cambridge Bay	**145**	69 10N	105 0W
Cambridge Gulf	**114**	14 55S	128 15 E
Cambridgeshire □	**25**	52 12N	0 7 E
Camden, Ark., U.S.A.	**168**	33 40N	92 50W
Camden, N.J., U.S.A.	**164**	39 57N	75 7W
Camden, S.C., U.S.A.	**165**	34 17N	80 34W
Cameroon ■	**131**	6 0N	12 30 E
Cameroun, Mt.	**131**	4 13N	9 10 E
Cametá	**188**	2 12S	49 30W
Camiri	**187**	20 3S	63 31W
Camocim	**189**	2 55S	40 50W
Campagna	**46**	40 40N	15 5 E
Campania □	**49**	40 50N	14 45 E
Campbell I.	**15**	52 30S	169 0 E
Campbell River	**154**	50 5N	125 20W
Campbellton	**148**	47 57N	66 43W
Campbelltown, Australia	**117**	34 4S	150 49 E
Campbeltown, U.K.	**30**	57 34N	4 2W
Campeche	**177**	19 51N	90 32W
Campeche □	**177**	19 0N	90 30W
Campeche, B. de	**177**	20 0N	94 0W
Camperdown	**119**	38 14S	143 9 E
Camperville	**153**	51 59N	100 9W
Campina Grande	**189**	7 20S	35 47W
Campinas	**188**	22 50S	47 0W
Campo Grande	**188**	20 25S	54 40W
Campos	**188**	21 50S	41 20W
Camrose	**155**	53 0N	112 50W
Can Tho	**95**	10 2N	105 46 E
Canada ■	**139**	60 0N	100 0W
Cañada de Gómez	**190**	32 40S	61 30W
Canadian →	**158**	35 27N	95 3W
Çanakkale Boğazi	**80**	40 0N	26 0 E
Cananea	**174**	30 57N	110 18W
Canarias, Islas	**126**	28 30N	16 0W
Canary Is. = Canarias, Islas	**126**	28 30N	16 0W
Canaveral, C.	**170**	28 28N	80 31W
Canberra	**117**	35 15S	149 8 E
Candala	**133**	11 30N	49 58 E
Candia = Iráklion	**55**	35 20N	25 12 E
Canea = Khaniá	**55**	35 30N	24 4 E
Çankırı	**80**	40 40N	33 37 E
Canmore	**155**	51 7N	115 18W
Canna	**32**	57 3N	6 33W
Cannanore	**90**	11 53N	75 27 E
Cannes	**37**	43 32N	7 0 E
Cannock	**28**	52 42N	2 2W
Canora	**152**	51 40N	102 30W
Canowindra	**117**	33 35S	148 38 E
Canso	**149**	45 20N	61 0W
Cantabrian Mts. = Cantábrica, Cordillera	**50**	43 0N	5 10W
Cantábrica, Cordillera	**50**	43 0N	5 10W
Canterbury	**25**	51 17N	1 5 E
Canterbury □	**123**	43 45S	171 19 E

Canterbury Bight	**123**	44 16S	171 55E
Canterbury Plains	**123**	43 55S	171 22E
Canton = Guangzhou	**99**	23 5N	113 10E
Canton, Ill., U.S.A.	**166**	40 32N	90 0W
Canton, Miss., U.S.A.	**169**	32 40N	90 1W
Canton, Ohio, U.S.A.	**167**	40 47N	81 22W
Canutama	**185**	6 30S	64 20W
Cap-Chat	**148**	49 6N	66 40W
Cap-de-la-Madeleine	**151**	46 22N	72 31W
Cap-Haïtien	**180**	19 40N	72 20W
Cape Barren I.	**119**	40 25S	148 15E
Cape Breton I.	**149**	46 0N	60 30W
Cape Coast	**130**	5 5N	1 15W
Cape Dorset	**146**	64 14N	76 32W
Cape Fear →	**165**	34 30N	78 25W
Cape Girardeau	**169**	37 20N	89 30W
Cape May	**164**	39 1N	74 53W
Cape Montague	**149**	46 5N	62 25W
Cape Province ☐	**136**	32 0S	23 0E
Cape Town	**136**	33 55S	18 22E
Cape Verde Is. ■	**9**	17 10N	25 20W
Cape York Peninsula	**115**	12 0S	142 30E
Caquetá →	**184**	1 15S	69 15W
Caracal	**57**	44 8N	24 22E
Caracas	**184**	10 30N	66 55W
Caratinga	**188**	19 50S	42 10W
Carberry	**153**	49 50N	99 25W
Carbonara, C.	**48**	39 8N	9 30E
Carbondale	**166**	37 45N	89 10W
Carbonear	**149**	47 42N	53 13W
Carcassonne	**37**	43 13N	2 20E
Carcross	**144**	60 13N	134 45W
Cárdenas, Cuba	**178**	23 0N	81 30W
Cárdenas, Mexico	**177**	21 0N	99 40W
Cardiff	**27**	51 28N	3 11W
Cardigan	**26**	52 6N	4 41W
Cardigan B.	**26**	52 30N	4 30W
Cardston	**155**	49 15N	113 20W
Cardwell	**121**	18 14S	146 2E
Caribbean Sea	**181**	15 0N	75 0W
Cariboo Mts.	**155**	53 0N	121 0W
Caribou	**148**	46 55N	68 0W
Caribou Mts.	**145**	59 12N	115 40W
Carinhanha	**188**	14 15S	44 46W
Carinthia ☐ = Kärnten ☐	**45**	46 52N	13 30E
Carlisle, U.K.	**28**	54 54N	2 55W
Carlisle, U.S.A.	**164**	40 12N	77 10W
Carlow	**35**	52 50N	6 58W
Carlow ☐	**35**	52 43N	6 50W
Carlsbad, Calif., U.S.A.	**173**	33 11N	117 25W
Carlsbad, N. Mex., U.S.A.	**161**	32 20N	104 14W
Carlyle	**152**	49 40N	102 20W
Carmacks	**144**	62 5N	136 16W
Carman	**153**	49 30N	98 0W
Carmarthen	**26**	51 52N	4 20W
Carmarthen B.	**27**	51 40N	4 30W
Carnarvon	**120**	24 51S	113 42E
Carnegie, L.	**114**	26 5S	122 30E
Carniche, Alpi	**47**	46 36N	13 0E
Carnsore Pt.	**35**	52 10N	6 20W
Caroline Is.	**122**	8 0N	150 0E
Caroona	**116**	31 24S	150 26E
Carpathians, Mts.	**17**	49 50N	21 0E
Carpaţii Meridionali	**57**	45 30N	25 0E
Carpentaria, G. of	**115**	14 0S	139 0E
Carrara	**46**	44 5N	10 7E
Carrick-on-Shannon	**34**	53 57N	8 7W
Carrick-on-Suir	**35**	52 22N	7 30W
Carrickfergus	**34**	54 43N	5 50W
Carrickmacross	**34**	54 0N	6 43W
Carroll	**166**	42 2N	94 55W
Carrollton	**170**	33 36N	85 5W
Carse of Gowrie	**31**	56 30N	3 10W
Carson City	**172**	39 12N	119 46W
Carstairs	**31**	55 42N	3 41W
Cartagena, Colombia	**184**	10 25N	75 33W
Cartagena, Spain	**51**	37 38N	0 59W
Cartago, Colombia	**184**	4 45N	75 55W
Cartago, C. Rica	**179**	9 50N	85 52W
Cartersville	**169**	34 11N	84 48W
Carthage	**168**	37 10N	94 20W
Cartwright	**147**	53 41N	56 58W
Caruaru	**189**	8 15S	35 55W
Carúpano	**185**	10 39N	63 15W
Caruthersville	**169**	36 10N	89 40W
Carvin	**38**	50 30N	2 57E
Casablanca	**126**	33 36N	7 36W
Casas Grandes	**174**	30 22N	107 57W
Cascade Ra.	**171**	47 0N	121 30W
Casilda	**190**	33 10S	61 10W
Casino	**116**	28 52S	153 3E
Casiquiare →	**184**	2 1N	67 7W
Casma	**186**	9 30S	78 20W
Casper	**163**	42 52N	106 20W
Caspian Sea	**70**	43 0N	50 0E
Cassiar Mts.	**144**	59 30N	130 30W
Castellón de la Plana	**51**	39 58N	0 3W
Castelsarrasin	**36**	44 2N	1 7E
Casterton	**119**	37 30S	141 30E
Castilla La Nueva	**50**	39 45N	3 20W
Castilla La Vieja	**50**	41 55N	4 0W
Castle Douglas	**31**	54 57N	3 57W
Castlebar	**34**	53 52N	9 17W
Castleblaney	**34**	54 7N	6 44W
Castlegar	**155**	49 20N	117 40W
Castlemaine	**117**	37 2S	144 12E
Castlereagh	**34**	53 47N	8 30W
Castletown	**28**	58 35N	3 22W
Castletown Bearhaven	**35**	51 40N	9 54W
Castor	**155**	52 15N	111 50W
Castres	**37**	43 37N	2 13E
Castricum	**40**	52 33N	4 40E
Castries	**180**	14 0N	60 50W
Castro	**192**	42 30S	73 50W
Cat I.	**178**	24 30N	75 30W
Catacáos	**186**	5 20S	80 45W
Catalonia = Cataluña ☐	**51**	41 40N	1 15E
Cataluña ☐	**51**	41 40N	1 15E
Catamarca	**190**	28 30S	65 50W
Catanduanes	**112**	13 50N	124 20E
Catánia	**49**	37 31N	15 4E
Catanzaro	**49**	38 54N	16 38E
Catoche, C.	**177**	21 35N	87 5W
Catskill Mts.	**164**	42 15N	74 15W
Cauca →	**184**	8 54N	74 28W
Caucasus Mts. = Bolshoi Kavkas	**70**	42 50N	44 0E
Caudry	**38**	50 7N	3 22E
Cauquenes	**190**	36 0S	72 22W
Cavaillon	**37**	43 50N	5 2E
Cavan	**34**	54 0N	7 22W
Cawnpore = Kanpur	**91**	26 28N	80 20E
Caxias	**188**	4 55S	43 20W
Caxias do Sul	**191**	29 10S	51 10W
Cayenne	**185**	5 0N	52 18W
Cayes, Les	**180**	18 15N	73 46W
Cayman Is.	**178**	19 40N	80 30W
Ceanannus Mor	**34**	53 42N	6 53W
Ceará = Fortaleza	**189**	3 45S	38 35W
Ceará ☐	**189**	5 0S	40 0W
Cebu	**112**	10 18N	123 54E
Cedar →	**166**	41 17N	91 21W
Cedar City	**162**	37 41N	113 3W
Cedar Falls	**166**	42 39N	92 29W
Cedar L.	**152**	53 10N	100 0W
Cedar Rapids	**166**	42 0N	91 38W
Cedartown	**169**	34 1N	85 15W
Ceduna	**118**	32 7S	133 46E
Cegléd	**59**	47 11N	19 47E
Ceiba, La	**179**	15 40N	86 50W
Celaya	**177**	20 31N	100 37W
Celebes = Sulawesi ☐	**113**	2 0S	120 0E
Celebes Sea	**113**	3 0N	123 0E
Center	**168**	31 50N	94 10W
Centerville	**166**	40 45N	92 57W
Central ☐	**31**	56 10N	4 30W
Central, Cordillera	**184**	5 0N	75 0W
Central African Republic ■	**129**	7 0N	20 0E
Central Auckland ☐	**122**	37 30S	175 30E
Central Makran Range	**88**	26 30N	64 15E
Central Russian Uplands	**17**	54 0N	36 0E
Central Siberian Plateau	**77**	65 0N	105 0E

Centralia	**166**	38 32N	89 5W
Cephalonia = Kefallinía	**54**	38 20N	20 30 E
Ceram = Seram	**113**	3 10S	129 0 E
Ceram Sea = Seram Sea	**113**	2 30S	128 30 E
Cerignola	**49**	41 17N	15 53 E
Cerigo = Kíthira	**55**	36 9N	23 0 E
Cerritos	**177**	22 26N	100 17W
Cesena	**47**	44 9N	12 14 E
Ceskomoravská Vrchovina	**59**	49 30N	15 40 E
Ceský Těšin	**59**	49 45N	18 39 E
Cessnock	**117**	32 50S	151 21 E
Cetinje	**52**	42 23N	18 59 E
Ceuta	**126**	35 52N	5 18W
Cévennes	**37**	44 10N	3 50 E
Ceylon = Sri Lanka ■	**90**	7 30N	80 50 E
Chachapoyas	**186**	6 15S	77 50W
Chachoengsao	**95**	13 42N	101 5 E
Chad ■	**131**	15 0N	17 15 E
Chad, L. = Tchad, L.	**131**	13 30N	14 30 E
Chadron	**163**	42 50N	103 0W
Chagos Arch.	**76**	6 0S	72 0 E
Chāh Bahār	**85**	25 20N	60 40 E
Chakradharpur	**92**	22 45N	85 40 E
Chala	**186**	15 48S	74 20W
Chalcis = Khalkís	**55**	38 27N	23 42 E
Chalhuanca	**186**	14 15S	73 15W
Chalisgaon	**91**	20 30N	75 10 E
Challapata	**187**	18 53S	66 50W
Chalon-sur-Saône	**37**	46 48N	4 50 E
Châlons-sur-Marne	**37**	48 58N	4 20 E
Chambal →	**91**	26 29N	79 15 E
Chambersburg	**164**	39 53N	77 41W
Chambéry	**37**	45 34N	5 55 E
Chamonix	**37**	45 55N	6 51 E
Champagne	**37**	49 0N	4 40 E
Champaign	**167**	40 8N	88 14W
Champlain, L.	**151**	44 30N	73 20W
Chañaral	**190**	26 23S	70 40W
Chandigarh	**89**	30 43N	76 47 E
Chandler	**118**	27 0S	133 19 E
Chang Jiang →	**99**	31 48N	121 10 E
Changchiak'ou = Zhangjiakou	**98**	40 48N	114 55 E
Ch'angchou = Changzhou	**99**	31 47N	119 58 E
Changchun	**98**	43 57N	125 17 E
Changde	**99**	29 4N	111 35 E
Changhai = Shanghai	**99**	31 15N	121 26 E
Changsha	**99**	28 12N	113 0 E
Changzhi	**98**	36 10N	113 6 E
Changzhou	**99**	31 47N	119 58 E
Channel Is.	**36**	49 30N	2 40W
Channel-Port aux Basques	**149**	47 30N	59 9W
Chanthaburi	**95**	12 38N	102 12 E
Chantilly	**39**	49 12N	2 29 E
Chanute	**166**	37 45N	95 25W
Chao Phraya →	**94**	13 32N	100 36 E
Ch'aoan	**99**	23 41N	116 33 E
Chapala, L. de	**175**	20 15N	103 0W
Chapayevsk	**68**	53 0N	49 40 E
Chapel Hill	**165**	35 53N	79 3W
Chapleau	**150**	47 50N	83 24W
Charagua	**187**	19 45S	63 10W
Charaña	**187**	17 30S	69 25W
Chard	**27**	50 52N	2 59W
Chardzhou	**70**	39 6N	63 34 E
Chari →	**131**	12 58N	14 31 E
Chārīkār	**87**	35 0N	69 10 E
Charleroi	**42**	50 24N	4 27 E
Charles, C.	**165**	37 10N	75 59W
Charles City	**166**	43 2N	92 41W
Charleston, S.C., U.S.A.	**170**	32 47N	79 56W
Charleston, W. Va., U.S.A.	**165**	38 24N	81 36W
Charleville – Rath Luirc	**35**	52 21N	8 40W
Charleville	**116**	26 24S	146 15 E
Charleville-Mézières	**37**	49 44N	4 40 E
Charlotte, Mich., U.S.A.	**167**	42 36N	84 48W
Charlotte, N.C., U.S.A.	**165**	35 16N	80 46W
Charlotte Amalie	**180**	18 22N	64 56W
Charlotte Harbor	**170**	26 58N	82 4W
Charlottenburg	**43**	52 31N	13 15 E
Charlottesville	**165**	38 1N	78 30W
Charlottetown	**149**	46 14N	63 8W
Charlton, Australia	**117**	36 16S	143 24 E
Charlton, U.S.A.	**166**	40 59N	93 20W
Charters Towers	**121**	20 5S	146 13 E
Chartres	**39**	48 29N	1 30 E
Chascomús	**191**	35 30S	58 0W
Château-du-Loir	**39**	47 40N	0 25 E
Château-Thierry	**39**	49 3N	3 20 E
Châteaubriant	**36**	47 43N	1 23W
Châteaudun	**39**	48 3N	1 20 E
Châteauroux	**37**	46 50N	1 40 E
Châtellerault	**36**	46 50N	0 30 E
Chatham, N.B., Canada	**148**	47 2N	65 28W
Chatham, Ont., Canada	**141**	42 24N	82 11W
Chatham, U.K.	**25**	51 22N	0 32 E
Chatta-Hantō	**106**	34 45N	136 55 E
Chattahoochee →	**170**	30 43N	84 51W
Chattanooga	**169**	35 2N	85 17W
Chaumont	**37**	48 7N	5 8 E
Chauny	**38**	49 37N	3 12 E
Cheboksary	**68**	56 8N	47 12 E
Cheboygan	**150**	45 38N	84 29W
Checheno-Ingush A.S.S.R. □	**70**	43 30N	45 29 E
Chegdomyn	**75**	51 7N	133 1 E
Chegga	**126**	25 27N	5 40W
Chehalis	**171**	46 44N	122 59W
Cheju Do	**99**	33 29N	126 34 E
Chekiang = Zhejiang □	**99**	29 0N	120 0 E
Chelforó	**190**	39 0S	66 33W
Chelkar Tengiz, Solonchak	**70**	48 0N	62 30 E
Chełm	**58**	51 8N	23 30 E
Chełmża	**58**	53 10N	18 39 E
Cheltenham	**24**	51 55N	2 5W
Chelyabinsk	**71**	55 10N	61 24 E
Chemainus	**154**	48 55N	123 42W
Chemnitz = Karl-Marx-Stadt	**43**	50 50N	12 55 E
Chemult	**171**	43 14N	121 47W
Chen, Gora	**73**	65 16N	141 50 E
Chencha	**132**	6 15N	37 32 E
Chenchiang = Zhenjiang	**99**	32 11N	119 26 E
Chengchou = Zhengzhou	**99**	34 45N	113 34 E
Chengde	**98**	40 59N	117 58 E
Chengdu	**99**	30 38N	104 2 E
Ch'engtu = Chengdu	**99**	30 38N	104 2 E
Cheo Reo	**95**	13 25N	108 28 E
Chepstow	**27**	51 38N	2 40W
Cher →	**36**	47 21N	0 29 E
Cherbourg	**36**	49 39N	1 40W
Cheremkhovo	**74**	53 8N	103 1 E
Cherepovets	**68**	59 5N	37 55 E
Cherkassy	**68**	49 27N	32 4 E
Chernigov	**68**	51 28N	31 20 E
Chernovtsy	**68**	48 15N	25 52 E
Chernoye	**72**	70 30N	89 10 E
Cherokee	**166**	42 40N	95 30W
Cherrapunji	**93**	25 17N	91 47 E
Cherskiy	**73**	68 45N	161 18 E
Cherskogo Khrebet	**73**	65 0N	143 0 E
Cherwell →	**25**	51 46N	1 18W
Chesapeake	**165**	36 43N	76 15W
Chesapeake Bay	**165**	38 0N	76 12W
Cheshire □	**28**	53 14N	2 30W
Cheshskaya Guba	**69**	67 20N	47 0 E
Chester, U.K.	**28**	53 12N	2 53W
Chester, Pa., U.S.A.	**164**	39 54N	75 20W
Chester, S.C., U.S.A.	**165**	34 44N	81 13W
Chesterfield	**28**	53 14N	1 26W
Chesterfield Inlet	**145**	63 30N	90 45W
Chetumal	**177**	18 30N	88 18W
Cheviot, The	**31**	55 29N	2 8W
Cheviot Hills	**31**	55 20N	2 30W
Chew Bahir	**132**	4 40N	36 50 E
Cheyenne	**163**	41 9N	104 49W
Cheyenne →	**163**	44 40N	101 15W
Chhapra	**92**	25 48N	84 44 E
Chiamussu = Jiamusi	**98**	46 40N	130 26 E
Chiang Mai	**94**	18 47N	98 59 E
Chiapa →	**177**	16 42N	93 0W
Chiapas □	**177**	16 30N	92 30W
Chiba	**107**	35 30N	140 7 E
Chibougamau	**151**	49 56N	74 24W

Chicago	**167**	41 53N	87 40W
Chicago Heights	**167**	41 29N	87 37W
Chichagof I.	**143**	58 0N	136 0W
Chichester	**25**	50 50N	0 47W
Chichibu	**107**	36 5N	139 10 E
Ch'ich'ihaerh = Qiqihar	**98**	47 26N	124 0 E
Chiclayo	**186**	6 42S	79 50W
Chico	**172**	39 45N	121 54W
Chicopee	**164**	42 6N	72 37W
Chicoutimi	**148**	48 28N	71 5W
Chidambaram	**90**	11 20N	79 45 E
Chidley C.	**146**	60 23N	64 26W
Chigasaki	**107**	35 19N	139 24 E
Chihli, G. of = Bo Hai	**98**	39 0N	120 0 E
Chihuahua	**174**	28 38N	106 5W
Chihuahua □	**174**	28 30N	106 0W
Chikugo	**108**	33 14N	130 28 E
Chilapa	**177**	17 40N	99 11W
Childress	**161**	34 30N	100 15W
Chile ■	**190**	35 0S	72 0W
Chilin = Jilin	**98**	43 44N	126 30 E
Chilka L.	**92**	19 40N	85 25 E
Chillán	**190**	36 40S	72 10W
Chillicothe, Mo., U.S.A.	**166**	39 45N	93 30W
Chillicothe, Ohio, U.S.A.	**167**	39 20N	82 58W
Chilliwack	**154**	49 10N	121 54W
Chiloé, I. de	**192**	42 30S	73 50W
Chilpancingo	**177**	17 30N	99 30W
Chiltern Hills	**25**	51 44N	0 42W
Chimborazo	**184**	1 29S	78 55W
Chimbote	**186**	9 0S	78 35W
Chimkent	**71**	42 18N	69 36 E
Chin □	**93**	22 0N	93 0 E
China ■	**79**	30 0N	110 0 E
Chinan = Jinan	**98**	36 38N	117 1 E
Chinandega	**179**	12 35N	87 12W
Chincha Alta	**186**	13 25S	76 7W
Chinchilla	**116**	26 45S	150 38 E
Chinchou = Jinzhou	**98**	41 5N	121 3 E
Chindwin →	**93**	21 26N	95 15 E
Ch'ingtao = Qingdao	**98**	36 5N	120 20 E
Chinju	**98**	35 12N	128 2 E
Chinnampo	**98**	38 52N	125 10 E
Chino	**107**	35 59N	138 9 E
Chinon	**36**	47 10N	0 15 E
Chippenham	**24**	51 27N	2 7W
Chippewa Falls	**166**	44 55N	91 22W
Chiquián	**186**	10 10S	77 0W
Chiquimula	**177**	14 51N	89 37W
Chiquinquira	**184**	5 37N	73 50W
Chirala	**90**	15 50N	80 26 E
Chirchik	**71**	41 29N	69 35 E
Chita	**74**	52 0N	113 35 E
Chitral	**89**	35 50N	71 56 E
Chitré	**179**	7 59N	80 27W
Chittagong	**93**	22 19N	91 48 E
Chittagong □	**93**	24 5N	91 0 E
Chivilcoy	**190**	34 55S	60 0W
Chkalov = Orenburg	**70**	51 45N	55 6 E
Chōfu	**107**	35 39N	139 33 E
Choix	**174**	26 43N	108 17W
Chojnice	**58**	53 42N	17 32 E
Cholet	**36**	47 4N	0 52W
Choluteca	**179**	13 20N	87 14W
Chon Buri	**95**	13 21N	101 1 E
Chongjin	**98**	41 47N	129 50 E
Chŏngju	**98**	36 39N	127 27 E
Chongqing	**99**	29 35N	106 25 E
Chŏnju	**98**	35 50N	127 4 E
Chonos, Arch. de los	**192**	45 0S	75 0W
Chorley	**28**	53 39N	2 39W
Chorzów	**58**	50 18N	18 57 E
Chōshi	**107**	35 45N	140 51 E
Christchurch, N.Z.	**123**	43 33S	172 47 E
Christchurch, U.K.	**24**	50 44N	1 33W
Christianshåb	**147**	68 50N	51 18W
Christmas I. = Kiritimati	**123**	1 58N	157 27W
Christmas I.	**111**	10 30S	105 40 E
Ch'uanchou = Quanzhou	**99**	24 55N	118 34 E
Chūbu □	**106**	36 45N	137 30 E
Chubut →	**192**	43 20S	65 5W
Chūgoku □	**109**	35 0N	133 0 E
Chūgoku-Sanchi	**109**	35 0N	133 0 E
Chukotskiy Khrebet	**73**	68 0N	175 0 E
Chukotskoye More	**73**	68 0N	175 0W
Chula Vista	**173**	32 39N	117 8W
Chulman	**74**	56 52N	124 52 E
Chulucanas	**186**	5 8S	80 10W
Chumikan	**75**	54 40N	135 10 E
Chumphon	**94**	10 35N	99 14 E
Chunchŏn	**98**	37 58N	127 44 E
Chungking = Chongqing	**99**	29 35N	106 25 E
Chuquibamba	**186**	15 47S	72 44W
Chur	**44**	46 52N	9 32 E
Churchill →, Man., Canada	**143**	58 47N	94 12W
Churchill →, Nfld., Canada	**147**	53 19N	60 10W
Churchill, C.	**143**	58 46N	93 12W
Churchill Falls	**147**	53 36N	64 19W
Churchill Pk.	**144**	58 10N	125 10W
Churu	**89**	28 20N	74 50 E
Chuvash A.S.S.R. □	**68**	55 30N	47 0 E
Chuxiong	**101**	25 2N	101 28 E
Cicero	**167**	41 48N	87 48W
Ciego de Avila	**178**	21 50N	78 50W
Ciénaga	**184**	11 1N	74 15W
Cienfuegos	**178**	22 10N	80 30W
Cimarron →	**161**	36 10N	96 17W
Cincinnati	**167**	39 10N	84 26W
Cinto, Mt.	**36**	42 24N	8 54 E
Ciotat, La	**37**	43 12N	5 36 E
Circle	**142**	65 50N	144 10W
Circleville	**167**	39 35N	82 57W
Cirebon	**111**	6 45S	108 32 E
Cirencester	**24**	51 43N	1 59W
Citlaltépetl, Volcán	**177**	19 1N	97 16W
Ciudad Acuña	**174**	29 20N	100 58W
Ciudad Bolívar	**185**	8 5N	63 36W
Ciudad Camargo, Chihuahua, Mexico	**174**	27 40N	105 10W
Ciudad Camargo, Tamaulipas, Mexico	**176**	26 19N	98 50W
Ciudad de Valles	**177**	21 59N	99 1W
Ciudad del Carmen	**177**	18 38N	91 50W
Ciudad Guayana	**185**	8 0N	62 30W
Ciudad Guzmán	**175**	19 41N	103 29W
Ciudad Juárez	**174**	31 44N	106 29W
Ciudad Madero	**177**	22 16N	97 50W
Ciudad Mante	**177**	22 44N	98 57W
Ciudad Obregón	**174**	27 29N	109 56W
Ciudad Real	**50**	38 59N	3 55W
Ciudad Rodrigo	**50**	40 35N	6 32W
Ciudad Trujillo = Santo Domingo	**180**	18 30N	64 54W
Ciudad Victoria	**177**	23 44N	99 8W
Civril	**80**	38 20N	29 43 E
Cizre	**81**	37 19N	42 10 E
Clare	**119**	33 50S	138 37 E
Clare □	**35**	52 20N	9 0W
Clare →	**35**	53 22N	9 5W
Clare I.	**34**	53 48N	10 0W
Claremont	**164**	43 23N	72 20W
Claremore	**168**	36 40N	95 37W
Claremorris	**34**	53 45N	9 0W
Claresholm	**155**	50 0N	113 33W
Clark Fork →	**162**	48 9N	116 15W
Clarksburg	**164**	39 18N	80 21W
Clarksdale	**169**	34 12N	90 33W
Clarkston	**171**	46 28N	117 2W
Clarksville	**169**	36 32N	87 20W
Clear, C.	**20**	51 26N	9 30W
Clearwater, Canada	**155**	51 38N	120 2W
Clearwater, U.S.A.	**170**	27 58N	82 45W
Cleburne	**168**	32 18N	97 25W
Clee Hills	**24**	52 26N	2 35W
Cleethorpes	**29**	53 33N	0 2W
Cleeve Hill	**24**	51 54N	2 0W
Clermont, Australia	**121**	22 49S	147 39 E
Clermont, France	**39**	49 23N	2 24 E
Clermont-Ferrand	**37**	45 46N	3 4 E
Clevedon	**27**	51 26N	2 52W
Cleveland, Miss., U.S.A.	**169**	33 43N	90 43W
Cleveland, Ohio, U.S.A.	**167**	41 28N	81 43W

Cleveland, Tenn., U.S.A.	**169**	35 9N	84 52W
Cleveland, Tex., U.S.A.	**169**	30 18N	95 0W
Cleveland □	**29**	54 35N	1 8 E
Cleveleys	**28**	53 52N	3 3W
Clew B.	**34**	53 54N	9 50W
Clifton Beach	**121**	16 46 S	145 39 E
Clifton Forge	**165**	37 49N	79 51W
Clinton, Canada	**150**	43 37N	81 32W
Clinton, Iowa, U.S.A.	**166**	41 50N	90 12W
Clinton, Mass., U.S.A.	**164**	42 26N	71 40W
Clinton, Mo., U.S.A.	**166**	38 20N	93 46W
Clinton, Okla., U.S.A.	**161**	35 30N	99 0W
Clinton, S.C., U.S.A.	**165**	34 30N	81 54W
Clinton Colden L.	**145**	63 58N	107 27W
Clonakilty	**35**	51 37N	8 53W
Cloncurry	**115**	20 40 S	140 28 E
Clones	**34**	54 10N	7 13W
Clonmel	**35**	52 22N	7 42W
Clovis	**161**	34 20N	103 10W
Cluj-Napoca	**56**	46 47N	23 38 E
Clunes	**117**	37 20 S	143 45 E
Clwyd □	**26**	53 5N	3 20W
Clyde →	**31**	55 56N	4 29W
Clyde, Firth of	**30**	55 20N	5 0W
Clydebank	**31**	55 54N	4 25W
Coahuila □	**174**	27 20N	102 0W
Coaldale	**155**	49 45N	112 35W
Coalinga	**173**	36 10N	120 21W
Coalville	**29**	52 43N	1 21W
Coast Mts.	**144**	55 0N	129 0W
Coast Ranges	**173**	41 0N	123 0W
Coatbridge	**31**	55 52N	4 2W
Coatepeque	**177**	14 46N	91 55W
Coats I.	**146**	62 30N	83 0W
Coats Land	**14**	77 0 S	25 0W
Coatzacoalcos	**177**	18 9N	94 25W
Cobalt	**151**	47 25N	79 42W
Cobán	**177**	15 30N	90 21W
Cobar	**116**	31 27 S	145 48 E
Cóbh	**35**	51 50N	8 18W
Cobham	**118**	30 18 S	142 7 E
Cobourg	**151**	43 58N	78 10W
Cobram	**117**	35 54 S	145 40 E
Cocanada = Kakinada	**92**	16 57N	82 11 E
Cochabamba	**187**	17 26 S	66 10W
Cochin China = Nam-Phan	**95**	10 30N	106 0 E
Cochran	**170**	32 25N	83 23W
Cochrane	**151**	49 0N	81 0W
Cockburn, Canal	**192**	54 30 S	72 0W
Coco →	**179**	15 0N	83 8W
Coco Chan.	**94**	13 50N	93 25 E
Cocos Is.	**111**	12 10 S	96 55 E
Cod, C.	**164**	42 8N	70 10W
Codajás	**185**	3 55 S	62 0W
Codó	**185**	4 30 S	43 55W
Cœur d'Alene	**171**	47 45N	116 51W
Coffs Harbour	**116**	30 16 S	153 5 E
Cohoes	**164**	42 47N	73 42W
Cohuna	**117**	35 45 S	144 15 E
Coiba, I.	**179**	7 30N	81 40W
Coihaique	**192**	45 30 S	71 45W
Coimbatore	**90**	11 2N	76 59 E
Coimbra	**50**	40 15N	8 27W
Cojimies	**184**	0 20N	80 0W
Cojutepequé	**177**	13 41N	88 54W
Colac	**117**	38 21 S	143 35 E
Colchester	**25**	51 54N	0 55 E
Coldstream	**31**	55 39N	2 14W
Coleman	**155**	49 40N	114 30W
Coleraine, Australia	**119**	37 36 S	141 40 E
Coleraine, U.K.	**34**	55 8N	6 40W
Colima	**175**	19 14N	103 43W
Colima □	**175**	19 10N	104 0W
Coll	**30**	56 40N	6 35W
College Park	**170**	33 42N	84 27W
Collie	**120**	33 22 S	116 8 E
Collingwood	**151**	44 29N	80 13W
Collinsville	**121**	20 30 S	147 56 E
Collooney	**34**	54 11N	8 28W
Colmar	**37**	48 5N	7 20 E
Colne	**28**	53 51N	2 11W
Cologne = Köln	**42**	50 56N	6 58 E
Colomb-Béchar = Béchar	**127**	31 38N	2 18W
Colômbia	**188**	20 10 S	48 40W
Colombia ■	**184**	3 45N	73 0W
Colombo	**90**	6 56N	79 58 E
Colón, Cuba	**178**	22 42N	80 54W
Colón, Panama	**179**	9 20N	79 54W
Colonia	**191**	34 25 S	57 50W
Colonsay	**30**	56 4N	6 12W
Colorado □	**163**	37 40N	106 0W
Colorado →, Argentina	**190**	39 50 S	62 8W
Colorado →, Calif., U.S.A.	**173**	34 45N	114 40W
Colorado →, Tex., U.S.A.	**161**	28 36N	95 58W
Colorado Desert	**160**	34 20N	116 0W
Colorado Plateau	**161**	36 40N	110 30W
Colorado Springs	**163**	38 55N	104 50W
Columbia, Miss., U.S.A.	**169**	31 16N	89 50W
Columbia, Mo., U.S.A.	**166**	38 58N	92 20W
Columbia, S.C., U.S.A.	**165**	34 0N	81 0W
Columbia, Tenn., U.S.A.	**169**	35 40N	87 0W
Columbia →	**171**	46 15N	124 5W
Columbia Basin	**171**	47 30N	118 30W
Columbretes, Is.	**51**	39 50N	0 50 E
Columbus, Ga., U.S.A.	**170**	32 30N	84 58W
Columbus, Ind., U.S.A.	**167**	39 14N	85 55W
Columbus, Miss., U.S.A.	**169**	33 30N	88 26W
Columbus, Ohio, U.S.A.	**167**	39 57N	83 1W
Colwyn Bay	**26**	53 17N	3 44W
Comeragh Mts.	**35**	52 17N	7 35W
Comilla	**93**	23 28N	91 10 E
Comitán	**177**	16 18N	92 9W
Committee B.	**146**	68 30N	86 30W
Communism Pk. = Kommunizma, Pik	**71**	39 0N	72 2 E
Como	**46**	45 48N	9 5 E
Como, L. di	**46**	46 5N	9 17 E
Comodoro Rivadavia	**192**	45 50 S	67 40W
Comorin, C.	**90**	8 3N	77 40 E
Comoro Is. ■	**125**	12 10 S	44 15 E
Comox	**154**	49 42N	124 55W
Compiègne	**38**	49 24N	2 50 E
Côn Dao	**95**	8 45N	106 45 E
Conakry	**130**	9 29N	13 49W
Conceição da Barra	**189**	18 35 S	39 45W
Concepción, Argentina	**191**	27 20 S	65 35W
Concepción, Chile	**190**	36 50 S	73 0W
Concepción, Est. de	**192**	50 30 S	74 55W
Concepción del Oro	**174**	24 38N	101 25W
Concepción del Uruguay	**190**	32 35 S	58 20W
Conchos, R. →	**174**	29 35N	104 25W
Concord, Calif., U.S.A.	**172**	37 59N	122 2W
Concord, N.C., U.S.A.	**165**	35 28N	80 35W
Concord, N.H., U.S.A.	**164**	43 12N	71 30W
Concordia, Argentina	**190**	31 20 S	58 2W
Concordia, U.S.A.	**161**	39 35N	97 40W
Condamine	**155**	26 56 S	150 9 E
Condé	**38**	50 26N	3 34 E
Condobolin	**117**	33 4 S	147 6 E
Congleton	**28**	53 10N	2 12W
Congo = Zaïre →	**134**	6 4 S	12 24 E
Congo (Kinshasa) ■ = Zaïre ■	**134**	3 0 S	23 0 E
Congo ■	**134**	1 0 S	16 0 E
Congo Basin	**124**	0 10 S	24 30 E
Conjeeveram = Kanchipuram	**90**	12 52N	79 45 E
Connacht	**34**	53 23N	8 40W
Conneaut	**164**	41 55N	80 32W
Connecticut □	**164**	41 40N	72 40W
Connecticut →	**157**	41 17N	72 21W
Connemara	**34**	53 29N	9 45W
Connors Ra.	**121**	21 40 S	149 10 E
Consett	**28**	54 52N	1 50W
Constance = Konstanz	**44**	47 39N	9 10 E
Constance, L. = Bodensee	**44**	47 35N	9 25 E
Constanța	**57**	44 14N	28 38 E
Constantine	**127**	36 25N	6 42 E
Contamana	**186**	7 19 S	74 55W
Conway = Conwy	**26**	53 17N	3 50W
Conway = Conwy →	**26**	53 18N	3 50W
Conway, N.H., U.S.A.	**148**	43 58N	71 8W
Conway, S.C., U.S.A.	**165**	33 49N	79 2W

Conwy	**26**	53 17N	3 50W
Conwy →	**26**	53 18N	3 50W
Cook, Mt.	**123**	43 36S	170 9 E
Cook Inlet	**142**	59 0N	151 0W
Cook Is.	**123**	17 0S	160 0W
Cook Strait	**123**	41 15S	174 29 E
Cookeville	**169**	36 12N	85 30W
Cookstown	**34**	54 40N	6 43W
Coolah	**116**	31 48S	149 41 E
Coolamon	**117**	34 46S	147 8 E
Coolangatta	**116**	28 11S	153 29 E
Coolgardie	**120**	30 55S	121 8 E
Cooma	**117**	36 12S	149 8 E
Coonabarabran	**116**	31 14S	149 18 E
Coonamble	**116**	30 56S	148 27 E
Cooper Cr. →	**118**	12 7S	132 41 E
Coorong, The	**119**	35 50S	139 20 E
Coorow	**120**	29 53S	116 2 E
Coos Bay	**171**	43 26N	124 7W
Cootamundra	**117**	34 36S	148 1 E
Copenhagen = København	**61**	55 41N	12 34 E
Copiapó	**190**	27 30S	70 20W
Copper Center	**142**	62 10N	145 25W
Coppermine	**145**	67 50N	115 5W
Coppermine →	**145**	67 49N	116 4W
Coquilhatville = Mbandaka	**134**	0 1N	18 18 E
Coquimbo	**190**	30 0S	71 20W
Coracora	**186**	15 5S	73 45W
Coral Gables	**170**	25 45N	80 16W
Coral Harbour	**146**	64 8N	83 10W
Coral Sea	**121**	15 0S	150 0 E
Corbeil-Essonnes	**39**	48 36N	2 26 E
Corbin	**165**	37 0N	84 3W
Corby	**25**	52 29N	0 41W
Cordele	**170**	31 55N	83 49W
Córdoba, Argentina	**190**	31 20S	64 10W
Córdoba, Mexico	**177**	18 53N	96 56W
Córdoba, Spain	**50**	37 50N	4 50W
Córdoba, Sierra de	**190**	31 10S	64 25W
Cordova	**142**	60 36N	145 45W
Corfu = Kérkira	**54**	39 38N	19 50 E
Corinth = Kórinthos	**54**	37 56N	22 55 E
Corinth	**169**	34 54N	88 30W
Corinth, G. of = Korinthiakós Kólpos	**54**	38 16N	22 30 E
Corinto, Brazil	**188**	18 20S	44 30W
Corinto, Nic.	**179**	12 30N	87 10W
Cork	**35**	51 54N	8 30W
Cork □	**35**	51 50N	8 50W
Corlu	**80**	41 11N	27 49 E
Corn Is. = Maiz, Islas del	**179**	12 15N	83 4W
Corner Brook	**140**	48 57N	57 58W
Cornwall	**151**	45 2N	74 44W
Cornwall □	**27**	50 26N	4 40W
Coro	**184**	11 25N	69 41W
Coroatá	**188**	4 8S	44 0W
Corocoro	**187**	17 15S	68 28W
Coroico	**187**	16 0S	67 50W
Coromandel Coast	**90**	12 30N	81 0 E
Corona	**173**	33 49N	117 36W
Coronado	**173**	32 45N	117 9W
Coronation Gulf	**145**	68 25N	110 0W
Coronel	**190**	37 0S	73 10W
Coronel Pringles	**190**	38 0S	61 30W
Corowa	**117**	35 58S	146 21 E
Corozal	**177**	9 19N	75 18W
Corpus Christi	**161**	27 50N	97 28W
Corrib, L.	**34**	53 5N	9 10W
Corrientes	**190**	27 30S	58 45W
Corrientes, C., Colombia	**184**	5 30N	77 34W
Corrientes, C., Cuba	**178**	21 43N	84 30W
Corrientes, C., Mexico	**175**	20 25N	105 42W
Corrigin	**120**	32 20S	117 53 E
Corse	**36**	42 0N	9 0 E
Corsica = Corse	**36**	42 0N	9 0 E
Corsicana	**168**	32 5N	96 30W
Cortez	**163**	37 24N	108 35W
Cortland	**164**	42 35N	76 11W
Corum	**80**	40 30N	34 57 E
Corumbá	**187**	19 0S	57 30W
Coruña, La	**50**	43 20N	8 25W
Corunna = Coruña, La	**50**	43 20N	8 25W
Corvallis	**171**	44 36N	123 15W
Cosamaloapan	**177**	18 23N	95 50W
Cosenza	**49**	39 17N	16 14 E
Coshocton	**167**	40 17N	81 51W
Costa Blanca	**51**	38 25N	0 10W
Costa Brava	**51**	41 30N	3 0 E
Costa del Sol	**50**	36 30N	4 30W
Costa Dorada	**51**	40 45N	1 15 E
Costa Rica ■	**179**	10 0N	84 0W
Cotagaita	**187**	20 45S	65 40W
Côte d'Or	**37**	47 10N	4 50 E
Coteau des Prairies	**156**	44 30N	97 0W
Cotonou	**131**	6 20N	2 25 E
Cotopaxi, Vol.	**184**	0 40S	78 30W
Cotswold Hills	**24**	51 42N	2 10W
Cottbus	**43**	51 44N	14 20 E
Coulommiers	**39**	48 50N	3 3 E
Council	**142**	64 55N	163 45W
Council Bluffs	**166**	41 20N	95 50W
Courantyne →	**185**	5 55N	57 5W
Courtrai = Kortrijk	**42**	50 50N	3 17 E
Coventry	**24**	52 25N	1 31W
Covington, Ga., U.S.A.	**170**	33 36N	83 50W
Covington, Ky., U.S.A.	**167**	39 5N	84 30W
Cowdenbeath	**31**	56 7N	3 20W
Cowes	**25**	50 45N	1 18W
Cowra	**117**	33 49S	148 42 E
Coxim	**188**	18 30S	54 55W
Cracow = Kraków	**58**	50 4N	19 57 E
Craigavon = Lurgan	**34**	54 28N	6 20W
Craiova	**57**	44 21N	23 48 E
Cranbrook, Australia	**120**	34 18S	117 33 E
Cranbrook, Canada	**155**	49 30N	115 46W
Crateús	**189**	5 10S	40 39W
Crato	**189**	7 10S	39 25W
Crawfordsville	**167**	40 2N	86 51W
Crawley	**24**	51 7N	0 10W
Creil	**39**	49 15N	2 34 E
Cremona	**46**	45 8N	10 2 E
Crépy-en-Valois	**39**	49 14N	2 54 E
Cres	**52**	44 58N	14 25 E
Crescent City	**172**	41 45N	124 12W
Creston, Canada	**155**	49 10N	116 31W
Creston, U.S.A.	**166**	41 0N	94 20W
Crestview	**169**	30 45N	86 35W
Crete = Kríti	**55**	35 15N	25 0 E
Creuse →	**36**	47 0N	0 34 E
Creusot, Le	**37**	46 50N	4 24 E
Crewe	**28**	53 6N	2 28W
Criciúma	**191**	28 40S	49 23W
Crieff	**31**	56 22N	3 50W
Crimea = Krymskiy P-ov.	**68**	45 0N	34 0 E
Crişul Alb →	**56**	46 42N	21 17 E
Crişul Negru →	**56**	46 38N	22 26 E
Crna Gora	**52**	42 10N	21 30 E
Crna Gora □	**52**	42 40N	19 20 E
Croatia = Hrvatska □	**52**	45 20N	18 0 E
Crockett	**168**	31 20N	95 30W
Cromarty	**33**	57 40N	4 2W
Cromer	**29**	52 56N	1 18 E
Crooked I.	**180**	22 50N	74 10W
Crookwell	**117**	34 28S	149 24 E
Cross Fell	**28**	54 44N	2 29W
Cross L.	**153**	54 45N	97 30W
Crosse, La	**166**	43 48N	91 13W
Crowley	**168**	30 15N	92 20W
Crowsnest Pass	**155**	49 40N	114 40W
Cruz, C.	**178**	19 50N	77 50W
Cruz Alta	**191**	28 45S	53 40W
Cruz del Eje	**190**	30 45S	64 50W
Cruzeiro do Sul	**186**	7 35S	72 35W
Crystal Brook	**119**	33 21S	138 12 E
Cu Lao Hon	**95**	10 54N	108 18 E
Cuando →	**134**	14 0S	19 30 E
Cuanza →	**134**	9 2S	13 30 E
Cuba ■	**178**	22 0N	79 0W
Cubango →	**134**	18 50S	22 25 E
Cucuí	**184**	1 12N	66 50W
Cúcuta	**184**	7 54N	72 31W
Cuddalore	**90**	11 46N	79 45 E

Cuddapah	**90**	14 30N	78 47 E
Cue	**120**	27 25 S	117 54 E
Cuenca, Ecuador	**184**	2 50 S	79 9W
Cuenca, Spain	**51**	40 5N	2 10W
Cuenca, Serranía de	**51**	39 55N	1 50W
Cuernavaca	**177**	18 55N	99 15W
Cuevo	**187**	20 15 S	63 30W
Cuiabá	**188**	15 30 S	56 0W
Cuillin Hills	**32**	57 14N	6 15W
Cuitzeo, L. de	**175**	19 55N	101 5W
Culcairn	**117**	35 41 S	147 3 E
Culiacán	**174**	24 48N	107 24W
Cullarin Range	**117**	34 30 S	149 30 E
Culloden Moor	**33**	57 29N	4 7W
Culverden	**123**	42 47 S	172 49 E
Cumaná	**185**	10 30N	64 5W
Cumberland	**164**	39 40N	78 43W
Cumberland →	**169**	36 15N	87 0W
Cumberland Is.	**121**	20 35 S	149 10 E
Cumberland Pen.	**146**	67 0N	64 0W
Cumberland Plat.	**169**	36 0N	84 30W
Cumberland Sd.	**146**	65 30N	66 0W
Cumbria □	**28**	54 35N	2 55W
Cumbrian Mts.	**28**	54 30N	3 0W
Cumbum	**90**	15 40N	79 10 E
Cummins	**119**	34 16 S	135 43 E
Cumnock	**31**	55 27N	4 18W
Cunene →	**134**	17 20 S	11 50 E
Cunnamulla	**116**	28 2 S	145 38 E
Curaçao	**181**	12 10N	69 0W
Curaray →	**184**	2 20 S	74 5W
Curiapo	**185**	8 33N	61 5W
Curicó	**190**	34 55 S	71 20W
Curitiba	**191**	25 20 S	49 10W
Curtis Group	**117**	39 30 S	146 37 E
Curuá →	**188**	5 23 S	54 22W
Curuçá	**188**	0 43 S	47 50W
Curuzú Cuatiá	**191**	29 50 S	58 5W
Cushing	**168**	35 59N	96 46W
Cusihuiriáchic	**174**	28 14N	106 50W
Cuthbert	**170**	31 47N	84 47W
Cuttack	**92**	20 25N	85 57 E
Cuxhaven	**42**	53 51N	8 41 E
Cuyahoga Falls	**167**	41 8N	81 30W
Cuzco, Bolivia	**187**	20 0 S	66 50W
Cuzco, Peru	**186**	13 32 S	72 0W
Cwmbran	**27**	51 39N	3 0W
Cypress Hills	**152**	49 40N	109 30W
Cyprus ■	**80**	35 0N	33 0 E
Cyrenaica	**124**	27 0N	23 0 E
Czechoslovakia ■	**59**	49 0N	17 0 E
Czeremcha	**58**	52 31N	23 21 E
Częstochowa	**58**	50 49N	19 7 E
Da →	**95**	21 15N	105 20 E
Da Hinggan Ling	**98**	48 0N	121 0 E
Da Nang	**95**	16 4N	108 13 E
Da Yunhe →	**99**	34 25N	120 5 E
Daba Shan	**99**	32 0N	109 0 E
Dacca = Dhaka	**92**	23 43N	90 26 E
Dacca □ = Dhaka □	**93**	24 25N	90 25 E
Dadanawa	**185**	2 50N	59 30W
Dadra and Nagar Haveli □	**91**	20 5N	73 0 E
Daghestan A.S.S.R. □	**70**	42 30N	47 0 E
Dahomey = Benin ■	**131**	10 0N	2 0 E
Dai-Sen	**109**	35 22N	133 32 E
Daiō-Misaki	**106**	34 15N	136 45 E
Daisetsu-Zan	**103**	43 30N	142 57 E
Daito	**109**	35 19N	132 58 E
Dajarra	**115**	21 42 S	139 30 E
Dakar	**130**	14 34N	17 29W
Dakhla	**126**	23 50N	15 53W
Dakhla, El Wâhât el-	**128**	25 30N	28 50 E
Đakovica	**52**	42 22N	20 26 E
Dalandzadgad	**98**	43 27N	104 30 E
Dalbeattie	**31**	54 55N	3 50W
Dalby	**116**	27 10 S	151 17 E
Dalhousie	**148**	48 5N	66 26W
Dali	**99**	25 40N	100 10 E
Dalian	**98**	38 50N	121 40 E
Daliang Shan	**99**	28 0N	102 45 E
Dallas, Oreg., U.S.A.	**171**	45 0N	123 15W
Dallas, Tex., U.S.A.	**168**	32 50N	96 50W
Dalmacija □	**52**	43 20N	17 0 E
Dalmatia = Dalmacija □	**52**	43 20N	17 0 E
Daloa	**130**	7 0N	6 30W
Dalton	**169**	34 47N	84 58W
Daly Waters	**114**	16 15 S	133 24 E
Daman	**91**	20 25N	72 57 E
Damaraland	**136**	21 0 S	17 0 E
Damascus = Dimashq	**80**	33 30N	36 18 E
Damāvand	**86**	35 47N	52 0 E
Damāvand, Qolleh-ye	**86**	35 56N	52 10 E
Dampier	**114**	20 41 S	116 42 E
Dampier Arch.	**114**	20 38 S	116 32 E
Danbury	**164**	41 23N	73 29W
Dandenong	**117**	38 0 S	145 15 E
Dandong	**98**	40 10N	124 20 E
Dangriga	**177**	17 0N	88 13W
Dannevirke	**122**	40 12 S	176 8 E
Dansville	**164**	42 32N	77 41W
Danville, Ill., U.S.A.	**167**	40 10N	87 40W
Danville, Ky., U.S.A.	**167**	37 40N	84 45W
Danville, Va., U.S.A.	**165**	36 40N	79 20W
Danzig = Gdańsk	**58**	54 22N	18 40 E
Dar es Salaam	**135**	6 50 S	39 12 E
Darbhanga	**92**	26 15N	85 55 E
Dardanelles = Çanakkale Boğazi	**80**	40 0N	26 0 E
Dârfûr	**129**	13 40N	24 0 E
Dargan Ata	**70**	40 29N	62 10 E
Dargaville	**122**	35 57 S	173 52 E
Darién, G. del	**184**	9 0N	77 0W
Darjeeling = Darjiling	**92**	27 3N	88 18 E
Darjiling	**92**	27 3N	88 18 E
Darling →	**119**	34 4 S	141 54 E
Darling Downs	**116**	27 30 S	150 30 E
Darling Ra.	**120**	32 30 S	116 0 E
Darlington	**28**	54 33N	1 33W
Darmstadt	**42**	49 51N	8 40 E
Darnley, C.	**14**	68 0 S	69 0 E
Dart →	**27**	50 24N	3 36W
Dartmoor	**27**	50 36N	4 0W
Dartmouth, Canada	**149**	44 40N	63 30W
Dartmouth, U.K.	**27**	50 21N	3 35W
Darwin	**114**	12 25 S	130 51 E
Dasht-e Kavīr	**86**	34 30N	55 0 E
Dasht-e Lūt	**85**	31 30N	58 0 E
Dasht-e Mārgow	**87**	30 40N	62 30 E
Datia	**91**	25 39N	78 27 E
Datong	**98**	40 6N	113 18 E
Daugavpils	**68**	55 53N	26 32 E
Dauphin	**153**	51 9N	100 5W
Dauphiné	**37**	45 15N	5 25 E
Davangere	**90**	14 25N	75 55 E
Davao	**112**	7 0N	125 40 E
Davenport	**166**	41 30N	90 40W
Daventry	**24**	52 16N	1 10W
David	**179**	8 30N	82 30W
Davis Sea	**15**	66 0 S	92 0 E
Davis Str.	**146**	65 0N	58 0W
Davos	**44**	46 48N	9 49 E
Dawson	**144**	64 10N	139 30W
Dawson Creek	**155**	55 45N	120 15W
Dawson Range	**121**	24 30 S	149 48 E
Daylesford	**117**	37 21 S	144 9 E
Dayr az Zawr	**81**	35 20N	40 5 E
Dayton, Ohio, U.S.A.	**167**	39 45N	84 10W
Dayton, Wash., U.S.A.	**171**	46 20N	118 10W
Daytona Beach	**170**	29 14N	81 0W
De Aar	**136**	30 39 S	24 0 E
De Land	**170**	29 1N	81 19W
De Ridder	**168**	30 48N	93 15W
De Soto	**166**	38 7N	90 33W
Deakin	**114**	30 46 S	128 0 E
Deal	**25**	51 13N	1 25 E
Dean, Forest of	**24**	51 50N	2 35W
Deán Funes	**190**	30 20 S	64 20W
Dease →	**144**	59 56N	128 32W
Dease Lake	**144**	58 25N	130 6W

Death Valley	**173**	36 19N	116 52W
Deauville	**38**	49 23N	0 2 E
Debar	**52**	41 31N	20 30 E
Debre Markos	**132**	10 20N	37 40 E
Debre Tabor	**132**	11 50N	38 26 E
Debrecen	**59**	47 33N	21 42 E
Decatur, Ala., U.S.A.	**169**	34 35N	87 0W
Decatur, Ga., U.S.A.	**170**	33 47N	84 17W
Decatur, Ill., U.S.A.	**166**	39 50N	89 0W
Deccan	**76**	18 0N	79 0 E
Dedéagach = Alexandroúpolis	**55**	40 50N	25 54 E
Dee →, Scotland, U.K.	**33**	57 4N	2 7W
Dee →, Wales, U.K.	**26**	53 15N	3 7W
Deepwater	**116**	29 25S	151 51 E
Deer Lake	**149**	49 11N	57 27W
Defiance	**167**	41 20N	84 20W
Deh Bīd	**85**	30 39N	53 11 E
Dehra Dun	**89**	30 20N	78 4 E
Dej	**56**	47 10N	23 52 E
Del Rio	**161**	29 23N	100 50W
Delano	**173**	35 48N	119 13W
Delaware □	**164**	39 0N	75 40W
Delaware →	**164**	39 20N	75 25W
Delaware B.	**157**	38 50N	75 0W
Delft	**40**	52 1N	4 22 E
Delfzijl	**41**	53 20N	6 55 E
Delgado, C.	**137**	10 45S	40 40 E
Delgo	**129**	20 6N	30 40 E
Delhi	**89**	28 38N	77 17 E
Delice →	**80**	39 45N	34 15 E
Delicias	**174**	28 13N	105 28W
Delong, Ostrova	**72**	76 40N	149 20 E
Deloraine	**119**	41 30S	146 40 E
Delray Beach	**170**	26 27N	80 4W
Demanda, Sierra de la	**50**	42 15N	3 0W
Dembidolo	**132**	8 34N	34 50 E
Deming	**161**	32 10N	107 50W
Demopolis	**169**	32 30N	87 48W
Den Burg	**40**	53 3N	4 47 E
Den Haag = 's-Gravenhage	**40**	52 7N	4 17 E
Den Helder	**40**	52 57N	4 45 E
Den Oever	**40**	52 56N	5 2 E
Denain	**38**	50 20N	3 22 E
Denbigh	**26**	53 12N	3 26W
Denham	**120**	25 56S	113 31 E
Deniliquin	**117**	35 30S	144 58 E
Denison	**168**	33 50N	96 40W
Denizli	**80**	37 42N	29 2 E
Denmark	**120**	34 59S	117 25 E
Denmark ■	**61**	55 30N	9 0 E
Denmark Str.	**13**	66 0N	30 0W
Denton	**168**	33 12N	97 10W
D'Entrecasteaux Is.	**115**	9 0S	151 0 E
Denver	**163**	39 45N	105 0W
Deolali	**91**	19 58N	73 50 E
Deoria	**92**	26 31N	83 48 E
Deosai Mts.	**89**	35 40N	75 0 E
Dera Ghazi Khan	**89**	30 5N	70 43 E
Dera Ismail Khan	**89**	31 50N	70 50 E
Derby	**28**	52 55N	1 28W
Derby □	**28**	52 55N	1 28W
Derg, L.	**35**	53 0N	8 20W
Derry = Londonderry	**34**	55 0N	7 20W
Derryveagh Mts.	**34**	55 0N	8 40W
Derwent →, Cumbria, U.K.	**28**	54 42N	3 22W
Derwent →, Derby, U.K.	**29**	52 53N	1 17W
Derwent →, N. Yorks., U.K.	**29**	53 45N	0 57W
Derwent Water, L.	**28**	54 35N	3 9W
Des Moines	**166**	41 35N	93 37W
Des Moines →	**166**	40 23N	91 25W
Deschutes →	**171**	45 30N	121 0W
Dese	**133**	11 5N	39 40 E
Despeñaperros, Paso	**50**	38 24N	3 30W
Dessau	**43**	51 49N	12 15 E
Dessye = Dese	**133**	11 5N	39 40 E
Desvrès	**38**	50 40N	1 48 E
Detroit	**167**	42 23N	83 5W
Deurne	**41**	51 27N	5 49 E
Deutsche Bucht	**42**	54 10N	7 51 E
Devakottai	**90**	9 55N	78 45 E
Deventer	**41**	52 15N	6 10 E
Devizes	**24**	51 21N	2 0W
Devon I.	**13**	75 10N	85 0W
Devonport, Australia	**119**	41 10S	146 22 E
Devonport, N.Z.	**122**	36 49S	174 49 E
Devonport, U.K.	**27**	50 23N	4 11W
Devonshire □	**27**	50 50N	3 40W
Dewsbury	**28**	53 42N	1 38W
Dezfūl	**84**	32 20N	48 30 E
Dezhneva, Mys	**73**	66 5N	169 40W
Dhahran = Az Zahrān	**84**	26 10N	50 7 E
Dhaka	**92**	23 43N	90 26 E
Dhaka □	**93**	24 25N	90 25 E
Dhamar	**83**	14 30N	44 20 E
Dhar	**91**	22 35N	75 26 E
Dharmapuri	**90**	12 10N	78 10 E
Dharwad	**90**	15 22N	75 15 E
Dhidhimótikhon	**55**	41 22N	26 29 E
Dhikti	**55**	35 8N	25 22 E
Dhodhekánisos	**55**	36 35N	27 0 E
Dhuburi	**92**	26 2N	89 59 E
Dhule	**91**	20 58N	74 50 E
Di Linh, Cao Nguyen	**95**	11 30N	108 0 E
Diamantina	**188**	18 17S	43 40W
Diamantina →	**115**	26 45S	139 10 E
Diamantino	**188**	14 30S	56 30W
Dibrugarh	**93**	27 29N	94 55 E
Dickinson	**163**	46 50N	102 48W
Didsbury	**155**	51 35N	114 10W
Diefenbaker L.	**152**	51 0N	106 55W
Dieppe	**38**	49 54N	1 4 E
Dieren	**41**	52 3N	6 6 E
Digby	**148**	44 38N	65 50W
Digne	**37**	44 5N	6 12 E
Dijlah, Nahr →	**81**	31 0N	47 25 E
Dijon	**37**	47 20N	5 0 E
Dila	**133**	6 21N	38 22 E
Dillon	**165**	34 26N	79 20W
Dimashq	**80**	33 30N	36 18 E
Dimboola	**119**	36 28S	142 7 E
Dîmboviţa →	**57**	44 14N	26 13 E
Dimitrovgrad	**53**	42 5N	25 35 E
Dimitrovo = Pernik	**53**	42 35N	23 2 E
Dinan	**36**	48 28N	2 2W
Dinara Planina	**52**	44 0N	16 30 E
Dinaric Alps = Dinara Planina	**52**	44 0N	16 30 E
Dindigul	**90**	10 25N	78 0 E
Dingle	**35**	52 9N	10 17W
Dingle B.	**35**	52 3N	10 20W
Dingwall	**33**	57 36N	4 26W
Dinuba	**173**	36 31N	119 22W
Dire Dawa	**133**	9 35N	41 45 E
Diriamba	**179**	11 51N	86 19W
Dirranbandi	**116**	28 33S	148 17 E
Disappointment L.	**114**	23 20S	122 40 E
Discovery B.	**119**	38 10S	140 40 E
Disko	**146**	69 45N	53 30W
Diss	**25**	52 23N	1 6 E
District of Columbia □	**164**	38 55N	77 0W
Diu	**91**	20 45N	70 58 E
Dives-sur-Mer	**39**	49 18N	0 8W
Dixon	**166**	41 50N	89 30W
Dixon Entrance	**154**	54 30N	132 0W
Diyarbakir	**81**	37 55N	40 18 E
Djakarta = Jakarta	**111**	6 9S	106 49 E
Djelfa	**130**	34 40N	3 15 E
Djerid, Chott	**127**	33 42N	8 30 E
Djibouti	**133**	11 30N	43 5 E
Djibouti ■	**133**	12 0N	43 0 E
Djoum	**131**	2 41N	12 35 E
Dmitriya Lapteva, Proliv	**72**	73 0N	140 0 E
Dnepr →	**68**	46 30N	32 18 E
Dnepropetrovsk	**68**	48 30N	35 0 E
Dnestr →	**68**	46 18N	30 17 E
Dnestrovski = Belgorod	**68**	50 35N	36 35 E
Dnieper = Dnepr →	**68**	46 30N	32 18 E
Dniester = Dnestr →	**68**	46 18N	30 17 E
Dobruja	**57**	44 30N	28 15 E
Dodecanese = Dhodhekánisos	**55**	36 35N	27 0 E
Dodge City	**161**	37 42N	100 0W

Dodoma	**135**	6 8S	35 45 E
Doesburg	**41**	52 1N	6 9 E
Doetinchem	**41**	51 59N	6 18 E
Dogger Bank	**124**	54 50N	2 0 E
Doi Luang	**95**	18 30N	101 0 E
Dojran	**54**	41 10N	22 45 E
Dokkum	**41**	53 20N	5 59 E
Dolbeau	**148**	48 53N	72 18W
Dole	**37**	47 7N	5 31 E
Dolgellau	**26**	52 44N	3 53W
Dolgelley = Dolgellau	**26**	52 44N	3 53W
Dolomites = Dolomiti	**47**	46 30N	11 40 E
Dolomiti	**47**	46 30N	11 40 E
Dolores	**191**	36 20S	57 40W
Dolphin and Union Str.	**145**	69 5N	114 45W
Domel I. = Letsôk-aw Kyun	**94**	11 30N	98 25 E
Dominica ■	**180**	15 20N	61 20W
Dominican Rep. ■	**180**	19 0N	70 30W
Don →, U.K.	**33**	57 14N	2 5W
Don →, U.S.S.R.	**68**	47 4N	39 18 E
Donaghadee	**34**	54 38N	5 32W
Donau →	**42**	48 10N	17 0 E
Doncaster	**29**	53 31N	1 9W
Dondra Head	**90**	5 55N	80 40 E
Donegal	**34**	54 39N	8 8W
Donegal □	**34**	54 53N	8 0W
Donegal B.	**34**	54 30N	8 35W
Donetsk	**68**	48 0N	37 45 E
Dongara	**120**	29 14S	114 57 E
Dongen	**40**	51 38N	4 56 E
Dongting Hu	**99**	29 18N	112 45 E
Donnelly's Crossing	**122**	35 42S	173 38 E
Donnybrook	**120**	33 34S	115 48 E
Doon →	**31**	55 26N	4 41W
Dorada, La	**184**	5 30N	74 40W
Dorchester	**27**	50 42N	2 28W
Dorchester, C.	**146**	65 27N	77 27W
Dordogne □	**36**	45 5N	0 40 E
Dordrecht	**40**	51 48N	4 39 E
Dornoch	**33**	57 52N	4 0W
Dorrigo	**116**	30 20S	152 44 E
Dorris	**172**	41 59N	121 58W
Dorset □	**27**	50 48N	2 25W
Dortmund	**42**	51 32N	7 28 E
Dothan	**169**	31 10N	85 25W
Douai	**38**	50 21N	3 4 E
Douala	**131**	4 0N	9 45 E
Douarnenez	**36**	48 6N	4 21W
Douglas, U.K.	**28**	54 9N	4 29W
Douglas, U.S.A.	**170**	31 32N	82 52W
Doullens	**38**	50 10N	2 20 E
Dounreay	**33**	58 34N	3 44W
Dourados	**188**	22 9S	54 50W
Douro →	**50**	41 8N	8 40W
Douro Litoral □	**50**	41 10N	8 20W
Dove →	**28**	52 51N	1 36W
Dover, U.K.	**25**	51 7N	1 19 E
Dover, Del., U.S.A.	**164**	39 10N	75 31W
Dover, N.H., U.S.A.	**164**	43 12N	70 51W
Dover, Str. of	**38**	51 0N	1 30 E
Dovey →	**26**	52 32N	4 0W
Downham Market	**25**	52 36N	0 22 E
Downpatrick	**34**	54 20N	5 43W
Drachten	**41**	53 7N	6 5 E
Dragoman, Prokhod	**53**	43 0N	22 53 E
Draguignan	**37**	43 30N	6 27 E
Drakensberg	**137**	31 0S	28 0 E
Dráma	**55**	41 9N	24 10 E
Drammen	**60**	59 42N	10 12 E
Drau = Drava →	**59**	45 33N	18 55 E
Drava →	**59**	45 33N	18 55 E
Drayton Valley	**155**	53 12N	114 58W
Drenthe □	**41**	52 52N	6 40 E
Dresden	**43**	51 2N	13 45 E
Dreux	**39**	48 44N	1 23 E
Driffield	**29**	54 0N	0 25W
Drin i zi →	**52**	41 37N	20 28 E
Drina →	**52**	44 53N	19 21 E
Drogheda	**34**	53 45N	6 20W
Droitwich	**24**	52 16N	2 10W
Dronne →	**36**	45 2N	0 9W
Dronning Maud Land	**14**	72 30S	12 0 E
Drumheller	**155**	51 25N	112 40W
Drummond Ra.	**121**	23 45S	147 10 E
Drummondville	**151**	45 55N	72 25W
Dryden	**153**	49 47N	92 50W
Du Bois	**164**	41 8N	78 46W
Du Quoin	**166**	38 0N	89 10W
Dubai = Dubayy	**85**	25 18N	55 20 E
Dubawnt →	**145**	64 33N	100 6W
Dubawnt, L.	**143**	63 4N	101 42W
Dubayy	**85**	25 18N	55 20 E
Dubbo	**116**	32 11S	148 35 E
Dublin, Ireland	**35**	53 20N	6 18W
Dublin, U.S.A.	**170**	32 30N	82 34W
Dublin □	**34**	53 24N	6 20W
Dubrovnik	**52**	42 39N	18 6 E
Dubuque	**166**	42 30N	90 41W
Dudley	**24**	52 30N	2 5W
Dugi Otok	**52**	44 0N	15 0 E
Duisburg	**42**	51 27N	6 42 E
Duluth	**150**	46 48N	92 10W
Dumbarton	**31**	55 58N	4 35W
Dumfries	**31**	55 4N	3 37W
Dumfries & Galloway □	**31**	55 0N	4 0W
Dun Laoghaire	**35**	53 17N	6 9W
Dunărea →	**57**	45 30N	8 15 E
Dunaújváros	**59**	47 0N	18 57 E
Dunbar	**31**	56 0N	2 32W
Dunblane	**31**	56 10N	3 58W
Duncan, Canada	**154**	48 45N	123 40W
Duncan, U.S.A.	**161**	34 25N	98 0W
Duncan Pass.	**94**	11 0N	92 30 E
Dundalk	**34**	54 1N	6 25W
Dundas, Canada	**151**	43 17N	79 59W
Dundas, Greenland	**13**	77 0N	69 0W
Dundee	**31**	56 29N	3 0W
Dundrum	**34**	54 17N	5 50W
Dunedin	**123**	45 50S	170 33 E
Dunedoo	**116**	32 0S	149 25 E
Dunfermline	**31**	56 5N	3 28W
Dungannon	**34**	54 30N	6 47W
Dungarvan	**35**	52 6N	7 40W
Dungeness	**25**	50 54N	0 59 E
Dungog	**117**	32 22S	151 46 E
Dunhuang	**100**	40 8N	94 36 E
Dunkeld	**33**	56 34N	3 36W
Dunkerque	**38**	51 2N	2 20 E
Dunkery Beacon	**27**	51 15N	3 37W
Dunkirk = Dunkerque	**38**	51 2N	2 20 E
Dunkirk	**164**	42 30N	79 18W
Dúnleary = Dun Laoghaire	**35**	53 17N	6 9W
Dunmore	**164**	41 27N	75 38W
Dunn	**165**	35 18N	78 36W
Dunnet Hd.	**33**	58 38N	3 22W
Duns	**31**	55 47N	2 20W
Dunsmuir	**172**	41 10N	122 18W
Dunstan Mts.	**123**	44 53S	169 35 E
Durance →	**37**	43 55N	4 45 E
Durango, Mexico	**174**	24 3N	104 39W
Durango, U.S.A.	**163**	37 16N	107 50W
Durango □	**174**	24 50N	104 50W
Durant	**168**	34 0N	96 25W
Durazno	**191**	33 25S	56 31W
Durban	**137**	29 49S	31 1 E
Durg	**92**	21 15N	81 22 E
Durham, U.K.	**28**	54 47N	1 34W
Durham, U.S.A.	**165**	36 0N	78 55W
Durham □	**28**	54 42N	1 45W
Durmitor	**52**	43 10N	19 0 E
Durness	**32**	58 34N	4 45W
D'Urville I.	**122**	40 50S	173 55 E
Dushanbe	**71**	38 33N	68 48 E
Düsseldorf	**42**	51 15N	6 46 E
Duwādimi	**82**	24 35N	44 15 E
Duyun	**99**	26 18N	107 29 E
Duzce	**80**	40 50N	31 10 E
Duzdab = Zāhedān	**86**	29 30N	60 50 E
Dvina, Sev. →	**69**	64 32N	40 30 E
Dvinsk = Daugavpils	**68**	55 53N	26 32 E
Dyer, C.	**146**	66 40N	61 0W
Dyersburg	**169**	36 2N	89 20W

Dyfed □	**26**	52 0N	4 30W
Dysart	**121**	22 32S	148 23 E
Dzamin Üüd	**98**	43 50N	111 58 E
Dzerzhinsk	**68**	53 40N	27 1 E
Dzhalal-Abad	**71**	40 56N	73 0 E
Dzhalinda	**75**	53 26N	124 0 E
Dzhambul	**71**	42 54N	71 22 E
Dzhardzhan	**72**	68 10N	124 10 E
Dzhetygara	**71**	52 11N	61 12 E
Dzhezkazgan	**71**	47 44N	67 40 E
Dzhugdzur, Khrebet	**75**	57 30N	138 0 E
Dzuumod	**98**	47 45N	106 58 E
Eagle	**142**	64 44N	141 7W
Eagle Pass	**161**	28 45N	100 35W
Eagle River	**150**	45 55N	89 17W
Ealing	**25**	51 30N	0 19W
Earn →	**31**	56 20N	3 19W
Easley	**165**	34 52N	82 35W
East Angus	**148**	45 30N	71 40W
East Bengal	**92**	24 0N	90 0 E
East Beskids = Vychodné Beskydy	**59**	49 30N	22 0 E
East C.	**122**	37 42S	178 35 E
East Chicago	**167**	41 40N	87 30W
East China Sea	**99**	30 5N	126 0 E
East Falkland	**192**	51 30S	58 30W
East Germany ■	**43**	52 0N	12 0 E
East Indies	**77**	0 0	120 0 E
East Kilbride	**31**	55 46N	4 10W
East Liverpool	**164**	40 39N	80 35W
East London	**137**	33 0S	27 55 E
East Main = Eastmain	**140**	52 10N	78 30W
East Pakistan = Bangladesh ■	**92**	24 0N	90 0 E
East Point	**170**	33 40N	84 28W
East St. Louis	**166**	38 37N	90 4W
East Schelde → = Oosterschelde	**40**	51 33N	4 0 E
East Siberian Sea	**73**	73 0N	160 0 E
East Sussex □	**25**	51 0N	0 20 E
Eastbourne, N.Z.	**123**	41 19S	174 55 E
Eastbourne, U.K.	**25**	50 46N	0 18 E
Eastern Ghats	**90**	14 0N	78 50 E
Eastleigh	**25**	50 58N	1 21W
Eastmain	**140**	52 10N	78 30W
Eastmain →	**140**	52 27N	78 26W
Easton	**164**	40 41N	75 15W
Eau Claire	**166**	44 46N	91 30W
Eau Claire, L. à l'	**146**	56 10N	74 25W
Ebbw Vale	**26**	51 47N	3 12W
Eboli	**49**	40 39N	15 2 E
Ebro →	**51**	40 43N	0 54 E
Echizen-Misaki	**106**	35 59N	135 57 E
Echo Bay	**145**	46 29N	84 4W
Echuca	**117**	36 10S	144 20 E
Ecuador ■	**184**	2 0S	78 0W
Ed Dâmer	**129**	17 27N	34 0 E
Edam	**40**	52 31N	5 3 E
Eddystone	**27**	50 11N	4 16W
Ede	**41**	52 4N	5 40 E
Eden	**117**	37 3S	149 55 E
Eden →	**28**	54 57N	3 2W
Edenhope	**119**	37 4S	141 19 E
Edge Hill	**24**	52 7N	1 28W
Edhessa	**54**	40 48N	22 5 E
Edinburgh	**31**	55 57N	3 12W
Edirne	**80**	41 40N	26 34 E
Edmonton, Australia	**121**	17 2S	145 46 E
Edmonton, Canada	**155**	53 30N	113 30W
Edmundston	**148**	47 23N	68 20W
Edson	**155**	53 35N	116 28W
Edward, L.	**132**	0 25S	29 40 E
Edward VII Land	**15**	80 0S	150 0W
Edwards Plat.	**161**	30 30N	101 5W
Effingham	**167**	39 8N	88 30W
Égadi, Ísole	**48**	37 55N	12 16 E
Eger	**59**	47 53N	20 27 E
Egmont, Mt.	**122**	39 17S	174 5 E
Eğridir Gölü	**80**	37 53N	30 50 E
Egypt ■	**128**	28 0N	31 0 E
Eifel	**42**	50 10N	6 45 E
Eigg	**32**	56 54N	6 10W
Eil	**133**	8 0N	49 50 E
Eindhoven	**41**	51 26N	5 30 E
Eirunepé	**187**	6 35S	69 53W
El Aaiún	**126**	27 9N	13 12W
El Cajon	**173**	32 49N	117 0W
El Callao	**185**	7 18N	61 50W
El Centro	**173**	32 50N	115 40W
El Cerro	**187**	17 30S	61 40W
El Dere	**133**	3 50N	47 8 E
El Djouf	**126**	20 0N	11 30 E
El Dorado	**168**	33 10N	92 40W
El Escorial	**50**	40 35N	4 7W
El Faiyûm	**128**	29 19N	30 50 E
El Fâsher	**129**	13 33N	25 26 E
El Ferrol	**50**	43 29N	8 15W
El Fuerte	**174**	26 25N	108 39W
El Geteina	**129**	14 50N	32 27 E
El Iskandarîya	**128**	31 0N	30 0 E
El Jadida	**126**	33 11N	8 17W
El Khârga	**128**	25 30N	30 33 E
El Khartûm	**129**	15 31N	32 35 E
El Mahalla el Kubra	**128**	31 0N	31 0 E
El Minyâ	**128**	28 7N	30 33 E
El Obeid	**129**	13 8N	30 10 E
El Oro	**177**	27 15N	103 30W
El Paso	**161**	31 50N	106 30W
El Progreso	**177**	15 26N	87 51W
El Qâhira	**128**	30 1N	31 14 E
El Qasr	**128**	25 44N	28 42 E
El Salvador ■	**177**	13 50N	89 0W
El Suweis	**128**	29 58N	32 31 E
El Tigre	**185**	8 44N	64 15W
El Turbio	**192**	51 45S	72 5W
Elat	**80**	29 30N	34 56 E
Elâzığ	**81**	38 37N	39 14 E
Elba	**46**	42 48N	10 15 E
Elbasani	**52**	41 9N	20 9 E
Elbe →	**42**	53 50N	9 0 E
Elbert, Mt.	**163**	39 5N	106 27W
Elberton	**165**	34 7N	82 51W
Elbeuf	**39**	49 17N	1 2 E
Elbing = Elbląg	**58**	54 10N	19 25 E
Elbląg	**58**	54 10N	19 25 E
Elbrus	**70**	43 21N	42 30 E
Elburg	**41**	52 26N	5 50 E
Elburz Mts. = Alborz, Reshteh-ye Kūhhā-ye	**86**	36 0N	52 0 E
Elche	**51**	38 15N	0 42W
Eldorado	**174**	24 20N	107 22W
Eldorado Springs	**166**	37 54N	93 59W
Eldoret	**132**	0 30N	35 17 E
Eleanora, Peak	**120**	32 57S	121 9 E
Electra	**161**	34 0N	99 0W
Elephant Butte Res.	**161**	33 45N	107 30W
Eleuthera	**178**	25 0N	76 20W
Elgin, U.K.	**33**	57 39N	3 20W
Elgin, Ill., U.S.A.	**167**	42 0N	88 20W
Elgin, Oreg., U.S.A.	**171**	45 37N	118 0W
Elgon, Mt.	**132**	1 10N	34 30 E
Elisabethville = Lubumbashi	**135**	11 40S	27 28 E
Elizabeth, Australia	**119**	34 42S	138 41 E
Elizabeth, U.S.A.	**164**	40 37N	74 12W
Elizabeth City	**165**	36 18N	76 16W
Elizabethton	**165**	36 20N	82 13W
Elizabethtown	**167**	37 40N	85 54W
Elk Point	**152**	53 54N	110 55W
Elkhart	**167**	41 42N	85 55W
Elkins	**165**	38 53N	79 53W
Elko	**172**	40 50N	115 50W
Ellensburg	**171**	47 0N	120 30W
Ellery, Mt.	**117**	37 28S	148 47 E
Ellesmere I.	**13**	79 30N	80 0W
Ellesmere Port	**28**	53 17N	2 55W
Ellice Is. = Tuvalu ■	**122**	8 0S	178 0 E
Elliot Lake	**150**	46 25N	82 35W
Ellore = Eluru	**92**	16 48N	81 8 E
Ellsworth Land	**14**	76 0S	89 0W

Ellsworth Mts.	**14**	78 30S	85 0W
Elmhurst	**167**	41 52N	87 58W
Elmira	**164**	42 8N	76 49W
Elrose	**152**	51 12N	108 0W
Eluru	**92**	16 48N	81 8 E
Elvas	**50**	38 50N	7 10W
Elwood	**167**	40 20N	85 50W
Ely	**172**	39 10N	114 50W
Elyria	**167**	41 22N	82 8W
Emāmrūd	**86**	36 30N	55 0 E
Emba →	**70**	46 38N	53 14 E
Emden	**42**	53 22N	7 12 E
Emerald	**121**	23 32S	148 10 E
Emilia-Romagna □	**46**	44 33N	10 40 E
Emmeloord	**41**	52 44N	5 46 E
Emmen	**41**	52 48N	6 57 E
Empalme	**174**	27 58N	110 51W
Emporia, Kans., U.S.A.	**158**	38 25N	96 10W
Emporia, Va., U.S.A.	**165**	36 41N	77 32W
Ems →	**42**	52 37N	9 26 E
En Nahud	**129**	12 45N	28 25 E
Ena	**106**	35 25N	137 25 E
Ena-San	**106**	35 26N	137 36 E
Encarnación	**191**	27 15S	55 50W
Encarnación de Díaz	**175**	21 31N	102 14W
Encontrados	**184**	9 3N	72 14W
Enderby	**155**	50 35N	119 10W
Enderby Land	**14**	66 0S	53 0 E
Endicott	**164**	42 6N	76 2W
Engaño, C.	**180**	18 30N	68 20W
Engels	**68**	51 28N	46 6 E
Enggano	**111**	5 20S	102 40 E
England □	**21**	53 0N	2 0W
English Bazar = Ingraj Bazar	**92**	24 58N	88 10 E
English Channel	**16**	50 0N	2 0W
Enid	**161**	36 26N	97 52W
Enkhuizen	**40**	52 42N	5 17 E
Ennedi	**129**	17 15N	22 0 E
Ennis	**35**	52 51N	8 59W
Enniscorthy	**35**	52 30N	6 35W
Enniskillen	**34**	54 20N	7 40W
Enriquillo, L.	**180**	18 20N	72 5W
Enschede	**41**	52 13N	6 53 E
Ensenada	**174**	31 52N	116 37W
Enshū-Nada	**106**	34 27N	137 38 E
Entebbe	**132**	0 4N	32 28 E
Enterprise	**171**	45 30N	117 18W
Entre Ríos □	**190**	30 30S	58 30W
Enugu	**131**	6 20N	7 30 E
Enzan	**107**	35 42N	138 44 E
Eólie, I.	**49**	38 30N	14 50 E
Epe	**41**	52 21N	5 59 E
Épernay	**39**	49 3N	3 56 E
Ephesus	**80**	37 50N	27 33 E
Épinal	**37**	48 10N	6 27 E
Epping	**25**	51 42N	0 8 E
Equatorial Guinea ■	**134**	2 0S	8 0 E
Er Rif	**126**	35 1N	4 1W
Erāwadī Myit → = Irrawaddy →	**93**	15 50N	95 6 E
Ercha	**73**	69 45N	147 20 E
Erciyaş Dağı	**80**	38 30N	35 30 E
Erebus, Mt.	**15**	77 35S	167 0 E
Erechim	**191**	27 35S	52 15W
Ereğli	**80**	41 15N	31 30 E
Erfurt	**43**	50 58N	11 2 E
Erg Chech	**126**	50 59N	11 0 E
Erie	**164**	42 10N	80 7W
Erie, L.	**151**	42 15N	81 0W
Erímanthos	**54**	37 57N	21 50 E
Erimo-misaki	**103**	41 50N	143 15 E
Eritrea □	**132**	14 0N	41 0 E
Ermoúpolis = Síros	**55**	37 28N	24 57 E
Erne, Lough	**34**	54 26N	7 46W
Erode	**90**	11 24N	77 45 E
Erramala Hills	**90**	15 30N	78 15 E
Erris Hd.	**34**	54 19N	10 0W
Erzgebirge	**43**	50 25N	13 0 E
Erzincan	**81**	39 46N	39 30 E
Erzurum	**81**	39 57N	41 15 E
Es Sînâ'	**128**	29 0N	34 0 E
Esan-Misaki	**103**	41 40N	141 10 E
Esashi	**103**	41 52N	140 7 E
Esbjerg	**61**	55 29N	8 29 E
Escanaba	**150**	45 44N	87 5W
Escondido	**173**	33 9N	117 4W
Escuintla	**177**	14 20N	90 48W
Eşfahān	**85**	33 0N	53 0 E
Esh Sham = Dimashq	**80**	33 30N	36 18 E
Esk →	**29**	54 27N	0 36W
Eskilstuna	**60**	59 22N	16 32 E
Eskimo Pt.	**145**	61 10N	94 15W
Eskişehir	**80**	39 50N	30 35 E
Eslāmābād-e Gharb	**84**	34 10N	46 30 E
Esmeraldas	**184**	1 0N	79 40W
Espanola	**151**	46 15N	81 46W
Esperance	**114**	33 45S	121 55 E
Espinazo, Sierra del = Espinhaço, Serra do	**188**	17 30S	43 30W
Espinhaço, Serra do	**188**	17 30S	43 30W
Espírito Santo □	**189**	20 0S	40 45W
Essaouira	**126**	31 32N	9 42W
Essen	**42**	51 28N	6 59 E
Essequibo →	**185**	6 50N	58 30W
Essex □	**25**	51 48N	0 30 E
Estados, I. de los	**192**	54 40S	64 30W
Estelí	**179**	13 9N	86 22W
Estevan	**152**	49 10N	102 59W
Estherville	**166**	43 25N	94 50W
Estonian S.S.R. □	**68**	58 30N	25 30 E
Estoril	**50**	38 42N	9 23W
Estrêla, Serra da	**50**	40 10N	7 45W
Estremadura	**50**	39 0N	9 0W
Étampes	**39**	48 26N	2 10 E
Étaples	**38**	50 30N	1 39 E
Etawah	**91**	26 48N	79 6 E
Ethiopia ■	**133**	8 0N	40 0 E
Ethiopian Highlands	**132**	10 0N	37 0 E
Etna	**49**	37 45N	15 0 E
Etosha Pan	**136**	18 40S	16 30 E
Etzatlán	**175**	20 46N	104 5W
Euboea = Évvoia	**55**	38 30N	24 0 E
Euclid	**167**	41 32N	81 31W
Eucumbene, L.	**117**	36 2S	148 40 E
Eufaula	**169**	35 20N	95 33W
Eugene	**171**	44 0N	123 8W
Eupen	**42**	50 37N	6 3 E
Euphrates = Furāt, Nahr al →	**84**	31 0N	47 25 E
Eureka, Calif., U.S.A.	**172**	40 50N	124 0W
Eureka, Nev., U.S.A.	**172**	39 32N	116 2W
Euroa	**117**	36 44S	145 35 E
Europa, Pta. de	**50**	36 3N	5 21W
Europa Pt. = Europa, Pta. de	**50**	36 3N	5 21W
Europoort	**40**	51 57N	4 10 E
Euston	**119**	34 30S	142 46 E
Eutsuk L.	**154**	53 20N	126 45W
Evans Head	**116**	29 7S	153 27 E
Evanston	**167**	42 0N	87 40W
Evansville	**167**	38 0N	87 35W
Everard, L.	**118**	31 30S	135 0 E
Everest, Mt.	**92**	28 5N	86 58 E
Everett	**171**	48 0N	122 10W
Everglades	**170**	26 0N	80 30W
Evesham	**24**	52 6N	1 57W
Évora	**50**	38 33N	7 57W
Évreux	**39**	49 0N	1 8 E
Évvoia	**55**	38 30N	24 0 E
Excelsior Springs	**166**	39 20N	94 10W
Exe →	**27**	50 38N	3 27W
Exeter	**27**	50 43N	3 31W
Exmoor	**27**	51 10N	3 59W
Exmouth	**27**	50 37N	3 26W
Extremadura □	**50**	39 30N	6 5W
Eyasi, L.	**135**	3 30S	35 0 E
Eye Pen.	**32**	58 13N	6 10W
Eyre, L.	**118**	29 30S	137 26 E
Eyre Mts.	**123**	45 25S	168 25 E
Eyre Pen.	**119**	33 30S	137 17 E

Facatativá	**184**	4 49N	74 22W
Faddeyevskiy, Ostrov	**72**	76 0N	150 0 E
Fair Hd.	**34**	55 14N	6 10W
Fairbanks	**142**	64 50N	147 50W
Fairfield, N.Z.	**123**	45 54S	170 24 E
Fairfield, Ala., U.S.A.	**169**	33 30N	87 0W
Fairfield, Calif., U.S.A.	**172**	38 14N	122 1W
Fairfield, Tex., U.S.A.	**168**	31 40N	96 0W
Fairmont, Minn., U.S.A.	**166**	43 37N	94 30W
Fairmont, W. Va., U.S.A.	**164**	39 29N	80 10W
Fairview	**155**	56 5N	118 25W
Fairweather, Mt.	**143**	58 55N	137 45W
Faisalabad	**89**	31 30N	73 5 E
Faizabad	**92**	26 45N	82 10 E
Fajardo	**180**	18 20N	65 39W
Fakenham	**29**	52 50N	0 51 E
Falam	**93**	23 0N	93 45 E
Falkirk	**31**	56 0N	3 47W
Falkland Is.	**192**	51 30S	59 0W
Falköping	**60**	58 12N	13 33 E
Fall River	**164**	41 45N	71 5W
Falls City	**166**	40 0N	95 40W
Falmouth, Jamaica	**180**	18 30N	77 40W
Falmouth, U.K.	**27**	50 9N	5 5W
Famagusta	**80**	35 8N	33 55 E
Farāh	**87**	32 20N	62 7 E
Farāh □	**87**	32 25N	62 10 E
Fareham	**25**	50 52N	1 11W
Farewell, C.	**122**	40 29S	172 43 E
Farewell C. = Farvel, Kap	**147**	59 48N	43 55W
Fargo	**156**	46 52N	96 40W
Farmington, N.H., U.S.A.	**157**	43 25N	71 3W
Farmington, N. Mex., U.S.A.	**161**	36 45N	108 28W
Farnborough	**25**	51 17N	0 46W
Faro	**50**	37 2N	7 55W
Faroe Is.	**16**	62 0N	7 0W
Fars □	**85**	29 30N	55 0 E
Fársala	**54**	39 17N	22 23 E
Farvel, Kap	**147**	59 48N	43 55W
Fāryāb □	**87**	36 0N	65 0 E
Fatehgarh	**89**	27 25N	79 35 E
Fatehpur, Raj., India	**92**	28 0N	74 40 E
Fatehpur, Ut. P., India	**89**	25 56N	81 13 E
Faxaflói	**64**	64 29N	23 0W
Fayetteville, Ark., U.S.A.	**168**	36 0N	94 5W
Fayetteville, N.C., U.S.A.	**165**	35 0N	78 58W
Fazilka	**89**	30 27N	74 2 E
Fdérik	**126**	22 40N	12 45W
Fear, C.	**165**	33 51N	78 0W
Fécamp	**38**	49 45N	0 22 E
Feilding	**122**	40 13S	175 35 E
Feira de Santana	**189**	12 15S	38 57W
Felixstowe	**25**	51 58N	1 22 E
Fengjie	**99**	31 5N	109 36 E
Fens, The	**29**	52 45N	0 2 E
Fenyang	**98**	37 19N	111 46 E
Ferfer	**133**	5 4N	45 9 E
Fergana	**71**	40 23N	71 19 E
Fergus Falls	**156**	46 18N	96 7W
Fermoy	**35**	52 4N	8 18W
Fernando de Noronha	**189**	4 0S	33 10W
Fernando Póo = Bioko	**131**	3 30N	8 40 E
Fernie	**155**	49 30N	115 5W
Ferrara	**47**	44 50N	11 36 E
Ferté-Bernard, La	**39**	48 10N	0 40 E
Fès	**126**	34 0N	5 0W
Feuilles →	**146**	58 47N	70 4W
Feyẕābād	**87**	37 7N	70 33 E
Fezzan	**124**	27 0N	15 0 E
Fianarantsoa	**137**	21 26S	47 5 E
Fichtelgebirge	**43**	50 10N	12 0 E
Fife □	**31**	56 13N	3 2W
Fife Ness	**31**	56 17N	2 35W
Fiji ■	**122**	17 20S	179 0 E
Filey	**29**	54 13N	0 18W
Findlay	**167**	41 0N	83 41W
Finisterre, C.	**50**	42 50N	9 19W
Finland ■	**67**	63 0N	27 0 E
Finland, G. of	**67**	60 0N	26 0 E
Finlay →	**144**	57 0N	125 10W
Finley	**117**	35 38S	145 35 E
Firenze	**47**	43 47N	11 15 E
Firozabad	**89**	27 10N	78 25 E
Fishguard	**26**	51 59N	4 59W
Fiskenæsset	**147**	63 5N	50 45W
Fitchburg	**164**	42 35N	71 47W
Fitzgerald	**170**	31 45N	83 16W
Fitzroy →	**121**	23 32S	150 52 E
Fiume = Rijeka	**52**	45 20N	14 21 E
Flagstaff	**160**	35 10N	111 40W
Flamborough Hd.	**29**	54 8N	0 4W
Flannan Is.	**32**	58 9N	7 52W
Flattery, C.	**171**	48 21N	124 43W
Flèche, La	**39**	47 42N	0 4W
Fleetwood	**28**	53 55N	3 1W
Flekkefjord	**60**	58 18N	6 39 E
Flensburg	**43**	54 46N	9 28 E
Flers	**36**	48 47N	0 33W
Flin Flon	**152**	54 46N	101 53W
Flinders I.	**117**	40 0S	148 0 E
Flinders Ranges	**118**	31 30S	138 30 E
Flinders Reefs	**121**	17 37S	148 31 E
Flint, U.K.	**26**	53 15N	3 7W
Flint, U.S.A.	**167**	43 5N	83 40W
Flint →	**170**	30 52N	84 38W
Flodden	**31**	55 37N	2 8W
Flora	**167**	38 40N	88 30W
Florence = Firenze	**47**	43 47N	11 15 E
Florence, Ala., U.S.A.	**169**	34 50N	87 40W
Florence, S.C., U.S.A.	**165**	34 12N	79 44W
Flores, Guat.	**177**	16 59N	89 50W
Flores, Indonesia	**113**	8 35S	121 0 E
Flores Sea	**113**	6 30S	124 0 E
Floriano	**188**	6 50S	43 0W
Florianópolis	**191**	27 30S	48 30W
Florida	**191**	34 7S	56 10W
Florida □	**170**	28 30N	82 0W
Florida, Straits of	**159**	25 0N	80 0W
Florida B.	**159**	25 0N	81 20W
Florida Keys	**159**	25 0N	80 40W
Flórina	**54**	40 48N	21 26 E
Flushing = Vlissingen	**40**	51 26N	3 34 E
Fly →	**115**	8 25S	143 0 E
Foam Lake	**152**	51 40N	103 32W
Fóggia	**49**	41 28N	15 31 E
Foix	**36**	42 58N	1 38 E
Folda	**64**	64 41N	10 50 E
Folkestone	**25**	51 5N	1 11 E
Follette, La	**169**	36 23N	84 9W
Fond-du-Lac, Canada	**145**	59 19N	107 12W
Fond-du-Lac, U.S.A.	**167**	43 46N	88 26W
Fontainebleau	**39**	48 24N	2 40 E
Fonte Boa	**184**	2 33S	66 0W
Foochow = Fuzhou	**99**	26 5N	119 16 E
Forbes	**117**	33 22S	148 0 E
Forestburg	**155**	52 35N	112 1W
Forestville	**148**	48 48N	69 2W
Forfar	**33**	56 40N	2 53W
Forlì	**47**	44 14N	12 2 E
Formby Pt.	**28**	53 33N	3 7W
Formentera	**51**	38 43N	1 27 E
Formosa = Taiwan ■	**99**	23 30N	121 0 E
Formosa	**191**	26 15S	58 10W
Forrest City	**169**	35 0N	90 50W
Fort Albany	**140**	52 15N	81 35W
Fort Augustus	**32**	57 9N	4 40W
Fort Chipewyan	**145**	58 42N	111 8W
Fort Collins	**163**	40 30N	105 4W
Fort-Coulonge	**151**	45 50N	76 45W
Fort-de-France	**180**	14 36N	61 2W
Fort Dodge	**166**	42 29N	94 10W
Fort Frances	**153**	48 36N	93 24W
Fort Franklin	**145**	65 10N	123 30W
Fort George	**140**	53 50N	79 0W
Fort Good-Hope	**144**	66 14N	128 40W
Fort Hertz = Putao	**93**	27 28N	97 30 E
Fort Kent	**148**	47 12N	68 30W
Fort-Lamy = Ndjamena	**131**	12 10N	14 59 E
Fort Lauderdale	**170**	26 10N	80 5W
Fort Liard	**144**	60 14N	123 30W
Fort Mackay	**143**	57 12N	111 41W
Fort Macleod	**155**	49 45N	113 30W

Fort McMurray	**155**	56 44N	111 7W
Fort McPherson	**144**	67 30N	134 55W
Fort Madison	**166**	40 39N	91 20W
Fort Morgan	**163**	40 10N	103 50W
Fort Myers	**170**	26 39N	81 51W
Fort Nelson	**144**	58 50N	122 44W
Fort Nelson →	**144**	59 32N	124 0W
Fort Payne	**169**	34 25N	85 44W
Fort Peck L.	**163**	47 40N	107 0W
Fort Pierce	**170**	27 29N	80 19W
Fort Providence	**145**	61 3N	117 40W
Fort Qu'Appelle	**152**	50 45N	103 50W
Fort Resolution	**145**	61 10N	113 40W
Fort Rupert	**140**	51 30N	78 40W
Fort St. James	**154**	54 30N	124 10W
Fort St. John	**155**	56 15N	120 50W
Fort Sandeman	**88**	31 20N	69 31 E
Fort Saskatchewan	**155**	53 40N	113 15W
Fort Scott	**166**	37 50N	94 40W
Fort Severn	**140**	56 0N	87 40W
Fort Shevchenko	**70**	43 40N	51 20 E
Fort Simpson	**144**	61 45N	121 15W
Fort Smith, Canada	**145**	60 0N	111 51W
Fort Smith, U.S.A.	**168**	35 25N	94 25W
Fort Smith Region □	**145**	63 0N	120 0W
Fort Trinquet = Bir Mogrein	**126**	25 10N	11 25W
Fort Valley	**170**	32 33N	83 52W
Fort Vermilion	**145**	58 24N	116 0W
Fort Wayne	**167**	41 5N	85 10W
Fort William	**32**	56 48N	5 8W
Fort Worth	**168**	32 45N	97 25W
Fort Yukon	**142**	66 35N	145 20W
Fortaleza	**189**	3 45S	38 35W
Forth →	**31**	56 9N	4 18W
Forth, Firth of	**31**	56 5N	2 55W
Fortuna	**172**	40 38N	124 8W
Foshan	**99**	23 4N	113 5 E
Foster	**117**	38 40S	146 15 E
Fougères	**36**	48 21N	1 14W
Foula, I.	**30**	60 10N	2 5W
Foulness I.	**24**	51 36N	0 55 E
Fourmies	**38**	50 1N	4 2 E
Foúrnoi	**55**	37 36N	26 32 E
Fouta Djalon	**130**	11 20N	12 10W
Foveaux Str.	**123**	46 42S	168 10 E
Fowey	**27**	50 20N	4 39W
Foxe Basin	**146**	66 0N	77 0W
Foxe Chan.	**146**	65 0N	80 0W
Foxe Pen.	**146**	65 0N	76 0W
Foxton	**122**	40 29S	175 18 E
Foyle, Lough	**34**	55 6N	7 8W
Foynes	**35**	52 37N	9 5W
Franca	**188**	20 33S	47 30W
France ■	**37**	47 0N	3 0 E
Franche-Comté	**37**	46 30N	5 50 E
François	**180**	14 38N	60 57W
Franeker	**41**	53 12N	5 33 E
Frankfort, Ind., U.S.A.	**167**	40 20N	86 33W
Frankfort, Ky., U.S.A.	**165**	38 12N	84 52W
Frankfurt am Main	**42**	50 7N	8 40 E
Frankfurt an der Oder	**43**	52 50N	14 31 E
Fränkische Alb	**43**	49 20N	11 30 E
Franklin, La., U.S.A.	**168**	29 45N	91 30W
Franklin, N.H., U.S.A.	**164**	43 28N	71 39W
Franklin, W. Va., U.S.A.	**165**	38 38N	79 21W
Franklin D. Roosevelt L.	**162**	48 30N	118 16W
Franklin Mts.	**145**	65 0N	125 0W
Franklin Str.	**145**	72 0N	96 0W
Frankston	**117**	38 8S	145 8 E
Franz	**150**	48 25N	84 30W
Fraser →	**154**	49 7N	123 11W
Fraser, Mt.	**120**	25 35S	118 20 E
Fraser I.	**116**	25 15S	153 10 E
Fraserburgh	**33**	57 41N	2 0W
Fray Bentos	**190**	33 10S	58 15W
Frederick	**164**	39 25N	77 23W
Fredericksburg	**165**	38 16N	77 29W
Fredericton	**148**	45 57N	66 40W
Frederikshavn	**61**	57 28N	10 31 E
Fredrikstad	**60**	59 13N	10 57 E
Freeport, Bahamas	**178**	26 30N	78 47W
Freeport, Ill., U.S.A.	**166**	42 18N	89 40W
Freeport, N.Y., U.S.A.	**164**	40 39N	73 35W
Freeport, Tex., U.S.A.	**158**	28 55N	95 22W
Freetown	**130**	8 30N	13 17W
Freiberg	**42**	50 55N	13 20 E
Freibourg = Fribourg	**44**	46 49N	7 9 E
Fréjus	**37**	43 25N	6 44 E
Fremantle	**120**	32 7S	115 47 E
Fremont, Calif., U.S.A.	**172**	37 32N	122 1W
Fremont, Nebr., U.S.A.	**166**	41 30N	96 30W
French Guiana ■	**185**	4 0N	53 0W
French Pass	**123**	40 55S	173 55 E
French Terr. of Afars & Issas = Djibouti ■	**133**	12 0N	43 0 E
Fresnillo	**175**	23 10N	102 53W
Fresno	**173**	36 47N	119 50W
Fria, C.	**136**	18 0S	12 0 E
Frías	**190**	28 40S	65 5W
Fribourg	**44**	46 49N	7 9 E
Friendly, Is. = Tonga ■	**123**	19 50S	174 30W
Friesland □	**41**	53 5N	5 50 E
Frio, C.	**182**	22 50S	41 50W
Friuli-Venezia Giulia □	**47**	46 0N	13 0 E
Frobisher B.	**146**	62 30N	66 0W
Frobisher Bay	**146**	63 44N	68 31W
Frobisher L.	**152**	56 20N	108 15W
Frome	**27**	51 16N	2 17W
Frome, L.	**118**	30 45S	139 45 E
Frome Downs	**118**	31 13S	139 45 E
Front Range	**163**	40 0N	105 40W
Front Royal	**164**	38 55N	78 10W
Frontera	**177**	18 32N	92 38W
Frostburg	**164**	39 43N	78 57W
Frunze	**71**	42 54N	74 46 E
Frutal	**188**	20 0S	49 0W
Fuchou = Fuzhou	**99**	26 5N	119 16 E
Fuchū, Hiroshima, Japan	**109**	34 34N	133 14 E
Fuchū, Tōkyō, Japan	**107**	35 40N	139 29 E
Fuerte, R. →	**174**	25 54N	109 22W
Fuji	**107**	35 9N	138 39 E
Fuji-no-miya	**107**	35 10N	138 40 E
Fuji-San	**107**	35 22N	138 44 E
Fuji-yoshida	**107**	35 30N	138 46 E
Fujian □	**99**	26 0N	118 0 E
Fujieda	**107**	34 52N	138 16 E
Fujisawa	**107**	35 22N	139 29 E
Fukaya	**107**	36 12N	139 12 E
Fukien = Fujian □	**99**	26 0N	118 0 E
Fukuchiyama	**106**	35 19N	135 9 E
Fukue-Shima	**104**	32 40N	128 45 E
Fukui	**106**	36 0N	136 10 E
Fukuoka	**108**	33 39N	130 21 E
Fukushima	**103**	37 44N	140 28 E
Fukuyama	**109**	34 35N	133 20 E
Fulton, Mo., U.S.A.	**166**	38 50N	91 55W
Fulton, N.Y., U.S.A.	**164**	43 20N	76 22W
Funabashi	**107**	35 45N	140 0 E
Funchal	**126**	32 38N	16 54W
Fundación	**184**	10 31N	74 11W
Fundy, B. of	**148**	45 0N	66 0W
Furāt, Nahr al →	**84**	31 0N	47 25 E
Furneaux Group	**119**	40 10S	147 50 E
Furness	**28**	54 14N	3 8W
Fürth	**43**	49 29N	11 0 E
Fury and Hecla Str.	**146**	69 56N	84 0W
Fushun	**98**	41 50N	123 55 E
Fuxin	**98**	42 5N	121 48 E
Fuzhou	**99**	26 5N	119 16 E
Fylde	**28**	53 50N	2 58W
Fyn	**61**	55 20N	10 30 E
Fyne, L.	**30**	56 0N	5 20W
Gabès, Golfe de	**127**	34 0N	10 30 E
Gabon ■	**134**	0 10S	10 0 E
Gaborone	**137**	24 45S	25 57 E
Gachsārān	**85**	30 15N	50 45 E
Gadag	**90**	15 30N	75 45 E
Gadsden	**169**	34 1N	86 0W
Gaeta	**49**	41 12N	13 35 E

Gaffney	**165**	35 3N	81 40W
Gagnon	**141**	51 50N	68 5W
Gainesville, Fla., U.S.A.	**170**	29 38N	82 20W
Gainesville, Ga., U.S.A.	**165**	34 17N	83 47W
Gainesville, Tex., U.S.A.	**168**	33 40N	97 10W
Gainsborough	**29**	53 23N	0 46W
Gairdner L.	**118**	31 30S	136 0E
Galápagos	**10**	0 0	89 0W
Galas →	**96**	4 55N	101 57E
Galashiels	**31**	55 37N	2 50W
Galaţi	**57**	45 27N	28 2E
Galatina	**49**	40 10N	18 10E
Galdhøpiggen	**60**	61 38N	8 18E
Galesburg	**166**	40 57N	90 23W
Galicia □	**50**	42 43N	7 45W
Galilee, L.	**121**	22 20S	145 50E
Gallatin	**169**	36 24N	86 27W
Galle	**90**	6 5N	80 10E
Gallinas, Pta.	**184**	12 28N	71 40W
Gallipoli = Gelibolu	**80**	40 28N	26 43E
Gallípoli	**49**	40 8N	18 0E
Gällivare	**66**	67 9N	20 40E
Galloway	**31**	55 0N	4 25W
Galloway, Mull of	**30**	54 38N	4 50W
Gallup	**161**	35 30N	108 45W
Galty Mts.	**35**	52 22N	8 10W
Galveston	**168**	29 15N	94 48W
Galveston B.	**168**	29 30N	94 50W
Galway	**35**	53 16N	9 4W
Galway □	**34**	53 16N	9 3W
Gamagori	**106**	34 50N	137 14E
Gambia ■	**130**	13 25N	16 0W
Gambia →	**130**	13 28N	16 34W
Gand = Gent	**42**	51 2N	3 42E
Gander	**149**	48 58N	54 35W
Gandhi Sagar	**91**	24 40N	75 40E
Gandi	**131**	12 55N	5 49E
Ganga →	**92**	23 20N	90 30E
Ganges = Ganga →	**92**	23 20N	90 30E
Gangtok	**92**	27 20N	88 37E
Gannett Pk.	**163**	43 15N	109 38W
Gansu □	**98**	36 0N	104 0E
Ganzhou	**99**	25 51N	114 56E
Gao	**130**	16 15N	0 5W
Gaoxiong	**99**	22 38N	120 18E
Garachiné	**179**	8 0N	78 12W
Garanhuns	**189**	8 50S	36 30W
Garberville	**172**	40 11N	123 50W
Garda, L. di	**46**	45 40N	10 40E
Garden City	**161**	38 0N	100 45W
Garden Grove	**173**	33 47N	117 55W
Gardēz	**87**	33 37N	69 9E
Garmsār	**86**	35 20N	52 25E
Garonne →	**36**	45 2N	0 36W
Garoua	**131**	9 19N	13 21E
Garrison Res. = Sakakawea, L.	**163**	47 30N	102 0W
Garry L.	**145**	65 58N	100 18W
Garvie Mts.	**123**	45 30S	168 50E
Garwa = Garoua	**131**	9 19N	13 21E
Gary	**167**	41 35N	87 20W
Garzón	**184**	2 10N	75 40W
Gascogne	**36**	43 45N	0 20E
Gascony = Gascogne	**36**	43 45N	0 20E
Gaspé	**148**	48 52N	64 30W
Gaspé, C. de	**148**	48 48N	64 7W
Gaspé, Pén. de	**148**	48 45N	65 40W
Gastonia	**165**	35 17N	81 10W
Gastre	**192**	42 20S	69 15W
Gata, C. de	**51**	36 41N	2 13W
Gateshead	**28**	54 57N	1 37W
Gauhati	**93**	26 10N	91 45E
Gävle	**60**	60 40N	17 9E
Gävleborgs län □	**60**	61 30N	16 15E
Gawilgarh Hills	**91**	21 15N	76 45E
Gawler	**119**	34 30S	138 42E
Gawler Ranges	**114**	32 30S	135 45E
Gaxun Nur	**100**	42 22N	100 30E
Gaya	**92**	24 47N	85 4E
Gaylord	**150**	45 1N	84 41W
Gayndah	**116**	25 35S	151 32E

Gaza	**80**	31 30N	34 28E
Gaziantep	**80**	37 6N	37 23E
Gdańsk	**58**	54 22N	18 40E
Gdańska, Zatoka	**58**	54 30N	19 20E
Gdynia	**58**	54 35N	18 33E
Gedaref	**129**	14 2N	35 28E
Geelong	**117**	38 10S	144 22E
Gejiu	**99**	23 20N	103 10E
Gelderland □	**41**	52 5N	6 10E
Geldermalsen	**40**	51 53N	5 17E
Geldrop	**41**	51 25N	5 32E
Geleen	**41**	50 57N	5 49E
Gelibolu	**80**	40 28N	26 43E
Gelsenkirchen	**42**	51 30N	7 5E
Gemert	**41**	51 33N	5 41E
General Alvear	**190**	35 0S	67 40W
General Pico	**190**	35 45S	63 50W
Geneva = Genève	**44**	46 12N	6 9E
Geneva	**164**	42 53N	77 0W
Geneva, L. = Léman, Lac	**44**	46 26N	6 30E
Genève	**44**	46 12N	6 9E
Genk	**41**	50 58N	5 32E
Genkai-Nada	**108**	34 0N	130 0E
Gennargentu, Mti. del	**48**	40 0N	9 10E
Genoa = Génova	**46**	44 24N	8 56E
Génova	**46**	44 24N	8 56E
Génova, Golfo di	**46**	44 0N	9 0E
Gent	**42**	51 2N	3 42E
George, L.	**132**	0 5N	30 10E
George River = Port Nouveau-Québec	**146**	58 30N	65 59W
George Town	**96**	5 25N	100 15E
Georgetown, Australia	**119**	18 17S	143 33E
Georgetown, Canada	**151**	43 40N	79 56W
Georgetown, Guyana	**185**	6 50N	58 12W
Georgetown, U.S.A.	**170**	33 22N	79 15W
Georgia □	**170**	32 0N	82 0W
Georgian B.	**151**	45 15N	81 0W
Georgian S.S.R. □	**70**	42 0N	43 0E
Gera	**43**	50 53N	12 11E
Geraldton, Australia	**120**	28 48S	114 32E
Geraldton, Canada	**150**	49 44N	86 59W
Gereshk	**87**	31 47N	64 35E
Germany, East ■	**18**	52 0N	12 0E
Germany, West ■	**18**	52 0N	9 0E
Germiston	**137**	26 15S	28 10E
Gerona	**51**	41 58N	2 46E
Ghana ■	**130**	6 0N	1 0W
Ghat	**127**	24 59N	10 11E
Ghawdex = Gozo	**49**	36 0N	14 13E
Ghaziabad	**89**	28 42N	77 26E
Ghazipur	**92**	25 38N	83 35E
Ghaznī	**87**	33 30N	68 28E
Ghaznī □	**87**	32 10N	68 20E
Ghent = Gent	**42**	51 2N	3 42E
Ghowr □	**87**	34 0N	64 20E
Ghulam Mohammad Barrage	**88**	25 30N	68 20E
Giant's Causeway	**34**	55 15N	6 30W
Gibara	**178**	21 9N	76 11W
Gibraltar	**50**	36 7N	5 22W
Gibraltar, Str. of	**50**	35 55N	5 40W
Gien	**39**	47 40N	2 36E
Gifu	**106**	35 30N	136 45E
Gigha	**30**	55 42N	5 45W
Gijón	**50**	43 32N	5 42W
Gila →	**173**	32 43N	114 33W
Gīlān □	**81**	37 0N	50 0E
Gilbert Is. = Kiribati ■	**122**	1 0N	176 0E
Gilford I.	**154**	50 40N	126 30W
Gilgandra	**116**	31 43S	148 39E
Gilgit	**89**	35 50N	74 15E
Gillingham	**25**	51 23N	0 34E
Gingin	**120**	31 22S	115 54E
Gippsland	**117**	37 45S	147 15E
Girardot	**184**	4 18N	74 48W
Giresun	**81**	40 55N	38 30E
Gironde →	**36**	45 32N	1 7W
Girvan	**30**	55 15N	4 50W
Gisborne	**122**	38 39S	178 5E
Gisors	**39**	49 15N	1 47E
Gizhiga	**73**	62 3N	160 30E

Gizhiginskaya, Guba	**73**	61 0N	158 0 E
Giżycko	**58**	54 2N	21 48 E
Gjoa Haven	**145**	68 20N	96 8W
Glace Bay	**149**	46 11N	59 58W
Gladstone, Queens., Australia	**121**	23 52S	151 16 E
Gladstone, S. Austral., Australia	**118**	33 15S	138 22 E
Gláma	**64**	65 48N	23 0W
Glasgow, U.K.	**31**	55 52N	4 14W
Glasgow, U.S.A.	**169**	37 2N	85 55W
Glastonbury	**27**	51 9N	2 42W
Gleiwitz = Gliwice	**58**	50 22N	18 41 E
Glen Coe	**32**	56 40N	5 0W
Glen Innes	**116**	29 44S	151 44 E
Glen Mor	**33**	57 12N	4 37 E
Glenburgh	**120**	25 26S	116 6 E
Glendale	**173**	34 7N	118 18W
Glendive	**163**	47 7N	104 40W
Glenelg	**119**	34 58S	138 31 E
Glenns Ferry	**172**	43 0N	115 15W
Glenorchy	**119**	42 49S	147 18 E
Glenrothes	**31**	56 12N	3 11W
Glens Falls	**164**	43 20N	73 40W
Gliwice	**58**	50 22N	18 41 E
Głogów	**58**	51 37N	16 5 E
Glossop	**28**	53 27N	1 56W
Gloucester	**24**	51 52N	2 15W
Gloucestershire □	**24**	51 44N	2 10W
Gloversville	**164**	43 5N	74 18W
Gniezno	**58**	52 30N	17 35 E
Go Cong	**95**	10 22N	106 40 E
Goa	**91**	15 33N	73 59 E
Goa □	**90**	15 33N	73 59 E
Goat Fell	**30**	55 37N	5 11W
Goba	**133**	7 1N	39 59 E
Gobi	**98**	44 0N	111 0 E
Gobō	**106**	33 53N	135 10 E
Godavari →	**91**	16 25N	82 18 E
Godbout	**148**	49 20N	67 38W
Goderich	**150**	43 45N	81 41W
Godhra	**91**	22 49N	73 40 E
Gods L.	**153**	54 40N	94 15W
Godthåb	**147**	64 10N	51 35W
Goeie Hoop, Kaap die	**136**	34 24S	18 30 E
Goeree	**40**	51 50N	4 0 E
Goes	**40**	51 30N	3 55 E
Gogama	**151**	47 35N	81 43W
Goiânia	**188**	16 43S	49 20W
Goiás □	**188**	12 10S	48 0W
Goirle	**40**	51 31N	5 4 E
Gojō	**106**	34 21N	135 42 E
Gökçeada	**55**	40 10N	25 50 E
Gold Coast, Australia	**116**	28 0S	153 25 E
Gold Coast, W. Afr.	**124**	4 0N	1 40W
Golden Bay	**122**	40 40S	172 50 E
Golden Gate	**172**	37 54N	122 30W
Golden Hinde	**154**	49 40N	125 44W
Golden Vale	**35**	52 33N	8 17W
Goldfield	**172**	37 45N	117 13W
Goldsboro	**165**	35 24N	77 59W
Goldsworthy	**114**	20 21S	119 30 E
Golfo Aranci	**48**	41 0N	9 35 E
Gomel	**68**	52 28N	31 0 E
Gómez Palacio	**174**	25 34N	103 30W
Gonābād	**86**	34 15N	58 45 E
Gonaïves	**180**	19 20N	72 42W
Gonda	**92**	27 9N	81 58 E
Gonder	**132**	12 39N	37 30 E
Good Hope, C. of = Goeie Hoop, Kaap die	**136**	34 24S	18 30 E
Goole	**29**	53 42N	0 52W
Goondiwindi	**116**	28 30S	150 21 E
Goose Bay	**147**	53 15N	60 20W
Gorakhpur	**92**	26 47N	83 23 E
Gordonvale	**121**	17 5S	145 50 E
Gore, Ethiopia	**132**	8 12N	35 32 E
Gore, N.Z.	**123**	46 5S	168 58 E
Gorey	**35**	52 41N	6 18W
Gorinchem	**40**	51 50N	4 59 E
Gorki = Gorkiy	**68**	56 20N	44 0 E
Gorkiy	**68**	56 20N	44 0 E
Görlitz	**43**	51 10N	14 59 E
Gorna Oryakhovitsa	**53**	43 7N	25 40 E
Gort	**35**	53 4N	8 50W
Gorzów Wielkopolski	**58**	52 43N	15 15 E
Gosford	**117**	33 23S	151 18 E
Gospič	**52**	44 35N	15 23 E
Gosport	**25**	50 48N	1 8W
Göteborg	**60**	57 43N	11 59 E
Göteborgs och Bohus län □	**60**	58 30N	11 30 E
Gotemba	**107**	35 18N	138 56 E
Gotha	**43**	50 56N	10 42 E
Gotland	**60**	57 30N	18 33 E
Gōtsu	**109**	35 0N	132 14 E
Gottwaldov	**59**	49 14N	17 40 E
Gouda	**40**	52 1N	4 42 E
Gouin, Rés.	**151**	48 35N	74 40W
Goulburn	**117**	34 44S	149 44 E
Goundam	**130**	16 25N	3 45W
Gournay-en-Bray	**38**	49 29N	1 44 E
Governador Valadares	**188**	18 15S	41 57W
Governor's Harbour	**178**	25 10N	76 14W
Gower, The	**27**	51 35N	4 10W
Goya	**190**	29 10S	59 10W
Gozo	**49**	36 0N	14 13 E
Graaff-Reinet	**136**	32 13S	24 32 E
Gracias a Dios, C.	**179**	15 0N	83 10W
Grafton	**116**	29 38S	152 58 E
Graham	**165**	36 5N	79 22W
Graham I.	**154**	53 40N	132 30W
Graham Land	**14**	65 0S	64 0W
Grahamstown	**137**	33 19S	26 31 E
Grain Coast	**124**	4 20N	10 0W
Grampian □	**33**	57 0N	3 0W
Grampian Mts.	**33**	56 50N	4 0W
Grampians, The	**119**	37 0S	142 20 E
Gran Chaco	**190**	25 0S	61 0W
Gran Sasso d'Italia	**47**	42 25N	13 30 E
Granada, Nic.	**179**	11 58N	86 0W
Granada, Spain	**50**	37 10N	3 35W
Granby	**151**	45 25N	72 45W
Grand Bank	**149**	47 6N	55 48W
Grand Bassam	**130**	5 10N	3 49W
Grand Canyon	**160**	36 3N	112 9W
Grand Cayman	**178**	19 20N	81 20W
Grand Cess	**130**	4 40N	8 12W
Grand Falls	**149**	48 56N	55 40W
Grand Forks, Canada	**155**	49 0N	118 30W
Grand Forks, U.S.A.	**156**	48 0N	97 3W
Grand Island	**163**	40 59N	98 25W
Grand Junction	**163**	39 0N	108 30W
Grand Mère	**151**	46 36N	72 40W
Grand Portage	**150**	47 58N	89 41W
Grand Rapids, Canada	**153**	53 12N	99 19W
Grand Rapids, U.S.A.	**167**	42 57N	86 40W
Grand St.-Bernard, Col. du	**44**	45 53N	7 11 E
Grand Teton	**163**	43 54N	111 50W
Grand View	**153**	51 10N	100 42W
Grande →, Bolivia	**187**	15 51S	64 39W
Grande →, Brazil	**188**	20 6S	51 4W
Grande, B.	**192**	50 30S	68 20W
Grande, La	**171**	45 15N	118 0W
Grande, La →	**140**	53 50N	79 0W
Grande Baleine, R. de la →	**140**	55 16N	77 47W
Grande de Santiago, R. →	**175**	21 36N	105 26W
Grande Prairie	**155**	55 10N	118 50W
Grande-Rivière	**148**	48 26N	64 30W
Grange, La	**170**	33 4N	85 0W
Grangemouth	**31**	56 1N	3 43W
Grangeville	**162**	45 57N	116 4W
Granite City	**166**	38 45N	90 3W
Grant, Mt.	**172**	38 34N	118 48W
Grantham	**29**	52 55N	0 39W
Grantown-on-Spey	**33**	57 19N	3 36W
Grants Pass	**171**	42 30N	123 22W
Grass Valley	**172**	39 18N	121 0W
Grasse	**37**	43 38N	6 56 E
Gravelbourg	**152**	49 50N	106 35W
Gravelines	**38**	51 0N	2 10 E
's-Gravenhage	**40**	52 7N	4 17 E

Gravesend	**25**	51 25N	0 22 E
Grayling	**167**	44 40N	84 42W
Graz	**45**	47 4N	15 27 E
Great Abaco I.	**178**	26 25N	77 10W
Great Australian Bight	**114**	33 30S	130 0 E
Great Bahama Bank	**178**	23 15N	78 0W
Great Barrier I.	**122**	36 11S	175 25 E
Great Barrier Reef	**121**	18 0S	146 50 E
Great Basin	**172**	40 0N	116 30W
Great Bear L.	**145**	65 30N	120 0W
Great Britain	**16**	54 0N	2 15W
Great Divide, The	**117**	35 0S	149 17 E
Great Dividing Ra.	**121**	23 0S	146 0 E
Great Exuma I.	**178**	23 30N	75 50W
Great Falls	**163**	47 27N	111 12W
Great Inagua I.	**180**	21 0N	73 20W
Great Indian Desert = Thar Desert	**89**	28 0N	72 0 E
Great Orme's Head	**26**	53 20N	3 52W
Great Ouse →	**29**	52 47N	0 22 E
Great Plains	**138**	47 0N	105 0W
Great Salt Lake	**162**	41 0N	112 30W
Great Salt Lake Desert	**162**	40 20N	113 50W
Great Slave L.	**145**	61 23N	115 38W
Great Wall	**98**	38 30N	109 30 E
Great Whernside	**28**	54 9N	1 59W
Great Yarmouth	**29**	52 40N	1 45 E
Greater Antilles	**181**	17 40N	74 0W
Greater Manchester □	**28**	53 30N	2 15W
Greater Sunda Is.	**111**	2 30S	110 0 E
Gredos, Sierra de	**50**	40 20N	5 0W
Greece ■	**54**	40 0N	23 0 E
Greeley	**163**	40 30N	104 40W
Green →, Ky., U.S.A.	**167**	37 54N	87 30W
Green →, Utah, U.S.A.	**163**	38 11N	109 53W
Green Bay	**167**	44 30N	88 0W
Greenfield	**164**	42 38N	72 38W
Greenland □	**147**	66 0N	45 0W
Greenland Sea	**13**	73 0N	10 0W
Greenock	**30**	55 57N	4 46W
Greensboro	**165**	36 7N	79 46W
Greenville, Ala., U.S.A.	**169**	31 50N	86 37W
Greenville, Mich., U.S.A.	**167**	43 12N	85 14W
Greenville, Miss., U.S.A.	**168**	33 25N	91 0W
Greenville, N.C., U.S.A.	**165**	35 37N	77 26W
Greenville, S.C., U.S.A.	**165**	34 54N	82 24W
Greenville, Tenn., U.S.A.	**165**	36 13N	82 51W
Greenwood, Miss., U.S.A.	**169**	33 30N	90 4W
Greenwood, S.C., U.S.A.	**165**	34 13N	82 13W
Grenada	**169**	33 45N	89 50W
Grenada ■	**180**	12 10N	61 40W
Grenoble	**37**	45 12N	5 42 E
Grenville	**117**	37 46S	143 52 E
Gretna Green	**31**	55 0N	3 3W
Grey Range	**116**	27 0S	143 30 E
Grey Res.	**149**	48 20N	56 30W
Greymouth	**123**	42 29S	171 13 E
Griffin	**170**	33 17N	84 14W
Griffith	**117**	34 18S	146 2 E
Grimsby	**29**	53 35N	0 5W
Grimshaw	**155**	56 10N	117 40W
Grinnell	**166**	41 45N	92 43W
Grodno	**68**	53 42N	23 52 E
Groningen	**41**	53 15N	6 35 E
Groningen □	**41**	53 16N	6 40 E
Grootfontein	**136**	19 31S	18 6 E
Groznyy	**70**	43 20N	45 45 E
Grudziądz	**58**	53 30N	18 47 E
Grytviken	**14**	53 50S	37 10W
Gt. Stour = Stour →	**25**	51 15N	1 20 E
Guadalajara, Mexico	**175**	20 40N	103 20W
Guadalajara, Spain	**50**	40 37N	3 12W
Guadalquivir →	**50**	36 47N	6 22W
Guadalupe = Guadeloupe ■	**180**	16 20N	61 40W
Guadalupe Bravos	**174**	31 23N	106 7W
Guadarrama, Sierra de	**50**	41 0N	4 0W
Guadeloupe ■	**180**	16 20N	61 40W
Guadiana →	**50**	37 14N	7 22W
Guadix	**50**	37 18N	3 11W
Guaíra	**191**	24 5S	54 10W
Guajará-Mirim	**187**	10 50S	65 20W
Gualeguay	**190**	33 10S	59 14W
Gualeguaychú	**190**	33 3S	59 31W
Guam	**10**	13 27N	144 45 E
Guanabacoa	**178**	23 8N	82 18W
Guanacaste, Cordillera del	**179**	10 40N	85 4W
Guanahani = San Salvador	**178**	24 0N	74 40W
Guanajay	**178**	22 56N	82 42W
Guanajuato	**177**	21 1N	101 15W
Guanajuato □	**177**	21 0N	101 0W
Guanare	**184**	8 42N	69 12W
Guangdong □	**99**	23 0N	113 0 E
Guangxi Zhuangzu Zizhiqu □	**99**	24 0N	109 0 E
Guangzhou	**99**	23 5N	113 10 E
Guantánamo	**178**	20 10N	75 14W
Guaporé →	**187**	11 55S	65 4W
Guaqui	**187**	16 41S	68 54W
Guarapuava	**191**	25 20S	51 30W
Guarda	**50**	40 32N	7 20W
Guardafui, C. = Asir, Ras	**133**	11 55N	51 10 E
Guatemala	**177**	14 40N	90 22W
Guatemala ■	**177**	15 40N	90 30W
Guaviare →	**184**	4 3N	67 44W
Guayama	**180**	17 59N	66 7W
Guayaquil	**184**	2 15S	79 52W
Guayaquil, G. de	**186**	3 10S	81 0W
Guaymas	**174**	27 56N	110 54W
Guddu Barrage	**89**	28 30N	69 50 E
Gudur	**90**	14 12N	79 55 E
Guelph	**151**	43 35N	80 20W
Guernica	**50**	43 19N	2 40W
Guernsey	**36**	49 30N	2 35W
Guerrero □	**177**	17 40N	100 0W
Guilin	**99**	25 18N	110 15 E
Guimarães	**188**	2 9S	44 42W
Guinea ■	**130**	10 20N	10 0W
Guinea, Gulf of	**130**	3 0N	2 30 E
Guinea-Bissau ■	**130**	12 0N	15 0W
Güines	**178**	22 50N	82 0W
Guiyang	**99**	26 32N	106 40 E
Guizhou □	**99**	27 0N	107 0 E
Gujarat □	**91**	23 20N	71 0 E
Gujranwala	**89**	32 10N	74 12 E
Gujrat	**89**	32 40N	74 2 E
Gulbarga	**91**	17 20N	76 50 E
Gulf, The	**85**	27 0N	50 0 E
Gulfport	**169**	30 21N	89 3W
Gulgong	**116**	32 20S	149 49 E
Gull Lake	**152**	50 10N	108 29W
Gümüsane	**81**	40 30N	39 30 E
Guna	**91**	24 40N	77 19 E
Gundagai	**117**	35 3S	148 6 E
Gunnedah	**116**	30 59S	150 15 E
Gunningbar Cr. →	**116**	31 14S	147 6 E
Guntakal	**90**	15 11N	77 27 E
Guntersville	**169**	34 18N	86 16W
Guntur	**92**	16 23N	80 30 E
Gurdaspur	**89**	32 5N	75 31 E
Gurgaon	**89**	28 27N	77 1 E
Gurkha	**92**	28 5N	84 40 E
Gurupi →	**188**	1 13S	46 6W
Guryev	**70**	47 5N	52 0 E
Gusau	**131**	12 12N	6 40 E
Guthrie	**168**	35 55N	97 30W
Guyana ■	**185**	5 0N	59 0W
Guyenne	**36**	44 30N	0 40 E
Guyra	**116**	30 15S	151 40 E
Gwalior	**91**	26 12N	78 10 E
Gwent □	**27**	51 45N	2 55W
Gweru	**137**	19 28S	29 45 E
Gwynedd □	**26**	53 0N	4 0W
Gyaring Hu	**101**	34 50N	97 40 E
Gydanskiy P-ov.	**69**	70 0N	78 0 E
Gympie	**116**	26 11S	152 38 E
Gyoda	**107**	36 10N	139 30 E
Gyöngyös	**59**	47 48N	20 0 E
Györ	**59**	47 41N	17 40 E
Gypsumville	**153**	51 45N	98 40W

Ha 'Arava	**80**	30 50N	35 20 E
Ha Giang	**95**	22 50N	104 59 E
Haarlem	**40**	52 23N	4 39 E
Habana, La	**178**	23 8N	82 22W
Hachijō-Jima	**105**	33 5N	139 45 E
Hachinohe	**103**	40 30N	141 29 E
Hachiōji	**107**	35 40N	139 20 E
Hadera	**80**	32 27N	34 55 E
Hadhramaut = Haḑramawt	**83**	15 30N	49 30 E
Hadiya	**82**	25 30N	36 56 E
Haḑramawt	**83**	15 30N	49 30 E
Hadrians Wall	**28**	55 0N	2 30W
Haeju	**98**	38 3N	125 45 E
Haerhpin = Harbin	**98**	45 48N	126 40 E
Hafar al Bāţin	**82**	28 25N	46 0 E
Hafnarfjörður	**64**	64 4N	21 57W
Haft-Gel	**84**	31 30N	49 32 E
Hagen	**42**	51 21N	7 29 E
Hagerstown	**164**	39 39N	77 46W
Hagi	**108**	34 30N	131 22 E
Hags Hd.	**35**	52 57N	9 30W
Hague, The = 's-Gravenhage	**40**	52 7N	4 17 E
Hai'an	**99**	32 37N	120 27 E
Haifa = Hefa	**80**	32 46N	35 0 E
Haikou	**99**	20 1N	110 16 E
Ḩā'il	**82**	27 28N	41 45 E
Hailar	**98**	49 10N	119 38 E
Hailey	**162**	43 30N	114 15W
Haileybury	**151**	47 30N	79 38W
Hainan	**99**	19 0N	110 0 E
Hainan Dao	**99**	19 0N	109 30 E
Haiphong	**95**	20 47N	106 41 E
Haiti ■	**180**	19 0N	72 30W
Hakken-Zan	**106**	34 10N	135 54 E
Hakodate	**103**	41 45N	140 44 E
Ḩalab	**80**	36 10N	37 15 E
Halaib	**129**	22 12N	36 30 E
Halberstadt	**43**	51 53N	11 2 E
Halfmoon Bay	**123**	46 50S	168 5 E
Halifax, Canada	**148**	44 38N	63 35W
Halifax, U.K.	**28**	53 43N	1 51W
Halifax B.	**121**	18 50S	147 0 E
Hallands län □	**61**	56 50N	12 50 E
Halle	**43**	51 29N	12 0 E
Halls Creek	**114**	18 16S	127 38 E
Halmahera	**113**	0 40N	128 0 E
Halmstad	**61**	56 41N	12 52 E
Hälsingborg = Helsingborg	**61**	56 3N	12 42 E
Hamada	**109**	34 56N	132 4 E
Hamadān	**81**	34 52N	48 32 E
Hamadān □	**81**	35 0N	49 0 E
Hamāh	**80**	35 5N	36 40 E
Hamakita	**107**	34 45N	137 47 E
Hamamatsu	**106**	34 45N	137 45 E
Hamar	**60**	60 48N	11 7 E
Hamburg	**43**	53 32N	9 59 E
Hämeenlinna	**67**	61 0N	24 28 E
Hamelin Pool	**120**	26 22S	114 20 E
Hameln	**42**	52 7N	9 24 E
Hamhung	**98**	39 54N	127 30 E
Hamilton, Australia	**119**	37 45S	142 2 E
Hamilton, Bermuda	**180**	32 15N	64 45W
Hamilton, Canada	**151**	43 15N	79 50W
Hamilton, N.Z.	**122**	37 47S	175 19 E
Hamilton, U.K.	**31**	55 47N	4 2W
Hamilton, U.S.A.	**167**	39 20N	84 35W
Hamm	**42**	51 40N	7 49 E
Hammerfest	**67**	70 39N	23 41 E
Hammond, Ind., U.S.A.	**167**	41 40N	87 30W
Hammond, La., U.S.A.	**169**	30 32N	90 30W
Hampshire □	**25**	51 3N	1 20W
Hampshire Downs	**25**	51 10N	1 10W
Hampton	**165**	37 4N	76 18W
Hanamaki	**103**	39 23N	141 7 E
Hancock	**150**	47 10N	88 40W
Handa	**106**	34 53N	137 0 E
Handan	**98**	36 35N	114 28 E
Haney	**154**	49 12N	122 40W
Hanford	**173**	36 23N	119 39W
Hangayn Nuruu	**100**	47 30N	100 0 E
Hangchou = Hangzhou	**99**	30 18N	120 11 E
Hangö	**67**	59 50N	22 57 E
Hangu	**98**	39 18N	117 53 E
Hangzhou	**99**	30 18N	120 11 E
Hanna	**155**	51 40N	111 54W
Hannibal	**166**	39 42N	91 22W
Hannover	**42**	52 23N	9 43 E
Hanoi	**95**	21 5N	105 55 E
Hanover = Hannover	**42**	52 23N	9 43 E
Hanover, N.H., U.S.A.	**148**	43 43N	72 17W
Hanover, Pa., U.S.A.	**164**	39 46N	76 59W
Hansi	**89**	29 10N	75 57 E
Hanyū	**107**	36 10N	139 32 E
Hanzhong	**99**	33 10N	107 1 E
Haora	**92**	22 37N	88 20 E
Haparanda	**67**	65 52N	24 8 E
Ḩaraḑ, Si. Arabia	**83**	24 22N	49 0 E
Ḩaraḑ, Yemen	**83**	16 26N	43 5 E
Harare	**137**	17 43S	31 2 E
Harbin	**98**	45 48N	126 40 E
Harbour Breton	**149**	47 29N	55 50W
Harbour Grace	**149**	47 40N	53 22W
Hardap Dam	**136**	24 32S	17 50 E
Hardenberg	**41**	52 34N	6 37 E
Harderwijk	**41**	52 21N	5 38 E
Hardinxveld	**40**	51 49N	4 53 E
Hardwar = Haridwar	**89**	29 58N	78 9 E
Harer	**133**	9 20N	42 8 E
Harfleur	**38**	49 30N	0 10 E
Hargeisa	**133**	9 30N	44 2 E
Hari →	**111**	1 16S	104 5 E
Haridwar	**89**	29 58N	78 9 E
Harima-Nada	**109**	34 30N	134 35 E
Harīrūd →	**86**	34 20N	62 30 E
Harlech	**26**	52 52N	4 7W
Harlingen, Neth.	**41**	53 11N	5 25 E
Harlingen, U.S.A.	**161**	26 20N	97 50W
Harlow	**25**	51 47N	0 9 E
Harney Basin	**171**	43 30N	119 0W
Härnösand	**66**	62 38N	18 0 E
Harriman	**169**	36 0N	84 35W
Harris	**32**	57 50N	6 55W
Harris L.	**118**	31 10S	135 10 E
Harrisburg, Ill., U.S.A.	**167**	37 42N	88 30W
Harrisburg, Pa., U.S.A.	**164**	40 18N	76 52W
Harrison	**168**	36 10N	93 4W
Harrison, C.	**147**	54 55N	57 55W
Harrison B.	**142**	70 25N	151 30W
Harrisonburg	**165**	38 28N	78 52W
Harrogate	**28**	53 59N	1 32W
Harrow	**25**	51 35N	0 15W
Hartford	**164**	41 47N	72 41W
Hartland Pt.	**27**	51 2N	4 32W
Hartlepool	**29**	54 42N	1 11W
Hartsville	**165**	34 23N	80 2W
Harvey, Australia	**120**	33 5S	115 54 E
Harvey, U.S.A.	**167**	41 40N	87 40W
Harwich	**25**	51 56N	1 18 E
Haryana □	**89**	29 0N	76 10 E
Hashima	**106**	35 20N	136 40 E
Hashimoto	**106**	34 19N	135 37 E
Hastings, N.Z.	**122**	39 39S	176 52 E
Hastings, U.K.	**25**	50 51N	0 36 E
Hastings, U.S.A.	**163**	40 34N	98 22W
Hastings Ra.	**116**	31 15S	152 14 E
Hatano	**107**	35 22N	139 14 E
Hathras	**89**	27 36N	78 6 E
Hatteras, C.	**165**	35 10N	75 30W
Hattiesburg	**169**	31 20N	89 20W
Hatvan	**59**	47 40N	19 45 E
Hau Bon = Cheo Reo	**95**	13 25N	108 28 E
Hauraki Gulf	**122**	36 35S	175 5 E
Haut Atlas	**126**	32 30N	5 0W
Havana = Habana, La	**178**	23 8N	82 22W
Havant	**25**	50 51N	0 59W
Havelock	**151**	44 26N	77 53W
Haverfordwest	**26**	51 48N	4 59W
Haverhill	**164**	42 50N	71 2W
Havre	**163**	48 34N	109 40W
Havre, Le	**38**	49 30N	0 5 E
Hawaii □	**160**	20 30N	157 0W
Hawaiian Is.	**160**	20 30N	156 0W

Hawea Lake	**123**	44 28S	169 19 E
Hawera	**122**	39 35S	174 19 E
Hawick	**31**	55 25N	2 48W
Hawke B.	**122**	39 25S	177 20 E
Hawke's Bay □	**122**	39 45S	176 35 E
Hawkesbury	**151**	45 37N	74 37W
Hawthorne	**172**	38 31N	118 37W
Hay, Australia	**117**	34 30S	144 51 E
Hay, U.K.	**26**	52 4N	3 9W
Hay River	**145**	60 51N	115 44W
Hayward's Heath	**25**	51 0N	0 5W
Hazard	**165**	37 18N	83 10W
Hazaribag	**92**	23 58N	85 26 E
Hazebrouck	**38**	50 42N	2 31 E
Hazelton	**154**	55 20N	127 42W
Hazleton	**164**	40 58N	76 0W
Healdsburg	**172**	38 33N	122 51W
Healesville	**117**	37 35S	145 30 E
Heanor	**29**	53 1N	1 20W
Hearst	**150**	49 40N	83 41W
Hebei □	**98**	39 0N	116 0 E
Hebel	**116**	28 58S	147 47 E
Hebrides	**16**	57 30N	7 0W
Hebron = Al Khalīl	**80**	31 32N	35 6 E
Hebron	**147**	58 5N	62 30W
Hecate Str.	**154**	53 10N	130 30W
Hechuan	**99**	30 2N	106 12 E
Hedmark fylke □	**60**	61 17N	11 40 E
Heemstede	**40**	52 22N	4 37 E
Heerenveen	**41**	52 57N	5 55 E
Heerlen	**41**	50 55N	6 0 E
Hefa	**80**	32 46N	35 0 E
Hefei	**99**	31 52N	117 18 E
Hegang	**98**	47 20N	130 19 E
Heidelberg	**42**	49 23N	8 41 E
Heilbronn	**42**	49 8N	9 13 E
Heilongjiang □	**98**	48 0N	126 0 E
Heilunkiang = Heilongjiang □	**98**	48 0N	126 0 E
Heinze Is.	**94**	14 25N	97 45 E
Hekimhan	**81**	38 50N	38 0 E
Hekinan	**106**	34 52N	137 0 E
Hekla	**16**	63 56N	19 35W
Helena, Ark., U.S.A.	**169**	34 30N	90 35W
Helena, Mont., U.S.A.	**163**	46 40N	112 0W
Helensburgh	**30**	56 0N	4 44W
Helmand →	**87**	31 12N	61 34 E
Helmond	**41**	51 29N	5 41 E
Helmsdale	**33**	58 7N	3 40W
Helsingborg	**61**	56 3N	12 42 E
Helsinki	**67**	60 15N	25 3 E
Helston	**27**	50 7N	5 17W
Helvellyn	**28**	54 31N	3 1W
Hemel Hempstead	**25**	51 45N	0 28W
Hempstead	**164**	30 5N	96 5W
Henan □	**99**	34 0N	114 0 E
Henderson	**165**	36 20N	78 25W
Hendersonville	**165**	35 21N	82 28W
Hengelo	**41**	52 16N	6 48 E
Hengyang	**99**	26 51N	112 30 E
Hénin-Beaumont	**38**	50 25N	2 58 E
Hennebont	**36**	47 49N	3 19W
Henrietta Maria C.	**140**	55 9N	82 20W
Henty	**117**	35 30S	147 0 E
Henzada	**93**	17 38N	95 26 E
Herāt	**87**	34 20N	62 7 E
Herāt □	**87**	35 0N	62 0 E
Herbert →	**121**	18 31S	146 17 E
Herbiers, Les	**36**	46 52N	1 0W
Hercegnovi	**52**	42 30N	18 33 E
Hercegovina = Bosna i Hercegovina □	**52**	44 0N	18 0 E
Hereford	**24**	52 4N	2 42W
Hereford and Worcester □	**24**	52 10N	2 30W
Herford	**42**	52 7N	8 40 E
Hermosillo	**174**	29 4N	110 58W
Heroica = Caborca	**174**	30 40N	112 10W
Heroica Nogales = Nogales	**174**	31 20N	110 56W
Heron Bay	**150**	48 40N	86 25W
Herrin	**166**	37 50N	89 0W
Hertford □	**25**	51 51N	0 5W
's-Hertogenbosch	**40**	51 42N	5 17 E
Hesse = Hessen □	**42**	50 40N	9 20 E
Hessen □	**42**	50 40N	9 20 E
Hewett, C.	**146**	70 16N	67 45W
Hexham	**28**	54 58N	2 7W
Heysham	**28**	54 5N	2 53W
Heywood	**119**	38 8S	141 37 E
Hi-no-Misaki	**109**	35 26N	132 38 E
Hialeach	**170**	25 49N	80 17W
Hibiki-Nada	**108**	34 0N	130 0 E
Hickory	**165**	35 46N	81 17W
Hida-Gawa →	**106**	35 26N	137 3 E
Hida-Sammyaku	**106**	36 30N	137 40 E
Hida-Sanchi	**106**	36 10N	137 0 E
Hidaka	**109**	35 30N	134 44 E
Hidalgo □	**177**	20 30N	99 0W
Hidalgo del Parral	**174**	26 56N	105 40W
Higashi-matsuyama	**107**	36 2N	139 25 E
Higashiōsaka	**106**	34 40N	135 37 E
Higasi-Suidō	**108**	34 0N	129 30 E
High Atlas = Haut Atlas	**126**	32 30N	5 0W
High Point	**165**	35 57N	79 58W
High Prairie	**155**	55 30N	116 30W
Highland □	**32**	57 30N	5 0W
Highland Park	**167**	42 10N	87 50W
Ḩijārah, Şaḩrā' al	**84**	30 25N	44 30 E
Hikari	**108**	33 58N	131 58 E
Hikone	**106**	35 15N	136 10 E
Hildesheim	**43**	52 9N	9 55 E
Hillegom	**40**	52 18N	4 35 E
Hillsboro	**171**	45 31N	123 0W
Hillston	**117**	33 30S	145 31 E
Hilo	**160**	19 44N	155 5W
Hilversum	**40**	52 14N	5 10 E
Himachal Pradesh □	**89**	31 30N	77 0 E
Himalaya, Mts.	**101**	29 0N	84 0 E
Hime-Jima	**108**	33 43N	131 40 E
Himeji	**109**	34 50N	134 40 E
Himi	**106**	36 50N	137 0 E
Ḥimş	**80**	34 40N	36 45 E
Hinchinbrook I.	**121**	18 20S	146 15 E
Hinckley	**25**	52 33N	1 21W
Hindmarsh	**119**	34 54S	138 34 E
Hindu Kush	**89**	36 0N	71 0 E
Hindupur	**90**	13 49N	77 32 E
Hines Creek	**155**	56 20N	118 40W
Hingoli	**91**	19 41N	77 15 E
Hinton	**165**	37 40N	80 51W
Hirado	**108**	33 22N	129 33 E
Hirakarta	**106**	34 48N	135 40 E
Hirakud Dam	**92**	21 32N	83 45 E
Hirata	**109**	35 24N	132 49 E
Hiratsuka	**107**	35 19N	139 21 E
Hirosaki	**103**	40 34N	140 28 E
Hiroshima	**109**	34 24N	132 30 E
Hirson	**38**	49 55N	4 4 E
Hispaniola	**180**	19 0N	71 0W
Hita	**108**	33 20N	130 58 E
Hitachi	**107**	36 36N	140 39 E
Hitachiota	**107**	36 30N	140 30 E
Hitchin	**25**	51 57N	0 16W
Hitoyoshi	**108**	32 13N	130 45 E
Hitra	**65**	63 30N	8 45 E
Hiuchi-Nada	**109**	34 5N	133 20 E
Ho Chi Minh City = Thanh Pho Ho Chi Minh	**95**	10 58N	106 40 E
Hoa Binh	**95**	20 50N	105 20 E
Hobart	**119**	42 50S	147 21 E
Hobbs	**161**	32 40N	103 3W
Hodaka-Dake	**106**	36 17N	137 39 E
Hódmezővásárhely	**59**	46 28N	20 22 E
Hoek van Holland	**40**	52 0N	4 7 E
Hofsjökull	**64**	64 49N	18 48W
Hōfu	**108**	34 3N	131 34 E
Hogan Group	**117**	39 13S	147 1 E
Hoh Xil Shan	**101**	35 0N	89 0 E
Hohhot	**98**	40 52N	111 40 E
Hōjō	**109**	33 58N	132 46 E
Hokitika	**123**	42 42S	171 0 E
Hokkaidō □	**103**	43 30N	143 0 E
Holbrook	**117**	35 42S	147 18 E
Holderness	**29**	53 45N	0 5W

Holdrege	**163**	40 26N	99 22W
Holguín	**178**	20 50N	76 20W
Holland	**167**	42 47N	86 7W
Holly Springs	**169**	34 45N	89 25W
Hollywood, Calif., U.S.A.	**173**	34 7N	118 25W
Hollywood, Fla., U.S.A.	**170**	26 0N	80 9W
Holsteinsborg	**147**	66 40N	53 30W
Holsworthy	**27**	50 48N	4 21W
Holt	**64**	63 33N	19 48W
Holy I., Scotland, U.K.	**31**	55 31N	5 4W
Holy I., Wales, U.K.	**26**	53 17N	4 37W
Holyhead	**26**	53 18N	4 38W
Holyoke	**164**	42 14N	72 37W
Hombori	**130**	15 20N	1 38W
Home Hill	**121**	19 43S	147 25 E
Homer	**142**	59 40N	151 35W
Homs = Ḩimş	**80**	34 40N	36 45 E
Honan = Henan □	**99**	34 0N	114 0 E
Hondo	**108**	32 27N	130 12 E
Honduras ■	**179**	14 40N	86 30W
Honduras, Golfo de	**177**	16 50N	87 0W
Hong Kong ■	**99**	22 11N	114 14 E
Hongha →	**95**	22 0N	104 0 E
Hongshui He →	**99**	23 48N	109 30 E
Honiton	**27**	50 48N	3 11W
Honolulu	**160**	21 19N	157 52W
Honshū	**106**	36 0N	138 0 E
Hoogeveen	**41**	52 44N	6 30 E
Hook Hd.	**35**	52 8N	6 57W
Hook of Holland = Hoek van Holland	**40**	52 0N	4 7 E
Hoorn	**40**	52 38N	5 4 E
Hope, Canada	**154**	49 25N	121 25 E
Hope, U.S.A.	**168**	33 40N	93 36W
Hope Town	**178**	26 35N	76 57W
Hopedale	**147**	55 28N	60 13W
Hopei = Hebei □	**98**	39 0N	116 0 E
Hopelchén	**177**	19 46N	89 51W
Hopetoun, Vic., Australia	**119**	35 42S	142 22 E
Hopetoun, W. Austral., Australia	**120**	33 57S	120 7 E
Hopkinsville	**169**	36 52N	87 26W
Hoquiam	**171**	46 50N	123 55W
Hordaland fylke □	**60**	60 25N	6 15 E
Hormoz	**85**	27 35N	55 0 E
Hormuz Str.	**85**	26 30N	56 30 E
Horn, Cape = Hornos, Cabo de	**192**	55 50S	67 30W
Hornavan	**66**	66 15N	17 30 E
Hornell	**164**	42 23N	77 41W
Hornos, Cabo de	**192**	55 50S	67 30W
Hornsby	**117**	33 42S	151 2 E
Hornsea	**29**	53 55N	0 10W
Horqin Youyi Qianqi	**98**	46 5N	122 3 E
Horsens	**61**	55 52N	9 51 E
Horsham	**119**	36 44S	142 13 E
Horton →	**145**	69 56N	126 52W
Hoshiarpur	**89**	31 30N	75 58 E
Hospet	**90**	15 15N	76 20 E
Hospitalet de Llobregat	**51**	41 21N	2 6 E
Hoste, I.	**192**	55 0S	69 0W
Hot Springs	**168**	34 30N	93 0W
Houghton	**150**	47 9N	88 39W
Houghton-le-Spring	**28**	54 51N	1 28W
Houhora	**122**	34 49S	173 9 E
Houlton	**148**	46 5N	67 50W
Houma	**169**	29 35N	90 44W
Houston, Canada	**154**	54 25N	126 39W
Houston, U.S.A.	**168**	29 50N	95 20W
Houtman Abrolhos	**120**	28 43S	113 48 E
Hovd	**100**	48 2N	91 37 E
Hove	**25**	50 50N	0 10W
Howe, C.	**117**	37 30S	150 0 E
Howrah = Haora	**92**	22 37N	88 20 E
Hoy I.	**33**	58 50N	3 15W
Hrádec Králové	**58**	50 15N	15 50 E
Hrvatska □	**52**	45 20N	18 0 E
Hsiamen = Xiamen	**99**	24 25N	118 4 E
Hsian = Xi'an	**99**	34 15N	109 0 E
Hsinhailien = Lianyungang	**99**	34 40N	119 11 E
Hsüchou = Xuzhou	**99**	34 18N	117 10 E
Hua Hin	**94**	12 34N	99 58 E
Huacho	**186**	11 10S	77 35W
Huainan	**99**	32 38N	116 58 E
Huallaga →	**186**	5 0S	75 30W
Huambo	**134**	12 42S	15 54 E
Huancane	**187**	15 10S	69 44W
Huancavelica	**186**	12 50S	75 5W
Huancayo	**186**	12 5S	75 12W
Huanchaca	**187**	20 15S	66 40W
Huang Hai = Yellow Sea	**99**	35 0N	123 0 E
Huang Ho →	**98**	37 30N	118 50 E
Huangshi	**99**	30 10N	115 3 E
Huánuco	**186**	9 55S	76 15W
Huaraz	**186**	9 30S	77 32W
Huascarán	**186**	9 8S	77 36W
Huasco	**190**	28 30S	71 15W
Huatabampo	**174**	26 50N	109 38W
Huautla	**177**	17 51N	100 5W
Hubei □	**99**	31 0N	112 0 E
Hubli-Dharwad = Dharwad	**90**	15 22N	75 15 E
Huddersfield	**28**	53 38N	1 49W
Hudiksvall	**66**	61 43N	17 10 E
Hudson	**164**	42 15N	73 46W
Hudson →	**164**	40 42N	74 2W
Hudson Bay	**146**	52 51N	102 23W
Hudson Str.	**146**	62 0N	70 0W
Hudson's Hope	**155**	56 0N	121 54W
Hue	**95**	16 30N	107 35 E
Huehuetenango	**177**	15 20N	91 28W
Huelva	**50**	37 18N	6 57W
Huesca	**51**	42 8N	0 25W
Hughenden	**121**	20 52S	144 10 E
Huila, Nevado del	**184**	3 0N	76 0W
Huinca Renancó	**190**	34 51S	64 22W
Huixtla	**177**	15 9N	92 28W
Huizen	**40**	52 18N	5 14 E
Hukawng Valley	**93**	26 30N	96 30 E
Hull, Canada	**151**	45 25N	75 44W
Hull, U.K.	**29**	53 45N	0 20W
Hulst	**40**	51 17N	4 2 E
Hulun Nur	**98**	49 0N	117 30 E
Humaitá	**187**	27 2S	58 31W
Humber →	**29**	53 40N	0 10W
Humberside □	**29**	53 50N	0 30W
Humboldt, Canada	**152**	52 15N	105 9W
Humboldt, U.S.A.	**169**	35 50N	88 55W
Humboldt →	**172**	40 2N	118 31W
Hume, L.	**117**	36 0S	147 0 E
Húnaflói	**64**	65 50N	20 50W
Hunan □	**99**	27 30N	111 30 E
Hunedoara	**56**	45 40N	22 50 E
Hungary ■	**59**	47 20N	19 20 E
Hungary, Plain of	**17**	47 0N	20 0 E
Hungnam	**98**	39 49N	127 45 E
Hunsrück	**42**	49 30N	7 0 E
Hunstanton	**29**	52 57N	0 30 E
Hunter Ra.	**117**	32 45S	150 15 E
Huntingdon	**25**	52 20N	0 11W
Huntington, Ind., U.S.A.	**167**	40 52N	85 30W
Huntington, W. Va., U.S.A.	**165**	38 20N	82 30W
Huntington Beach	**173**	33 40N	118 0W
Huntly	**122**	37 34S	175 11 E
Huntsville, Canada	**151**	45 20N	79 14W
Huntsville, Ala., U.S.A.	**169**	34 45N	86 35W
Huntsville, Tex., U.S.A.	**168**	30 45N	95 35W
Huonville	**119**	43 0S	147 5 E
Hupeh □ = Hubei □	**99**	31 0N	112 0 E
Huron, L.	**150**	45 0N	83 0W
Hurricane	**173**	37 10N	113 12W
Húsavík	**64**	66 3N	17 21W
Hutchinson	**161**	38 3N	97 59W
Hvar	**52**	43 11N	16 28 E
Hwang Ho = Huang Ho →	**98**	37 30N	118 50 E
Hwange	**137**	18 18S	26 30 E
Hyden	**120**	32 24S	118 53 E
Hyderabad, India	**91**	17 22N	78 29 E
Hyderabad, Pakistan	**88**	25 23N	68 24 E
Hyères	**37**	43 8N	6 9 E
Hyndman Pk.	**162**	43 50N	114 10W
Hythe	**24**	51 4N	1 5 E
Hyūga	**108**	32 25N	131 35 E

Iaşi	**57**	47 10N	27 40 E
Ibadan	**131**	7 22N	3 58 E
Ibagué	**184**	4 20N	75 20W
Ibara	**109**	34 36N	133 28 E
Ibaraki	**106**	34 49N	135 34 E
Ibarra	**184**	0 21N	78 7W
Iberian Peninsula	**16**	40 0N	5 0W
Ibiza	**51**	38 54N	1 26 E
Ibuki-Sanchi	**106**	35 25N	136 18 E
Ibusuki	**108**	31 12N	130 40 E
Icá	**186**	14 0S	75 48W
Içá →	**184**	2 55S	67 58W
Iceland ■	**64**	65 0N	19 0W
Icha	**73**	55 30N	156 0 E
Ich'ang = Yichang	**99**	30 40N	111 20 E
Ichchapuram	**92**	19 10N	84 40 E
Ichihara	**107**	35 28N	140 5 E
Ichikawa	**107**	35 44N	139 55 E
Ichinomiya	**106**	35 18N	136 48 E
Ichinoseki	**103**	38 55N	141 8 E
Idaho □	**162**	44 10N	114 0W
Idaho Falls	**163**	43 30N	112 1W
Ídhi Óros	**55**	35 15N	24 45 E
Ídhra	**55**	37 20N	23 28 E
Ierápetra	**55**	35 0N	25 44 E
Ife	**131**	7 30N	4 31 E
Igloolik	**146**	69 20N	81 49W
Iguaçu →	**191**	25 36S	54 36W
Iguaçu, Cat. del	**191**	25 41S	54 26W
Iguaçu Falls = Iguaçu, Cat. del	**191**	25 41S	54 26W
Iguala de la Independencia	**177**	18 21N	99 32W
Iguassu = Iguaçu →	**191**	25 36S	54 36W
Iida	**107**	35 35N	137 50 E
Iisalmi	**67**	63 32N	27 10 E
Iizuka	**108**	33 38N	130 42 E
IJmuiden	**40**	52 28N	4 35 E
IJsselmeer	**40**	52 45N	5 20 E
IJsselstein	**40**	52 1N	5 2 E
Ikaría	**55**	37 35N	26 10 E
Ikeda	**109**	34 1N	133 48 E
Iki	**108**	33 45N	129 42 E
Iki-Kaikyō	**108**	33 40N	129 45 E
Île-de-France	**37**	49 0N	2 20 E
Ilebo	**134**	4 17S	20 55 E
Ilfracombe	**27**	51 13N	4 8W
Ilhéus	**189**	14 49S	39 2W
Ili →	**71**	45 53N	77 10 E
Iliamna L.	**142**	59 35N	155 30W
Iliodhrómia	**55**	39 12N	23 50 E
Ilkeston	**29**	52 59N	1 19W
Illampu = Ancohuma, Nevada	**187**	16 0S	68 50W
Illinois □	**166**	40 15N	89 30W
Illinois →	**166**	38 55N	90 28W
Ilo	**187**	17 40S	71 20W
Iloilo	**112**	10 45N	122 33 E
Ilorin	**131**	8 30N	4 35 E
Imabari	**109**	34 4N	133 0 E
Imari	**108**	33 15N	129 52 E
Imatra	**67**	61 12N	28 48 E
Immingham	**29**	53 37N	0 12W
Imperial	**152**	51 21N	105 28W
Imphal	**92**	24 48N	93 56 E
Imroz = Gökçeada	**55**	40 10N	25 50 E
Ina	**107**	35 50N	138 0 E
Iñapari	**187**	11 0S	69 40W
Inari	**67**	68 54N	27 5 E
Inarijärvi	**67**	69 0N	28 0 E
Inazawa	**106**	35 15N	136 47 E
Inchon	**98**	37 27N	126 40 E
Indalsälven →	**66**	62 36N	17 30 E
Independence, Kans., U.S.A.	**166**	37 10N	95 43W
Independence, Mo., U.S.A.	**166**	39 3N	94 25W
India ■	**78**	20 0N	78 0 E
Indian Head	**152**	50 30N	103 41W
Indiana	**164**	40 38N	79 9W
Indiana □	**167**	40 0N	86 0W
Indianapolis	**167**	39 42N	86 10W
Indigirka →	**73**	70 48N	148 54 E
Indonesia ■	**111**	5 0S	115 0 E
Indore	**91**	22 42N	75 53 E
Indre →	**36**	47 16N	0 19 E
Indus →	**88**	24 20N	67 47 E
Indus, Mouth of the	**88**	24 0N	68 0 E
Inebolu	**80**	41 55N	33 40 E
İnegöl	**80**	40 5N	29 31 E
Ingersoll	**151**	43 4N	80 55W
Ingham	**121**	18 43S	146 10 E
Ingleborough	**28**	54 11N	2 23W
Inglewood, N.Z.	**122**	39 9S	174 14 E
Inglewood, U.S.A.	**173**	33 58N	118 21W
Ingolstadt	**43**	48 45N	11 26 E
Ingraj Bazar	**92**	24 58N	88 10 E
Inhambane	**137**	23 54S	35 30 E
Ining = Yining	**100**	43 58N	81 10 E
Inishmore	**35**	53 8N	9 45W
Inishowen	**34**	55 14N	7 15W
Inn →	**43**	48 35N	13 28 E
Innamincka	**118**	27 44S	140 46 E
Inner Hebrides	**32**	57 0N	6 30W
Inner Mongolia = Nei Monggol Zizhiqu □	**98**	42 0N	112 0 E
Innisfail, Australia	**121**	17 33S	146 5 E
Innisfail, Canada	**155**	52 0N	113 57W
In'no-shima	**109**	34 19N	133 10 E
Innsbruck	**45**	47 16N	11 23 E
Inoucdjouac	**146**	58 25N	78 15W
Inowrocław	**58**	52 50N	18 12 E
Inquisivi	**187**	16 50S	67 10W
Insein	**93**	16 50N	96 5 E
Interlaken	**44**	46 41N	7 50 E
Inuvik	**144**	68 16N	133 40W
Inuvik □	**144**	70 0N	130 0W
Inuyama	**106**	35 23N	136 56 E
Inveraray	**30**	56 13N	5 5W
Invercargill	**123**	46 24S	168 24 E
Inverell	**116**	29 45S	151 8 E
Invergordon	**33**	57 41N	4 10W
Inverness	**33**	57 29N	4 12W
Investigator Group	**119**	34 45S	134 20 E
Investigator Str.	**119**	35 30S	137 0 E
Ioánnina	**54**	39 42N	20 47 E
Iola	**166**	38 0N	95 20W
Iona	**30**	56 20N	6 25W
Ionian Is. = Iónioi Níoi	**54**	38 40N	20 0 E
Ionian Sea	**54**	37 30N	17 30 E
Iónioi Níoi	**54**	38 40N	20 0 E
Íos	**55**	36 41N	25 20 E
Iowa □	**166**	42 18N	93 30W
Iowa City	**166**	41 40N	91 35W
Iowa Falls	**166**	42 30N	93 15W
Ipiales	**184**	0 50N	77 37W
Ipin = Yibin	**99**	28 45N	104 32 E
Ípiros □	**54**	39 30N	20 30 E
Ipoh	**96**	4 35N	101 5 E
Ipswich, Australia	**116**	27 35S	152 40 E
Ipswich, U.K.	**25**	52 4N	1 9 E
Iquique	**187**	20 19S	70 5W
Iquitos	**186**	3 45S	73 10W
Iracoubo	**185**	5 30N	53 10W
Iráklion	**55**	35 20N	25 12 E
Iran ■	**86**	33 0N	53 0 E
Iran Ra.	**111**	2 20N	114 50 E
Irapuato	**177**	20 41N	101 28W
Iraq ■	**81**	33 0N	44 0 E
Irbid	**80**	32 35N	35 48 E
Ireland ■	**34**	53 0N	8 0W
Irian Jaya □	**113**	4 0S	137 0 E
Iriri →	**188**	3 52S	52 37W
Irish Republic ■	**20**	53 0N	8 0W
Irish Sea	**20**	54 0N	5 0W
Irkutsk	**74**	52 18N	104 20 E
Irō-Zaki	**107**	34 36N	138 51 E
Iron Gate = Portile de Fier	**56**	44 42N	22 30 E
Iron Knob	**118**	32 46S	137 8 E
Iron Mountain	**150**	45 49N	88 4W
Ironbridge	**24**	52 38N	2 29W
Ironton	**167**	38 35N	82 40W
Ironwood	**150**	46 30N	90 10W

Iroquois Falls	**151**	48 46N	80 41W
Irrawaddy →	**93**	15 50N	95 6 E
Irtysh →	**69**	61 4N	68 52 E
Irumu	**135**	1 32N	29 53 E
Irún	**51**	43 20N	1 52W
Irvine	**31**	55 37N	4 40W
Irvinestown	**34**	54 28N	7 38W
Ísafjörður	**64**	66 5N	23 9W
Isahaya	**108**	32 52N	130 2 E
Íschia	**49**	40 45N	13 51 E
Ise	**106**	34 25N	136 45 E
Ise-Wan	**106**	34 43N	136 43 E
Isère →	**37**	44 59N	4 51 E
Isesaki	**107**	36 19N	139 12 E
Ishikari-Wan	**103**	43 25N	141 1 E
Ishinomaki	**103**	38 32N	141 20 E
Ishioka	**107**	36 11N	140 16 E
Ishkuman	**89**	36 30N	73 50 E
Ishpeming	**150**	46 30N	87 40W
İskenderun	**80**	36 32N	36 10 E
Islamabad	**89**	33 40N	73 10 E
Island L.	**153**	53 47N	94 25W
Island Pond	**148**	48 25N	56 23W
Islay	**30**	55 46N	6 10W
Isle-Adam, L'	**39**	49 6N	2 14 E
Isle Royale	**150**	48 0N	88 50W
Isparta	**80**	37 47N	30 30 E
Israel ■	**80**	32 0N	34 50 E
Issoire	**37**	45 32N	3 15 E
Issyk-Kul, Ozero	**71**	42 25N	77 15 E
İstanbul	**80**	41 0N	29 0 E
Istra	**52**	45 10N	14 0 E
Istria = Istra	**52**	45 10N	14 0 E
Itabuna	**189**	14 48S	39 16W
Itaituba	**185**	4 10S	55 50W
Itajaí	**191**	27 50S	48 39W
Italy ■	**19**	42 0N	13 0 E
Itaquatiara	**185**	2 58S	58 30W
Itaquí	**191**	29 8S	56 30W
Itchen →	**24**	50 57N	1 20W
Ithaca = Itháki	**54**	38 25N	20 40 E
Ithaca	**164**	42 25N	76 30W
Itháki	**54**	38 25N	20 40 E
Ito	**107**	34 58N	139 5 E
Ituaçu	**189**	13 50S	41 18W
Ituiutaba	**188**	19 0S	49 25W
Iturup, Ostrov	**75**	45 0N	148 0 E
Ivano-Frankovsk	**68**	48 40N	24 40 E
Ivanovo, Byelorussian S.S.R., U.S.S.R.	**68**	52 7N	25 29 E
Ivanovo, R.S.F.S.R., U.S.S.R.	**68**	57 5N	41 0 E
Ivigtut	**147**	61 14N	48 12W
Iviza = Ibiza	**51**	38 54N	1 26 E
Ivory Coast ■	**130**	7 30N	5 0W
Iwai-Jima	**108**	33 47N	131 58 E
Iwaki	**105**	37 3N	140 55 E
Iwakuni	**109**	34 15N	132 8 E
Iwami	**109**	35 32N	134 15 E
Iwamizawa	**103**	43 12N	141 46 E
Iwanuma	**103**	38 7N	140 51 E
Iwata	**107**	34 42N	137 51 E
Iwo	**131**	7 39N	4 9 E
Ixiamas	**187**	13 50S	68 5W
Ixtepec	**177**	16 34N	95 6W
Ixtlán	**175**	20 11N	102 24W
Ixtlán de Juárez	**177**	17 23N	96 28W
Iyo	**109**	33 45N	132 45 E
Iyo-mishima	**109**	33 58N	133 30 E
Iyo-Nada	**109**	33 40N	132 20 E
Izamal	**177**	20 56N	89 1W
Izhevsk = Ustinov	**69**	56 51N	53 14 E
İzmir	**80**	38 25N	27 8 E
İzmit	**80**	40 45N	29 50 E
Izu-Hantō	**107**	34 45N	139 0 E
Izumi	**108**	32 5N	130 22 E
Izumi-sano	**106**	34 23N	135 18 E
Izumiotsu	**106**	34 30N	135 24 E
Izumo	**109**	35 20N	132 46 E
Jabalpur	**91**	23 9N	79 58 E
Jacarèzinho	**191**	23 5S	50 0W
Jackson, Mich., U.S.A.	**167**	42 18N	84 25W
Jackson, Miss., U.S.A.	**169**	32 20N	90 10W
Jackson, Tenn., U.S.A.	**169**	35 40N	88 50W
Jacksonville, Fla., U.S.A.	**170**	30 15N	81 38W
Jacksonville, Ill., U.S.A.	**166**	39 42N	90 15W
Jacksonville, N.C., U.S.A.	**165**	34 50N	77 29W
Jacksonville, Tex., U.S.A.	**168**	31 58N	95 19W
Jacmel	**180**	18 14N	72 32W
Jacobabad	**88**	28 20N	68 29 E
Jacques Cartier, Dét. de	**149**	50 0N	63 30W
Jadotville = Likasi	**135**	10 55S	26 48 E
Jaén, Peru	**186**	5 25S	78 40W
Jaén, Spain	**50**	37 44N	3 43W
Jaffa = Tel Aviv-Yafo	**80**	32 4N	34 48 E
Jaffna	**90**	9 45N	80 2 E
Jagdalpur	**92**	19 3N	82 0 E
Jaguariaíva	**191**	24 10S	49 50W
Jagüey Grande	**178**	22 35N	81 7W
Jahrom	**85**	28 30N	53 31 E
Jaipur	**91**	27 0N	75 50 E
Jakarta	**111**	6 9S	106 49 E
Jalalabad	**87**	34 30N	70 29 E
Jalapa, Guat.	**177**	14 39N	89 59W
Jalapa, Mexico	**177**	17 43N	92 49W
Jalgaon	**91**	21 0N	75 42 E
Jalisco □	**175**	20 20N	103 40W
Jalna	**91**	19 48N	75 38 E
Jalón →	**51**	41 47N	1 4W
Jalpaiguri	**92**	26 32N	88 46 E
Jamaica ■	**180**	18 10N	77 30W
Jamalpur, Bangla.	**92**	24 52N	89 56 E
Jamalpur, India	**92**	25 18N	86 28 E
Jambi	**111**	1 38S	103 30 E
James →	**163**	42 52N	97 18W
James B.	**140**	51 30N	80 0W
Jamestown, Australia	**118**	33 10S	138 32 E
Jamestown, N. Dak., U.S.A.	**163**	46 54N	98 42W
Jamestown, N.Y., U.S.A.	**164**	42 5N	79 18W
Jamkhandi	**91**	16 30N	75 15 E
Jammu	**89**	32 43N	74 54 E
Jammu & Kashmir □	**89**	34 25N	77 0 E
Jamnagar	**90**	22 30N	70 6 E
Jamshedpur	**92**	22 44N	86 12 E
Jan Mayen Is.	**13**	71 0N	9 0W
Janesville	**166**	42 39N	89 1W
Januária	**188**	15 25S	44 25W
Jaora	**91**	23 40N	75 10 E
Japan ■	**79**	36 0N	136 0 E
Japan, Sea of	**102**	40 0N	135 0 E
Japurá →	**185**	3 8S	64 46W
Jargalant = Hovd	**100**	48 2N	91 37 E
Jargeau	**39**	47 50N	2 1 E
Jarosław	**58**	50 2N	22 42 E
Jāsk	**85**	25 38N	57 45 E
Jasło	**59**	49 45N	21 30 E
Jasper, Canada	**155**	52 55N	118 5W
Jasper, U.S.A.	**169**	33 48N	87 16W
Jassy = Iaşi	**57**	47 10N	27 40 E
Jataí	**188**	17 58S	51 48W
Jaú	**188**	22 10S	48 30W
Jaunpur	**92**	25 46N	82 44 E
Java, I.	**111**	7 0S	110 0 E
Java Sea	**111**	4 35S	107 15 E
Javhlant = Ulyasutay	**100**	47 56N	97 28 E
Jean Marie River	**144**	61 32N	120 38W
Jean Rabel	**180**	19 50N	73 5W
Jedburgh	**31**	55 28N	2 33W
Jędrzejów	**58**	50 35N	20 15 E
Jefferson, Mt.	**171**	44 45N	121 50W
Jefferson City	**166**	38 34N	92 10W
Jeffersonville	**167**	38 20N	85 42W
Jelenia Góra	**58**	50 50N	15 45 E
Jena	**43**	50 56N	11 33 E
Jenkins	**165**	37 13N	82 41W
Jennings	**168**	30 10N	92 45W
Jeparit	**119**	36 8S	142 1 E
Jequié	**189**	13 51S	40 5W
Jequitinhonha	**189**	16 30S	41 0W
Jérémie	**180**	18 40N	74 10W

Jerez de García Salinas **175** 22 39N 103 0W
Jerez de la Frontera **50** 36 41N 6 7W
Jerez de los Caballeros **50** 38 20N 6 45W
Jericho **121** 23 38S 146 6E
Jerilderie **117** 35 20S 145 41E
Jerome **148** 47 37N 82 14W
Jersey, I. **36** 49 13N 2 7W
Jersey City **164** 40 41N 74 8W
Jerseyville **166** 39 5N 90 20W
Jerusalem **80** 31 47N 35 10E
Jesselton = Kota Kinabalu ... **112** 6 0N 116 4E
Jhang Maghiana **89** 31 15N 72 22E
Jhansi **91** 25 30N 78 36E
Jharsuguda **92** 21 56N 84 5E
Jhelum → **89** 31 20N 72 10E
Jhunjhunu **89** 28 10N 75 30E
Jiamusi **98** 46 40N 130 26E
Ji'an **99** 27 6N 114 59E
Jiangmen **99** 22 32N 113 0E
Jiangsu □ **99** 33 0N 120 0E
Jiangxi □ **99** 27 30N 116 0E
Jian'ou **99** 27 3N 118 17E
Jiao Xian **98** 36 18N 120 1E
Jiaozuo **99** 35 16N 113 12E
Jiaxing **99** 30 49N 120 45E
Jiayi **99** 23 30N 120 24E
Jibuti = Djibouti ■ **133** 12 0N 43 0E
Jiddah **82** 21 29N 39 10E
Jido **93** 29 2N 94 58E
Jihlava **59** 49 28N 15 35E
Jilin **98** 43 44N 126 30E
Jilong **99** 25 8N 121 42E
Jima **132** 7 40N 36 47E
Jiménez **174** 27 8N 104 54W
Jinan **98** 36 38N 117 1E
Jingdezhen **99** 29 20N 117 11E
Jining, Nei Mongol Zizhiqu, China **98** 41 5N 113 0E
Jining, Shandong, China **99** 35 22N 116 34E
Jinja **132** 0 25N 33 12E
Jinnah Barrage **89** 32 58N 71 33E
Jinotega **179** 13 6N 85 59W
Jinotepe **179** 11 50N 86 10W
Jinshi **99** 29 40N 111 50E
Jinzhou **98** 41 5N 121 3E
Jipijapa **184** 1 0S 80 40W
Jiquilpan de Juárez **175** 19 59N 102 43W
Jisr ash Shughūr **80** 35 49N 36 18E
Jiujiang **99** 29 42N 115 58E
Jixi **98** 45 20N 130 50E
João Pessoa **189** 7 10S 34 52W
Jodhpur **91** 26 23N 73 8E
Joensuu **67** 62 37N 29 49E
Jogjakarta = Yogyakarta **111** 7 49S 110 22E
Jōhana **106** 36 30N 136 57E
Johannesburg **137** 26 10S 28 2E
John o' Groats **33** 58 39N 3 3W
Johnson City, N.Y., U.S.A. .. **164** 42 7N 75 57W
Johnson City, Tenn., U.S.A. . **165** 36 18N 82 21W
Johnston **31** 51 45N 5 5W
Johnstown, N.Y., U.S.A. **164** 43 1N 74 20W
Johnstown, Pa., U.S.A. **164** 40 19N 78 53W
Johor □ **96** 2 5N 103 20E
Johor Baharu **96** 1 28N 103 46E
Joigny **39** 48 0N 3 20E
Joinvile **191** 26 15S 48 55E
Joliet **167** 41 30N 88 0W
Joliette **151** 46 3N 73 24W
Jolo **112** 6 0N 121 0E
Jonesboro **169** 35 50N 90 45W
Jönköping **60** 57 45N 14 10E
Jönköpings län □ **61** 57 30N 14 30E
Jonquière **148** 48 27N 71 14W
Joplin **168** 37 0N 94 31W
Jordan ■ **80** 31 0N 36 0E
Jordan → **80** 31 48N 35 32E
Jorhat **93** 26 45N 94 12E
José de San Martín **192** 44 4S 70 26W
Jowzjān □ **87** 36 10N 66 0E
Juan de Fuca Str. **142** 48 15N 124 0W
Juan Fernández, Arch. de **183** 33 50S 80 0W
Juàzeiro **189** 9 30S 40 30W
Juàzeiro do Norte **189** 7 10S 39 18W
Jubbulpore = Jabalpur **91** 23 9N 79 58E
Júcar → **51** 39 5N 0 10W
Juchitán de Zaragoza **177** 16 26N 95 1W
Jugoslavia = Yugoslavia ■ ... **52** 44 0N 20 0E
Juiz de Fora **188** 21 43S 43 19W
Juli **187** 16 10S 69 25W
Juliaca **187** 15 25S 70 10W
Julianehåb **147** 60 43N 46 0W
Jullundur **89** 31 20N 75 40E
Jumla **92** 29 15N 82 13E
Jumna = Yamuna → **92** 25 30N 81 53E
Junagadh **91** 21 30N 70 30E
Jundiaí **191** 24 30S 47 0W
Juneau **143** 58 20N 134 20W
Junee **117** 34 53S 147 35E
Junggar Pendi **100** 44 30N 86 0E
Junín **190** 34 33S 60 57W
Jura, Europe **37** 46 35N 6 5E
Jura, U.K. **30** 56 0N 5 50W
Jurado **184** 7 7N 77 46W
Juruá → **184** 2 37S 65 44W
Juruena **187** 13 0S 58 10W
Juruena → **187** 7 20S 58 3W
Juticalpa **179** 14 40N 86 12W
Jutland = Jylland **61** 56 25N 9 30E
Juventud, I. de la **178** 21 40N 82 40W
Jylland **61** 56 25N 9 30E
Jyväskylä **67** 62 14N 25 50E

Kaapstad = Cape Town **136** 33 55S 18 22E
Kabala **130** 9 38N 11 37W
Kabardino-Balkar-A.S.S.R. □ . **70** 43 30N 43 30E
Kabarega Falls **132** 2 15N 31 30E
Kabīr Kūh **84** 33 0N 47 30E
Kābul **87** 34 28N 69 11E
Kābul □ **87** 34 30N 69 0E
Kabwe **135** 14 30S 28 29E
Kachin □ **93** 26 0N 97 30E
Kadan Kyun **94** 12 30N 98 20E
Kadina **119** 34 0S 137 43E
Kaduna **131** 10 30N 7 21E
Kaédi **126** 16 9N 13 28W
Kāf **80** 31 25N 37 29E
Kafirévs, Ákra **55** 38 9N 24 38E
Kafue → **135** 15 30S 26 0E
Kaga **106** 36 16N 136 15E
Kagoshima **108** 31 35N 130 33E
Kagoshima-Wan **108** 31 25N 130 40E
Kai, Kepulauan **113** 5 55S 132 45W
Kaieteur Falls **185** 5 1N 59 10W
Kaifeng **99** 34 49N 114 30E
Kaikoura Ra. **123** 41 59S 173 41E
Kailua **160** 19 39N 156 0W
Kaimanawa Mts. **122** 39 15S 175 56E
Kainan **106** 34 9N 135 12E
Kainji Res. **131** 10 1N 4 40E
Kaipara Harbour **122** 36 25S 174 14E
Kaiserslautern **42** 49 30N 7 43E
Kaitaia **122** 35 8S 173 17E
Kajaani **67** 64 17N 27 46E
Kajana = Kajaani **67** 64 17N 27 46E
Kakabeka Falls **150** 48 24N 89 37W
Kakamigahara **106** 35 28N 136 48E
Kakanui Mts. **123** 45 10S 170 30E
Kakegawa **107** 34 45N 138 1E
Kakinada **92** 16 57N 82 11E
Kakogawa **109** 34 46N 134 51E
Kalabáka **54** 39 42N 21 39E
Kalahari **136** 24 0S 21 30E
Kalamata **54** 37 3N 22 10E
Kalamazoo **167** 42 20N 85 35W
Kalamazoo → **167** 42 40N 86 12W
Kalat **88** 29 8N 66 31E
Kalaupapa **160** 21 12N 156 59W
Kalemie **135** 5 55S 29 9E
Kalgan = Zhangjiakou **98** 40 48N 114 55E
Kalgoorlie-Boulder **120** 30 40S 121 22E

Kálimnos	**55**	37 0N	27 0 E
Kalinin	**68**	56 55N	35 55 E
Kaliningrad	**68**	54 42N	20 32 E
Kalispell	**162**	48 10N	114 22W
Kalisz	**58**	51 45N	18 8 E
Kalmar	**61**	56 40N	16 20 E
Kalmar län □	**61**	57 25N	16 0 E
Kalmyk A.S.S.R. □	**70**	46 5N	46 1 E
Kalocsa	**59**	46 32N	19 0 E
Kaluga	**68**	54 35N	36 10 E
Kama →	**68**	55 45N	52 0 E
Kamaishi	**103**	39 16N	141 53 E
Kamakura	**107**	35 19N	139 33 E
Kamaran	**82**	15 21N	42 35 E
Kamchatka, P-ov.	**73**	57 0N	160 0 E
Kamenka	**69**	53 10N	44 5 E
Kamensk Uralskiy	**69**	56 25N	62 2 E
Kamenskoye	**73**	62 45N	165 30 E
Kameoka	**106**	35 0N	135 35 E
Kameyama	**106**	34 51N	136 27 E
Kami-koshiki-Jima	**108**	31 50N	129 52 E
Kamioka	**106**	36 25N	137 15 E
Kamloops	**155**	50 40N	120 20W
Kampala	**132**	0 20N	32 30 E
Kampar	**96**	4 18N	101 9 E
Kampen	**41**	52 33N	5 53 E
Kampot	**95**	10 36N	104 10 E
Kampuchea = Cambodia ■	**95**	12 15N	105 0 E
Kamsack	**152**	51 34N	101 54W
Kamui-Misaki	**103**	43 20N	140 21 E
Kamyshin	**68**	50 10N	45 24 E
Kananga	**134**	5 55S	22 18 E
Kanawha →	**165**	38 50N	82 8W
Kanazawa	**106**	36 30N	136 38 E
Kanchenjunga	**92**	27 50N	88 10 E
Kanchipuram	**90**	12 52N	79 45 E
Kandahar = Qandahār	**87**	31 32N	65 30 E
Kandalaksha	**69**	67 9N	32 30 E
Kandi	**131**	11 7N	2 55 E
Kandos	**117**	32 45S	149 58 E
Kandy	**90**	7 18N	80 43 E
Kangar	**97**	6 27N	100 12 E
Kangaroo I.	**119**	35 45S	137 0 E
Kangean Is.	**113**	6 55S	115 23 E
Kangnŭng	**98**	37 45N	128 54 E
Kangto	**93**	27 50N	92 35 E
Kaniapiskau →	**146**	56 40N	69 30W
Kanin, P-ov.	**69**	68 0N	45 0 E
Kaniva	**119**	36 22S	141 18 E
Kankakee	**167**	41 6N	87 50W
Kankakee →	**167**	41 23N	88 16W
Kankan	**130**	10 23N	9 15W
Kanmuri-Yama	**109**	34 30N	132 4 E
Kannapolis	**165**	35 32N	80 37W
Kano	**131**	12 2N	8 30 E
Kan'onji	**109**	34 7N	133 39 E
Kanoya	**108**	31 25N	130 50 E
Kanpur	**91**	26 28N	80 20 E
Kansas □	**161**	38 40N	98 0W
Kansas →	**158**	39 7N	94 36W
Kansas City, Kans., U.S.A.	**166**	39 0N	94 40W
Kansas City, Mo., U.S.A.	**166**	39 3N	94 30W
Kansk	**74**	56 20N	95 37 E
Kansu = Gansu □	**98**	36 0N	104 0 E
Kantō □	**107**	36 15N	139 30 E
Kantō-Sanchi	**107**	35 59N	138 50 E
Kanuma	**107**	36 34N	139 42 E
Kaohsiung = Gaoxiong	**99**	22 38N	120 18 E
Kaolack	**130**	14 5N	16 8W
Kāpīsā □	**87**	35 0N	69 20 E
Kapoeta	**129**	4 50N	33 35 E
Kapuas →	**111**	0 25S	109 20 E
Kapunda	**119**	34 20S	138 56 F
Kapuskasing	**150**	49 25N	82 30W
Kaputar, Mt.	**116**	30 15S	150 10 E
Kara Bogaz Gol, Zaliv	**70**	41 0N	53 30 E
Kara Kalpak A.S.S.R. □	**70**	43 0N	60 0 E
Kara Kum = Karakum, Peski	**70**	39 30N	60 0 E
Kara Sea	**69**	75 0N	70 0 E
Karabük	**80**	41 12N	32 37 E
Karachi	**88**	24 53N	67 0 E
Karad	**91**	17 15N	74 10 E
Karadeniz Boğazı	**80**	41 10N	29 10 E
Karaganda	**71**	49 50N	73 10 E
Karaj	**86**	35 48N	51 0 E
Karakoram Pass	**89**	35 33N	77 50 E
Karakoram Ra.	**89**	35 30N	77 0 E
Karakum, Peski	**70**	39 30N	60 0 E
Karaman	**80**	37 14N	33 13 E
Karamea Bight	**123**	41 22S	171 40 E
Karasuk	**71**	53 44N	78 2 E
Karatau, Khrebet	**71**	43 30N	69 30 E
Karbalā	**84**	32 36N	44 3 E
Karelian A.S.S.R. □	**68**	65 30N	32 30 E
Karen	**94**	12 49N	92 53 E
Kariba Lake	**137**	16 40S	28 25 E
Karimata I.	**111**	1 40S	109 0 E
Karimnagar	**91**	18 26N	79 10 E
Karimunjawa, Kepulauan	**111**	5 50S	110 30 E
Kariya	**106**	34 58N	137 1 E
Karl-Marx-Stadt	**43**	50 50N	12 55 E
Karlskrona	**61**	56 10N	15 35 E
Karlsruhe	**42**	49 3N	8 23 E
Karlstad	**60**	59 23N	13 30 E
Karnal	**89**	29 42N	77 2 E
Karnaphuli Res.	**93**	22 40N	92 20 E
Karnataka □	**90**	13 15N	77 0 E
Kärnten □	**45**	46 52N	13 30 E
Kárpathos	**55**	35 37N	27 10 E
Kars	**81**	40 40N	43 5 E
Karshi	**70**	38 53N	65 48 E
Kasai →	**134**	3 30S	16 10 E
Kasaoka	**109**	34 30N	133 30 E
Kaseda	**108**	31 25N	130 19 E
Kāshān	**86**	34 5N	51 30 E
Kashi	**100**	39 30N	76 2 E
Kashihara	**106**	34 27N	135 46 E
Kashima	**108**	33 7N	130 6 E
Kashima-Nada	**107**	36 0N	140 45 E
Kashiwa	**107**	35 52N	139 59 E
Kāshmar	**86**	35 16N	58 26 E
Kashmir	**78**	34 0N	76 0 E
Kashun Noerh = Gaxun Nur	**100**	42 22N	100 30 E
Kásos	**55**	35 20N	26 55 E
Kassala	**129**	16 0N	36 0 E
Kassel	**42**	51 19N	9 32 E
Kastoría	**54**	40 30N	21 19 E
Kasugai	**106**	35 12N	136 59 E
Kasukabe	**107**	35 58N	139 49 E
Kasumiga-Ura	**107**	36 0N	140 25 E
Kasur	**89**	31 5N	74 25 E
Katanning	**120**	33 40S	117 33 E
Katha	**93**	24 10N	96 30 E
Katherîna, Gebel	**128**	28 30N	33 57 E
Katherine	**114**	14 27S	132 20 E
Kathiawar	**91**	22 20N	71 0 E
Katihar	**92**	25 34N	87 36 E
Katmandu	**92**	27 45N	85 20 E
Katoomba	**117**	33 41S	150 19 E
Katowice	**58**	50 17N	19 5 E
Katsuta	**107**	36 25N	140 31 E
Katsuura	**107**	35 10N	140 20 E
Katsuyama	**106**	36 3N	136 30 E
Kattegatt	**61**	57 0N	11 20 E
Katwijk-aan-Zee	**40**	52 12N	4 24 E
Kauai	**160**	22 0N	159 30W
Kaukauna	**167**	44 20N	88 13W
Kaunas	**68**	54 54N	23 54 E
Kawachi-Nagano	**106**	34 28N	135 31 E
Kawagoe	**107**	35 55N	139 29 E
Kawaguchi	**107**	35 52N	139 45 E
Kawanoe	**109**	34 1N	133 34 E
Kawarau	**122**	45 3S	168 45 E
Kawasaki	**107**	35 35N	139 42 E
Kayah □	**93**	19 15N	97 15 E
Kayes	**130**	14 25N	11 30W
Kayseri	**80**	38 45N	35 30 E
Kazachinskoye	**74**	56 16N	107 36 E
Kazachye	**72**	70 52N	135 58 E
Kazakh S.S.R. □	**71**	50 0N	70 0 E
Kazan	**68**	55 48N	49 3 E
Kazanlúk	**53**	42 38N	25 20 E

Kāzerūn 85 29 38N 51 40 E
Kazo 107 36 7N 139 36 E
Kéa 55 37 35N 24 22 E
Keaau 160 19 37N 155 3W
Kebnekaise 66 67 53N 18 33 E
Kecskemét 59 46 57N 19 42 E
Kedah □ 96 5 50N 100 40 E
Kediri 111 7 51S 112 1 E
Keeling Is. = Cocos Is. 111 12 10S 96 55 E
Keene 164 42 57N 72 17W
Keetmanshoop 136 26 35S 18 8 E
Keewatin 153 49 46N 94 34W
Keewatin □ 145 63 20N 95 0W
Kefallinía 54 38 20N 20 30 E
Keflavík 64 64 2N 22 35W
Keighley 28 53 52N 1 54W
Keith, Australia 119 36 6S 140 20 E
Keith, U.K. 33 57 33N 2 58W
Kelang 96 3 2N 101 26 E
Kelantan □ 96 5 10N 102 0 E
Kelantan → 96 6 13N 102 14 E
Kellerberrin 120 31 36S 117 38 E
Kellogg 162 47 30N 116 5W
Kells = Ceanannus Mor 34 53 42N 6 53W
Kelowna 155 49 50N 119 25W
Kelso, U.K. 31 55 36N 2 27W
Kelso, U.S.A. 171 46 10N 122 57W
Keluang 96 2 3N 103 18 E
Kelvington 152 52 10N 103 30W
Kemerovo 71 55 20N 86 5 E
Kemi 67 65 44N 24 34 E
Kemi → 67 67 30N 28 30 E
Kempsey 116 31 1S 152 50 E
Kendal 28 54 19N 2 44W
Keng Tung 93 21 0N 99 30 E
Kenitra 126 34 15N 6 40W
Kenmare 35 51 52N 9 35W
Kennewick 171 46 11N 119 2W
Keno Hill 144 63 57N 135 18W
Kenora 153 49 47N 94 29W
Kenosha 167 42 33N 87 48W
Kent 164 41 8N 81 20W
Kent □ 25 51 12N 0 40 E
Kent Group 117 39 30S 147 20 E
Kent Pen. 145 68 30N 107 0W
Kentucky □ 167 37 20N 85 0W
Kentucky → 167 38 41N 85 11W
Kenya ■ 133 1 0N 38 0 E
Kenya, Mt. 132 0 10S 37 18 E
Keokuk 166 40 25N 91 24W
Kepsut 80 39 40N 28 9 E
Kerala □ 90 11 0N 76 15 E
Kerang 117 35 40S 143 55 E
Kerch 68 45 20N 36 20 E
Kerki 70 37 50N 65 12 E
Kérkira 54 39 38N 19 50 E
Kerkrade 41 50 53N 6 4 E
Kermadec Is. 122 30 0S 178 15W
Kermān 85 30 15N 57 1 E
Kermān □ 85 30 0N 57 0 E
Kermānshāh = Bākhtarān 84 34 23N 47 0 E
Kerrobert 152 52 0N 109 11W
Kerry □ 35 52 7N 9 35W
Kerulen → 98 48 48N 117 0 E
Kestenga 68 66 0N 31 50 E
Keswick 28 54 35N 3 9W
Ketchikan 143 55 25N 131 40W
Kettering 156 39 41N 84 10W
Kewanee 166 41 18N 89 55W
Keweenaw B. 150 46 56N 88 23W
Key West 159 24 33N 82 0W
Keyser 164 39 26N 79 0W
Khabarovsk 75 48 30N 135 5 E
Khalkhāl 81 37 37N 48 32 E
Khalkís 55 38 27N 23 42 E
Khalmer Yu 69 67 58N 65 1 E
Khambhat 91 22 23N 72 33 E
Khambhat, G. of 91 20 45N 72 30 E
Khamir 82 16 0N 44 0 E
Khānābād 87 36 45N 69 5 E
Khānaqīn 81 34 23N 45 25 E
Khandwa 91 21 49N 76 22 E
Khanewal 89 30 20N 71 55 E
Khaniá 55 35 30N 24 4 E
Khanka, Ozero 75 45 0N 132 24 E
Kharagpur 92 22 20N 87 25 E
Kharkov 68 49 58N 36 20 E
Khartoum = El Khartûm 129 15 31N 32 35 E
Khashm el Girba 129 14 59N 35 58 E
Khaskovo 53 41 56N 25 30 E
Khatanga 72 72 0N 102 20 E
Khatanga → 72 72 55N 106 0 E
Khenchela 127 35 28N 7 11 E
Kherson 68 46 35N 32 35 E
Kheta → 72 71 54N 102 6 E
Khíos, I. 55 38 20N 26 0 E
Khmer Rep. = Cambodia ■ 95 12 15N 105 0 E
Khojak P. 88 30 55N 66 30 E
Kholm 87 36 45N 67 40 E
Khon Kaen 95 16 30N 102 47 E
Khoper → 68 49 30N 42 20 E
Khorāsān □ 86 34 0N 58 0 E
Khorat = Nakhon Ratchasima 95 14 59N 102 12 E
Khorat, Cao Nguyen 95 15 30N 102 50 E
Khorog 71 37 30N 71 36 E
Khorramābād 84 33 30N 48 25 E
Khorrāmshahr 84 30 29N 48 15 E
Khulna 92 22 45N 89 34 E
Khulna □ 92 22 25N 89 35 E
Khushab 89 32 20N 72 20 E
Khūzestān □ 84 31 0N 49 0 E
Khvor 86 33 45N 55 0 E
Khvoy 81 38 35N 45 0 E
Khyber Pass 89 34 10N 71 8 E
Kiama 117 34 40S 150 50 E
Kiangsi = Jiangxi □ 99 27 30N 116 0 E
Kiangsu = Jiangsu □ 99 33 0N 120 0 E
Kichiga 73 59 50N 163 5 E
Kicking Horse Pass 155 51 28N 116 16W
Kidderminster 24 52 24N 2 13W
Kidnappers, C. 122 39 38S 177 5 E
Kiel 43 54 16N 10 8 E
Kielce 58 50 52N 20 42 E
Kieler Bucht 42 54 30N 10 30 E
Kiev = Kiyev 68 50 30N 30 28 E
Kigali 135 1 59S 30 4 E
Kii-Hantō 106 34 0N 135 45 E
Kii-Sanchi 106 34 20N 136 0 E
Kii-Suidō 109 33 40N 135 0 E
Kikládhes □ 55 37 0N 25 0 E
Kikuchi 108 32 59N 130 47 E
Kilcoy 116 26 59S 152 30 E
Kildare □ 35 53 10N 6 50W
Kilimanjaro 132 3 7S 37 20 E
Kilis 80 36 50N 37 10 E
Kilkenny 35 52 40N 7 17W
Kilkenny □ 35 52 35N 7 15W
Killala B. 34 54 20N 9 12W
Killarney, Canada 153 49 10N 99 40W
Killarney, Ireland 35 52 2N 9 30W
Killary Harbour 34 53 38N 9 52W
Killiecrankie, Pass of 33 56 44N 3 46W
Kilmarnock 31 55 36N 4 30W
Kilmore 117 37 25S 144 53 E
Kilrush 35 52 39N 9 30W
Kimba 118 33 8S 136 23 E
Kimberley, Australia 114 16 20S 127 0 E
Kimberley, Canada 155 49 40N 115 59W
Kimberley, S. Africa 136 28 43S 24 46 E
Kinabalu 112 6 3N 116 14 E
Kincardine 150 44 10N 81 40W
Kindersley 152 51 30N 109 10W
Kindia 130 10 0N 12 52W
King Frederick VI Land =
Kong Frederik VI.s Kyst 147 63 0N 43 0W
King George Is. 140 57 20N 80 30W
King I. = Kadan Kyun 94 12 30N 98 20 E
King I., Australia 119 39 50S 144 0 E
King I., Canada 154 52 10N 127 40W
King Sd. 114 16 50S 123 20 E
King William I. 145 69 10N 97 25W
Kingaroy 116 26 32S 151 51 E

Kingman	**173**	35 12N	114 2W
King's Lynn	**29**	52 45N	0 25 E
Kingscote	**119**	35 40S	137 38 E
Kingsport	**165**	36 33N	82 36W
Kingston, Canada	**151**	44 14N	76 30W
Kingston, Jamaica	**180**	18 0N	76 50W
Kingston, N.Z.	**123**	45 20S	168 43 E
Kingston, U.S.A.	**164**	41 55N	74 0W
Kingston South East	**119**	36 51S	139 55 E
Kingstown	**180**	13 10N	61 10W
Kingsville	**150**	42 2N	82 45W
Kingussie	**33**	57 5N	4 2W
Kinistino	**152**	52 57N	105 2W
Kinki □	**106**	33 30N	136 0 E
Kinnairds Hd.	**33**	57 40N	2 0W
Kinsale, Old Hd. of	**35**	51 37N	8 32W
Kinshasa	**134**	4 20S	15 15 E
Kinston	**165**	35 18N	77 35W
Kintyre	**30**	55 30N	5 35W
Kintyre, Mull of	**30**	55 17N	5 55W
Kinu-Gawa →	**107**	35 36N	139 57 E
Kiparissía	**54**	37 15N	21 40 E
Kirensk	**74**	57 50N	107 55 E
Kirgiz S.S.R. □	**71**	42 0N	75 0 E
Kiribati ■	**122**	1 0N	176 0 E
Kırıkkale	**80**	39 51N	33 32 E
Kirin = Jilin	**98**	43 44N	126 30 E
Kiritimati	**123**	1 58N	157 27W
Kirkcaldy	**31**	56 7N	3 10W
Kirkcudbright	**31**	54 50N	4 3W
Kirkee	**91**	18 34N	73 56 E
Kirkintilloch	**31**	55 57N	4 10W
Kirkland Lake	**151**	48 9N	80 2W
Kirksville	**166**	40 8N	92 35W
Kirkūk	**81**	35 30N	44 21 E
Kirkwall	**33**	58 59N	2 59W
Kirov	**69**	58 35N	49 40 E
Kirovabad	**70**	40 45N	46 20 E
Kirovograd	**68**	48 35N	32 20 E
Kirthar Range	**88**	27 0N	67 0 E
Kiruna	**66**	67 52N	20 15 E
Kiryū	**107**	36 24N	139 20 E
Kisangani	**135**	0 35N	25 15 E
Kisarazu	**107**	35 23N	139 55 E
Kiselevsk	**71**	54 5N	86 39 E
Kishangarh	**89**	27 50N	70 30 E
Kishinev	**68**	47 0N	28 50 E
Kishiwada	**106**	34 28N	135 22 E
Kiskunfelégyháza	**59**	46 42N	19 53 E
Kiso-Gawa →	**106**	35 20N	136 45 E
Kisumu	**132**	0 3S	34 45 E
Kita	**130**	13 5N	9 25W
Kita-Ura	**107**	36 0N	140 34 E
Kitakami-Gawa →	**103**	38 25N	141 19 E
Kitakyūshū	**108**	33 50N	130 50 E
Kitale	**132**	1 0N	35 0 E
Kitami	**103**	43 48N	143 54 E
Kitchener	**151**	43 27N	80 29W
Kíthira	**55**	36 9N	23 0 E
Kíthnos	**55**	37 26N	24 27 E
Kitikmeot □	**145**	70 0N	110 0W
Kitimat	**154**	54 3N	128 38W
Kitsuki	**108**	33 25N	131 37 E
Kittakittaooloo, L.	**118**	28 3S	138 14 E
Kitwe	**135**	12 54S	28 13 E
Kiyev	**68**	50 30N	30 28 E
Klagenfurt	**45**	46 38N	14 20 E
Klaipeda	**68**	55 43N	21 10 E
Klamath →	**172**	41 40N	124 4W
Klamath Falls	**171**	42 20N	121 50W
Klamath Mts.	**172**	41 20N	123 0W
Kleena Kleene	**154**	52 0N	124 59W
Klondike	**144**	64 0N	139 26W
Kluane L.	**144**	61 15N	138 40W
Klyuchevsk, mt.	**73**	55 50N	160 30 E
Knaresborough	**28**	54 1N	1 29W
Knockmealdown Mts.	**35**	52 16N	8 0W
Knossos	**55**	35 16N	25 10 E
Knoxville, Iowa, U.S.A.	**166**	41 20N	93 5W
Knoxville, Tenn., U.S.A.	**165**	35 58N	83 57W
Ko Chang	**95**	12 0N	102 20 E
Ko Kut	**95**	11 40N	102 32 E
Koartac	**146**	60 55N	69 40W
Kobarid	**52**	46 15N	13 30 E
Kobayashi	**108**	31 56N	130 59 E
Kobdo = Hovd	**100**	48 2N	91 37 E
Kōbe	**106**	34 45N	135 10 E
København	**61**	55 41N	12 34 E
Koblenz	**42**	50 21N	7 36 E
Kobroor, Kepulauan	**113**	6 10S	134 30 E
Kočani	**53**	41 55N	22 25 E
Kōchi	**109**	33 30N	133 35 E
Kochiu = Gejiu	**99**	23 20N	103 10 E
Kodaira	**107**	35 44N	139 29 E
Kodiak I.	**142**	57 30N	152 45W
Kōfu	**107**	35 40N	138 30 E
Koga	**107**	36 11N	139 43 E
Kogota	**103**	38 33N	141 3 E
Koh-i-Bābā	**87**	34 30N	67 0 E
Kohat	**89**	33 40N	71 29 E
Kokand	**71**	40 30N	70 57 E
Kokchetav	**71**	53 20N	69 25 E
Koko Kyunzu	**94**	14 10N	93 25 E
Kokomo	**167**	40 30N	86 6W
Kokopo	**115**	4 22S	152 19 E
Koksoak →	**146**	58 30N	68 10W
Kokubu	**108**	31 44N	130 46 E
Kola Pen. = Kolskiy Poluostrov	**69**	67 30N	38 0 E
Kolar	**90**	13 12N	78 15 E
Kolar Gold Fields	**90**	12 58N	78 16 E
Kolarovgrad	**53**	43 18N	26 55 E
Kolding	**61**	55 30N	9 29 E
Kolguyev, Ostrov	**69**	69 20N	48 30 E
Kolhapur	**91**	16 43N	74 15 E
Köln	**42**	50 56N	6 58 E
Koło	**58**	52 14N	18 40 E
Kolomna	**68**	55 8N	38 45 E
Kolskiy Poluostrov	**69**	67 30N	38 0 E
Kolyma →	**73**	69 30N	161 0 E
Komagene	**107**	35 44N	137 58 E
Komaki	**106**	35 17N	136 55 E
Komandorskiye, Is.	**73**	55 0N	167 0 E
Komárno	**59**	47 49N	18 5 E
Komatsu	**106**	36 25N	136 30 E
Komatsujima	**109**	34 0N	134 35 E
Komi A.S.S.R. □	**69**	64 0N	55 0 E
Kommunizma, Pik	**71**	39 0N	72 2 E
Komoro	**107**	36 19N	138 26 E
Kompong Cham	**95**	12 0N	105 30 E
Kompong Chhnang	**95**	12 20N	104 35 E
Kompong Som	**95**	10 38N	103 30 E
Komsomolets, Ostrov	**72**	80 30N	95 0 E
Komsomolsk	**75**	50 30N	137 0 E
Konarhá □	**87**	35 30N	71 3 E
Kong	**130**	8 54N	4 36W
Kong, Koh	**95**	11 20N	103 0 E
Kong Christian X.s Land	**13**	74 0N	29 0W
Kong Frederik VI.s Kyst	**147**	63 0N	43 0W
Kong Frederik VIII.s Land	**13**	78 30N	26 0W
Kongor	**129**	7 1N	31 27 E
Königsberg = Kaliningrad	**68**	54 42N	20 32 E
Konin	**58**	52 12N	18 15 E
Konjic	**52**	43 42N	17 58 E
Konosha	**68**	61 0N	40 5 E
Konstanz	**44**	47 39N	9 10 E
Kontagora	**131**	10 23N	5 27 E
Konya	**80**	37 52N	32 35 E
Konya Ovasi	**80**	38 30N	33 0 E
Koolyanobbing	**120**	30 48S	119 36 E
Kopaonik Planina	**52**	43 10N	21 50 E
Kopeysk	**71**	55 7N	61 37 E
Kopparberg	**60**	60 52N	15 0 E
Koppeh Dāgh	**86**	38 0N	58 0 E
Korab	**52**	41 44N	20 40 E
Korça	**52**	40 37N	20 50 E
Korčula	**52**	42 57N	17 8 E
Kordestān □	**81**	36 0N	47 0 E
Korea Bay	**98**	39 0N	124 0 E
Korea Strait	**104**	34 0N	129 30 E
Korhogo	**130**	9 29N	5 28W
Korinthiakós Kólpos	**54**	38 16N	22 30 E

Kórinthos	**54**	37 56N	22 55 E
Kōriyama	**105**	37 24N	140 23 E
Koroit	**119**	38 18S	142 24 E
Kortrijk	**42**	50 50N	3 17 E
Koryakskiy Khrebet	**73**	61 0N	171 0 E
Kos	**55**	36 50N	27 15 E
Kosciusko	**169**	33 3N	89 34W
Kosciusko, Mt.	**117**	36 27S	148 16 E
Koshigaya	**107**	35 54N	139 48 E
K'oshih = Kashi	**100**	39 30N	76 2 E
Koshiki-Rettō	**108**	31 45N	129 49 E
Kōshoku	**107**	36 38N	138 6 E
Košice	**59**	48 42N	21 15 E
Kosovska-Mitrovica	**52**	42 54N	20 52 E
Kôstî	**129**	13 8N	32 43 E
Kostroma	**68**	57 50N	40 58 E
Koszalin	**58**	53 50N	16 8 E
Kota	**91**	25 14N	75 49 E
Kota Baharu	**96**	6 7N	102 14 E
Kota Kinabalu	**112**	6 0N	116 4 E
Kotelnich	**68**	58 20N	48 10 E
Kotka	**67**	60 28N	26 58 E
Kotlas	**69**	61 15N	47 0 E
Kotor	**52**	42 25N	18 47 E
Kotuy →	**77**	71 54N	102 6 E
Kotzebue	**142**	66 50N	162 40W
Kowloon	**99**	22 20N	114 15 E
Kōyama	**108**	31 20N	130 56 E
Koyukuk →	**142**	64 56N	157 30W
Kozáni	**55**	40 19N	21 47 E
Kozhikode = Calicut	**90**	11 15N	75 43 E
Kōzu-Shima	**107**	34 13N	139 10 E
Kra, Isthmus of = Kra, Kho Khot	**94**	10 15N	99 30 E
Kra, Kho Khot	**94**	10 15N	99 30 E
Kragujevac	**52**	44 2N	20 56 E
Kraków	**58**	50 4N	19 57 E
Kraljevo	**52**	43 44N	20 41 E
Krasnodar	**68**	45 5N	39 0 E
Krasnovodsk	**70**	40 0N	52 52 E
Krasnoyarsk	**74**	56 8N	93 0 E
Krasnyy Kut	**68**	50 50N	47 0 E
Kratie	**95**	12 32N	106 10 E
Kravanh, Chuor Phnum	**95**	12 0N	103 32 E
Krefeld	**42**	51 20N	6 32 E
Kremenchug	**68**	49 5N	33 25 E
Krishna →	**91**	15 57N	80 59 E
Krishnanagar	**92**	23 24N	88 33 E
Kristiansand	**60**	58 9N	8 1 E
Kristianstad	**61**	56 2N	14 9 E
Kristianstads län □	**61**	56 15N	14 0 E
Kristiansund	**65**	63 7N	7 45 E
Kríti	**55**	35 15N	25 0 E
Krivoy Rog	**68**	47 51N	33 20 E
Krk	**52**	45 8N	14 40 E
Kronobergs län □	**61**	56 45N	14 30 E
Kronshtadt	**68**	60 5N	29 45 E
Krotoszyn	**58**	51 42N	17 23 E
Krugersdorp	**137**	26 5S	27 46 E
Krung Thep = Bangkok	**94**	13 45N	100 35 E
Kruševac	**52**	43 35N	21 28 E
Krymskiy P-ov.	**68**	45 0N	34 0 E
Kuala Dungun	**96**	4 45N	103 25 E
Kuala Kangsar	**96**	4 46N	100 56 E
Kuala Lipis	**96**	4 10N	102 3 E
Kuala Lumpur	**96**	3 9N	101 41 E
Kuala Pilah	**96**	2 45N	102 15 E
Kuala Trengganu	**96**	5 20N	103 8 E
Kuangchou = Guangzhou	**99**	23 5N	113 10 E
Kuantan	**96**	3 49N	103 20 E
Kubak	**88**	27 10N	63 10 E
Kuban →	**68**	45 20N	37 30 E
Kubokawa	**109**	33 12N	133 8 E
Kuchinoerabu-Jima	**104**	30 28N	130 11 E
Kucing	**111**	1 33N	110 25 E
Kudamatsu	**108**	34 0N	131 52 E
Kueiyang = Guiyang	**99**	26 32N	106 40 E
Kūh-e-Jebāl Bārez	**85**	29 0N	58 0 E
Kūh-e Sorkh	**86**	35 30N	58 45 E
Kūhhā-ye-Bashākerd	**85**	26 45N	59 0 E
Kūhhā-ye Sabalān	**81**	38 15N	47 45 E
Kuji	**103**	40 11N	141 46 E
Kuldja = Yining	**100**	43 58N	81 10 E
Kulunda	**71**	52 35N	78 57 E
Kumagaya	**107**	36 9N	139 22 E
Kumamoto	**108**	32 45N	130 45 E
Kumano	**106**	33 54N	136 5 E
Kumano-Nada	**106**	33 47N	136 20 E
Kumasi	**130**	6 41N	1 38W
Kumon Bum	**93**	26 30N	97 15 E
Kunashir, Ostrov	**75**	44 0N	146 0 E
Kunimi-Dake	**109**	32 33N	131 1 E
Kunlun Shan	**100**	36 0N	86 30 E
Kunming	**101**	25 1N	102 41 E
Kunsan	**98**	35 59N	126 45 E
Kuopio	**67**	62 53N	27 35 E
Kupang	**113**	10 19S	123 39 E
Kurashiki	**109**	34 40N	133 50 E
Kurayoshi	**109**	35 26N	133 50 E
Kure	**109**	34 14N	132 32 E
Kurgan	**71**	55 26N	65 18 E
Kuril Is. = Kurilskiye Ostrova	**75**	45 0N	150 0 E
Kurilskiye Ostrova	**75**	45 0N	150 0 E
Kurnool	**90**	15 45N	78 0 E
Kurobe-Gawe →	**106**	36 55N	137 25 E
Kurri Kurri	**117**	32 50S	151 28 E
Kursk	**68**	51 42N	36 11 E
Kuršumlija	**52**	43 9N	21 19 E
Kurume	**108**	33 15N	130 30 E
Kurunegala	**90**	7 30N	80 23 E
Kusatsu	**106**	34 58N	135 57 E
Kushikino	**108**	31 44N	130 16 E
Kushima	**108**	31 29N	131 14 E
Kushimoto	**106**	33 28N	135 47 E
Kushiro	**103**	43 0N	144 25 E
Kushka	**70**	35 20N	62 18 E
Kushtia	**92**	23 55N	89 5 E
Kuskokwim Bay	**142**	59 50N	162 56W
Kustanay	**71**	53 10N	63 35 E
Kusu	**108**	33 16N	131 9 E
Kütahya	**80**	39 30N	30 2 E
Kutaisi	**70**	42 19N	42 40 E
Kutaraja = Banda Aceh	**111**	5 35N	95 20 E
Kutno	**58**	52 15N	19 23 E
Kuujjuaq	**146**	58 6N	68 15W
Kuwait = Al Kuwayt	**84**	29 30N	47 30 E
Kuwait ■	**84**	29 30N	47 30 E
Kuwana	**106**	35 0N	136 43 E
Kuybyshev	**68**	53 8N	50 6 E
Kwakoegron	**185**	5 12N	55 25W
Kwangju	**98**	35 9N	126 54 E
Kwangsi-Chuang = Guangxi Zhuangzu Zizhiqu □	**99**	24 0N	109 0 E
Kwangtung = Guangdong □	**99**	23 0N	113 0 E
Kweichow = Guizhou □	**99**	27 0N	107 0 E
Kwinana New Town	**120**	32 15S	115 47 E
Kyabram	**117**	36 19S	145 4 E
Kyaukpadaung	**93**	20 52N	95 8 E
Kyle of Lochalsh	**32**	57 17N	5 43W
Kyneton	**117**	37 10S	144 29 E
Kyō-ga-Saki	**106**	35 45N	135 15 E
Kyoga, L.	**132**	1 35N	33 0 E
Kyogle	**116**	28 40S	153 0 E
Kyōto	**106**	35 0N	135 45 E
Kyrenia	**80**	35 20N	33 20 E
Kyūshū	**108**	33 0N	131 0 E
Kyūshū □	**108**	33 0N	131 0 E
Kyūshū-Sanchi	**108**	32 35N	131 17 E
Kyustendil	**53**	42 16N	22 41 E
Kyzyl	**74**	51 50N	94 30 E
Kyzylkum, Peski	**70**	42 30N	65 0 E
Kzyl-Orda	**71**	44 48N	65 28 E
Labe = Elbe →	**42**	53 50N	9 0 E
Laboulaye	**190**	34 10S	63 30W
Labrador, Coast of □	**147**	53 20N	61 0W
Lábrea	**187**	7 15S	64 51W
Lac la Martre	**145**	63 8N	117 16W
Laccadive Is. = Lakshadweep Is.	**78**	10 0N	72 30 E

Lachine	**151**	45 30N	73 40W
Lachute	**151**	45 39N	74 21W
Lackawanna	**164**	42 49N	78 50W
Lacombe	**155**	52 30N	113 44W
Laconia	**148**	43 32N	71 30W
Ladakh Ra.	**89**	34 0N	78 0 E
Ladoga, L. = Ladozhskoye Ozero	**68**	61 15N	30 30 E
Ladozhskoye Ozero	**68**	61 15N	30 30 E
Ladysmith	**154**	49 0N	123 49W
Lae	**115**	6 40S	147 2 E
Lafayette, Ind., U.S.A.	**167**	40 25N	86 54W
Lafayette, La., U.S.A.	**168**	30 18N	92 0W
Laghmān □	**87**	34 20N	70 0 E
Laghouat	**127**	33 50N	2 59 E
Lagny	**39**	48 52N	2 40 E
Lagos, Nigeria	**131**	6 25N	3 27 E
Lagos, Portugal	**50**	37 5N	8 41W
Lagos de Moreno	**175**	21 21N	101 55W
Laguna	**191**	28 30S	48 50W
Laguna Beach	**173**	33 31N	117 52W
Laguna Madre	**158**	27 0N	97 20W
Lagunas, Chile	**187**	21 0S	69 45W
Lagunas, Peru	**186**	5 10S	75 35W
Lahore	**89**	31 32N	74 22 E
Lahti	**67**	60 58N	25 40 E
Lahtis = Lahti	**67**	60 58N	25 40 E
Laï	**131**	9 25N	16 18 E
Laidley	**116**	27 39S	152 20 E
Lairg	**33**	58 1N	4 24W
Laja, R. de la →	**177**	20 55N	100 46W
Lajes	**191**	27 48S	50 20W
Lake Cargelligo	**117**	33 15S	146 22 E
Lake Charles	**168**	30 15N	93 10W
Lake City, Fla., U.S.A.	**170**	30 10N	82 40W
Lake City, S.C., U.S.A.	**165**	33 51N	79 44W
Lake Grace	**120**	33 7S	118 28 E
Lake Harbour	**146**	62 50N	69 50W
Lake Worth	**170**	26 36N	80 3W
Lakeland	**170**	28 0N	82 0W
Lakes Entrance	**117**	37 50S	148 0 E
Lakewood	**167**	41 28N	81 50W
Lakshadweep Is.	**78**	10 0N	72 30 E
Lala Ghat	**93**	24 30N	92 40 E
Lalitpur	**91**	24 42N	78 28 E
Lamar	**163**	38 9N	102 35W
Lambi Kyun	**96**	10 50N	98 20 E
Lameroo	**119**	35 19S	140 33 E
Lamía	**54**	38 55N	22 26 E
Lammermuir Hills	**31**	55 50N	2 40W
Lamon Bay	**112**	14 30N	122 20 E
Lampa	**187**	15 22S	70 22W
Lampang	**94**	18 16N	99 32 E
Lampeter	**26**	52 6N	4 6W
Lamu	**133**	2 16S	40 55 E
Lanark	**31**	55 40N	3 48W
Lancang Jiang →	**101**	21 40N	101 10 E
Lancashire □	**28**	53 40N	2 30W
Lancaster, U.K.	**28**	54 3N	2 48W
Lancaster, U.S.A.	**164**	40 4N	76 19W
Lancaster Sd.	**146**	74 13N	84 0W
Lanchow = Lanzhou	**99**	36 1N	103 52 E
Landes, Les	**36**	44 20N	1 0W
Land's End	**27**	50 4N	5 43W
Landskrona	**61**	55 53N	12 50 E
Lanett	**169**	33 0N	85 15W
Langjökull	**64**	64 39N	20 12W
Langlade	**149**	46 50N	56 20W
Langøya	**64**	68 45N	14 50 E
Langres, Plateau de	**37**	47 45N	5 3 E
Languedoc	**37**	43 58N	4 0 E
Lannion	**36**	48 46N	3 29W
Lansing	**167**	42 47N	84 40W
Lanzhou	**99**	36 1N	103 52 E
Laois □	**35**	53 0N	7 20W
Laon	**38**	49 33N	3 35 E
Laona	**150**	45 32N	88 41W
Laos ■	**95**	17 45N	105 0 E
Lapeer	**167**	43 3N	83 20W
Lapland = Lappland	**67**	68 7N	24 0 E
Lappland	**67**	68 7N	24 0 E
Laptev Sea	**72**	76 0N	125 0 E
Laramie	**163**	41 20N	105 38W
Laramie Mts.	**163**	42 0N	105 30W
Laredo	**161**	27 34N	99 29W
Laren	**40**	52 16N	5 14 E
Largs	**30**	55 48N	4 51W
Lárisa	**54**	39 49N	22 28 E
Larkana	**88**	27 32N	68 18 E
Larnaca	**80**	35 0N	33 35 E
Larne	**34**	54 52N	5 50W
Laryak	**69**	61 15N	80 0 E
Las Cruces	**161**	32 18N	106 50W
Las Lajas	**190**	38 30S	70 25W
Las Palmas	**126**	28 7N	15 26W
Las Vegas, N. Mex., U.S.A.	**161**	35 35N	105 10W
Las Vegas, Nev., U.S.A.	**173**	36 10N	115 5W
Lashio	**93**	22 56N	97 45 E
Latacunga	**184**	0 50S	78 35W
Latakia = Al Lādhiqīyah	**80**	35 30N	35 45 E
Latium = Lazio □	**46**	42 10N	12 30 E
Latrobe	**119**	41 14S	146 30 E
Latur	**91**	18 25N	76 40 E
Latvian S.S.R. □	**68**	56 50N	24 0 E
Lauchhammer	**43**	51 35N	13 48 E
Launceston, Australia	**119**	41 24S	147 8 E
Launceston, U.K.	**27**	50 38N	4 21W
Launglon Bok	**94**	13 50N	97 54 E
Laurel	**169**	31 41N	89 9W
Laurens	**165**	34 32N	82 2W
Laurentian Plat.	**138**	52 0N	70 0W
Laurinburg	**165**	34 50N	79 25W
Lausanne	**44**	46 32N	6 38 E
Laut, Pulau	**111**	3 40S	116 10 E
Laut Ketil, Kepulauan	**113**	4 45S	115 40 E
Lauzon	**148**	46 48N	71 10W
Laval	**36**	48 4N	0 48W
Lávrion	**55**	37 40N	24 4 E
Lawrence, Kans., U.S.A.	**166**	39 0N	95 10W
Lawrence, Mass., U.S.A.	**164**	42 40N	71 9W
Lawrenceburg	**169**	35 12N	87 19W
Lawton	**161**	34 33N	98 25W
Lazio □	**46**	42 10N	12 30 E
Lea →	**25**	51 30N	0 10W
Leader	**152**	50 50N	109 30W
Leadhills	**31**	55 25N	3 47W
Leadville	**163**	39 17N	106 23W
Leamington, Canada	**150**	42 3N	82 36W
Leamington, U.K.	**24**	52 18N	1 32W
Leavenworth	**166**	39 25N	95 0W
Lebanon, Mo., U.S.A.	**166**	37 40N	92 40W
Lebanon, Oreg., U.S.A.	**171**	44 31N	122 57W
Lebanon, Pa., U.S.A.	**164**	40 20N	76 28W
Lebanon, Tenn., U.S.A.	**169**	36 15N	86 20W
Lebanon ■	**80**	34 0N	36 0 E
Lecce	**49**	40 20N	18 10 E
Ledbury	**24**	52 3N	2 25W
Leduc	**155**	53 15N	113 30W
Leeds	**28**	53 48N	1 34W
Leek	**28**	53 7N	2 2W
Leerdam	**40**	51 54N	5 6 E
Leesburg	**170**	28 47N	81 52W
Leeton	**117**	34 33S	146 23 E
Leeuwarden	**41**	53 15N	5 48 E
Leeuwin, C.	**120**	34 20S	115 9 E
Leeward Is.	**181**	16 30N	63 30W
Leghorn = Livorno	**46**	43 32N	10 18 E
Legnica	**58**	51 12N	16 10 E
Leicester	**25**	52 39N	1 9W
Leicester □	**25**	52 40N	1 10W
Leichhardt	**121**	33 53S	151 9 E
Leiden	**40**	52 9N	4 30 E
Leigh Creek South	**118**	30 38S	138 26 E
Leinster	**120**	27 51S	120 36 E
Leinster □	**35**	53 0N	7 10W
Leinster, Mt.	**35**	52 38N	6 47W
Leipzig	**43**	51 20N	12 23 E
Leith	**31**	55 59N	3 10W
Leith Hill	**24**	51 10N	0 23W
Leitrim	**34**	54 0N	8 5W
Lek →	**40**	51 54N	4 35 E
Leleque	**192**	42 28S	71 0W

Léman, Lac **44** 46 26N 6 30 E
Lemmer **41** 52 51N 5 43 E
Lena → **72** 72 52N 126 40 E
Leninabad **71** 40 17N 69 37 E
Leninakan **70** 40 47N 43 50 E
Leningrad **68** 59 55N 30 20 E
Leninsk-Kuznetskiy **71** 54 44N 86 10 E
Leninskoye **75** 47 56N 132 38 E
Lenoir City **165** 35 40N 84 20W
Lens, Belgium **38** 50 33N 3 54 E
Lens, France **37** 50 26N 2 50 E
Lensk **74** 60 48N 114 55 E
Leominster, U.K. **24** 52 15N 2 43W
Leominster, U.S.A. **164** 42 32N 71 45W
León, Mexico **177** 21 7N 101 40W
León, Nic. **179** 12 20N 86 51W
León, Spain **50** 42 38N 5 34W
León □ **50** 42 40N 5 55W
Leongatha **117** 38 30S 145 58 E
Léopold II, Lac = Mai-Ndombe, L. **134** 2 0S 18 20 E
Léopoldville = Kinshasa **134** 4 20S 15 15 E
Lérida **51** 41 37N 0 39 E
Lerwick **30** 60 10N 1 10W
Lesbos, I. = Lésvos **55** 39 10N 26 20 E
Lesotho ■ **137** 29 40S 28 0 E
Lesozavodsk **75** 45 30N 133 29 E
Lesser Antilles **181** 15 0N 61 0W
Lesser Slave L. **155** 55 30N 115 25W
Lésvos **55** 39 10N 26 20 E
Letchworth **25** 51 58N 0 13W
Lethbridge **155** 49 45N 112 45W
Leti, Kepulauan **113** 8 10S 128 0 E
Leticia **184** 4 9S 70 0W
Letsôk-aw Kyun **94** 11 30N 98 25 E
Letterkenny **34** 54 57N 7 42W
Leuven **42** 50 52N 4 42 E
Levanger **65** 63 45N 11 19 E
Levin **122** 40 37S 175 18 E
Lévis **148** 46 48N 71 9W
Levkás **54** 38 40N 20 43 E
Levkôsia = Nicosia **80** 35 10N 33 25 E
Lewes **25** 50 53N 0 2 E
Lewis **32** 58 10N 6 40W
Lewis, Butt of **32** 58 30N 6 12W
Lewis Ra. **162** 48 0N 113 15W
Lewisporte **149** 49 15N 55 3W
Lewiston **148** 44 3N 70 10 E
Lexington, Ky., U.S.A. **165** 38 6N 84 30W
Lexington, Mo., U.S.A. **166** 39 7N 93 55W
Lexington, N.C., U.S.A. **165** 35 50N 80 13W
Lexington, Oreg., U.S.A. **171** 45 29N 119 46W
Lexington Park **165** 38 16N 76 27W
Leyte **112** 11 0N 125 0 E
Lhasa **101** 29 50N 91 3 E
Lhazê **101** 29 5N 87 38 E
Lianyungang **99** 34 40N 119 11 E
Liaoning □ **98** 41 40N 122 30 E
Liaoyuan **98** 42 58N 125 2 E
Liard → **144** 61 51N 121 18W
Libau = Liepaja **68** 56 30N 21 0 E
Liberec **58** 50 47N 15 7 E
Liberia ■ **130** 6 30N 9 30W
Lîbîya, Sahrâ' **128** 27 35N 25 0 E
Libreville **134** 0 25N 9 26 E
Libya ■ **127** 27 0N 17 0 E
Lichfield **28** 52 40N 1 50W
Liechtenstein ■ **44** 47 8N 9 35 E
Liège **42** 50 38N 5 35 E
Liegnitz = Legnica **58** 51 12N 16 10 E
Lienyünchiangshih = Lianyungang **99** 34 40N 119 11 E
Liepaja **68** 56 30N 21 0 E
Liévin **38** 50 24N 2 47 E
Liffey → **35** 53 21N 6 20W
Lifford **34** 54 50N 7 30W
Liguria □ **46** 44 30N 9 0 E
Ligurian Sea **46** 43 20N 9 0 E
Lihou Reefs and Cays **121** 17 25S 151 40 E
Lihue **160** 21 59N 159 24W
Likasi **135** 10 55S 26 48 E
Lille, Belgium **38** 51 15N 4 50 E
Lille, France **37** 50 38N 3 3 E
Lille Bælt **61** 55 20N 9 45 E
Lillehammer **60** 61 8N 10 30 E
Lillers **38** 50 35N 2 28 E
Lillooet **154** 50 44N 121 57W
Lilongwe **137** 14 0S 33 48 E
Lima, Peru **186** 12 0S 77 0W
Lima, U.S.A. **167** 40 42N 84 5W
Limassol **80** 34 42N 33 1 E
Limavady **34** 55 3N 6 58W
Limbe **137** 15 55S 35 2 E
Limburg □ **41** 51 20N 5 55 E
Limeira **188** 22 35S 47 28W
Limerick **35** 52 40N 8 38W
Limerick □ **35** 52 30N 8 50W
Limfjorden **61** 56 55N 9 0 E
Límnos **55** 39 50N 25 5 E
Limoges **36** 45 50N 1 15 E
Limón **179** 10 0N 83 2W
Limousin **36** 46 0N 1 0 E
Limpopo → **137** 25 15S 33 30 E
Linares, Chile **190** 35 50S 71 40W
Linares, Mexico **176** 24 50N 99 40W
Linares, Spain **50** 38 10N 3 40W
Lincoln, Argentina **190** 34 55S 61 30W
Lincoln, U.K. **29** 53 14N 0 32W
Lincoln, Ill., U.S.A. **166** 40 10N 89 20W
Lincoln, Maine, U.S.A. **148** 45 27N 68 29W
Lincoln, Nebr., U.S.A. **156** 40 50N 96 42W
Lincoln □ **29** 53 14N 0 32W
Lincoln Sea **12** 84 0N 55 0W
Lincoln Wolds **29** 53 20N 0 5W
Lindsay, Canada **151** 44 22N 78 43W
Lindsay, U.S.A. **173** 36 14N 119 6W
Línea de la Concepción, La **50** 36 15N 5 23W
Lingga, Kepulauan **111** 0 10S 104 30 E
Linguéré **130** 15 25N 15 5W
Linköping **60** 58 28N 15 36 E
Linlithgow **31** 55 58N 3 38W
Linxia **99** 35 36N 103 10 E
Linz **45** 48 18N 14 18 E
Lion, G. du **37** 43 0N 4 0 E
Lípari, Is. **49** 38 30N 14 50 E
Lipetsk **68** 52 37N 39 35 E
Lippe → **42** 51 39N 6 38 E
Lisboa **50** 38 42N 9 10W
Lisbon = Lisboa **50** 38 42N 9 10W
Lisburn **34** 54 30N 6 9W
Lisburne, C. **142** 68 50N 166 0W
Lisieux **39** 49 10N 0 12 E
Lismore **116** 28 44S 153 21 E
Lister, Mt. **15** 78 0S 162 0 E
Listowel **35** 52 27N 9 30W
Litchfield **166** 39 10N 89 40W
Lithgow **117** 33 25S 150 8 E
Lithuanian S.S.R. □ **68** 55 30N 24 0 E
Little Andaman I. **94** 10 40N 92 15 E
Little Barrier I. **122** 36 12S 175 8 E
Little Current **150** 45 55N 82 0W
Little Falls **164** 43 3N 74 50W
Little Minch **32** 57 35N 6 45W
Little Rann **91** 23 25N 71 25 E
Little Rock **168** 34 41N 92 10W
Littlehampton **25** 50 48N 0 32W
Liuzhou **99** 24 22N 109 22 E
Liverpool, Australia **117** 33 54S 150 58 E
Liverpool, Canada **148** 44 5N 64 41W
Liverpool, U.K. **28** 53 25N 3 0W
Liverpool Plains **116** 31 15S 150 15 E
Livingston, Guat. **177** 15 50N 88 50W
Livingston, U.K. **31** 55 52N 3 33W
Livingston, Mont., U.S.A. **163** 45 40N 110 40W
Livingston, Tex., U.S.A. **168** 30 44N 94 54W
Livingstone **135** 17 46S 25 52 E
Livonia **167** 42 25N 83 23W
Livorno **46** 43 32N 10 18 E
Lizard Pt. **27** 49 57N 5 11W
Ljubljana **52** 46 4N 14 33 E
Ljusnan → **66** 61 12N 17 8 E
Llandeilo **26** 51 53N 4 0W

Llandovery	**26**	51 59N	3 49W
Llandrindod Wells	**26**	52 15N	3 23W
Llandudno	**26**	53 19N	3 51W
Llanelli	**27**	51 41N	4 11W
Llanes	**50**	43 25N	4 50W
Llangollen	**26**	52 58N	3 10W
Llanidloes	**26**	52 28N	3 31W
Llano Estacado	**161**	34 0N	103 0W
Llanos	**184**	5 0N	71 35W
Lloydminster	**152**	53 17N	110 0W
Loc Ninh	**95**	11 50N	106 34 E
Lochaber	**32**	56 55N	5 0W
Lochboisdale	**32**	57 10N	7 20W
Lochem	**41**	52 9N	6 26 E
Lochgilphead	**30**	56 2N	5 37W
Lochinver	**32**	58 9N	5 15W
Lochmaddy	**32**	57 36N	7 10W
Lochy, L.	**32**	56 58N	4 55W
Lock Haven	**164**	41 7N	77 31W
Lockhart	**117**	35 14S	146 40 E
Lockport	**164**	43 12N	78 42W
Lodi	**172**	38 12N	121 16W
Łódź	**58**	51 45N	19 27 E
Lofoten	**64**	68 30N	15 0 E
Logan, Utah, U.S.A.	**163**	41 45N	111 50W
Logan, W. Va., U.S.A.	**165**	37 51N	81 59W
Logan, Mt	**144**	60 31N	140 22W
Logansport	**167**	40 45N	86 21W
Logroño	**51**	42 28N	2 27W
Loire →	**36**	47 16N	2 10W
Loja	**184**	3 59S	79 16W
Lokka	**67**	67 55N	27 35 E
Lolland	**61**	54 45N	11 30 E
Lom	**53**	43 48N	23 12 E
Lomami →	**134**	0 46N	24 16 E
Lombardia □	**46**	45 35N	9 45 E
Lombardy = Lombardia □	**46**	45 35N	9 45 E
Lombok	**113**	8 45S	116 30 E
Lomé	**130**	6 9N	1 20 E
Lomond, L.	**31**	56 8N	4 38W
Lompoc	**173**	34 41N	120 32W
Łomza	**58**	53 10N	22 2 E
London, Canada	**150**	42 59N	81 15W
London, U.K.	**25**	51 30N	0 5W
Londonderry	**34**	55 0N	7 20W
Londrina	**191**	23 18S	51 10W
Long Beach	**173**	33 46N	118 12W
Long I., Bahamas	**178**	23 20N	75 10W
Long I., U.S.A.	**164**	40 50N	73 20W
Long Range Mts.	**149**	49 30N	57 30W
Long Xuyen	**95**	10 19N	105 28 E
Longford, Australia	**119**	41 32S	147 3 E
Longford, Ireland	**34**	53 43N	7 50W
Longford □	**34**	53 42N	7 45W
Longlac	**150**	49 45N	86 25W
Longmont	**163**	40 10N	105 4W
Longreach	**121**	23 28S	144 14 E
Longview, Tex., U.S.A.	**168**	32 30N	94 45W
Longview, Wash., U.S.A.	**171**	46 9N	122 58W
Looe	**27**	50 24N	4 25W
Loop Hd.	**35**	52 34N	9 55W
Lop Nor	**100**	40 20N	90 10 E
Lopez, C.	**134**	0 47S	8 40 E
Lorain	**167**	41 28N	82 55W
Lorca	**51**	37 41N	1 42W
Lord Howe I.	**122**	31 33S	159 6 E
Lordsburg	**161**	32 22N	108 45W
Lorient	**36**	47 45N	3 23W
Lorn	**30**	56 26N	5 10W
Lorn, Firth of	**30**	56 20N	5 40W
Lorraine	**37**	49 0N	6 0 E
Los Alamos	**161**	35 57N	106 17W
Los Andes	**190**	32 50S	70 40W
Los Angeles, Chile	**190**	37 28S	72 23W
Los Angeles, U.S.A.	**173**	34 0N	118 10W
Los Angeles Aqueduct	**173**	35 25N	118 0W
Los Hermanos	**181**	11 45N	84 25W
Los Mochis	**174**	25 45N	108 57W
Los Testigos	**181**	11 23N	63 6W
Lošinj	**52**	44 30N	14 30 E
Lossiemouth	**33**	57 43N	3 17W
Lot →	**36**	44 18N	0 20 E
Lota	**190**	37 5S	73 10W
Lothian □	**31**	55 50N	3 0W
Loughborough	**29**	52 46N	1 11W
Loughrea	**35**	53 11N	8 33W
Louisbourg	**149**	45 55N	60 0W
Louise I.	**154**	52 55N	131 50W
Louisiana □	**168**	30 50N	92 0W
Louisville, Ky., U.S.A.	**167**	38 15N	85 45W
Louisville, Miss., U.S.A.	**169**	33 7N	89 3W
Lourdes	**36**	43 6N	0 3W
Lourenço-Marques = Maputo	**137**	25 58S	32 32 E
Louth	**29**	53 23N	0 0 E
Louth □	**34**	53 55N	6 30W
Louvain = Leuven	**42**	50 52N	4 42 E
Louviers	**39**	49 12N	1 10 E
Lowell	**164**	42 38N	71 19W
Lower Austria = Niederösterreich □	**45**	48 25N	15 40 E
Lower California = Baja California	**174**	31 10N	115 12W
Lower Hutt	**123**	41 10S	174 55 E
Lower Saxony = Niedersachsen □	**42**	52 45N	9 0 E
Lowestoft	**25**	52 29N	1 44 E
Łowicz	**58**	52 6N	19 55 E
Loxton	**119**	34 28S	140 31 E
Loyalty Is. = Loyauté, Is.	**122**	21 0S	167 30 E
Loyang = Luoyang	**99**	34 40N	112 26 E
Loyauté, Is.	**122**	21 0S	167 30 E
Lualaba →	**135**	0 26N	25 20 E
Luan Chau	**95**	21 38N	103 24 E
Luanda	**134**	8 50S	13 15 E
Luang Prabang	**95**	19 52N	102 10 E
Luarca	**50**	43 32N	6 32W
Lubbock	**161**	33 40N	101 53W
Lübeck	**43**	53 52N	10 41 E
Lublin	**58**	51 12N	22 38 E
Lubnān, J.	**80**	33 50N	35 45 E
Lubumbashi	**135**	11 40S	27 28 E
Lucca	**46**	43 50N	10 30 E
Luce Bay	**30**	54 45N	4 48W
Lučenec	**59**	48 18N	19 42 E
Lucerne = Luzern	**44**	47 3N	8 18 E
Lucknow	**92**	26 50N	81 0 E
Lüda = Dalian	**98**	38 50N	121 40 E
Lüderitz	**136**	26 41S	15 8 E
Ludhiana	**89**	30 57N	75 56 E
Ludington	**167**	43 58N	86 27W
Ludlow	**24**	52 23N	2 42W
Ludwigshafen	**42**	49 27N	8 27 E
Lufkin	**168**	31 25N	94 40W
Lugano	**44**	46 0N	8 57 E
Lugansk = Voroshilovgrad	**68**	48 38N	39 15 E
Lugo	**50**	43 2N	7 35W
Lugovoye	**71**	42 55N	72 43 E
Luján	**190**	34 45S	59 5W
Łuków	**58**	51 55N	22 23 E
Lule älv →	**67**	65 35N	22 10 E
Luleå	**67**	65 35N	22 10 E
Lüleburgaz	**80**	41 23N	27 22 E
Lulua →	**134**	6 30S	22 50 E
Luluabourg = Kananga	**134**	5 55S	22 18 E
Lumberton	**165**	34 37N	78 59W
Lundy	**27**	51 10N	4 41W
Lune →	**28**	54 0N	2 51W
Lüneburg	**43**	53 15N	10 23 E
Lüneburg Heath = Lüneburger Heide	**43**	53 0N	10 0 E
Lüneburger Heide	**43**	53 0N	10 0 E
Lūni →	**91**	24 41N	71 14 E
Luoyang	**99**	34 40N	112 26 E
Lurgan	**34**	54 28N	6 20W
Lusaka	**135**	15 28S	28 16 E
Luta = Dalian	**98**	38 50N	121 40 E
Luton	**25**	51 53N	0 24W
Lutsk	**68**	50 50N	25 15 E
Luvua →	**135**	6 50S	27 30 E
Luxembourg	**42**	49 37N	6 9 E
Luxembourg ■	**42**	50 0N	6 0 E
Luzern	**44**	47 3N	8 18 E

Luzhou	**99**	28 52N	105 20 E
Luziânia	**188**	16 20S	48 0W
Luzon	**112**	16 0N	121 0 E
Lvov	**68**	49 50N	24 0 E
Lyakhovskiye, Ostrova	**72**	73 40N	141 0 E
Lyallpur = Faisalabad	**89**	31 30N	73 5 E
Lyell I.	**154**	52 40N	131 35W
Lyell Range	**123**	41 38S	172 20 E
Lyme Regis	**27**	50 44N	2 57W
Lymington	**24**	50 46N	1 32W
Lynchburg	**165**	37 23N	79 10W
Lynn	**164**	42 28N	70 57W
Lynn Lake	**152**	56 51N	101 3W
Lynton	**27**	51 14N	3 50W
Lyon	**37**	45 46N	4 50 E
Lyons = Lyon	**37**	45 46N	4 50 E
Lytham St. Anne's	**28**	53 45N	2 58W
Lyttelton	**122**	43 35S	172 44 E
Ma'ān	**80**	30 12N	35 44 E
Ma'anshan	**99**	31 44N	118 29 E
Ma'arrat an Nu'mān	**80**	35 43N	36 43 E
Maas →	**40**	51 45N	4 32 E
Maaseik	**41**	51 6N	5 45 E
Maastricht	**41**	50 50N	5 40 E
Mablethorpe	**29**	53 21N	0 14 E
McAlester	**168**	34 57N	95 46W
Macao = Macau ■	**99**	22 16N	113 35 E
Macapá	**185**	0 5N	51 4W
Macau	**189**	5 0S	36 40W
Macau ■	**99**	22 16N	113 35 E
McBride	**155**	53 20N	120 19W
Macclesfield	**28**	53 16N	2 9W
McClure Str.	**12**	75 0N	119 0W
McComb	**169**	31 13N	90 30W
McCook	**163**	40 15N	100 35W
McDermitt	**172**	42 0N	117 45W
Macdonald L.	**114**	23 30S	129 0 E
Macdonnell Ranges	**114**	23 40S	133 0 E
McDouall Peak	**118**	29 51S	134 55 E
Macduff	**33**	57 40N	2 30W
Macedonia = Makedhonía □	**55**	40 39N	22 0 E
Maceió	**189**	9 40S	35 41W
Macfarlane, L.	**118**	32 0S	136 40 E
Macgillycuddy's Reeks	**35**	52 2N	9 45W
Machala	**184**	3 20S	79 57W
Machida	**107**	35 28N	139 23 E
Machilipatnam	**92**	16 12N	81 8 E
Machiques	**184**	10 4N	72 34W
Machynlleth	**26**	52 36N	3 51W
Mackay	**121**	21 8S	149 11 E
Mackay, L.	**114**	22 30S	129 0 E
McKeesport	**164**	40 21N	79 50W
Mackenzie →	**144**	69 10N	134 20W
Mackenzie Bay	**12**	69 0N	137 30W
Mackenzie Mts.	**144**	64 0N	130 0W
McKinley, Mt.	**142**	63 2N	151 0W
McKinley Sea	**13**	84 0N	10 0W
McKinney	**168**	33 10N	96 40W
Macksville	**116**	30 40S	152 56 E
Maclean	**116**	29 26S	153 16 E
McLennan	**155**	55 42N	116 50W
MacLeod Lake	**154**	54 58N	123 0W
M'Clintock Chan.	**145**	72 0N	102 0W
McMinnville, Oreg., U.S.A.	**171**	45 16N	123 11W
McMinnville, Tenn., U.S.A.	**169**	35 43N	85 45W
McMurdo Sd.	**15**	77 0S	170 0 E
McMurray = Fort McMurray	**155**	56 44N	111 7W
McNaughton L.	**155**	52 0N	118 10W
Macomb	**166**	40 25N	90 40W
Mâcon, France	**37**	46 19N	4 50 E
Mâcon, U.S.A.	**170**	32 50N	83 37W
McPherson	**161**	38 25N	97 40W
Macpherson Ra.	**116**	28 15S	153 15 E
Macquarie →	**116**	30 5S	147 30 E
Macquarie Is.	**15**	54 36S	158 55 E
MacRobertson Land	**14**	71 0S	64 0 E
Macroom	**35**	51 54N	8 57W
Madagascar ■	**137**	20 0S	47 0 E
Madang	**115**	5 12S	145 49 E
Madaripur	**93**	23 19N	90 15 E
Made	**40**	51 41N	4 49 E
Madeira	**126**	32 50N	17 0W
Madeira →	**185**	3 22S	58 45W
Madeleine, Îs. de la	**149**	47 30N	61 40W
Madera	**173**	37 0N	120 1W
Madhya Pradesh □	**91**	21 50N	81 0 E
Madison, Fla., U.S.A.	**170**	30 29N	83 39W
Madison, Ind., U.S.A.	**167**	38 42N	85 20W
Madison, Wis., U.S.A.	**166**	43 5N	89 25W
Madisonville	**167**	37 20N	87 30W
Madiun	**111**	7 38S	111 32 E
Madras = Tamil Nadu □	**90**	11 0N	77 0 E
Madras, India	**90**	13 8N	80 19 E
Madras, U.S.A.	**171**	44 40N	121 10W
Madre, Laguna	**176**	25 0N	97 30W
Madre de Dios →	**187**	10 59S	66 8W
Madre del Sur, Sa.	**177**	17 0N	100 0W
Madre Occidental, Sa.	**174**	25 0N	105 0W
Madre Oriental, Sa.	**177**	22 0N	99 30W
Madrid	**50**	40 25N	3 45W
Madura, Selat	**111**	7 30S	113 20 E
Madurai	**90**	9 55N	78 10 E
Madurantakam	**90**	12 30N	79 50 E
Mae Rim	**94**	18 54N	98 57 E
Maebashi	**107**	36 24N	139 4 E
Maesteg	**27**	51 36N	3 40W
Maestra, Sierra	**178**	20 15N	77 0W
Mafeking	**152**	52 40N	101 10W
Maffra	**117**	37 53S	146 58 E
Mafia	**135**	7 45S	39 50 E
Mafikeng	**136**	25 50S	25 38 E
Mafra	**191**	26 10S	50 0W
Magadan	**73**	59 38N	150 50 E
Magallanes, Estrecho de	**192**	52 30S	75 0W
Magangué	**184**	9 14N	74 45W
Magdalena, Bolivia	**187**	13 13S	63 57W
Magdalena, Mexico	**174**	30 38N	110 57W
Magdalena →	**184**	11 6N	74 51W
Magdeburg	**43**	52 8N	11 36 E
Magelang	**111**	7 29S	110 13 E
Magellan's Str. = Magallanes, Estrecho de	**192**	52 30S	75 0W
Magherafelt	**34**	54 44N	6 37W
Magnitogorsk	**71**	53 27N	59 4 E
Magog	**148**	45 18N	72 9W
Magosa = Famagusta	**80**	35 8N	33 55 E
Magrath	**155**	49 25N	112 50W
Mahābād	**81**	36 50N	45 45 E
Mahajanga □	**137**	17 0S	47 0 E
Mahakam →	**111**	0 35S	117 17 E
Maḥallāt	**86**	33 55N	50 30 E
Mahanadi →	**92**	20 20N	86 25 E
Maharashtra □	**91**	20 30N	75 30 E
Mahbubnagar	**91**	16 45N	77 59 E
Mahia Pen.	**122**	39 9S	177 55 E
Mahón	**51**	39 53N	4 16 E
Mahone Bay	**148**	44 30N	64 20W
Mahukona	**160**	20 11N	155 52W
Mai-Ndombe, L.	**134**	2 0S	18 20 E
Maidenhead	**25**	51 31N	0 42W
Maiduguri	**131**	12 0N	13 20 E
Maikala Ra.	**92**	22 0N	81 0 E
Main →	**42**	50 0N	8 18 E
Maine	**36**	48 0N	0 0 E
Maine □	**148**	45 20N	69 0W
Mainland, Orkney, U.K.	**33**	59 0N	3 10W
Mainland, Shetland, U.K.	**30**	60 15N	1 22W
Mainpuri	**89**	27 18N	79 4 E
Mainz	**42**	50 0N	8 17 E
Maiquetía	**184**	10 36N	66 57W
Maisi, Pta. de	**178**	20 10N	74 10W
Maitland, N.S.W., Australia	**117**	32 33S	151 36 E
Maitland, S. Austral., Australia	**119**	34 23S	137 40 E
Maiz, Islas del	**179**	12 15N	83 4W
Maizuru	**106**	35 25N	135 22 E
Majorca, I. = Mallorca	**51**	39 30N	3 0 E
Makarikari = Makgadikgadi Salt Pans	**136**	20 40S	25 45 E
Makasar = Ujung Pandang	**113**	5 10S	119 20 E

Makasar, Selat	**113**	1 0S	118 20 E
Makedhonía □	**55**	40 39N	22 0 E
Makena	**160**	20 39N	156 27W
Makeyevka	**68**	48 0N	38 0 E
Makgadikgadi Salt Pans	**136**	20 40S	25 45 E
Makhachkala	**70**	43 0N	47 30 E
Makkah	**82**	21 30N	39 54 E
Makó	**59**	46 14N	20 33 E
Makran Coast Range	**88**	25 40N	64 0 E
Makurazaki	**108**	31 15N	130 20 E
Makurdi	**131**	7 43N	8 35 E
Malabar Coast	**90**	11 0N	75 0 E
Malacca, Str. of	**111**	3 0N	101 0 E
Malad City	**162**	42 10N	112 20 E
Málaga	**50**	36 43N	4 23W
Malakal	**129**	9 33N	31 50 E
Malang	**111**	7 59S	112 45 E
Mälaren	**60**	59 30N	17 10 E
Malatya	**81**	38 25N	38 20 E
Malawi ■	**137**	13 0S	34 0 E
Malawi, L.	**137**	12 30S	34 30 E
Malay Pen.	**97**	7 25N	100 0 E
Malāyer	**84**	34 19N	48 51 E
Malaysia ■	**111**	5 0N	110 0 E
Malbaie, La	**148**	47 40N	70 10W
Malbork	**58**	54 3N	19 1 E
Malcolm	**120**	28 51S	121 25 E
Maldives ■	**78**	7 0N	73 0 E
Maldonado	**191**	35 0S	55 0W
Malebo, Pool	**134**	4 17S	15 20 E
Malegaon	**91**	20 30N	74 38 E
Mali ■	**130**	15 0N	2 0W
Mali Kyun	**94**	13 0N	98 20 E
Malin Hd.	**34**	55 18N	7 24W
Malindi	**133**	3 12S	40 5 E
Malines = Mechelen	**42**	51 2N	4 29 E
Mallaig	**32**	57 0N	5 50W
Mallorca	**51**	39 30N	3 0 E
Mallow	**35**	52 8N	8 40W
Malmédy	**42**	50 25N	6 2 E
Malmö	**61**	55 36N	12 59 E
Malmöhus län □	**61**	55 45N	13 30 E
Malone	**151**	44 50N	74 19W
Malta ■	**49**	35 50N	14 30 E
Malton	**29**	54 9N	0 48W
Maluku	**113**	1 0S	127 0 E
Malvern, U.K.	**24**	52 7N	2 19W
Malvern, U.S.A.	**168**	34 22N	92 50W
Malvern Hills	**24**	52 0N	2 19W
Malvinas, Is. = Falkland Is.	**192**	51 30S	59 0W
Mamers	**39**	48 21N	0 22 E
Mamoré →	**187**	10 23S	65 53W
Mamou	**130**	10 15N	12 0W
Man	**130**	7 30N	7 40W
Man, I. of	**28**	54 15N	4 30W
Mana, Fr. Gui.	**185**	5 45N	53 55W
Mana, U.S.A.	**160**	22 3N	159 45W
Manaar, Gulf of = Mannar, G. of	**90**	8 30N	79 0 E
Manacapuru	**185**	3 16S	60 37W
Manado	**113**	1 29N	124 51 E
Managua	**179**	12 6N	86 20W
Manaos = Manaus	**185**	3 0S	60 0W
Manapouri	**123**	45 34S	167 39 E
Manaung	**93**	18 45N	93 40 E
Manaus	**185**	3 0S	60 0W
Mancha, La	**50**	39 10N	2 54W
Manchester, U.K.	**28**	53 30N	2 15W
Manchester, U.S.A.	**164**	42 58N	71 29W
Mandalay	**93**	22 0N	96 4 E
Mandale = Mandalay	**93**	22 0N	96 4 E
Mandurah	**120**	32 36S	115 48 E
Manfredónia, G. di	**49**	41 30N	16 10 E
Mangalore	**90**	12 55N	74 47 E
Mangla Dam	**89**	33 9N	73 44 E
Mangole	**113**	1 50S	125 55 E
Mangonui	**122**	35 1S	173 32 E
Mangyshlak P-ov.	**70**	44 30N	52 30 E
Manhattan	**158**	39 10N	96 40W
Manicoré	**185**	5 48S	61 16W
Manicouagan →	**148**	49 30N	68 30W
Manila	**112**	14 40N	121 3 E
Manilla	**116**	30 45S	150 43 E
Manipur □	**93**	25 0N	94 0 E
Manisa	**80**	38 38N	27 30 E
Manistee	**167**	44 15N	86 20W
Manistique	**150**	45 59N	86 18W
Manitoba □	**153**	55 30N	97 0W
Manitoba, L.	**153**	51 0N	98 45W
Manitoulin I.	**150**	45 40N	82 30W
Manitowoc	**167**	44 8N	87 40W
Manizales	**184**	5 5N	75 32W
Manjil	**81**	36 46N	49 30 E
Manjimup	**120**	34 15S	116 6 E
Mankato	**166**	44 8N	93 59W
Manly	**117**	33 48S	151 17 E
Mannar, G. of	**90**	8 30N	79 0 E
Mannar I.	**90**	9 5N	79 45 E
Mannheim	**42**	49 28N	8 29 E
Mannum	**119**	34 50S	139 20 E
Manosque	**37**	43 49N	5 47 E
Manouane, L.	**148**	50 45N	70 45W
Mans, Le	**39**	48 0N	0 10 E
Mansel I.	**146**	62 0N	80 0W
Mansfield, Australia	**117**	37 4S	146 6 E
Mansfield, U.K.	**29**	53 8N	1 12W
Mansfield, U.S.A.	**167**	40 45N	82 30W
Manta	**184**	1 0S	80 40W
Mantes-la-Jolie	**39**	49 0N	1 41 E
Mantiqueira, Serra da	**188**	22 0S	44 0W
Mántova	**46**	45 20N	10 42 E
Mantua = Mántova	**46**	45 20N	10 42 E
Manu	**187**	12 10S	70 51W
Manukau	**122**	35 14S	173 13 E
Manyara, L.	**135**	3 40S	35 50 E
Manzanillo, Cuba	**178**	20 20N	77 31W
Manzanillo, Mexico	**175**	19 3N	104 20W
Manzhouli	**98**	49 35N	117 25 E
Mapimí	**174**	25 49N	103 51W
Maple	**152**	43 51N	79 31W
Maputo	**137**	25 58S	32 32 E
Maquinchao	**192**	41 15S	68 50W
Mar, Serra do	**191**	25 30S	49 0W
Mar Chiquita, L.	**190**	30 40S	62 50W
Mar del Plata	**191**	38 0S	57 30W
Mar Menor, L.	**51**	37 40N	0 45W
Marabá	**188**	5 20S	49 5W
Maracaibo	**184**	10 40N	71 37W
Maracaibo, Lago de	**184**	9 40N	71 30W
Maracay	**184**	10 15N	67 28W
Marajó, Ilha de	**188**	1 0S	49 30W
Maranhão = São Luís	**188**	2 39S	44 15W
Maranhão □	**188**	5 0S	46 0W
Marañón →	**186**	4 30S	73 35W
Maraş	**80**	37 37N	36 53 E
Marathón	**55**	38 11N	23 58 E
Marbella	**50**	36 30N	4 57W
Marble Bar	**114**	21 9S	119 44 E
March	**25**	52 33N	0 5 E
Marché	**36**	46 0N	1 20 E
Marche □	**47**	43 22N	13 10 E
Marchena	**50**	37 18N	5 23W
Marches = Marche □	**47**	43 22N	13 10 E
Mardan	**89**	34 20N	72 0 E
Mardin	**81**	37 20N	40 43 E
Mareeba	**121**	16 59S	145 28 E
Margarita	**175**	9 20N	79 55W
Margarita I.	**185**	11 0N	64 0W
Margate	**25**	51 23N	1 24 E
Mari, A.S.S.R. □	**68**	56 30N	48 0 E
Maria van Diemen, C.	**122**	34 29S	172 40 E
Marianao	**178**	23 8N	82 24W
Marianna	**169**	30 45N	85 15W
Maribor	**52**	46 36N	15 40 E
Maricourt	**146**	61 30N	72 0W
Marie-Galante	**180**	15 56N	61 16W
Marienberg	**41**	52 30N	6 35 E
Marietta, Ga., U.S.A.	**169**	34 0N	84 30W
Marietta, Ohio, U.S.A.	**164**	39 27N	81 27W
Marília	**188**	22 13S	50 0W
Marín	**50**	42 23N	8 42W
Marinette	**167**	45 4N	87 40W

Maringá	**191**	23 26S	52 2W
Marion, Ill., U.S.A.	**166**	37 45N	88 55W
Marion, Ind., U.S.A.	**167**	40 35N	85 40W
Marion, Ohio, U.S.A.	**167**	40 38N	83 8W
Marken	**40**	52 26N	5 12 E
Market Drayton	**28**	52 55N	2 30W
Market Harborough	**25**	52 29N	0 55W
Market Rasen	**29**	53 24N	0 20W
Markham Mt.	**15**	83 0S	164 0 E
Marlborough	**24**	51 26N	1 44W
Marlborough □	**123**	41 45S	173 33 E
Marlborough Downs	**24**	51 25N	1 55W
Marlin	**168**	31 25N	96 50W
Marmagao	**91**	15 25N	73 56 E
Marmara, Sea of = Marmara Denizi	**80**	40 45N	28 15 E
Marmara Denizi	**80**	40 45N	28 15 E
Marmaris	**80**	36 50N	28 14 E
Marne →	**39**	8 23N	18 36 E
Maroochydore	**116**	26 29S	153 5 E
Marquesas Is.	**123**	9 30S	140 0W
Marquette	**150**	46 30N	87 21W
Marrakech	**126**	31 9N	8 0W
Marree	**118**	29 39S	138 1 E
Marsabit	**133**	2 18N	38 0 E
Marseille	**37**	43 18N	5 23 E
Marseilles = Marseille	**37**	43 18N	5 23 E
Marshall, Minn., U.S.A.	**166**	44 25N	95 45W
Marshall, Mo., U.S.A.	**166**	39 8N	93 15W
Marshall, Tex., U.S.A.	**168**	32 29N	94 20W
Marshalltown	**166**	42 5N	92 56W
Marshfield	**166**	44 42N	90 10W
Martaban, G. of	**93**	16 5N	96 30 E
Martha's Vineyard	**164**	41 25N	70 35W
Martigues	**37**	43 24N	5 4 E
Martinique	**180**	14 40N	61 0W
Martinsburg	**164**	39 30N	77 57W
Martinsville, Ind., U.S.A.	**167**	39 29N	86 23W
Martinsville, Va., U.S.A.	**165**	36 41N	79 52W
Marton	**122**	40 4S	175 23 E
Marugame	**109**	34 15N	133 40 E
Maruoka	**106**	36 9N	136 16 E
Marwar	**91**	25 43N	73 45 E
Mary	**70**	37 40N	61 50 E
Maryborough = Port Laoise	**35**	53 2N	7 20W
Maryborough, Queens., Australia	**116**	25 31S	152 37 E
Maryborough, Vic., Australia	**117**	37 0S	143 44 E
Maryland □	**164**	39 10N	76 40W
Maryport	**28**	54 43N	3 30W
Marysville	**172**	39 14N	121 40W
Maryville	**165**	35 50N	84 0W
Marzūq	**127**	25 53N	13 57 E
Masan	**98**	35 11N	128 32 E
Masaya	**179**	12 0N	86 7W
Masbate, I.	**112**	12 21N	123 36 E
Mascota	**175**	20 32N	104 49W
Maseru	**137**	29 18S	27 30 E
Mashhad	**86**	36 20N	59 35 E
Masisea	**186**	8 35S	74 22W
Masjed Soleyman	**84**	31 55N	49 18 E
Mask, L.	**34**	53 36N	9 24W
Mason City	**166**	43 9N	93 12W
Masqat	**83**	23 37N	58 36 E
Massachusetts □	**164**	42 25N	72 0W
Massawa = Mitsiwa	**132**	15 35N	39 25 E
Massena	**151**	44 52N	74 55W
Massif Central	**37**	45 30N	2 21 E
Massillon	**167**	40 47N	81 30W
Mastanli = Momchilgrad	**53**	41 33N	25 23 E
Masterton	**123**	40 56S	175 39 E
Mastūrah	**82**	23 7N	38 52 E
Masuda	**108**	34 40N	131 51 E
Matachewan	**151**	47 56N	80 39W
Matadi	**134**	5 52S	13 31 E
Matagalpa	**179**	13 0N	85 58W
Matamoros, Coahuila, Mexico	**174**	25 32N	103 15W
Matamoros, Puebla, Mexico	**177**	18 2N	98 17W
Matane	**148**	48 50N	67 33W
Matanzas	**178**	23 0N	81 40W
Matapan, C. = Taínaron, Ákra	**54**	36 22N	22 27 E
Matarani	**186**	77 0S	72 10W
Matehuala	**177**	23 39N	100 39W
Mathura	**89**	27 30N	77 40 E
Matlock	**28**	53 8N	1 32W
Mato Grosso □	**188**	14 0S	55 0W
Mato Grosso, Planalto do	**188**	15 0S	59 57W
Matopo Hills	**137**	20 36S	28 20 E
Matrah	**83**	23 37N	58 30 E
Matsubara	**106**	34 33N	135 34 E
Matsudo	**107**	35 47N	139 54 E
Matsue	**109**	35 25N	133 10 E
Matsumoto	**107**	36 15N	138 0 E
Matsusaka	**106**	34 34N	136 32 E
Matsutō	**106**	36 31N	136 34 E
Matsuura	**108**	33 20N	129 49 E
Matsuyama	**109**	33 45N	132 45 E
Mattancheri	**90**	9 50N	76 15 E
Mattawa	**151**	46 20N	78 45W
Matterhorn	**44**	45 58N	7 39 E
Matucana	**186**	11 55S	76 25W
Maturín	**185**	9 45N	63 11W
Mau Ranipur	**91**	25 16N	79 8 E
Maubeuge	**38**	50 17N	3 57 E
Maudin Sun	**93**	16 0N	94 30 E
Maui	**160**	20 45N	156 20 E
Maulamyaing	**93**	16 30N	97 40 E
Mauna Kea	**160**	19 50N	155 28W
Mauna Loa	**160**	21 8N	157 10W
Maungmagan Kyunzu	**94**	14 0N	97 48 E
Mauritania ■	**126**	20 50N	10 0W
Mauritius ■	**9**	20 0S	57 0 E
Mawlaik	**93**	23 40N	94 26 E
May Pen	**180**	17 58N	77 15W
Maya →	**75**	54 31N	134 41 E
Mayagüez	**180**	18 12N	67 9W
Mayerthorpe	**155**	53 57N	115 8W
Mayfield	**169**	36 45N	88 40W
Maykop	**70**	44 35N	40 25 E
Maynooth	**34**	53 22N	6 38W
Mayo	**144**	63 38N	135 57W
Mayo □	**34**	53 47N	9 7W
Mayor I.	**122**	37 16S	176 17 E
Maysville	**167**	38 39N	83 46W
Mazagán = El Jadida	**126**	33 11N	8 17W
Mazán	**186**	3 30S	73 0W
Mazar-e Sharīf	**87**	36 41N	67 0 E
Mazarredo	**192**	47 10S	66 50W
Mazatenango	**177**	14 35N	91 30W
Mazatlán	**175**	23 13N	106 25W
Mbandaka	**134**	0 1N	18 18 E
Mdina	**49**	35 51N	14 25 E
Mead, L.	**173**	36 1N	114 44W
Meadville	**164**	41 39N	80 9W
Meander River	**145**	59 2N	117 42W
Meath □	**34**	53 32N	6 40W
Meaux	**39**	48 58N	2 50 E
Mecca = Makkah	**82**	21 30N	39 54 E
Mechelen	**42**	51 2N	4 29 E
Mecklenburger Bucht	**42**	54 20N	11 40 E
Medan	**111**	3 40N	98 38 E
Medellín	**184**	6 15N	75 35W
Medford	**171**	42 20N	122 52W
Mediaş	**57**	46 9N	24 22 E
Medicine Hat	**152**	50 0N	110 45W
Medina = Al Madīnah	**82**	24 35N	39 52 E
Medina	**167**	41 9N	81 50W
Medina del Campo	**50**	41 18N	4 55W
Mediterranean Sea	**124**	35 0N	15 0 E
Medley	**152**	54 25N	110 16W
Médoc	**36**	45 10N	0 56W
Medvezhi, Ostrava	**73**	71 0N	161 0 E
Medway →	**25**	51 28N	0 45 E
Meekatharra	**120**	26 32S	118 29 E
Meerut	**89**	29 1N	77 42 E
Mega	**133**	3 57N	38 19 E
Mégantic, L.	**148**	45 32N	70 53W
Mégara	**55**	37 58N	23 22 E
Meghalaya □	**93**	25 50N	91 0 E
Mei Xian	**99**	24 16N	116 6 E
Meknès	**126**	33 57N	5 33W
Mekong →	**95**	9 30N	106 15 E

Melaka	**96**	2 15N	102 15 E
Melaka □	**96**	2 15N	102 15 E
Melanesia	**122**	4 0S	155 0 E
Melbourne	**117**	37 50S	145 0 E
Melchor Muzquiz	**174**	27 53N	101 31W
Melfort	**152**	52 50N	104 37W
Melilla	**126**	35 21N	2 57W
Melitopol	**68**	46 50N	35 22 E
Melo	**191**	32 20S	54 10W
Melrose	**31**	53 35N	2 44W
Melton Mowbray	**29**	52 46N	0 52W
Melun	**39**	48 32N	2 39 E
Melville	**152**	50 55N	102 50W
Melville, L.	**147**	53 30N	60 0W
Melville I., Australia	**114**	11 30S	131 0 E
Melville I., Canada	**12**	75 30N	112 0W
Melville Pen.	**146**	68 0N	84 0W
Memel = Klaipeda	**68**	55 43N	21 10 E
Memphis	**169**	35 7N	90 0W
Menai Strait	**26**	53 14N	4 10W
Ménaka	**131**	15 59N	2 18 E
Menan = Chao Phraya →	**94**	13 32N	100 36 E
Menasha	**167**	44 13N	88 27W
Mende	**37**	44 31N	3 30 E
Mendip Hills	**27**	51 17N	2 40W
Mendocino	**172**	39 26N	123 50W
Mendoza	**190**	32 50S	68 52W
Menindee	**118**	32 20S	142 25 E
Menindee, L.	**118**	32 20S	142 25 E
Menominee	**150**	45 9N	87 39W
Menorca	**51**	40 0N	4 0 E
Mentawai, Kepulauan	**111**	2 0S	99 0 E
Menzies	**120**	29 40S	120 58 E
Meppel	**41**	52 42N	6 12 E
Merbein	**119**	34 10S	142 2 E
Merca	**133**	1 48N	44 50 E
Merced	**172**	37 18N	120 30W
Mercedes, Buenos Aires, Argentina	**190**	34 40S	59 30W
Mercedes, Corrientes, Argentina	**191**	29 10S	58 5W
Mercedes, San Luis, Argentina	**190**	33 40S	65 21W
Mercedes, Uruguay	**191**	33 12S	58 0W
Mere	**24**	51 5N	2 16W
Mergui Arch. = Myeik Kyunzu	**94**	11 30N	97 30 E
Mérida, Mexico	**177**	20 58N	89 37W
Mérida, Spain	**50**	38 55N	6 25W
Mérida, Venezuela	**184**	8 24N	71 8W
Mérida, Cord. de	**182**	9 0N	71 0W
Meriden	**164**	41 33N	72 47W
Meridian	**169**	32 20N	88 42W
Merowe	**129**	18 29N	31 46 E
Merredin	**120**	31 28S	118 18 E
Merrill	**156**	45 11N	89 41W
Merritt	**155**	50 10N	120 45W
Merriwa	**116**	32 6S	150 22 E
Mersey →	**28**	53 20N	2 56W
Merseyside □	**28**	53 25N	2 55W
Mersin	**80**	36 51N	34 36 E
Merthyr Tydfil	**27**	51 45N	3 23W
Méru	**39**	49 13N	2 8 E
Merville	**38**	50 38N	2 38 E
Mesa	**160**	33 20N	111 56W
Mesa, La	**173**	32 48N	117 5W
Meshed = Mashhad	**86**	36 20N	59 35 E
Mesolóngion	**54**	38 21N	21 28 E
Mesopotamia = Al Jazirah	**81**	33 30N	44 0 E
Mesquite	**173**	36 47N	114 6W
Messina, Italy	**49**	38 10N	15 32 E
Messina, S. Africa	**137**	22 20S	30 0 E
Messina, Str. di	**49**	38 5N	15 35 E
Messíni	**54**	37 4N	22 1 E
Meta →	**184**	6 12N	67 28W
Metairie	**169**	29 59N	90 9W
Metán	**190**	25 30S	65 0W
Metropolis	**169**	37 10N	88 47W
Metz	**37**	49 8N	6 10 E
Meuse →	**42**	50 45N	5 41 E
Mexia	**168**	31 38N	96 32W
Mexicali	**174**	32 40N	115 29W
México, Mexico	**177**	19 20N	99 10W
México, U.S.A.	**166**	39 10N	91 55W
México □	**177**	19 20N	99 30W
Mexico ■	**174**	20 0N	100 0W
Mexico, G. of	**138**	25 0N	90 0W
Mezen →	**69**	66 11N	43 59 E
Mhow	**91**	22 33N	75 50 E
Miahuatlán	**177**	16 21N	96 36W
Miami	**170**	25 45N	80 15W
Miami Beach	**170**	25 49N	80 6W
Mīāneh	**81**	37 30N	47 40 E
Mianwali	**89**	32 38N	71 28 E
Miaoli	**99**	24 37N	120 49 E
Miass	**69**	54 59N	60 6 E
Michigan □	**167**	44 40N	85 40W
Michigan, L.	**150**	44 0N	87 0W
Michigan City	**167**	41 42N	86 56W
Michikamau L.	**147**	54 20N	63 10W
Michipicoten	**150**	47 55N	84 55W
Michoacán □	**175**	19 10N	101 50W
Michurinsk	**68**	52 58N	40 27 E
Micronesia	**122**	11 0N	160 0 E
Mid Glamorgan □	**27**	51 40N	3 25W
Middelburg	**40**	51 30N	3 36 E
Middle Andaman I.	**94**	12 30N	92 30 E
Middlesboro	**165**	36 36N	83 43W
Middlesbrough	**29**	54 35N	1 14W
Middleton	**148**	44 57N	65 4W
Middletown, Conn., U.S.A.	**164**	41 37N	72 40W
Middletown, N.Y., U.S.A.	**164**	41 28N	74 28W
Middletown, Ohio, U.S.A.	**167**	39 29N	84 25W
Midland, Canada	**151**	44 45N	79 50W
Midland, Mich., U.S.A.	**167**	43 37N	84 17W
Midland, Tex., U.S.A.	**161**	32 0N	102 3W
Międzyrzec Podlaski	**58**	51 58N	22 45 E
Miercurea Ciuc	**57**	46 21N	25 48 E
Mieres	**50**	43 18N	5 48W
Migennes	**39**	47 58N	3 31 E
Mihara	**109**	34 24N	133 5 E
Miki	**109**	34 48N	134 59 E
Míkonos	**55**	37 30N	25 25 E
Mikuni-Tōge	**107**	36 50N	138 50 E
Mikura-Jima	**107**	33 52N	139 36 E
Milagro	**184**	2 11S	79 36W
Milan = Milano	**46**	45 28N	9 10 E
Milano	**46**	45 28N	9 10 E
Milâs	**80**	37 20N	27 50 E
Mildura	**119**	34 13S	142 9 E
Miles	**116**	26 40S	150 9 E
Miles City	**163**	46 24N	105 50W
Milford	**164**	38 52N	75 27W
Milford Haven	**27**	51 43N	5 2W
Milk →	**163**	48 5N	106 15W
Millau	**37**	44 8N	3 4 E
Millicent	**119**	37 34S	140 21 E
Millinocket	**148**	45 45N	68 45W
Millmerran	**116**	27 53S	151 16 E
Millom	**28**	54 13N	3 16W
Millville	**164**	39 22N	75 0W
Milne Inlet	**146**	72 30N	80 0W
Mílos	**55**	36 44N	24 25 E
Milton Keynes	**25**	52 3N	0 42W
Milwaukee	**167**	43 9N	87 58W
Milwaukie	**171**	45 27N	122 39W
Minamata	**108**	32 10N	130 30 E
Minas	**191**	34 20S	55 10W
Minas Gerais □	**188**	18 50S	46 0W
Minatitlán	**177**	17 59N	94 31W
Mindanao	**112**	8 0N	125 0 E
Mindanao Sea = Bohol Sea	**112**	9 0N	124 0 E
Minden	**168**	32 40N	93 20W
Mindoro	**112**	13 0N	121 0 E
Mindoro Strait	**112**	12 30N	120 30 E
Mine	**108**	34 12N	131 7 E
Minehead	**27**	51 12N	3 29W
Mineral Wells	**161**	32 50N	98 5W
Mingan	**148**	50 20N	64 0W
Mingenew	**120**	29 12S	115 21 E
Minho □	**50**	41 25N	8 20W
Minneapolis	**166**	44 58N	93 20W
Minnedosa	**153**	50 14N	99 50W

Minnesota □	**156**	46 40N	94 0W
Mino	**106**	35 32N	136 55 E
Mino-Kamo	**106**	35 23N	137 2 E
Mino-Mikawa-Kōgen	**106**	35 10N	137 23 E
Minorca = Menorca	**51**	40 0N	4 0 E
Minot	**163**	48 10N	101 15W
Minsk	**68**	53 52N	27 30 E
Mintaka Pass	**89**	37 0N	74 58 E
Miquelon, I.	**149**	47 2N	56 20W
Miraj	**91**	16 50N	74 45 E
Miranda do Douro	**50**	41 30N	6 16W
Mirpur Khas	**88**	25 30N	69 0 E
Mirzapur	**92**	25 10N	82 34 E
Mirzapur-cum-Vindhyachal = Mirzapur	**92**	25 10N	82 34 E
Miscou I.	**148**	47 57N	64 31W
Mishawaka	**167**	41 40N	86 8W
Mishima	**107**	35 10N	138 52 E
Miskitos, Cayos	**179**	14 26N	82 50W
Miskolc	**59**	48 7N	20 50 E
Misool	**113**	1 52S	130 10 E
Misrātah	**127**	32 24N	15 3 E
Mission City	**154**	49 10N	122 15W
Mississippi □	**169**	33 0N	90 0W
Mississippi →	**169**	29 0N	89 15W
Mississippi, Delta of the	**169**	29 15N	90 30W
Missoula	**162**	46 52N	114 0W
Missouri □	**166**	38 25N	92 30W
Missouri →	**166**	38 50N	90 8W
Mistassini L.	**151**	51 0N	73 30W
Mitaka	**107**	35 40N	139 33 E
Mitchell, Australia	**116**	26 29S	147 58 E
Mitchell, U.S.A.	**163**	43 40N	98 0W
Mitchell →	**115**	15 12S	141 35 E
Mitilíni	**55**	39 6N	26 35 E
Mito	**107**	36 20N	140 30 E
Mitsiwa	**132**	15 35N	39 25 E
Mitsukaidō	**107**	36 1N	139 59 E
Mittagong	**117**	34 28S	150 29 E
Mitú	**184**	1 8N	70 3W
Miura	**107**	35 12N	139 40 E
Miyake-Jima	**107**	34 0N	139 30 E
Miyako	**103**	39 40N	141 59 E
Miyakonojō	**108**	31 40N	131 5 E
Miyanojō	**108**	31 54N	130 27 E
Miyazaki	**108**	31 56N	131 30 E
Miyazu	**106**	35 35N	135 10 E
Miyoshi	**109**	34 48N	132 51 E
Mizamis = Ozamis	**112**	8 15N	123 50 E
Mizen Hd.	**35**	51 27N	9 50W
Mizoram □	**93**	23 30N	92 40 E
Mizunami	**106**	35 22N	137 15 E
Mława	**58**	53 9N	20 25 E
Mobara	**107**	35 25N	140 18 E
Moberley	**166**	39 25N	92 25W
Mobile	**169**	30 41N	88 3W
Mobutu Sese Seko, L.	**132**	1 30N	31 0 E
Moçâmedes = Namibe	**134**	15 7S	12 11 E
Moctezuma, R. →	**177**	21 59N	98 34W
Módena	**46**	44 39N	10 55 E
Modesto	**172**	37 43N	121 0W
Moe	**117**	38 12S	146 19 E
Moei →	**94**	17 25N	98 10 E
Moengo	**185**	5 45N	54 20W
Moffat	**31**	55 20N	3 27W
Mogadishu = Muqdisho	**133**	2 2N	45 25 E
Mogador = Essaouira	**126**	31 32N	9 42W
Mogami →	**103**	38 45N	140 0 E
Mogi das Cruzes	**191**	23 31S	46 11W
Mogilev	**68**	53 55N	30 18 E
Mointy	**71**	47 10N	73 18 E
Moisie	**148**	50 12N	66 1W
Mojave Desert	**173**	35 0N	116 30W
Mold	**26**	53 10N	3 10W
Moldavian S.S.R. □	**68**	47 0N	28 0 E
Molde	**65**	62 45N	7 9 E
Molfetta	**49**	41 12N	16 35 E
Moline	**166**	41 30N	90 30W
Molise □	**49**	41 45N	14 30 E
Mollendo	**187**	17 0S	72 0W
Mölndal	**60**	57 40N	12 3 E
Molong	**117**	33 5S	148 54 E
Molopo →	**136**	28 30S	20 13 E
Molotov = Perm	**69**	58 0N	57 10 E
Molucca Sea	**113**	4 0S	124 0 E
Moluccas = Maluku	**113**	1 0S	127 0 E
Mombasa	**135**	4 2S	39 43 E
Mombetsu	**103**	42 27N	142 4 E
Momchilgrad	**53**	41 33N	25 23 E
Mompós	**184**	9 14N	74 26W
Møn	**61**	54 57N	12 15 E
Mona, Canal de la	**180**	18 30N	67 45W
Monach Is.	**32**	57 32N	7 40W
Monaco ■	**37**	43 46N	7 23 E
Monaghan	**34**	54 15N	6 58W
Monaghan □	**34**	54 10N	7 0W
Monastir = Bitola	**52**	41 5N	21 10 E
Mönchengladbach	**42**	51 12N	6 23 E
Monchique	**50**	37 19N	8 38W
Monclova	**174**	26 50N	101 30W
Moncton	**148**	46 7N	64 51W
Monessen	**164**	40 9N	79 50W
Monforte	**50**	39 6N	7 25W
Mongalla	**129**	5 8N	31 42 E
Monghyr = Munger	**92**	25 23N	86 30 E
Mongolia ■	**98**	47 0N	103 0 E
Monmouth, U.K.	**26**	51 48N	2 43W
Monmouth, U.S.A.	**166**	40 50N	90 40W
Monroe, La., U.S.A.	**168**	32 32N	92 4W
Monroe, Mich., U.S.A.	**167**	41 55N	83 26W
Monroe, N.C., U.S.A.	**165**	35 2N	80 37W
Monrovia, Liberia	**130**	6 18N	10 47W
Monrovia, U.S.A.	**173**	34 7N	118 1W
Mons	**42**	50 27N	3 58 E
Mont-de-Marsan	**36**	43 54N	0 31W
Mont Laurier	**151**	46 35N	75 30W
Montague	**172**	41 47N	122 30W
Montana □	**163**	47 0N	110 0W
Montargis	**39**	48 0N	2 43 E
Montauban	**36**	44 0N	1 21 E
Montbéliard	**37**	47 31N	6 48 E
Montceau-les-Mines	**37**	46 40N	4 23 E
Montdidier	**38**	49 38N	2 35 E
Monte-Carlo	**37**	43 46N	7 23 E
Monte Caseros	**191**	30 10S	57 50W
Montego Bay	**180**	18 30N	78 0W
Montélimar	**37**	44 33N	4 45 E
Montemorelos	**176**	25 11N	99 42W
Montenegro = Crna Gora □	**52**	42 40N	19 20 E
Monterey	**173**	36 35N	121 57W
Montería	**184**	8 46N	75 53W
Monterrey	**176**	25 40N	100 30W
Montes Claros	**188**	16 30S	43 50W
Montevideo, Uruguay	**191**	34 50S	56 11W
Montevideo, U.S.A.	**166**	44 55N	95 40W
Montgomery = Sahiwal	**89**	30 45N	73 8 E
Montgomery, U.K.	**26**	52 34N	3 9W
Montgomery, U.S.A.	**169**	32 20N	86 20W
Montluçon	**37**	46 22N	2 36 E
Montmagny	**148**	46 58N	70 34W
Montmorency	**148**	46 53N	71 11W
Montpelier, Idaho, U.S.A.	**163**	42 15N	111 20W
Montpelier, Vt., U.S.A.	**151**	44 15N	72 38W
Montpellier	**37**	43 37N	3 52 E
Montréal	**151**	45 31N	73 34W
Montrose, U.K.	**33**	56 43N	2 28W
Montrose, U.S.A.	**163**	38 30N	107 52W
Montserrat	**180**	16 40N	62 10W
Monywa	**93**	22 7N	95 11 E
Monze, C.	**88**	24 47N	66 37 E
Mo'oka	**107**	36 26N	140 1 E
Moonta	**119**	34 6S	137 32 E
Moora	**120**	30 37S	115 58 E
Moorfoot Hills	**31**	55 44N	3 8W
Moorhead	**156**	46 51N	96 44W
Mooroopna	**117**	36 25S	145 22 E
Moose Jaw	**152**	50 24N	105 30W
Moosehead L.	**148**	45 34N	69 40W
Moosomin	**152**	50 9N	101 40W
Moosonee	**140**	51 17N	80 39W
Mopti	**130**	14 30N	4 0W
Moradabad	**89**	28 50N	78 50 E

Moranbah	**121**	22 1S	148 6 E
Moratuwa	**90**	6 45N	79 55 E
Morava →	**59**	48 10N	16 59 E
Moravian Hts. = Ceskomoravská Vrchovina	**59**	49 30N	15 40 E
Morawa	**120**	29 13S	116 0 E
Morawhanna	**185**	8 30N	59 40W
Moray Firth	**33**	57 50N	3 30W
Morden	**153**	49 15N	98 10W
Mordovian A.S.S.R.□	**68**	54 20N	44 30 E
Møre og Romsdal fylke □	**65**	62 30N	8 0 E
Morecambe	**28**	54 5N	2 52W
Morecambe B.	**28**	54 7N	3 0W
Moree	**116**	29 28S	149 54 E
Morehead City	**165**	34 46N	76 44W
Morelia	**175**	19 42N	101 7W
Morelos □	**177**	18 45N	99 0W
Morena, Sierra	**50**	38 20N	4 0W
Moresby I.	**154**	52 30N	131 40W
Morgan City	**168**	29 40N	91 15W
Morganton	**165**	35 46N	81 48W
Morgantown	**164**	39 39N	79 58W
Moriguchi	**106**	34 44N	135 34 E
Morlaix	**36**	48 36N	3 52W
Mornington	**117**	38 15S	145 5 E
Moro G.	**112**	6 30N	123 0 E
Morocco ■	**126**	32 0N	5 50W
Moroleón	**177**	20 8N	101 12W
Morón	**178**	22 8N	78 39W
Morotai	**113**	2 10N	128 30 E
Morrilton	**168**	35 10N	92 45W
Morrinhos	**188**	17 45S	49 10W
Morris	**153**	49 25N	97 22W
Morristown	**165**	36 18N	83 20W
Mortes, R. das →	**188**	11 45S	50 44W
Mortlake	**119**	38 5S	142 50 E
Moruya	**117**	35 58S	150 3 E
Morvern	**30**	56 38N	5 44W
Morwell	**117**	38 10S	146 22 E
Moscos Is.	**94**	14 0N	97 30 E
Moscow = Moskva	**68**	55 45N	37 35 E
Moscow	**171**	46 45N	116 59W
Mosel →	**42**	50 22N	7 36 E
Moselle = Mosel →	**42**	50 22N	7 36 E
Mosgiel	**123**	45 53S	170 21 E
Mosjøen	**65**	65 51N	13 12 E
Moskva	**68**	55 45N	37 35 E
Mosquera	**184**	2 35N	78 24W
Mosquitos, Golfo de los	**179**	9 15N	81 10W
Moss Vale	**117**	34 32S	150 25 E
Mosselbaai	**136**	34 11S	22 8 E
Mossman	**121**	16 21S	145 15 E
Mossoró	**189**	5 10S	37 15W
Mostaganem	**127**	35 54N	0 5 E
Mostar	**52**	43 22N	17 50 E
Mosul = Al Mawşil	**81**	36 15N	43 5 E
Motala	**60**	58 32N	15 1 E
Motherwell	**31**	55 48N	4 0W
Motihari	**92**	26 30N	84 55 E
Motueka	**123**	41 7S	173 1 E
Motul	**177**	21 6N	89 17W
Moúdhros	**55**	39 50N	25 18 E
Moule	**180**	16 20N	61 22W
Moulins	**37**	46 35N	3 19 E
Moultrie	**170**	31 11N	83 47W
Moundsville	**164**	39 53N	80 43W
Mount Airy	**165**	36 31N	80 37W
Mount Barker, S. Austral., Australia	**119**	35 5S	138 52 E
Mount Barker, W. Austral., Australia	**120**	34 38S	117 40 E
Mount Carmel	**167**	38 20N	87 48W
Mount Forest	**151**	43 59N	80 43W
Mount Gambier	**119**	37 50S	140 46 E
Mount Isa	**115**	20 42S	139 26 E
Mount Lofty Ra.	**119**	34 35S	139 5 E
Mount Magnet	**120**	28 2S	117 47 E
Mount Maunganui	**122**	37 40S	176 14 E
Mount Morgan	**121**	23 40S	150 25 E
Mount Pearl	**149**	47 31N	52 47W
Mount Pleasant, Mich., U.S.A.	**167**	43 35N	84 47W
Mount Pleasant, Tex., U.S.A.	**168**	33 5N	95 0W
Mount Sterling	**165**	38 0N	84 0W
Mount Vernon, Ill., U.S.A.	**166**	38 17N	88 57W
Mount Vernon, N.Y., U.S.A.	**164**	40 57N	73 49W
Mount Vernon, Wash., U.S.A.	**171**	48 25N	122 20W
Mount Whaleback	**114**	23 18S	119 44 E
Mountain City	**172**	41 54N	116 0W
Mountain View	**172**	37 26N	122 5W
Moura, Australia	**121**	24 35S	149 58 E
Moura, Brazil	**185**	1 32S	61 38W
Mourne →	**34**	54 45N	7 39W
Mourne Mts.	**34**	54 10N	6 0W
Moyale	**133**	3 30N	39 0 E
Mozambique ■	**137**	19 0S	35 0 E
Mozambique Chan.	**137**	20 0S	39 0 E
Mu Us Shamo	**98**	39 0N	109 0 E
Muaná	**188**	1 25S	49 15W
Muang Chiang Rai	**94**	19 52N	99 50 E
Muck	**32**	56 50N	6 15W
Mucuri	**189**	18 0S	39 36W
Mudanjiang	**98**	44 38N	129 30 E
Mudgee	**117**	32 32S	149 31 E
Muğla	**80**	37 15N	28 22 E
Mukden = Shenyang	**98**	41 50N	123 25 E
Mukhtuya = Lensk	**74**	60 48N	114 55 E
Mukinbudin	**120**	30 55S	118 5 E
Muktsar	**89**	30 30N	74 30 E
Mulchén	**190**	37 45S	72 20W
Mulgrave	**149**	45 38N	61 31W
Mulhacén	**50**	37 4N	3 20W
Mülheim	**42**	51 26N	6 53 E
Mulhouse	**37**	47 40N	7 20 E
Mull	**30**	56 27N	6 0W
Muller, Pegunungan	**111**	0 30N	113 30 E
Mullet Pen.	**34**	54 10N	10 2W
Mullewa	**120**	28 29S	115 30 E
Mullingar	**34**	53 31N	7 20W
Mullumbimby	**116**	28 30S	153 30 E
Multan	**89**	30 15N	71 36 E
Muna	**113**	5 0S	122 30 E
München	**43**	48 8N	11 33 E
Munchen-Gladbach = Mönchengladbach	**42**	51 12N	6 23 E
Muncie	**167**	40 10N	85 20W
Mundo Novo	**189**	11 50S	40 29W
Mungana	**121**	17 8S	144 27 E
Munger	**92**	25 23N	86 30 E
Munich = München	**43**	48 8N	11 33 E
Munising	**150**	46 25N	86 39W
Munku-Sardyk	**74**	51 45N	100 20 E
Münster	**42**	51 58N	7 37 E
Munster □	**35**	52 20N	8 40W
Muqdisho	**133**	2 2N	45 25 E
Murallón, Cuerro	**192**	49 48S	73 30W
Murchison →	**120**	27 45S	114 0 E
Murchison Falls = Kabarega Falls	**132**	2 15N	31 30 E
Murcia	**51**	38 20N	1 10W
Murcia □	**51**	37 50N	1 30W
Mureş →	**56**	46 15N	20 13 E
Mureşul = Mureş →	**56**	46 15N	20 13 E
Murfreesboro	**169**	35 50N	86 21W
Murgon	**116**	26 15S	151 54 E
Müritz See	**43**	53 25N	12 40 E
Murmansk	**69**	68 57N	33 10 E
Muroran	**103**	42 25N	141 0 E
Muroto	**109**	33 18N	134 9 E
Muroto-Misaki	**109**	33 15N	134 10 E
Murphysboro	**166**	37 50N	89 20W
Murray	**169**	36 40N	88 20W
Murray →	**119**	35 20S	139 22 E
Murray Bridge	**119**	35 6S	139 14 E
Murrumbidgee →	**117**	34 43S	143 12 E
Murrurundi	**116**	31 42S	150 51 E
Murtoa	**119**	36 35S	142 28 E
Murupara	**122**	38 28S	176 42 E
Murwillumbah	**116**	28 18S	153 27 E
Muş	**81**	38 45N	41 30 E
Musashino	**107**	35 42N	139 34 E
Muscat = Masqat	**83**	23 37N	58 36 E
Muscat & Oman = Oman ■	**83**	23 0N	58 0 E

Muscatine . . . 166 41 25N 91 5W
Musgrave Ras. . . . 114 26 0S 132 0E
Musi → . . . 111 2 20S 104 56E
Muskegon . . . 167 43 15N 86 17W
Muskegon → . . . 167 43 25N 86 0W
Muskegon Hts. . . . 167 43 12N 86 17W
Muskogee . . . 168 35 50N 95 25W
Musselburgh . . . 31 55 57N 3 3W
Muswellbrook . . . 116 32 16S 150 56E
Mutare . . . 137 18 58S 32 38E
Mutsu . . . 103 41 5N 140 55E
Mutsu-Wan . . . 103 41 5N 140 55E
Muzaffargarh . . . 89 30 5N 71 14E
Muzaffarnagar . . . 89 29 26N 77 40E
Muzaffarpur . . . 92 26 7N 85 23E
Mwanza . . . 135 2 30S 32 58E
Mweru, L. . . . 135 9 0S 28 40E
My Tho . . . 95 10 29N 106 23E
Myanaung . . . 93 18 18N 95 22E
Myeik Kyunzu . . . 94 11 30N 97 30E
Myingyan . . . 93 21 30N 95 20E
Myitkyina . . . 93 25 24N 97 26E
Mýrdalsjökull . . . 64 63 40N 19 6W
Myrtle Point . . . 171 43 0N 124 4W
Mysore . . . 90 12 17N 76 41E
Mysore □ = Karnataka □ . . . 90 13 15N 77 0E

Naaldwijk . . . 40 51 59N 4 13E
Nabari . . . 106 34 37N 136 5E
Nablus = Nābulus . . . 80 32 14N 35 15E
Nābulus . . . 80 32 14N 35 15E
Nacogdoches . . . 168 31 33N 94 39W
Nacozari . . . 174 30 24N 109 39W
Nadiad . . . 91 22 41N 72 56E
Nadym . . . 69 65 35N 72 42E
Nagahama . . . 106 35 23N 136 16E
Nagaland □ . . . 93 26 0N 94 30E
Nagano . . . 107 36 40N 138 10E
Nagaoka . . . 105 37 27N 138 51E
Nagappattinam . . . 90 10 46N 79 51E
Nagasaki . . . 108 32 47N 129 50E
Nagato . . . 108 34 19N 131 5E
Nagercoil . . . 90 8 12N 77 26E
Nagornyy . . . 75 55 58N 124 57E
Nagoya . . . 106 35 10N 136 50E
Nagpur . . . 91 21 8N 79 10E
Nahanni Butte . . . 144 61 2N 123 31W
Nahāvand . . . 84 34 10N 48 22E
Naicam . . . 152 52 30N 104 30W
Nain . . . 147 56 34N 61 40W
Nainpur . . . 91 22 30N 80 10E
Nairn . . . 33 57 35N 3 54W
Nairobi . . . 132 1 17S 36 48E
Naivasha . . . 132 0 40S 36 30E
Najafābād . . . 85 32 40N 51 15E
Najibabad . . . 89 29 40N 78 20E
Naka → . . . 107 36 20N 140 36E
Naka-no-Shima . . . 104 29 51N 129 46E
Nakama . . . 108 33 56N 130 43E
Nakamura . . . 109 33 0N 133 0E
Nakano . . . 107 36 45N 138 22E
Nakanojō . . . 107 36 35N 138 51E
Nakatsu . . . 108 33 34N 131 15E
Nakatsugawa . . . 106 35 29N 137 30E
Nakhichevan A.S.S.R. □ . . . 70 39 14N 45 30E
Nakhodka . . . 75 42 53N 132 54E
Nakhon Phanom . . . 95 17 23N 104 43E
Nakhon Ratchasima . . . 95 14 59N 102 12E
Nakhon Sawan . . . 94 15 35N 100 10E
Nakhon Si Thammarat . . . 96 8 29N 100 0E
Nakina . . . 140 50 10N 86 40W
Nakskov . . . 61 54 50N 11 8E
Nakuru . . . 132 0 15S 36 4E
Nalchik . . . 70 43 30N 43 33E
Nalgonda . . . 91 17 6N 79 15E
Nam Co . . . 101 30 30N 90 45E
Nam Dinh . . . 95 20 25N 106 5E
Nam-Phan . . . 95 10 30N 106 0E
Nam Tha . . . 95 20 58N 101 30E
Nam Tok . . . 94 14 21N 99 4E
Namaland . . . 136 24 30S 17 0E
Namangan . . . 71 41 0N 71 40E
Nambour . . . 116 26 32S 152 58E
Nambucca Heads . . . 116 30 37S 153 0E
Namerikawa . . . 106 36 46N 137 20E
Namib Desert = Namib-Woestyn . . . 124 22 30S 15 0E
Namib-Woestyn . . . 124 22 30S 15 0E
Namibe . . . 134 15 7S 12 11E
Namibia ■ . . . 136 22 0S 18 9E
Nampa . . . 171 43 34N 116 34W
Namsos . . . 65 64 29N 11 30E
Namur . . . 42 50 27N 4 52E
Nanaimo . . . 154 49 10N 124 0W
Nanango . . . 116 26 40S 152 0E
Nanao . . . 105 37 0N 137 0E
Nanchang . . . 99 28 42N 115 55E
Nanching = Nanjing . . . 99 32 2N 118 47E
Nanching . . . 99 32 3N 118 47E
Nancy . . . 37 48 42N 6 12E
Nanda Devi . . . 101 30 23N 79 59E
Nandan . . . 109 34 10N 134 42E
Nanded . . . 91 19 10N 77 20E
Nandurbar . . . 91 21 20N 74 15E
Nanga Parbat . . . 89 35 10N 74 35E
Nangarhár □ . . . 87 34 20N 70 0E
Nanjing . . . 99 32 2N 118 47E
Nanking = Nanching . . . 99 32 3N 118 47E
Nanking = Nanjing . . . 99 32 2N 118 47E
Nankoku . . . 109 33 39N 133 44E
Nanning . . . 99 22 48N 108 20E
Nanping . . . 99 26 38N 118 10E
Nantes . . . 36 47 12N 1 33W
Nanticoke . . . 164 41 12N 76 1W
Nanton . . . 155 50 21N 113 46W
Nanuque . . . 189 17 50S 40 21W
Napa . . . 172 38 18N 122 17W
Napier . . . 122 39 30S 176 56E
Naples = Nápoli . . . 49 40 50N 14 17E
Napo → . . . 186 3 20S 72 40W
Nápoli . . . 49 40 50N 14 17E
Nara, Japan . . . 106 34 40N 135 49E
Nara, Mali . . . 130 15 10N 7 20W
Naracoorte . . . 119 36 58S 140 45E
Narasapur . . . 92 16 26N 81 40E
Narayanganj . . . 92 23 40N 90 33E
Narayanpet . . . 91 16 45N 77 30E
Narbonne . . . 37 43 11N 3 0E
Narita . . . 107 35 47N 140 19E
Narmada → . . . 91 21 38N 72 36E
Narooma . . . 117 36 14S 150 4E
Narrabri . . . 116 30 19S 149 46E
Narrandera . . . 117 34 42S 146 31E
Narrogin . . . 120 32 58S 117 14E
Narromine . . . 116 32 12S 148 12E
Naruto . . . 109 34 11N 134 37E
Narvik . . . 64 68 28N 17 26E
Narym . . . 71 59 0N 81 30E
Naser, Buheirat en . . . 128 23 0N 32 30E
Nashua . . . 164 42 50N 71 25W
Nashville . . . 169 36 12N 86 46W
Nasik . . . 91 19 58N 73 50E
Nasirabad . . . 91 26 15N 74 45E
Nassau . . . 178 25 0N 77 20W
Nasser, L. = Naser, Buheirat en . . . 128 23 0N 32 30E
Nässjö . . . 60 57 39N 14 42E
Natal . . . 189 5 47S 35 13W
Natal □ . . . 137 28 30S 30 30E
Natashquan . . . 149 50 14N 61 46W
Natchez . . . 168 31 35N 91 25W
Natchitoches . . . 168 31 47N 93 4W
Nathalia . . . 117 36 1S 145 13E
National City . . . 173 32 39N 117 7W
Natuna Besar, Kepulauan . . . 111 4 0N 108 15E
Natuna Selatan, Kepulauan . . . 111 2 45N 109 0E
Nauru ■ . . . 122 1 0S 166 0E
Nauta . . . 186 4 31S 73 35W
Nautanwa . . . 92 27 20N 83 25E
Nautla . . . 177 20 20N 96 50W

Navarra □	**51**	42 40N	1 40W
Navojoa	**174**	27 0N	109 30W
Navsari	**91**	20 57N	72 59 E
Nawabshah	**88**	26 15N	68 25 E
Nawalgarh	**89**	27 50N	75 15 E
Náxos	**55**	37 8N	25 25 E
Nāy Band	**87**	27 20N	52 40 E
Nayakhan	**73**	61 56N	159 0 E
Nayarit □	**175**	22 0N	105 0W
Ndélé	**129**	8 25N	20 36 E
Ndjamena	**131**	12 10N	14 59 E
Ndola	**135**	13 0S	28 34 E
Neagh, Lough	**34**	54 35N	6 25W
Near Is.	**142**	53 0N	172 0 E
Neath	**27**	51 39N	3 49W
Nebraska □	**163**	41 30N	100 0W
Nebraska City	**166**	40 40N	95 52W
Nebrodi Mts.	**49**	37 55N	14 45 E
Neches →	**168**	29 55N	93 52W
Neckar →	**42**	49 31N	8 26 E
Necochea	**190**	38 30S	58 50W
Needles, The	**24**	50 39N	1 35W
Neenah	**167**	44 10N	88 30W
Neepawa	**153**	50 15N	99 30W
Negapatam = Nagappattinam	**90**	10 46N	79 51 E
Negeri Sembilan □	**96**	2 45N	102 10 E
Negotin	**53**	44 16N	22 37 E
Negra, Pta.	**186**	6 6S	81 10W
Negro →, Argentina	**190**	41 2S	62 47W
Negro →, Brazil	**185**	3 0S	60 0W
Negros	**112**	9 30N	122 40 E
Nehbandān	**85**	31 35N	60 5 E
Nei Monggol Zizhiqu □	**98**	42 0N	112 0 E
Neijiang	**99**	29 35N	104 55 E
Neiva	**184**	2 56N	75 18W
Nellore	**90**	14 27N	79 59 E
Nelson, Canada	**155**	49 30N	117 20W
Nelson, N.Z.	**123**	41 18S	173 16 E
Nelson, U.K.	**28**	53 50N	2 14W
Nelson →	**153**	54 33N	98 2W
Néma	**126**	16 40N	7 15W
Neman →	**68**	55 25N	21 10 E
Nemours	**39**	48 16N	2 40 E
Nemunas = Neman →	**68**	55 25N	21 10 E
Nemuro	**103**	43 20N	145 35 E
Nemuro-Kaikyō	**103**	43 30N	145 30 E
Nenagh	**35**	52 52N	8 11W
Nenana	**142**	64 30N	149 20W
Nene →	**29**	52 38N	0 13 E
Neosho	**168**	36 56N	94 28W
Neosho →	**168**	35 59N	95 10W
Nepal ■	**92**	28 0N	84 30 E
Nephi	**162**	39 43N	111 52W
Ness, Loch	**33**	57 15N	4 30W
Netanya	**80**	32 20N	34 51 E
Netherlands ■	**41**	52 0N	5 30 E
Netherlands Antilles ■	**181**	12 15N	69 0W
Netherlands Guiana = Surinam ■	**185**	4 0N	56 0W
Nettilling L.	**146**	66 30N	71 0W
Netzahualcoyotl, Presa	**177**	17 10N	93 30W
Neuchâtel	**44**	47 0N	6 55 E
Neuchâtel, Lac de	**44**	46 53N	6 50 E
Neuquén	**190**	38 55S	68 0 E
Neuse →	**165**	35 5N	76 30W
Neusiedler See	**45**	47 50N	16 47 E
Nevada	**166**	37 51N	94 22W
Nevada □	**172**	39 20N	117 0W
Nevada, Sierra, Spain	**50**	37 3N	3 15W
Nevada, Sierra, U.S.A.	**172**	39 0N	120 30W
Nevada City	**172**	39 20N	121 0W
Nevada de Sta. Marta, Sa.	**184**	10 55N	73 50W
Nevers	**37**	47 0N	3 9 E
New Albany	**167**	38 20N	85 50W
New Amsterdam	**185**	6 15N	57 36W
New Bedford	**164**	41 40N	70 52W
New Bern	**165**	35 8N	77 3W
New Braunfels	**161**	29 43N	98 9W
New Brighton	**123**	43 29S	172 43 E
New Britain, Papua N. G.	**115**	5 50S	150 20 E
New Britain, U.S.A.	**164**	41 41N	72 47W
New Brunswick	**164**	40 30N	74 28W
New Brunswick □	**148**	46 50N	66 30W
New Caledonia = Nouvelle Calédonie	**122**	21 0S	165 0 E
New Castile = Castilla La Nueva	**50**	39 45N	3 20W
New Castle, Ind., U.S.A.	**164**	39 55N	85 23W
New Castle, Pa., U.S.A.	**164**	41 0N	80 20W
New England Ra.	**116**	30 20S	151 45 E
New Forest	**24**	50 53N	1 40W
New Glasgow	**149**	45 35N	62 36W
New Hampshire □	**164**	43 40N	71 40W
New Haven	**164**	41 20N	72 54W
New Hebrides = Vanuatu ■	**122**	15 0S	168 0 E
New Iberia	**168**	30 2N	91 54W
New Ireland	**115**	3 20S	151 50 E
New Jersey □	**164**	40 30N	74 10W
New Kensington	**164**	40 36N	79 43W
New London	**164**	41 23N	72 8W
New Mexico □	**161**	34 30N	106 0W
New Norfolk	**119**	42 46S	147 2 E
New Orleans	**169**	30 0N	90 5W
New Philadelphia	**164**	40 29N	81 25W
New Plymouth	**122**	39 4S	174 5 E
New Providence	**178**	25 25N	78 35W
New Radnor	**26**	52 15N	3 10W
New Siberian Is. = Novosibirskiye Ostrova	**72**	75 0N	142 0 E
New South Wales □	**116**	33 0S	146 0 E
New Ulm	**166**	44 15N	94 30W
New Waterford	**149**	46 13N	60 4W
New Westminster	**154**	49 13N	122 55W
New York □	**164**	42 40N	76 0W
New York City	**164**	40 45N	74 0W
New Zealand ■	**122**	40 0S	176 0 E
Newark, N.J., U.S.A.	**164**	40 41N	74 12W
Newark, N.Y., U.S.A.	**164**	43 2N	77 10W
Newark, Ohio, U.S.A.	**167**	40 5N	82 24W
Newark-on-Trent	**29**	53 6N	0 48W
Newberry, Mich., U.S.A.	**150**	46 20N	85 32W
Newberry, S.C., U.S.A.	**165**	34 17N	81 37W
Newburgh	**164**	41 30N	74 1W
Newburyport	**164**	42 48N	70 50W
Newcastle, Australia	**117**	33 0S	151 46 E
Newcastle, Canada	**148**	47 1N	65 38W
Newcastle, U.K.	**34**	54 13N	5 54W
Newcastle Emlyn	**26**	52 2N	4 29W
Newcastle-under-Lyme	**28**	53 2N	2 15W
Newcastle-upon-Tyne	**28**	54 59N	1 37W
Newfoundland □	**149**	53 0N	58 0W
Newhaven	**25**	50 47N	0 4 E
Newmarket	**25**	52 15N	0 23 E
Newnan	**170**	33 22N	84 48W
Newport, Gwent, U.K.	**27**	51 35N	3 0W
Newport, I. of W., U.K.	**25**	50 42N	1 18W
Newport, Ark., U.S.A.	**168**	35 38N	91 15W
Newport, Ky., U.S.A.	**167**	39 5N	84 23W
Newport, Oreg., U.S.A.	**171**	44 41N	124 2W
Newport, R.I., U.S.A.	**164**	41 13N	71 19W
Newport, Vt., U.S.A.	**148**	44 57N	72 17W
Newport Beach	**173**	33 40N	117 58W
Newport News	**165**	37 2N	76 30W
Newquay	**27**	50 24N	5 6W
Newry	**34**	54 10N	6 20W
Newton, Iowa, U.S.A.	**166**	41 40N	93 3W
Newton, Mass., U.S.A.	**164**	42 21N	71 10W
Newton Abbot	**27**	50 32N	3 37W
Newton Stewart	**31**	54 57N	4 30W
Newtonmore	**33**	57 4N	4 7W
Newtown	**26**	52 31N	3 19W
Newtownards	**34**	54 37N	5 40W
Ngaoundéré	**131**	7 15N	13 35 E
Ngoring Hu	**101**	34 55N	97 5 E
Nguru	**131**	12 56N	10 29 E
Nha Trang	**95**	12 16N	109 10 E
Nhill	**119**	36 18S	141 40 E
Niagara Falls, Canada	**151**	43 7N	79 5W
Niagara Falls, U.S.A.	**164**	43 5N	79 0W

Niamey	**131**	13 27N	2 6 E
Nias	**111**	1 0N	97 30 E
Nicaragua ■	**179**	11 40N	85 30W
Nicaragua, Lago de	**179**	12 0N	85 30W
Nice	**37**	43 42N	7 14 E
Nichinan	**108**	31 38N	131 23 E
Nicobar Is.	**8**	9 0N	93 0 E
Nicosia	**80**	35 10N	33 25 E
Nicoya, Pen. de	**179**	9 45N	85 40W
Nidd →	**28**	54 1N	1 32W
Niederösterreich □	**45**	48 25N	15 40 E
Niedersachsen □	**42**	52 45N	9 0 E
Nieuw Nickerie	**185**	6 0N	56 59W
Niger ■	**131**	13 30N	10 0 E
Niger →	**131**	5 33N	6 33 E
Nigeria ■	**131**	8 30N	8 0 E
Nii-Jima	**107**	34 20N	139 15 E
Niigata	**103**	37 58N	139 0 E
Niihama	**109**	33 55N	133 16 E
Niimi	**109**	34 59N	133 28 E
Nijkerk	**41**	52 13N	5 30 E
Nijmegen	**41**	51 50N	5 52 E
Nikki	**131**	9 58N	3 12 E
Nikkō	**107**	36 45N	139 35 E
Nikolayev	**68**	46 58N	32 0 E
Nikolayevsk-na-Amur	**75**	53 8N	140 44 E
Nikolskoye	**73**	55 12N	166 0 E
Nikšić	**52**	42 50N	18 57 E
Nîl, Nahr en →	**128**	30 10N	31 6 E
Nîl el Abyad →	**129**	15 38N	32 31 E
Nîl el Azraq →	**129**	15 38N	32 31 E
Nile = Nîl, Nahr en →	**128**	30 10N	31 6 E
Niles	**164**	41 8N	80 40W
Nîmes	**37**	43 50N	4 23 E
Nimule	**129**	3 32N	32 3 E
Nīnawá	**81**	36 25N	43 10 E
Nineveh = Nīnawá	**81**	36 25N	43 10 E
Ningbo	**99**	29 51N	121 28 E
Ningde	**99**	26 38N	119 23 E
Ningpo = Ningbo	**99**	29 51N	121 28 E
Ningsia Hui A.R. = Ningxia Huizu Zizhiqu □	**98**	38 0N	106 0 E
Ningxia Huizu Zizhiqu □	**98**	38 0N	106 0 E
Niobrara →	**163**	42 45N	98 0W
Nioro du Sahel	**130**	15 15N	9 30W
Niort	**36**	46 19N	0 29W
Nipawin	**152**	53 20N	104 0W
Nipigon	**150**	49 0N	88 17W
Nipigon, L.	**150**	49 50N	88 30W
Niš	**53**	43 19N	21 58 E
Nişāb	**83**	14 25N	46 29 E
Nishinomiya	**106**	34 45N	135 20 E
Nishio	**106**	34 52N	137 3 E
Nishiwaki	**109**	34 59N	134 58 E
Niterói	**188**	22 52S	43 0W
Nith →	**31**	55 20N	3 5W
Nitra	**59**	48 19N	18 4 E
Nivernais	**37**	47 0N	3 40 E
Nizamabad	**91**	18 45N	78 7 E
Nizhne Kolymsk	**73**	68 34N	160 55 E
Nizhneudinsk	**74**	54 54N	99 3 E
Nizhnevartovsk	**69**	60 56N	76 38 E
Nizhniy Novgorod = Gorkiy	**68**	56 20N	44 0 E
Nizhniy Tagil	**69**	57 55N	59 57 E
Nizhnyaya Tunguska →	**74**	64 20N	93 0 E
Nizké Tatry	**59**	48 55N	20 0 E
Nkongsamba	**131**	4 55N	9 55 E
Noatak	**142**	67 32N	162 59W
Nobeoka	**108**	32 36N	131 41 E
Noda	**107**	35 56N	139 52 E
Nogales	**174**	31 20N	110 56W
Nōgata	**108**	33 48N	130 44 E
Nogent-le-Rotrou	**39**	48 20N	0 50 E
Noi →	**94**	14 50N	100 15 E
Noirmoutier, Î. de	**36**	46 58N	2 10W
Nojima-Zaki	**107**	34 54N	139 53 E
Nok Kundi	**88**	28 50N	62 45 E
Nome	**142**	64 30N	165 24W
Nong Khae	**95**	14 29N	100 53 E
Nong Khai	**95**	17 50N	102 46 E
Nonoava	**174**	27 28N	106 44W
Noord Brabant □	**40**	51 40N	5 0 E
Noord Holland □	**40**	52 30N	4 45 E
Noordbeveland	**40**	51 35N	3 50 E
Noordoostpolder	**41**	52 45N	5 45 E
Noordwijk aan Zee	**40**	52 14N	4 26 E
Nootka I.	**154**	49 32N	126 42W
Nord-Trøndelag fylke □	**65**	64 20N	12 0 E
Nordaustlandet	**13**	79 14N	23 0 E
Nordegg	**155**	52 29N	116 5W
Nordkapp	**67**	71 10N	25 44 E
Nordkinn	**67**	71 8N	27 40 E
Nordland fylke □	**65**	65 40N	13 0 E
Nordrhein-Westfalen □	**42**	51 45N	7 30 E
Nordvik	**72**	74 2N	111 32 E
Nore →	**35**	52 40N	7 20W
Norfolk	**165**	36 40N	76 15W
Norfolk □	**29**	52 39N	1 0 E
Norfolk I.	**122**	28 58S	168 3 E
Norilsk	**72**	69 20N	88 6 E
Norman	**168**	35 12N	97 30W
Norman Wells	**144**	65 17N	126 51W
Normandie	**39**	48 45N	0 10 E
Normandin	**151**	48 49N	72 31W
Normandy = Normandie	**39**	48 45N	0 10 E
Normanton	**115**	17 40S	141 10 E
Norquinco	**192**	41 51S	70 55W
Norristown	**164**	40 9N	75 21W
Norrköping	**60**	58 37N	16 11 E
Norrland □	**66**	66 50N	18 0 E
Norseman	**114**	32 8S	121 43 E
Norsk	**75**	52 30N	130 0 E
North Andaman I.	**94**	13 15N	92 40 E
North Battleford	**152**	52 50N	108 17W
North Bay	**151**	46 20N	79 30W
North Bend	**171**	43 28N	124 14W
North Berwick	**31**	56 4N	2 44W
North C.	**122**	34 23S	173 4 E
North Carolina □	**165**	35 30N	80 0W
North Channel, Br. Is.	**30**	55 0N	5 30W
North Channel, Canada	**150**	46 0N	83 0W
North Dakota □	**163**	47 30N	100 0W
North Downs	**25**	51 17N	0 30 E
North European Plain	**17**	55 0N	20 0 E
North I.	**122**	38 0S	175 0 E
North Korea ■	**98**	40 0N	127 0 E
North Minch	**32**	58 5N	5 55W
North Ossetian A.S.S.R. □	**70**	43 30N	44 30 E
North Platte	**163**	41 10N	100 50W
North Platte →	**163**	41 15N	100 45W
North Pole	**12**	90 0N	0 0 E
North Ronaldsay	**33**	59 20N	2 30W
North Saskatchewan →	**143**	53 15N	105 5W
North Sea	**16**	56 0N	4 0 E
North Sentinel I.	**94**	11 35N	92 15 E
North Sporades = Voríai Sporádhes	**55**	39 15N	23 30 E
North Sydney	**149**	46 12N	60 15W
North Tonawanda	**164**	43 5N	78 50W
North Uist	**32**	57 40N	7 15W
North Vancouver	**154**	49 25N	123 3W
North Walsham	**29**	52 49N	1 22 E
North West Frontier □	**89**	34 0N	71 0 E
North West Highlands	**32**	57 35N	5 2W
North West River	**147**	53 30N	60 10W
North West Territories □	**145**	67 0N	110 0W
North York Moors	**29**	54 25N	0 50W
North Yorkshire □	**28**	54 15N	1 25W
Northallerton	**28**	54 20N	1 26W
Northam	**120**	31 35S	116 42 E
Northampton, Australia	**120**	28 27S	114 33 E
Northampton, U.K.	**25**	52 14N	0 54W
Northampton, U.S.A.	**164**	42 22N	72 31W
Northampton □	**25**	52 16N	0 55W
Northcliffe	**120**	34 39S	116 7 E
Northern Circars	**92**	17 30N	82 30 E
Northern Ireland □	**34**	54 45N	7 0W
Northern Territory □	**114**	16 0S	133 0 E
Northfield	**166**	44 30N	93 10W
Northland □	**122**	35 30S	173 30 E

Northumberland □	**28**	55 12N	2 0W
Northumberland Is.	**121**	21 30S	149 50 E
Northumberland Str.	**148**	46 20N	64 0W
Northwich	**28**	53 16N	2 30W
Norton Sd.	**142**	64 0N	164 0W
Norwalk	**164**	41 9N	73 25W
Norway ■	**18**	63 0N	11 0 E
Norwegian Sea	**16**	66 0N	1 0 E
Norwich	**29**	52 38N	1 17 E
Nos Kaliakra	**53**	43 21N	28 30 E
Noshiro	**103**	40 12N	140 0 E
Noss Hd.	**33**	58 29N	3 4W
Nossob →	**136**	26 55S	20 37 E
Noteć →	**58**	52 44N	15 26 E
Notre Dame de Koartac = Koartac	**146**	60 55N	69 40W
Nottaway →	**140**	51 22N	78 55W
Nottingham	**29**	52 57N	1 10W
Nottingham □	**29**	53 10N	1 0W
Nouâdhibou	**126**	20 54N	17 0W
Nouâdhibou, Ras	**126**	20 50N	17 0W
Nouakchott	**126**	18 9N	15 58W
Noumea	**122**	22 17S	166 30 E
Nouveau Comptoir	**140**	53 0N	78 49W
Nouvelle Calédonie	**122**	21 0S	165 0 E
Nova Friburgo	**188**	22 16S	42 30W
Nova Granada	**188**	20 30S	49 20W
Nova Lisboa = Huambo	**134**	12 42S	15 54 E
Nova Scotia □	**149**	45 10N	63 0W
Novara	**46**	45 27N	8 36 E
Novaya Sibir, Ostrov	**72**	75 10N	150 0 E
Novaya Zemlya	**69**	75 0N	56 0 E
Novgorod	**68**	58 30N	31 25 E
Novi Pazar	**52**	43 12N	20 28 E
Novi Sad	**52**	45 18N	19 52 E
Novocherkassk	**68**	47 27N	40 5 E
Novokuznetsk	**71**	53 45N	87 10 E
Novomoskovsk	**68**	54 5N	38 15 E
Novorossiysk	**68**	44 43N	37 46 E
Novosibirsk	**71**	55 0N	83 5 E
Novosibirskiye Ostrova	**72**	75 0N	142 0 E
Nowgong	**93**	26 20N	92 50 E
Nowra	**117**	34 53S	150 35 E
Nowy Sącz	**59**	49 40N	20 41 E
Noyon	**38**	49 34N	3 0 E
Nûbîya, Es Sahrâ En	**129**	21 30N	33 30 E
Nueces →	**161**	27 50N	97 30W
Nueltin L.	**145**	60 30N	99 30W
Nueva Gerona	**178**	21 53N	82 49W
Nueva Rosita	**174**	27 57N	101 13W
Nuevitas	**178**	21 30N	77 20W
Nuevo Laredo	**176**	27 30N	99 30W
Nuevo Leon □	**176**	25 40N	100 0W
Nuhaka	**122**	39 3S	177 45 E
Nukey Bluff, Mt.	**118**	32 26S	135 29 E
Nukus	**70**	42 20N	59 7 E
Nulato	**142**	64 40N	158 10W
Nullarbor Plain	**114**	30 45S	129 0 E
Numan	**131**	9 29N	12 3 E
Numazu	**107**	35 7N	138 51 E
Numurkah	**117**	36 5S	145 26 E
Nuneaton	**25**	52 32N	1 29W
Nunivak	**142**	60 0N	166 0W
Nunspeet	**41**	52 21N	5 45 E
Nuoro	**48**	40 20N	9 20 E
Nuremburg = Nürnberg	**43**	49 26N	11 5 E
Nuriootpa	**119**	34 27S	139 0 E
Nürnberg	**43**	49 26N	11 5 E
Nurran, L. = Terewah, L.	**116**	29 52S	147 35 E
Nutak	**147**	57 28N	61 59W
Nuweveldberge	**136**	32 10S	21 45 E
Nuyts Arch.	**118**	32 35S	133 20 E
Nyaake	**130**	4 52N	7 37W
Nyainqentanglha Shan	**101**	30 0N	90 0 E
Nyasa, L. = Malawi, L.	**137**	12 30S	34 30 E
Nyíregyháza	**59**	47 58N	21 47 E
Nyngan	**116**	31 30S	147 8 E
Nysa	**58**	50 30N	17 22 E
Oahe L.	**163**	45 30N	100 25W
Oahu	**160**	21 30N	158 0W
Oak Hill	**165**	38 0N	81 7W
Oak Park	**167**	41 55N	87 45W
Oak Ridge	**169**	36 1N	84 12W
Oakengates	**28**	52 42N	2 29W
Oakey	**116**	27 25S	151 43 E
Oakham	**29**	52 40N	0 43W
Oakland	**172**	37 50N	122 18W
Oakridge	**171**	43 47N	122 31W
Oamaru	**123**	45 5S	170 59 E
Oaxaca	**177**	17 2N	96 40W
Oaxaca □	**177**	17 0N	96 30W
Ob →	**69**	66 45N	69 30 E
Oba	**150**	49 4N	84 7W
Obama	**106**	35 30N	135 45 E
Oban	**30**	56 25N	5 30W
Obbia	**133**	5 25N	48 30 E
Oberhausen	**42**	51 28N	6 50 E
Oberon	**117**	33 45S	149 52 E
Oberösterreich □	**45**	48 10N	14 0 E
Obi, Is.	**113**	1 30S	127 30 E
Obihiro	**103**	42 56N	143 12 E
Obskaya Guba	**69**	69 0N	73 0 E
Ocala	**170**	29 11N	82 5W
Ocampo	**174**	28 11N	108 23W
Ocaña	**184**	8 15N	73 20W
Occidental, Cordillera	**184**	5 0N	76 0W
Ocean City	**164**	39 18N	74 34W
Oceanside	**173**	33 13N	117 26W
Ochil Hills	**31**	56 14N	3 40W
Oconee →	**170**	31 58N	82 32W
Oconto	**167**	44 52N	87 53W
Ocotlán	**175**	20 21N	102 46W
Ōda	**109**	35 11N	132 30 E
Ódáðahraun	**64**	65 5N	17 0W
Odate	**103**	40 16N	140 34 E
Odawara	**107**	35 20N	139 6 E
Ödemiş	**80**	38 15N	28 0 E
Odense	**61**	55 22N	10 23 E
Oder →	**58**	53 33N	14 38 E
Odessa, U.S.A.	**161**	31 51N	102 23W
Odessa, U.S.S.R.	**68**	46 30N	30 45 E
Odra →	**58**	53 33N	14 38 E
Odžak	**52**	45 3N	18 18 E
Offaly □	**35**	53 15N	7 30W
Offenbach	**42**	50 6N	8 46 E
Oga-Hantō	**103**	39 58N	139 47 E
Ogaden	**133**	7 30N	45 30 E
Ōgaki	**106**	35 21N	136 37 E
Ogbomosho	**131**	8 1N	4 11 E
Ogden	**163**	41 13N	112 1W
Ogdensburg	**151**	44 40N	75 27W
Ohio □	**167**	40 20N	14 10 E
Ohio →	**167**	38 0N	86 0W
Ohrid	**52**	41 8N	20 52 E
Ohridsko, Jezero	**52**	41 8N	20 52 E
Oil City	**164**	41 26N	79 40W
Oise →	**38**	49 0N	2 4 E
Oisterwijk	**40**	51 35N	5 12 E
Ōita	**108**	33 14N	131 36 E
Ojos del Salado, Cerro	**190**	27 0S	68 40W
Oka →	**68**	56 20N	43 59 E
Okawa	**108**	33 9N	130 21 E
Okaya	**107**	36 0N	138 10 E
Okayama	**109**	34 40N	133 54 E
Okazaki	**106**	34 57N	137 10 E
Okeechobee, L.	**170**	27 0N	80 50W
Okehampton	**27**	50 44N	4 1W
Okha	**75**	53 40N	143 0 E
Okhotsk	**75**	59 20N	143 10 E
Okhotsk, Sea of	**77**	55 0N	145 0 E
Okhotsko Kolymskoye	**73**	63 0N	157 0 E
Oki-no-Shima	**109**	32 44N	132 33 E
Oki-Shotō	**109**	36 5N	133 15 E
Okinawa-Jima	**99**	26 32N	128 0 E
Oklahoma □	**161**	35 20N	97 30W
Oklahoma City	**161**	35 25N	97 30W
Okmulgee	**168**	35 38N	96 0W
Oktabrsk	**70**	49 28N	57 25 E
Oktyabrskoy Revolyutsii, Os.	**72**	79 30N	97 0 E

Oktyabrskoye	**69**	62 28N	66 3 E
Okuchi	**108**	32 4N	130 37 E
Okuru	**123**	43 55 S	168 55 E
Okushiri-Tō	**103**	42 15N	139 30 E
Olanchito	**179**	15 30N	86 30W
Öland	**61**	56 45N	16 38 E
Olary	**118**	32 18 S	140 19 E
Olavarría	**190**	36 55 S	60 20W
Old Castile = Castilla La Vieja	**50**	41 55N	4 0W
Old Town	**148**	45 0N	68 41W
Oldenburg	**42**	53 10N	8 10 E
Oldenzaal	**41**	52 19N	6 53 E
Oldham	**28**	53 33N	2 8W
Olds	**155**	51 50N	114 10W
Olekma →	**74**	60 22N	120 42 E
Olekminsk	**74**	60 25N	120 30 E
Olenek	**72**	68 28N	112 18 E
Olenek →	**72**	73 0N	120 10 E
Oléron, Île d'	**36**	45 55N	1 15W
Oleśnica	**58**	51 13N	17 22 E
Olifants →	**137**	24 5 S	31 20 E
Ólimbos, Óros	**54**	40 6N	22 23 E
Oliveira	**188**	20 39 S	44 50W
Oliver	**155**	49 13N	119 37W
Ollagüe	**187**	21 15 S	68 10W
Olney	**167**	38 40N	88 0W
Olomouc	**59**	49 38N	17 12 E
Olsztyn	**58**	53 48N	20 29 E
Olt →	**57**	43 50N	24 40 E
Olympia, Greece	**54**	37 39N	21 39 E
Olympia, U.S.A.	**171**	47 0N	122 58W
Olympic Mts.	**171**	47 50N	123 45W
Olympus, Mt. = Ólimbos, Óros	**54**	40 6N	22 23 E
Olympus, Mt.	**171**	47 52N	123 40W
Omachi	**107**	36 30N	137 50 E
Omae-Zaki	**107**	34 36N	138 14 E
Omagh	**34**	54 36N	7 20W
Omaha	**166**	41 15N	96 0W
Omak	**171**	48 24N	119 31W
Oman ■	**83**	23 0N	58 0 E
Oman, G. of	**83**	24 30N	58 30 E
Omdurmân	**129**	15 40N	32 28 E
Ome	**107**	35 47N	139 15 E
Omeo	**117**	37 6 S	147 36 E
Omihachiman	**106**	35 7N	136 3 E
Omiya	**107**	35 54N	139 38 E
Omo →	**132**	6 25N	36 10 E
Omolon →	**73**	68 42N	158 36 E
Omono-Gawa →	**103**	39 46N	140 3 E
Omsk	**71**	55 0N	73 12 E
Omura	**108**	32 56N	130 0 E
Omuta	**108**	33 0N	130 26 E
Onega	**68**	64 0N	38 10 E
Onega, L. = Onezhskoye Ozero	**68**	62 0N	35 30 E
Onehunga	**122**	36 55 S	174 48 E
Oneida	**164**	43 5N	75 40W
Onekotan, Ostrov	**75**	49 25N	154 45 E
Onezhskoye Ozero	**68**	62 0N	35 30 E
Ongerup	**120**	33 58 S	118 28 E
Ongole	**90**	15 33N	80 2 E
Onguren	**74**	53 38N	107 36 E
Onitsha	**131**	6 6N	6 42 E
Ono, Fukui, Japan	**106**	35 59N	136 29 E
Ono, Hyōgo, Japan	**109**	34 51N	134 56 E
Onoda	**108**	34 2N	131 25 E
Onomichi	**109**	34 25N	133 12 E
Onslow	**114**	21 40 S	115 12 E
Onslow B.	**165**	34 20N	77 20W
Ontake-San	**106**	35 53N	137 29 E
Ontario	**173**	34 2N	117 40W
Ontario □	**140**	52 0N	88 10W
Ontario, L.	**151**	43 40N	78 0W
Oodnadatta	**118**	27 33 S	135 30 E
Ooldea	**114**	30 27 S	131 50 E
Oostende	**42**	51 15N	2 50 E
Oosterhout	**40**	51 39N	4 47 E
Oosterschelde	**40**	51 33N	4 0 E
Opala	**73**	51 58N	156 30 E
Opava	**58**	49 57N	17 58 E
Opelousas	**168**	30 35N	92 7W
Ophir	**142**	63 10N	156 40W
Opole	**58**	50 42N	17 58 E
Oporto = Porto	**50**	41 8N	8 40W
Opp	**169**	31 19N	86 13W
Oppland fylke □	**60**	61 15N	9 40 E
Opua	**122**	35 19 S	174 9 E
Oradea	**56**	47 2N	21 58 E
Öræfajökull	**64**	64 2N	16 39W
Orai	**91**	25 58N	79 30 E
Oran, Algeria	**127**	35 45N	0 39W
Oran, Argentina	**190**	23 10 S	64 20W
Orange, Australia	**117**	33 15 S	149 7 E
Orange, France	**37**	44 8N	4 47 E
Orange, U.S.A.	**168**	30 10N	93 50W
Orange → = Oranje →	**136**	28 41 S	16 28 E
Orange, C.	**185**	4 20N	51 30W
Orangeburg	**170**	33 35N	80 53W
Oranje →	**136**	28 41 S	16 28 E
Oraşul Stalin = Braşov	**57**	45 38N	25 35 E
Orbost	**117**	37 40 S	148 29 E
Orchies	**38**	50 28N	3 14 E
Ordos = Mu Us Shamo	**98**	39 0N	109 0 E
Ordu	**81**	40 55N	37 53 E
Ordzhonikidze	**70**	43 0N	44 35 E
Ore Mts. = Erzgebirge	**43**	50 25N	13 0 E
Örebro	**60**	59 20N	15 18 E
Oregon □	**171**	44 0N	121 0W
Oregon City	**171**	45 21N	122 35W
Orel	**68**	52 57N	36 3 E
Orenburg	**70**	51 45N	55 6 E
Orense	**50**	42 19N	7 55W
Orepuki	**123**	46 19 S	167 46 E
Orford Ness	**24**	52 6N	1 31 E
Oriental, Cordillera	**184**	6 0N	73 0W
Orillia	**151**	44 40N	79 24W
Orinoco →	**185**	9 15N	61 30W
Orissa □	**92**	20 0N	84 0 E
Oristano	**48**	39 54N	8 35 E
Oristano, Golfo di	**48**	39 50N	8 22 E
Orizaba	**177**	18 51N	97 6W
Orkney Is.	**33**	59 0N	3 0W
Orland	**172**	39 46N	122 12W
Orlando	**170**	28 30N	81 25W
Orléanais	**39**	48 0N	2 0 E
Orléans	**39**	47 54N	1 52 E
Ormara	**88**	25 16N	64 33 E
Ormskirk	**28**	53 35N	2 53W
Örnsköldsvik	**66**	63 17N	18 40 E
Orocué	**184**	4 48N	71 20W
Oroville	**172**	39 31N	121 30W
Orsha	**68**	54 30N	30 25 E
Orsk	**70**	51 12N	58 34 E
Ortegal, C.	**50**	43 43N	7 52W
Orūmīyeh	**81**	37 40N	45 0 E
Orūmīyeh, Daryācheh-ye	**81**	37 50N	45 30 E
Oruro	**187**	18 0 S	67 9W
Oruzgān □	**87**	33 30N	66 0 E
Oryakhovo	**53**	43 40N	23 57 E
Osage →	**166**	38 35N	91 57W
Osaka	**106**	34 40N	135 30 E
Osceola	**169**	35 40N	90 0W
Ösel = Saaremaa	**68**	58 30N	22 30 E
Osh	**71**	40 37N	72 49 E
Oshawa	**151**	43 50N	78 50W
Oshima	**107**	33 55N	132 14 E
Oshkosh	**167**	44 3N	88 35W
Oshogbo	**131**	7 48N	4 37 E
Osijek	**52**	45 34N	18 41 E
Oskaloosa	**166**	41 18N	92 40W
Oslo	**60**	59 55N	10 45 E
Osmaniye	**80**	37 5N	36 10 E
Osnabrück	**42**	52 16N	8 2 E
Osorno	**190**	40 25 S	73 0W
Oss	**41**	51 46N	5 32 E
Ossa, Mt.	**119**	41 52 S	146 3 E
Ostend = Oostende	**42**	51 15N	2 50 E
Östergötlands län □	**60**	58 35N	15 45 E
Östersund	**66**	63 10N	14 38 E
Østfold fylke □	**60**	59 25N	11 25 E

Ostfriesische Inseln	**42**	53 45N	7 15 E
Ostia	**46**	41 40N	12 20 E
Ostrava	**59**	49 51N	18 18 E
Ostróda	**58**	53 42N	19 58 E
Ostrołeka	**58**	53 4N	21 32 E
Ostrów Mazowiecka	**58**	52 50N	21 51 E
Ostrów Wielkopolski	**58**	51 36N	17 44 E
Ōsumi-Kaikyō	**104**	30 55N	131 0 E
Ōsumi-Shotō	**104**	30 30N	130 0 E
Oswego	**164**	43 29N	76 30W
Oswestry	**28**	52 52N	3 3W
Ōta	**107**	36 18N	139 22 E
Otago □	**123**	44 44S	169 10 E
Ōtake	**109**	34 12N	132 13 E
Otaki	**122**	40 45S	175 10 E
Otaru	**103**	43 10N	141 0 E
Otaru-Wan = Ishikari-Wan	**103**	43 25N	141 1 E
Otira Gorge	**123**	42 53S	171 33 E
Otoineppu	**103**	44 44N	142 16 E
Otranto	**49**	40 9N	18 28 E
Otranto, C. d'	**49**	40 7N	18 30 E
Otranto, Str. of	**52**	40 15N	18 40 E
Ōtsu	**106**	35 0N	135 50 E
Ottawa, Canada	**151**	45 27N	75 42W
Ottawa, U.S.A.	**166**	38 40N	95 6W
Ottawa → = Outaouais →	**140**	45 27N	74 8W
Ottawa Is.	**146**	59 35N	80 10W
Otter Rapids, Ont., Canada	**151**	50 11N	81 39W
Otter Rapids, Sask., Canada	**152**	55 38N	104 44W
Ottumwa	**166**	41 0N	92 25W
Otwock	**58**	52 5N	21 20 E
Ouachita →	**168**	31 38N	91 49W
Ouachita Mts.	**168**	34 50N	94 30W
Ouagadougou	**130**	12 25N	1 30W
Ouahran = Oran	**127**	35 45N	0 39W
Ouargla	**127**	31 59N	5 16 E
Oubangi →	**131**	1 0N	17 50 E
Oudenbosch	**40**	51 35N	4 32 E
Oudtshoorn	**136**	33 35S	22 14 E
Ouessant, Île d'	**36**	48 28N	5 6W
Oujda	**127**	34 41N	1 55W
Oulu	**67**	65 1N	25 29 E
Oulujärvi	**67**	64 25N	27 15 E
Oulujoki →	**67**	65 1N	25 30 E
Ouse →	**29**	54 3N	0 7 E
Outaouais →	**140**	45 27N	74 8W
Outer Hebrides	**32**	57 30N	7 40W
Outlook	**152**	51 30N	107 0W
Outreau	**38**	50 40N	1 36 E
Ouyen	**119**	35 1S	142 22 E
Ovalle	**190**	30 33S	71 18W
Overflakkee	**40**	51 44N	4 10 E
Overijssel □	**41**	52 25N	6 35 E
Oviedo	**50**	43 25N	5 50W
Owaka	**123**	46 27S	169 40 E
Owase	**106**	34 7N	136 12 E
Owatonna	**166**	44 3N	93 10W
Owen Sound	**151**	44 35N	80 55W
Owen Stanley Range	**115**	8 30S	147 0 E
Owensboro	**167**	37 40N	87 5W
Owosso	**167**	43 0N	84 10W
Owyhee →	**171**	43 46N	117 2W
Oxford, U.K.	**25**	51 45N	1 15W
Oxford, U.S.A.	**165**	36 19N	78 36W
Oxford □	**25**	51 45N	1 15W
Oxford L.	**153**	54 51N	95 37W
Oxnard	**173**	34 10N	119 14W
Oyabe	**106**	36 47N	136 56 E
Oyama	**107**	36 18N	139 48 E
Oyana	**108**	32 32N	130 30 E
Oyo	**131**	7 46N	3 50 E
Oyonnax	**37**	46 16N	5 40 E
Ozamis	**112**	8 15N	123 50 E
Ozark	**169**	31 29N	85 39W
Ozark Plateau	**168**	37 20N	91 40W
Ozarks, L. of	**166**	38 10N	92 40W
Ozu, Ehime, Japan	**109**	33 30N	132 33 E
Ozu, Kumamoto, Japan	**108**	32 52N	130 52 E
Paarl	**136**	33 45S	18 56 E
Pabna	**92**	24 1N	89 18 E
Pacaraima, Sierra	**185**	4 0N	62 30W
Pacasmayo	**186**	7 20S	79 35W
Pachuca	**177**	20 10N	98 40W
Padang	**111**	1 0S	100 20 E
Pádova	**47**	45 24N	11 52 E
Padstow	**27**	50 33N	4 57W
Padua = Pádova	**47**	45 24N	11 52 E
Paducah	**169**	37 0N	88 40W
Pag	**52**	44 30N	14 50 E
Pagalu = Annobón	**131**	1 25S	5 36 E
Pagastikós Kólpos	**54**	39 15N	23 0 E
Page	**160**	36 57N	111 27W
Pahala	**160**	19 12N	155 25W
Pahang □	**96**	3 30N	102 45 E
Pahiatua	**122**	40 27S	175 50 E
Paignton	**27**	50 26N	3 33W
Painesville	**167**	41 42N	81 18W
Paint Hills = Nouveau Comptoir	**140**	53 0N	78 49W
Painted Desert	**160**	36 0N	111 30W
Paisley	**31**	55 51N	4 27W
Paita	**186**	5 11S	81 9W
Pak Sane	**95**	18 22N	103 39 E
Pakistan ■	**78**	30 0N	70 0 E
Pakistan, East = Bangladesh ■	**92**	24 0N	90 0 E
Pakokku	**93**	21 20N	95 0 E
Pakse	**95**	15 5N	105 52 E
Paktīā □	**87**	33 0N	69 15 E
Palanpur	**91**	24 10N	72 25 E
Palatka	**170**	29 40N	81 40W
Palawan	**112**	9 30N	118 30 E
Palembang	**111**	3 0S	104 50 E
Palencia	**50**	42 1N	4 34W
Palermo	**48**	38 8N	13 20 E
Palestine	**168**	31 42N	95 35W
Palghat	**90**	10 46N	76 42 E
Pali	**91**	25 50N	73 20 E
Palizada	**177**	18 15N	92 5W
Palk Bay	**90**	9 30N	79 15 E
Palk Strait	**90**	10 0N	79 45 E
Palm Is.	**121**	18 40S	146 35 E
Palm Springs	**173**	33 51N	116 35W
Palma, La	**179**	8 15N	78 0W
Palma de Mallorca	**51**	39 35N	2 39 E
Palma Soriano	**178**	20 15N	76 0W
Palmas, C.	**130**	4 27N	7 46W
Palmer Land	**14**	73 0S	60 0W
Palmerston North	**122**	40 21S	175 39 E
Palmi	**49**	38 21N	15 51 E
Palmira	**184**	3 32N	76 16W
Palmyra = Tudmur	**80**	34 36N	38 15 E
Palo Alto	**172**	37 25N	122 8W
Pamirs	**71**	37 40N	73 0 E
Pamlico Sd.	**165**	35 20N	76 0W
Pampa	**161**	35 35N	100 58W
Pampas	**190**	35 0S	63 0W
Pamplona	**51**	42 48N	1 38W
Panaca	**173**	37 51N	114 23W
Panaji	**91**	15 25N	73 50 E
Panamá	**179**	9 0N	79 25W
Panama ■	**179**	8 48N	79 55W
Panamá, Golfo de	**179**	8 4N	79 20W
Panama Canal	**175**	9 10N	79 37W
Panama City	**169**	30 10N	85 41W
Panay	**112**	11 10N	122 30 E
Pančevo	**52**	44 52N	20 41 E
Pandharpur	**91**	17 41N	75 20 E
Pangfou = Bengbu	**99**	32 58N	117 20 E
Pangkalpinang	**111**	2 0S	106 0 E
Pangnirtung	**140**	66 8N	65 54W
Panjim = Panaji	**91**	15 25N	73 50 E
Panjinad Barrage	**89**	29 22N	71 15 E
Pantelleria	**48**	36 52N	12 0 E
Pánuco	**177**	22 3N	98 10W
Paoting = Baoding	**98**	38 50N	115 28 E
Paot'ou = Baotou	**98**	40 32N	110 2 E
Papien Chiang = Da →	**95**	21 15N	105 20 E
Papua, Gulf of	**115**	9 0S	144 50 E

Papua New Guinea ■ **115** 8 0S 145 0E
Pará = Belém **188** 1 20S 48 30W
Pará □ **188** 3 20S 52 0W
Paracatu **188** 17 10S 46 50W
Paragua, La **185** 6 50N 63 20W
Paraguay ■ **191** 23 0S 57 0W
Paraguay → **191** 27 18S 58 38W
Paraíba = João Pessoa **189** 7 10S 34 52W
Paraíba □ **189** 7 0S 36 0W
Parakou **131** 9 25N 2 40E
Paramaribo **185** 5 50N 55 10W
Paraná **190** 31 45S 60 30W
Paraná □ **191** 24 30S 51 0W
Paraná → **190** 33 43S 59 15W
Paranaguá **191** 25 30S 48 30W
Paranaíba → **188** 20 6S 51 4W
Parbhani **91** 19 8N 76 52E
Parecis, Serra dos **187** 13 0S 60 0W
Parent **151** 47 55N 74 35W
Paria, Golfo de **180** 10 20N 62 0W
Parika **185** 6 50N 58 20W
Parintins **185** 2 40S 56 50W
Pariparit Kyun **94** 14 55S 93 45E
Paris, France **39** 48 50N 2 20E
Paris, Tenn., U.S.A. **169** 36 20N 88 20W
Paris, Tex., U.S.A. **168** 33 40N 95 30W
Park Range **163** 40 0N 106 30W
Parker **173** 34 8N 114 16W
Parkersburg **164** 39 18N 81 31W
Parkes **117** 33 9S 148 11E
Parma **46** 44 50N 10 20E
Parnaguá **188** 10 10S 44 38W
Parnaíba **189** 2 54S 41 47W
Parnaíba → **188** 3 0S 41 50W
Parnassós **54** 38 35N 22 30E
Pärnu **68** 58 28N 24 33E
Páros **55** 37 5N 25 12E
Parral **190** 36 10S 71 52W
Parramatta **117** 33 48S 151 1E
Parras **174** 25 30N 102 20W
Parrett → **27** 51 7N 2 58W
Parry Is. **12** 77 0N 110 0W
Parry Sound **151** 45 20N 80 0W
Parsons **166** 37 20N 95 17W
Paruro **187** 13 45S 71 50W
Parvān □ **87** 35 0N 69 0E
Pasadena, Calif., U.S.A. **173** 34 5N 118 9W
Pasadena, Tex., U.S.A. **168** 29 45N 95 14W
Pasaje **184** 3 23S 79 50W
Pascagoula **169** 30 21N 88 30W
Pasco **171** 46 10N 119 0W
Pasco, Cerro de **186** 10 45S 76 10W
Paso Robles **173** 35 40N 120 45W
Passero, C. **49** 36 42N 15 8E
Passo Fundo **191** 28 10S 52 20W
Pasto **184** 1 13N 77 17W
Patagonia **192** 45 0S 69 0W
Patan **91** 23 54N 72 14E
Patchogue **164** 40 46N 73 1W
Paterson **164** 40 55N 74 10W
Pathankot **89** 32 18N 75 45E
Patiala **89** 30 23N 76 26E
Patkai Bum **93** 27 0N 95 30E
Pátmos **55** 37 21N 26 36E
Patna **92** 25 35N 85 12E
Patos, Lag. dos **191** 31 20S 51 0E
Patos de Minas **188** 18 35S 46 32W
Pátrai **54** 38 14N 21 47E
Patuca → **179** 15 50N 84 18W
Pátzcuaro **175** 19 32N 101 36W
Pau **36** 43 19N 0 25W
Paulistana **189** 8 9S 41 9W
Paulo Afonso **189** 9 21S 38 15W
Pavia **46** 45 10N 9 10E
Pavlodar **71** 52 33N 77 0E
Pavlovo **74** 63 5N 115 25E
Pawtucket **164** 41 51N 71 22W
Payette **171** 44 0N 117 0W
Payne Bay = Bellin **146** 60 0N 70 0W
Payne L. **146** 59 30N 74 30W
Paynes Find **120** 29 15S 117 42E
Paysandú **191** 32 19S 58 8W
Paz, La, Argentina **190** 30 50S 59 45W
Paz, La, Bolivia **187** 16 20S 68 10W
Paz, La, Mexico **174** 24 10N 110 18W
Pazardzhik **53** 42 12N 24 20E
Peace → **145** 59 0N 111 25W
Peace River **155** 56 15N 117 18W
Peak, The **28** 53 24N 1 53W
Peak Hill **116** 32 47S 148 11E
Pearl City **160** 21 24N 158 0W
Pearl Harbor **160** 21 20N 158 0W
Peary Land **13** 82 40N 33 0W
Pebas **186** 3 10S 71 46W
Pechenga **69** 69 30N 31 25E
Pechora → **69** 68 13N 54 15E
Pechorskaya Guba **69** 68 40N 54 0E
Pecos **161** 31 25N 103 35W
Pecos → **161** 29 42N 102 30W
Pécs **59** 46 5N 18 15E
Pedro Afonso **188** 9 0S 48 10W
Pedro Juan Caballero **191** 22 30S 55 40W
Peebles **31** 55 40N 3 12W
Peekskill **164** 41 18N 73 57W
Peel **28** 54 14N 4 40W
Peel → **144** 67 0N 135 0W
Pegasus Bay **123** 43 20S 173 10E
Pegu **93** 17 20N 96 29E
Pegu Yoma **93** 19 0N 96 0E
Pehuajó **190** 35 45S 62 0W
Peip'ing = Beijing **98** 39 55N 116 20E
Pekalongan **111** 6 53S 109 40E
Pekan **96** 3 30N 103 25E
Pekanbaru **111** 0 30N 101 15E
Pekin **166** 40 35N 89 40W
Peking = Beijing **98** 39 55N 116 20E
Peleng **113** 1 20S 123 30E
Pelly → **144** 62 47N 137 19W
Pelly Bay **146** 68 38N 89 50W
Peloponnes = Pelopónnisos □ **54** 37 10N 22 0E
Pelopónnisos □ **54** 37 10N 22 0E
Peloro, C. **49** 38 15N 15 40E
Pelorus Sound **123** 40 59S 173 59E
Pelotas **191** 31 42S 52 23W
Pelvoux, Massif de **37** 44 52N 6 20E
Pematangsiantar **111** 2 57N 99 5E
Pemba **135** 5 0S 39 45E
Pembroke, Canada **151** 45 50N 77 7W
Pembroke, U.K. **27** 51 41N 4 57W
Pen-y-Ghent **28** 54 10N 2 15W
Penas, G. de **192** 47 0S 75 0W
Pench'i = Benxi **98** 41 20N 123 48E
Pendembu **130** 9 7N 12 14W
Pendleton **171** 45 35N 118 50W
Penetanguishene **151** 44 50N 79 55W
Penguin **119** 41 8S 146 6E
Penicuik **31** 55 50N 3 14W
Peninsular Malaysia □ **96** 4 0N 102 0E
Pennines **28** 54 50N 2 20W
Pennsylvania □ **164** 40 50N 78 0W
Penola **119** 37 25S 140 21E
Penonomé **179** 8 31N 80 21W
Penrith, Australia **117** 33 43S 150 38E
Penrith, U.K. **28** 54 40N 2 45W
Pensacola **169** 30 30N 87 10W
Pensacola Mts. **14** 84 0S 40 0W
Penshurst **119** 37 49S 142 20E
Penticton **155** 49 30N 119 38W
Pentland Firth **33** 58 43N 3 10W
Pentland Hills **31** 55 48N 3 25W
Penza **68** 53 15N 45 5E
Penzance **27** 50 7N 5 32W
Penzhinskaya Guba **73** 61 30N 163 0E
Peoria **166** 40 40N 89 40W
Perak □ **96** 5 0N 101 0E
Perche **36** 48 31N 1 1E
Pereira **184** 4 49N 75 43W
Perenjori **120** 29 26S 116 16E
Pergamino **190** 33 52S 60 30W
Périgueux **36** 45 10N 0 42E
Perlis □ **96** 6 30N 100 15E

Perm	**69**	58 0N	57 10 E
Pernambuco = Recife	**189**	8 0S	35 0W
Pernambuco □	**189**	8 0S	37 0W
Pernatty Lagoon	**118**	31 30S	137 12 E
Pernik	**53**	42 35N	23 2 E
Peron Pen.	**120**	26 0S	113 10 E
Péronne	**38**	49 55N	2 57 E
Perouse Str., La	**77**	45 40N	142 0 E
Perpignan	**37**	42 42N	2 53 E
Perry, Iowa, U.S.A.	**166**	41 48N	94 5W
Perry, Okla., U.S.A.	**168**	36 20N	97 20W
Persepolis	**85**	29 55N	52 50 E
Persia = Iran ■	**86**	33 0N	53 0 E
Persian Gulf = Gulf, The	**85**	27 0N	50 0 E
Perth, Australia	**120**	31 57S	115 52 E
Perth, Canada	**151**	44 55N	76 15W
Perth, U.K.	**31**	56 24N	3 27W
Perth Amboy	**164**	40 31N	74 16W
Peru	**167**	40 42N	86 0W
Peru ■	**186**	8 0S	75 0W
Perúgia	**46**	43 6N	12 24 E
Pervouralsk	**69**	56 55N	60 0 E
Pésaro	**47**	43 55N	12 53 E
Pescara	**47**	42 28N	14 13 E
Peshawar	**89**	34 2N	71 37 E
Pesqueria →	**176**	25 54N	99 11W
Petah Tiqwa	**80**	32 6N	34 53 E
Petaling Jaya	**96**	3 4N	101 42 E
Petaluma	**172**	38 13N	122 39W
Petatlán	**177**	17 31N	101 16W
Peterborough, Australia	**118**	32 58S	138 51 E
Peterborough, Canada	**151**	44 20N	78 20W
Peterborough, U.K.	**25**	52 35N	0 14W
Peterhead	**33**	57 30N	1 49W
Peterlee	**29**	54 45N	1 18W
Petersburg, Alaska, U.S.A.	**143**	56 50N	133 0W
Petersburg, Va., U.S.A.	**164**	37 17N	77 26W
Petit Goâve	**180**	18 27N	72 51W
Petitsikapau, L.	**147**	54 37N	66 25W
Petlad	**91**	22 30N	72 45 E
Petone	**123**	41 13S	174 53 E
Petoskey	**150**	45 22N	84 57W
Petrich	**53**	41 24N	23 13 E
Petrolia	**150**	42 54N	82 9W
Petrolina	**189**	9 24S	40 30W
Petropavlovsk	**71**	54 53N	69 13 E
Petropavlovsk-Kamchatskiy	**73**	53 3N	158 43 E
Petrópolis	**188**	22 33S	43 9W
Petrovaradin	**52**	45 16N	19 55 E
Petrozavodsk	**68**	61 41N	34 20 E
Pevek	**73**	69 41N	171 19 E
Pforzheim	**42**	48 53N	8 43 E
Phan Rang	**95**	11 34N	109 0 E
Phangan, Ko	**96**	9 45N	100 0 E
Phenix City	**169**	32 30N	85 0W
Philadelphia	**164**	40 0N	75 10W
Philippi	**55**	41 1N	24 16 E
Philippines ■	**112**	12 0N	123 0 E
Philippopolis = Plovdiv	**53**	42 8N	24 44 E
Phitsanulok	**94**	16 50N	100 12 E
Phnom Penh	**95**	11 33N	104 55 E
Phoenix	**160**	33 30N	112 10W
Phoenix Is.	**123**	3 30S	172 0W
Phra Chedi Sam Ong	**94**	15 16N	98 23 E
Phuket	**96**	7 52N	98 22 E
Piacenza	**46**	45 2N	9 42 E
Piauí □	**188**	7 0S	43 0W
Picardie	**38**	50 0N	2 15 E
Picardie, Plaine de	**37**	50 0N	2 0 E
Picardy = Picardie	**38**	50 0N	2 15 E
Picayune	**169**	30 31N	89 40W
Pickering	**29**	54 15N	0 46W
Picton, Australia	**117**	34 12S	150 34 E
Picton, N.Z.	**123**	41 18S	174 3 E
Pictou	**149**	45 41N	62 42W
Pidurutalagala	**90**	7 10N	80 50 E
Piedad, La	**175**	20 20N	102 1W
Piedmont = Piemonte □	**46**	45 0N	7 30 E
Piedmont Plat.	**165**	34 0N	81 30W
Piedras Negras	**174**	28 42N	100 31W
Piemonte □	**46**	45 0N	7 30 E
Pierre	**163**	44 23N	100 20W
Pietermaritzburg	**137**	29 35S	30 25 E
Pietrosul	**57**	47 35N	24 43 E
Pikeville	**165**	37 30N	82 30W
Pilcomayo →	**190**	25 21S	57 42W
Pilsen = Plzen	**43**	49 45N	13 22 E
Pimenta Bueno	**187**	11 35S	61 10W
Pinang □	**96**	5 20N	100 20 E
Pinar del Río	**178**	22 26N	83 40W
Pinaroo	**119**	35 17S	140 53 E
Pinawa	**153**	50 9N	95 50W
Pincher Creek	**155**	49 30N	113 57W
Pinczów	**58**	50 30N	20 35 E
Pindos Óros	**54**	40 0N	21 0 E
Pindus Mts. = Pindos Óros	**54**	40 0N	21 0 E
Pine Bluff	**168**	34 10N	92 0W
Pine Pass	**155**	55 25N	122 42W
Pineville	**168**	31 22N	92 30W
Ping →	**94**	15 42N	100 9 E
Pingdong	**99**	22 39N	120 30 E
Pingliang	**99**	35 35N	106 31 E
Pingxiang	**99**	22 6N	106 46 E
Piniós →	**54**	37 48N	21 20 E
Pinjarra	**120**	32 37S	115 52 E
Piombino	**46**	42 54N	10 30 E
Piotrków Trybunalski	**58**	51 23N	19 43 E
Piqua	**167**	40 10N	84 10W
Piracicaba	**188**	22 45S	47 40W
Piræus = Piraiévs	**55**	37 57N	23 42 E
Piraiévs	**55**	37 57N	23 42 E
Pirapora	**188**	17 20S	44 56W
Pírgos	**54**	37 40N	21 27 E
Pirin Planina	**53**	41 40N	23 30 E
Pirineos	**51**	42 40N	1 0 E
Pisa	**46**	43 43N	10 23 E
Pisagua	**187**	19 40S	70 15W
Pisco	**186**	13 50S	76 12W
Pistóia	**46**	43 57N	10 53 E
Pitcairn I.	**10**	25 5S	130 5W
Piteå	**67**	65 20N	21 25 E
Piteşti	**57**	44 52N	24 54 E
Pithiviers	**39**	48 10N	2 13 E
Pitlochry	**33**	56 43N	3 43W
Pitt I.	**154**	53 30N	129 50W
Pittsburg, Kans., U.S.A.	**166**	37 21N	94 43W
Pittsburg, Tex., U.S.A.	**168**	32 59N	94 58W
Pittsburgh	**164**	40 25N	79 55W
Pittsfield	**164**	42 28N	73 17W
Pittsworth	**116**	27 41S	151 37 E
Piura	**186**	5 15S	80 38W
Placentia	**149**	47 20N	54 0W
Placerville	**172**	38 47N	120 51W
Placetas	**178**	22 15N	79 44W
Plainfield	**164**	40 37N	74 28W
Plainview	**161**	34 10N	101 40W
Plaster Rock	**148**	46 53N	67 22W
Plata, La	**191**	35 0S	57 55W
Plata, Río de la	**191**	34 45S	57 30W
Platte →	**163**	39 16N	94 50W
Plattsburg	**151**	44 41N	73 30W
Plauen	**43**	50 29N	12 9 E
Pleasantville	**164**	39 25N	74 30W
Plenty, Bay of	**122**	37 45S	177 0 E
Plessisville	**148**	46 14N	71 47W
Pleven	**53**	43 26N	24 37 E
Płock	**58**	52 32N	19 40 E
Ploieşti	**57**	44 57N	26 5 E
Plovdiv	**53**	42 8N	24 44 E
Plymouth	**27**	50 23N	4 9W
Plzen	**43**	49 45N	13 22 E
Po →	**47**	44 57N	12 4 E
Po Hai = Bo Hai	**98**	39 0N	120 0 E
Pobeda	**73**	65 12N	146 12 E
Pobedy Pik	**71**	40 45N	79 58 E
Pocatello	**163**	42 50N	112 25W
Pochutla	**177**	15 50N	96 31W
Poços de Caldas	**188**	21 50S	46 33W
Podgorica = Titograd	**52**	42 30N	19 19 E
Podkamennaya Tunguska →	**74**	61 50N	90 13 E
Point Edward	**150**	43 0N	82 30W

Pointe-à-Pitre	**180**	16 10N	61 30W
Pointe Noire	**134**	4 48S	11 53E
Poissy	**39**	48 55N	2 0E
Poitiers	**36**	46 35N	0 20E
Poitou, Plaines et Seuil du	**36**	46 30N	0 1W
Pokaran	**91**	27 0N	71 50E
Pola = Pula	**52**	44 54N	13 57E
Poland ■	**58**	52 0N	20 0E
Polden Hills	**27**	51 7N	2 50W
Polesye	**17**	52 0N	28 10E
Polillo Is.	**112**	14 56N	122 0E
Políyiros	**55**	40 23N	23 25E
Pollachi	**90**	10 35N	77 0E
Polotsk	**68**	55 30N	28 50E
Poltava	**68**	49 35N	34 35E
Polynesia	**123**	10 0S	162 0W
Pomona	**173**	34 2N	117 49W
Pompano Beach	**170**	26 12N	80 6W
Ponca City	**168**	36 40N	97 5W
Ponce	**180**	18 1N	66 37W
Pond Inlet	**146**	72 40N	77 0W
Pondicherry	**90**	11 59N	79 50E
Ponnyadaung	**93**	22 0N	94 10E
Ponoka	**155**	52 42N	113 40W
Pont-Audemer	**39**	49 21N	0 30E
Ponta Grossa	**191**	25 7S	50 10W
Ponta Pora	**188**	22 20S	55 35W
Pontchartrain, L.	**169**	30 12N	90 0W
Pontefract	**29**	53 42N	1 19W
Pontevedra	**50**	42 26N	8 40W
Pontiac	**167**	42 40N	83 20W
Pontianak	**111**	0 3S	109 15E
Pontine Is. = Ponziane, Isole	**48**	40 55N	13 0E
Pontoise	**39**	49 3N	2 5E
Pontypool	**27**	51 42N	3 1W
Pontypridd	**27**	51 36N	3 21W
Ponziane, Isole	**48**	40 55N	13 0E
Poochera	**118**	32 43S	134 51E
Poole	**24**	50 42N	1 58W
Pooley I.	**154**	52 45N	128 15W
Poona = Pune	**91**	18 29N	73 57E
Poopó, Lago de	**187**	18 30S	67 35W
Popayán	**184**	2 27N	76 36W
Poplar Bluff	**169**	36 45N	90 22W
Popocatépetl, Volcán	**177**	19 2N	98 38W
Porcher I.	**154**	53 50N	130 30W
Porcupine →	**142**	66 35N	145 15W
Pori	**67**	61 29N	21 48E
Porkkala	**67**	59 59N	24 26E
Port Adelaide	**119**	34 46S	138 30E
Port Alberni	**154**	49 40N	124 50W
Port Albert	**115**	38 42S	146 42E
Port Alfred	**148**	48 18N	70 53W
Port Angeles	**171**	48 7N	123 30W
Port Antonio	**180**	18 10N	76 30W
Port Arthur	**168**	30 0N	94 0W
Port-au-Prince	**180**	18 40N	72 20W
Port Augusta	**118**	32 30S	137 50E
Port Blair	**94**	11 40N	92 30E
Port-Cartier	**148**	50 2N	66 50W
Port Chalmers	**123**	45 49S	170 30E
Port Colborne	**151**	42 50N	79 10W
Port Coquitlam	**154**	49 15N	122 45W
Port Darwin	**192**	51 50S	59 0W
Port-de-Paix	**180**	19 50N	72 50W
Port Elgin	**150**	44 25N	81 25W
Port Elizabeth	**136**	33 58S	25 40E
Port Erin	**28**	54 5N	4 45W
Port Etienne = Nouâdhibou	**126**	20 54N	17 0W
Port Fairy	**119**	38 22S	142 12E
Port Glasgow	**30**	55 57N	4 40W
Port Harcourt	**131**	4 40N	7 10E
Port Harrison = Inoucdjouac	**146**	58 25N	78 15W
Port Hawkesbury	**149**	45 36N	61 22W
Port Hope	**151**	43 56N	78 20W
Port Huron	**167**	43 0N	82 28W
Port Kembla	**117**	34 52S	150 49E
Port Laoise	**35**	53 2N	7 20W
Port Lavaca	**158**	28 38N	96 38W
Port Lincoln	**119**	34 42S	135 52E
Port Lyautey = Kenitra	**126**	34 15N	6 40W
Port Macquarie	**116**	31 25S	152 25E
Port Morant	**180**	17 54N	76 19W
Port Moresby	**115**	9 24S	147 8E
Port Nelson	**143**	57 3N	92 36W
Port Nolloth	**136**	29 17S	16 52E
Port Nouveau-Québec	**146**	58 30N	65 59W
Port of Spain	**180**	10 40N	61 31W
Port Phillip B.	**117**	38 10S	144 50E
Port Pirie	**118**	33 10S	138 1E
Port Said = Bûr Sa'îd	**128**	31 16N	32 18E
Port Simpson	**154**	54 30N	130 20W
Port Stanley	**150**	42 40N	81 10W
Port Sudan = Bûr Sûdân	**129**	19 32N	37 9E
Port Talbot	**27**	51 35N	3 48W
Port Townsend	**171**	48 7N	122 50W
Portadown	**34**	54 27N	6 26W
Portage La Prairie	**153**	49 58N	98 18W
Portarlington	**35**	53 10N	7 10W
Porte, La	**167**	41 36N	86 43W
Porterville	**173**	36 5N	119 0W
Porthcawl	**27**	51 28N	3 42W
Porthmadog	**26**	52 55N	4 13W
Portile de Fier	**56**	44 42N	22 30E
Portland, Australia	**119**	38 20S	141 35E
Portland, Maine, U.S.A.	**148**	43 40N	70 15W
Portland, Oreg., U.S.A.	**171**	45 35N	122 40W
Portland, Bill of	**24**	50 31N	2 27W
Portland Prom.	**146**	58 40N	78 33W
Porto	**50**	41 8N	8 40W
Pôrto Alegre	**191**	30 5S	51 10W
Porto Empédocle	**48**	37 18N	13 30E
Porto Mendes	**191**	24 30S	54 15W
Porto Novo	**131**	6 23N	2 42E
Pôrto Seguro	**189**	16 26S	39 5W
Pôrto Velho	**187**	8 46S	63 54W
Portoferráio	**46**	42 50N	10 20E
Portoscuso	**48**	39 12N	8 22E
Portovíejo	**184**	1 7S	80 28W
Portpatrick	**30**	54 50N	5 7W
Portree	**32**	57 25N	6 11W
Portrush	**34**	55 13N	6 40W
Portsmouth, Domin.	**180**	15 34N	61 27W
Portsmouth, U.K.	**25**	50 48N	1 6W
Portsmouth, N.H., U.S.A.	**164**	43 5N	70 45W
Portsmouth, Ohio, U.S.A.	**167**	38 45N	83 0W
Portsmouth, Va., U.S.A.	**165**	36 50N	76 20W
Porttipahta	**67**	68 5N	26 40E
Portugal ■	**50**	40 0N	7 0W
Portuguese-Guinea = Guinea-Bissau ■	**130**	12 0N	15 0W
Portuguese Timor ■ = Timor	**113**	9 0S	125 0E
Portumna	**35**	53 5N	8 12W
Porvenir	**192**	53 10S	70 16W
Posadas	**191**	27 30S	55 50W
Poshan = Boshan	**98**	36 28N	117 49E
Poste-de-la-Baleine	**140**	55 17N	77 45W
Potchefstroom	**137**	26 41S	27 7E
Potenza	**49**	40 40N	15 50E
Potomac →	**165**	38 0N	76 23W
Potosí	**187**	19 38S	65 50W
Potsdam, Germany	**43**	52 23N	13 4E
Potsdam, U.S.A.	**151**	44 40N	74 59W
Pottsville	**164**	40 39N	76 12W
Pouce Coupé	**155**	55 40N	120 10W
Poughkeepsie	**164**	41 40N	73 57W
Poulaphouca Res.	**35**	53 8N	6 30W
Póvoa de Varzim	**50**	41 25N	8 46W
Powell, L.	**163**	37 25N	110 45W
Powell River	**154**	49 50N	124 35W
Powys □	**26**	52 20N	3 20W
Poyang Hu	**99**	29 10N	116 10E
Poyarkovo	**75**	49 36N	128 41E
Poznań	**58**	52 25N	16 55E
Prachuap Khiri Khan	**94**	11 49N	99 48E
Prague = Praha	**58**	50 5N	14 22E
Praha	**58**	50 5N	14 22E
Prainha, Amazonas, Brazil	**187**	7 10S	60 30W
Prainha, Pará, Brazil	**185**	1 45S	53 30W
Prairie du Chien	**166**	43 1N	91 9W
Prato	**46**	43 53N	11 5E
Pratt	**161**	37 40N	98 45W

Prepansko Jezero	**52**	40 55N	21 0 E
Preparis North Channel	**94**	15 12N	93 40 E
Preparis South Channel	**94**	14 36N	93 40 E
Prescott	**160**	34 35N	112 30W
Preservation Inlet	**123**	46 8 S	166 35 E
Presidencia Roque Saenz Peña	**190**	26 45 S	60 30W
Presidente Prudente	**188**	22 5 S	51 25W
Presidio	**161**	29 30N	104 20W
Prespa, L. = Prepansko Jezero	**52**	40 55N	21 0 E
Presque Isle	**148**	46 40N	68 0W
Preston, Borders, U.K.	**28**	55 48N	2 18W
Preston, Lancs., U.K.	**21**	53 46N	2 42W
Prestonpans	**31**	55 58N	3 0W
Prestwick	**31**	55 30N	4 38W
Pretoria	**137**	25 44 S	28 12 E
Préveza	**55**	38 57N	20 47 E
Prichard	**169**	30 47N	88 5W
Prilep	**52**	41 21N	21 37 E
Prince Albert	**152**	53 15N	105 50W
Prince Albert Pen.	**145**	72 30N	116 0W
Prince Albert Sd.	**145**	70 25N	115 0W
Prince Charles I.	**146**	67 47N	76 12W
Prince Edward I. □	**148**	46 20N	63 20W
Prince George	**154**	53 55N	122 50W
Prince of Wales I., Canada	**145**	73 0N	99 0W
Prince of Wales I., U.S.A.	**143**	55 30N	133 0W
Prince Patrick I.	**12**	77 0N	120 0W
Prince Rupert	**154**	54 20N	130 20W
Princess Royal I.	**154**	53 0N	128 40W
Princeton	**155**	49 27N	120 30W
Principe, I. de	**131**	1 37N	7 27 E
Principe da Beira	**187**	12 20 S	64 30W
Pripet = Pripyat →	**68**	51 20N	30 9 E
Pripet Marshes = Polesye	**17**	52 0N	28 10 E
Pripyat →	**68**	51 20N	30 9 E
Pripyat Marshes = Polesye	**17**	52 0N	28 10 E
Priština	**52**	42 40N	21 13 E
Privolzhskaya Vozvyshennost	**17**	51 0N	46 0 E
Prizren	**52**	42 13N	20 45 E
Proddatur	**90**	14 45N	78 30 E
Progreso	**177**	21 17N	89 40W
Prokopyevsk	**71**	54 0N	86 45 E
Proserpine	**121**	20 21 S	148 36 E
Provence	**37**	43 40N	5 46 E
Providence	**164**	41 50N	71 28W
Provo	**163**	40 16N	111 37W
Prudhoe Bay	**142**	70 20N	148 20W
Pruszków	**58**	52 9N	20 49 E
Prut →	**57**	46 3N	28 10 E
Przemyśl	**58**	49 50N	22 45 E
Przeworsk	**58**	50 6N	22 32 E
Pskov	**68**	57 50N	28 25 E
Pucallpa	**186**	8 25 S	74 30W
Puebla	**177**	19 3N	98 12W
Puebla □	**177**	18 50N	98 0W
Pueblo	**163**	38 20N	104 40W
Puelches	**190**	38 5 S	65 51W
Puente Alto	**190**	33 32 S	70 35W
Puerto Armuelles	**179**	8 20N	82 51W
Puerto Ayacucho	**184**	5 40N	67 35W
Puerto Barrios	**177**	15 40N	88 32W
Puerto Cabello	**184**	10 28N	68 1W
Puerto Cabezas	**179**	14 0N	83 30W
Puerto Castilla	**179**	16 0N	86 0W
Puerto Cortes, C. Rica	**179**	8 55N	84 0W
Puerto Cortes, Hond.	**177**	15 51N	88 0W
Puerto Heath	**187**	12 34 S	68 39W
Puerto La Cruz	**185**	10 13N	64 38W
Puerto Libertad	**174**	29 55N	112 41W
Puerto Lobos	**192**	42 0 S	65 3W
Puerto Maldonado	**187**	12 30 S	69 10W
Puerto Montt	**190**	41 28 S	73 0W
Puerto Padre	**178**	21 13N	76 35W
Puerto Pinasco	**191**	22 36 S	57 50W
Puerto Plata	**180**	19 48N	70 45W
Puerto Quepos	**179**	9 29N	84 6W
Puerto Rico ■	**180**	18 15N	66 45W
Puerto Vallarta	**175**	20 37N	105 15W
Puertollano	**50**	38 43N	4 7W
Puget Sd.	**171**	47 15N	122 30W
Púglia □	**49**	41 0N	16 30 E
Pula	**52**	44 54N	13 57 E
Pulaski, Tenn., U.S.A.	**169**	35 10N	87 0W
Pulaski, Va., U.S.A.	**165**	37 4N	80 49W
Pulicat, L.	**90**	13 40N	80 15 E
Pullman	**171**	46 49N	117 10W
Punakha	**92**	27 42N	89 52 E
Punata	**187**	17 32 S	65 50W
Pune	**91**	18 29N	73 57 E
Punjab □, India	**89**	31 0N	76 0 E
Punjab □, Pakistan	**89**	30 0N	72 0 E
Puno	**187**	15 55 S	70 3W
Punta Alta	**190**	38 53 S	62 4W
Punta Arenas	**192**	53 10 S	71 0W
Punta Gorda	**177**	16 10N	88 45W
Puntabie	**118**	32 12 S	134 13 E
Puntarenas	**179**	10 0N	84 50W
Punto Fijo	**184**	11 50N	70 13W
Puquio	**186**	14 45 S	74 10W
Pur →	**69**	67 31N	77 55 E
Purbeck, Isle of	**24**	50 40N	2 5W
Purmerend	**40**	52 30N	4 58 E
Purnia	**92**	25 45N	87 31 E
Pursat	**95**	12 34N	103 50 E
Purus →	**185**	3 42 S	61 28W
Pusan	**98**	35 5N	129 0 E
Putao	**93**	27 28N	97 30 E
Putorana, Gory	**72**	69 0N	95 0 E
Putumayo →	**184**	3 7 S	67 58W
Puy, Le	**37**	45 2N	3 53 E
Puy-de-Dôme	**37**	45 46N	2 57 E
Puyallup	**171**	47 10N	122 22W
Pwllheli	**26**	52 54N	4 26W
Pyasina →	**72**	73 30N	87 0 E
Pyatigorsk	**70**	44 2N	43 6 E
Pyinmana	**93**	19 45N	96 12 E
Pyŏngyang	**98**	39 0N	125 30 E
Pyramid L.	**172**	40 0N	119 30W
Pyrénées	**124**	42 45N	0 18 E
Qā'emshahr	**86**	36 30N	52 55 E
Qahremānshahr = Bākhtarān	**84**	34 23N	47 0 E
Qaidam Pendi	**100**	37 0N	95 0 E
Qal'at al Akhḍar	**82**	28 0N	37 10 E
Qamar, Ghubbat al	**83**	16 20N	52 30 E
Qamdo	**101**	31 15N	97 6 E
Qandahār	**87**	31 32N	65 30 E
Qaṣr-e Qand	**85**	26 15N	60 45 E
Qatar ■	**85**	25 30N	51 15 E
Qāyen	**86**	33 40N	59 10 E
Qazvin	**81**	36 15N	50 0 E
Qena	**128**	26 10N	32 43 E
Qeshm	**85**	26 55N	56 10 E
Qilian Shan	**100**	38 30N	96 0 E
Qingdao	**98**	36 5N	120 20 E
Qinghai □	**101**	36 0N	98 0 E
Qinghai Hu	**100**	36 40N	100 10 E
Qinhuangdao	**98**	39 56N	119 30 E
Qiqihar	**98**	47 26N	124 0 E
Qom	**86**	34 40N	51 0 E
Qomsheh	**85**	32 0N	51 55 E
Qondūz □	**87**	36 50N	68 50 E
Qu Xian	**99**	30 48N	106 58 E
Quang Ngai	**95**	15 13N	108 58 E
Quantock Hills	**27**	51 8N	3 10W
Quanzhou	**99**	24 55N	118 34 E
Quatsino	**154**	50 30N	127 40W
Queanbeyan	**117**	35 17 S	149 14 E
Québec	**148**	46 52N	71 13W
Québec □	**140**	50 0N	70 0W
Queen Alexandra Ra.	**15**	85 0 S	170 0 E
Queen Charlotte	**154**	53 15N	132 2W
Queen Charlotte Is.	**154**	53 20N	132 10W
Queen Charlotte Str.	**154**	51 0N	128 0W
Queen Elizabeth Is.	**138**	76 0N	95 0W
Queen Mary Land	**15**	70 0 S	95 0 E
Queen Maud G.	**145**	68 15N	102 30W
Queen Maud Mts.	**15**	86 0 S	160 0W

Queenscliff	**117**	38 16S	144 39 E
Queensland □	**115**	22 0S	142 0 E
Queenstown, Australia	**119**	42 4S	145 35 E
Queenstown, N.Z.	**123**	45 1S	168 40 E
Quelimane	**137**	17 53S	36 58 E
Quelpart = Cheju Do	**99**	33 29N	126 34 E
Querétaro	**177**	20 36N	100 23W
Querétaro □	**177**	21 0N	99 55W
Quesnel	**154**	53 0N	122 30W
Quetta	**88**	30 15N	66 55 E
Quezaltenango	**177**	14 50N	91 30W
Quezon City	**112**	14 38N	121 0 E
Qui Nhon	**95**	13 40N	109 13 E
Quibdo	**184**	5 42N	76 40W
Quillabamba	**186**	12 50S	72 50W
Quilon	**90**	8 50N	76 38 E
Quilpie	**116**	26 35S	144 11 E
Quimper	**36**	48 0N	4 9W
Quincy, Calif., U.S.A.	**172**	39 56N	121 0W
Quincy, Fla., U.S.A.	**170**	30 34N	84 34W
Quincy, Ill., U.S.A.	**166**	39 55N	91 20W
Quincy, Mass., U.S.A.	**164**	42 14N	71 0W
Quintana Roo □	**177**	19 40N	88 30W
Quirindi	**116**	31 28S	150 40 E
Quitman	**170**	30 49N	83 35W
Quito	**184**	0 15S	78 35W
Quixadá	**189**	4 55S	39 0W
Quorn	**118**	32 25S	138 0 E
Quseir	**128**	26 7N	34 16 E
Raahe	**67**	64 40N	24 28 E
Raasay	**32**	57 25N	6 4W
Rabat	**126**	34 2N	6 48W
Rabaul	**115**	4 24S	152 18 E
Rābigh	**82**	22 50N	39 5 E
Race, C.	**149**	46 40N	53 5W
Rach Gia	**95**	10 5N	105 5 E
Racibórz	**58**	50 7N	18 18 E
Racine	**167**	42 41N	87 51W
Radium Hot Springs	**155**	50 35N	116 2W
Radnor Forest	**26**	52 17N	3 10W
Radom	**58**	51 23N	21 12 E
Radomir	**53**	42 37N	23 4 E
Radstock	**27**	51 17N	2 25W
Radville	**152**	49 30N	104 15W
Rae	**145**	62 50N	116 3W
Rae Bareli	**92**	26 18N	81 20 E
Raetihi	**122**	39 25S	175 17 E
Rafaela	**190**	31 10S	61 30W
Rafḥā	**82**	29 35N	43 35 E
Rafsanjān	**85**	30 30N	56 5 E
Ragama	**90**	7 0N	79 50 E
Raglan	**122**	37 55S	174 55 E
Ragusa	**49**	36 56N	14 42 E
Rahaeng = Tak	**94**	16 52N	99 8 E
Raichur	**91**	16 10N	77 20 E
Rainier, Mt.	**171**	46 50N	121 50W
Rainy L.	**153**	48 42N	93 10W
Rainy River	**153**	48 43N	94 29W
Raipur	**92**	21 17N	81 45 E
Rajahmundry	**92**	17 1N	81 48 E
Rajapalaiyam	**90**	9 25N	77 35 E
Rajasthan □	**91**	26 45N	73 30 E
Rajasthan Canal	**89**	28 0N	72 0 E
Rajkot	**91**	22 15N	70 56 E
Rajshahi □	**92**	25 0N	89 0 E
Raleigh	**165**	35 47N	78 39W
Raleigh B.	**165**	34 50N	76 15W
Rambouillet	**39**	48 40N	1 48 E
Rampur	**89**	28 50N	79 5 E
Ramsey	**28**	54 20N	4 21W
Rancagua	**190**	34 10S	70 50W
Ranchi	**92**	23 19N	85 27 E
Rangiora	**123**	43 19S	172 36 E
Rangoon	**93**	16 45N	96 20 E
Rangpur	**92**	25 42N	89 22 E
Raniwara	**91**	24 50N	72 10 E
Rankin Inlet	**145**	62 30N	93 0W
Rankins Springs	**117**	33 49S	146 14 E
Rannoch, L.	**33**	56 41N	4 20W
Rannoch Moor	**30**	56 38N	4 48W
Rapid City	**163**	44 0N	103 0W
Ras Dashen	**132**	13 8N	38 26 E
Rasa, Punta	**192**	40 50S	62 15W
Rasht	**81**	37 20N	49 40 E
Rat Is.	**142**	51 50N	178 15 E
Ratangarh	**89**	28 5N	74 35 E
Rath Luirc	**35**	52 21N	8 40W
Rathlin I.	**34**	55 18N	6 14W
Ratibor = Racibórz	**58**	50 7N	18 18 E
Ratlam	**91**	23 20N	75 0 E
Ratnagiri	**91**	16 57N	73 18 E
Rattray Hd.	**33**	57 38N	1 50W
Raub	**96**	3 47N	101 52 E
Raukumara Ra.	**122**	38 5S	177 55 E
Ravenna	**47**	44 28N	12 15 E
Ravenshoe	**121**	17 37S	145 29 E
Ravensthorpe	**120**	33 35S	120 2 E
Rawalpindi	**89**	33 38N	73 8 E
Rawlins	**163**	41 50N	107 20W
Ray, C.	**149**	47 33N	59 15W
Raymond	**155**	49 30N	112 35W
Razgrad	**53**	43 33N	26 34 E
Ré, Île de	**36**	46 12N	1 30W
Reading, U.K.	**25**	51 27N	0 57W
Reading, U.S.A.	**164**	40 20N	75 53W
Reay Forest	**32**	58 20N	4 55W
Rebun-Tō	**103**	45 23N	141 2 E
Recife	**189**	8 0S	35 0W
Reconquista	**190**	29 10S	59 45W
Recreo	**190**	29 25S	65 10W
Red →	**168**	31 0N	91 40W
Red Bluff	**172**	40 11N	122 11W
Red Cliffs	**119**	34 19S	142 11 E
Red Deer	**155**	52 20N	113 50W
Red Lake	**153**	51 3N	93 49W
Red Oak	**166**	41 0N	95 10W
Red Sea	**128**	25 0N	36 0 E
Red Tower Pass = Turnu Rosu Pasul	**57**	45 33N	24 17 E
Red Wing	**166**	44 32N	92 35W
Redcar	**29**	54 37N	1 4W
Redcliff	**152**	50 10N	110 50W
Redcliffe	**116**	27 12S	153 0 E
Redding	**172**	40 30N	122 25W
Redditch	**24**	52 18N	1 57W
Redlands	**173**	34 0N	117 11W
Redruth	**27**	50 14N	5 14W
Redwater	**155**	53 55N	113 6W
Redwood City	**172**	37 30N	122 15W
Ree, L.	**34**	53 35N	8 0W
Reedley	**173**	36 36N	119 27W
Regensburg	**43**	49 1N	12 7 E
Réggio di Calábria	**49**	38 7N	15 38 E
Réggio nell' Emilia	**46**	44 42N	10 38 E
Regina	**152**	50 27N	104 35W
Rehovot	**80**	31 54N	34 48 E
Reichenbach	**43**	50 36N	12 19 E
Reidsville	**165**	36 21N	79 40W
Reims	**39**	49 15N	4 0 E
Reina Adelaida, Arch.	**192**	52 20S	74 0W
Reindeer L.	**143**	57 15N	102 15W
Reliance	**145**	63 0N	109 20W
Remanso	**189**	9 41S	42 4W
Remarkable, Mt.	**118**	32 48S	138 10 E
Remscheid	**42**	51 11N	7 12 E
Rendsburg	**42**	54 18N	9 41 E
Renfrew, Canada	**151**	45 30N	76 40W
Renfrew, U.K.	**31**	55 52N	4 24W
Renkum	**41**	51 58N	5 43 E
Renmark	**119**	34 11S	140 43 E
Rennes	**36**	48 7N	1 41W
Reno	**172**	39 30N	119 50W
Republic	**150**	46 25N	87 59W
Republican →	**163**	39 3N	96 48W
Repulse Bay	**146**	66 30N	86 30W
Requena	**186**	5 5S	73 52W
Resht = Rasht	**81**	37 20N	49 40 E
Resistencia	**190**	27 30S	59 0W
Resolution I., Canada	**146**	61 30N	65 0W

Resolution I., N.Z.	**123**	45 40S	166 40E
Retalhuleu	**177**	14 33N	91 46W
Réthímnon	**55**	35 18N	24 30E
Réunion	**9**	22 0S	56 0E
Reval = Tallinn	**68**	59 22N	24 48E
Revelstoke	**155**	51 0N	118 10W
Revilla Gigedo, Is.	**139**	18 40N	112 0W
Rewa	**92**	24 33N	81 25E
Rewari	**89**	28 15N	76 40E
Rexburg	**163**	43 55N	111 50W
Rey Malabo	**131**	3 45N	8 50E
Reykjavík	**64**	64 10N	21 57E
Reynosa	**176**	26 5N	98 18W
Rhayader	**26**	52 19N	3 30W
Rhein →	**42**	51 52N	6 20E
Rheinland-Pfalz □	**42**	50 0N	7 0E
Rhin = Rhein →	**42**	51 52N	6 20E
Rhine = Rhein →	**42**	51 52N	6 20E
Rhineland-Palatinate □ = Rheinland-Pfalz □	**42**	50 0N	7 0E
Rhinelander	**150**	45 38N	89 29W
Rhode Island □	**164**	41 38N	71 37W
Rhodes = Ródhos	**55**	36 15N	28 10E
Rhodesia = Zimbabwe ■	**137**	20 0S	30 0E
Rhodope Mts. = Rhodopi Planina	**53**	41 40N	24 20E
Rhodopi Planina	**53**	41 40N	24 20E
Rhön	**42**	50 24N	9 58E
Rhondda	**27**	51 39N	3 30W
Rhône →	**37**	43 28N	4 42E
Rhum	**32**	57 0N	6 20W
Rhyl	**26**	53 19N	3 29W
Rhymney	**27**	51 45N	3 17W
Riachão	**188**	7 20S	46 37W
Riau, Kepulauan	**111**	0 30N	104 20E
Ribatejo □	**50**	39 15N	8 30W
Ribble →	**28**	54 13N	2 20W
Ribeirão Prêto	**188**	21 10S	47 50W
Riberalta	**187**	11 0S	66 0W
Riccarton	**123**	43 32S	172 37E
Richland	**171**	46 15N	119 15W
Richmond, Australia	**116**	20 43S	143 8E
Richmond, N.Z.	**123**	41 20S	173 12E
Richmond, N. Yorks., U.K.	**28**	54 24N	1 43W
Richmond, Surrey, U.K.	**25**	51 28N	0 18W
Richmond, Calif., U.S.A.	**172**	37 58N	122 21W
Richmond, Ind., U.S.A.	**167**	39 50N	84 50W
Richmond, Ky., U.S.A.	**165**	37 40N	84 20W
Richmond, Va., U.S.A.	**165**	37 33N	77 27W
Richwood	**165**	38 17N	80 32W
Ridgeway	**164**	42 56S	147 16E
Riga	**68**	56 53N	24 8E
Rīgestān □	**87**	30 15N	65 0E
Rigolet	**147**	54 10N	58 23W
Rijeka	**52**	45 20N	14 21E
Rijssen	**41**	52 19N	6 30E
Rijswijk	**40**	52 4N	4 22E
Rímini	**47**	44 3N	12 33E
Rîmnicu Vîlcea	**57**	45 9N	24 21E
Rimouski	**148**	48 27N	68 30W
Rinía	**55**	37 23N	25 13E
Rio Branco	**187**	9 58S	67 49W
Río Claro	**180**	10 20N	61 25W
Río Cuarto	**190**	33 10S	64 25W
Rio de Janeiro	**188**	23 0S	43 12W
Rio de Janeiro □	**188**	22 50S	43 0W
Río Gallegos	**192**	51 35S	69 15W
Rio Grande	**191**	32 0S	52 20W
Rio Grande →	**161**	25 57N	97 9W
Rio Grande do Norte □	**189**	5 40S	36 0W
Rio Grande do Sul □	**191**	30 0S	53 0W
Río Mulatos	**187**	19 40S	66 50W
Rio Negro	**191**	26 0S	50 0W
Rio Verde	**188**	17 50S	51 0W
Ríobamba	**184**	1 50S	78 45W
Ríohacha	**184**	11 33N	72 55W
Rioja, La	**190**	29 20S	67 0W
Rioja, La □	**50**	42 20N	2 20W
Ríosucio	**184**	7 27N	77 7W
Ripon	**28**	54 8N	1 31W
Rishiri-Tō	**103**	45 11N	141 15E
Ritchies Archipelago	**94**	12 5N	94 0E
Rivas	**179**	11 30N	85 50W
Riverhead	**164**	40 53N	72 40W
Riverside	**173**	34 0N	117 22W
Riverton	**153**	51 1N	97 0W
Riviera di Levante	**46**	44 23N	9 15E
Riviera di Ponente	**46**	43 50N	7 58E
Rivière-du-Loup	**148**	47 50N	69 30W
Riyadh = Ar Riyāḍ	**83**	24 41N	46 42E
Roanne	**37**	46 3N	4 4E
Roanoke, Ala., U.S.A.	**169**	33 9N	85 23W
Roanoke, Va., U.S.A.	**165**	37 19N	79 55W
Roanoke →	**165**	35 56N	76 43W
Roanoke Rapids	**165**	36 28N	77 42W
Robinvale	**119**	34 40S	142 45E
Roblin	**152**	51 14N	101 21W
Roboré	**187**	18 10S	59 45W
Robson, Mt.	**155**	53 10N	119 10W
Roca, C. da	**50**	38 40N	9 31W
Rocha	**191**	34 30S	54 25W
Rochdale	**28**	53 36N	2 10W
Roche-sur-Yon, La	**36**	46 40N	1 25W
Rochefort	**36**	45 56N	0 57W
Rochelle, La	**36**	46 10N	1 9W
Rochester, Minn., U.S.A.	**166**	44 1N	92 28W
Rochester, N.H., U.S.A.	**164**	43 19N	70 57W
Rochester, N.Y., U.S.A.	**164**	43 10N	77 40W
Rock Hill	**165**	34 55N	81 2W
Rock Island	**166**	41 30N	90 35W
Rock Sprs.	**163**	41 40N	109 10W
Rockall	**16**	57 37N	13 42W
Rockford	**166**	42 20N	89 0W
Rockglen	**152**	49 11N	105 57W
Rockhampton	**119**	23 22S	150 32E
Rockingham	**120**	32 15S	115 38E
Rockland	**148**	44 6N	69 6W
Rocky Mount	**165**	35 55N	77 48W
Rocky Mountain House	**155**	52 22N	114 55W
Rocky Mts.	**138**	55 0N	121 0W
Ródhos	**55**	36 15N	28 10E
Roebourne	**114**	20 44S	117 9E
Roermond	**41**	51 12N	6 0E
Roes Welcome Sd.	**146**	65 0N	87 0W
Rogaland fylke □	**60**	59 12N	6 20E
Rogers	**168**	36 20N	94 5W
Rohri	**88**	27 45N	68 51E
Rohtak	**89**	28 55N	76 43E
Rojo, C.	**177**	21 33N	97 20W
Rolla	**166**	37 56N	91 42W
Roma, Australia	**116**	26 32S	148 49E
Roma, Italy	**46**	41 54N	12 30E
Romaine →	**141**	50 18N	63 47W
Roman	**57**	46 57N	26 55E
Romana, La	**180**	18 27N	68 57W
Romania ■	**57**	46 0N	25 0E
Romans	**37**	45 3N	5 3E
Romanzof, C.	**142**	62 0N	165 50W
Rome = Roma	**46**	41 54N	12 30E
Rome, Ga., U.S.A.	**169**	34 20N	85 0W
Rome, N.Y., U.S.A.	**164**	43 14N	75 29W
Romilly	**39**	48 31N	3 44E
Romney Marsh	**25**	51 0N	1 0E
Rona	**32**	57 33N	6 0W
Rondônia □	**187**	11 0S	63 0W
Rong, Koh	**95**	10 45N	103 15E
Ronge, L. la	**152**	55 6N	105 17W
Roosendaal	**40**	51 32N	4 29E
Roraima □	**185**	2 0N	61 30W
Roraima, Mt.	**185**	5 10N	60 40W
Rosario, Argentina	**190**	33 0S	60 40W
Rosario, Brazil	**188**	3 0S	44 15W
Rosario, Mexico	**175**	22 58N	105 53W
Rosario, Paraguay	**191**	24 30S	57 35W
Rosário do Sul	**191**	30 15S	54 55W
Roscommon	**34**	53 38N	8 11W
Roscommon □	**34**	53 40N	8 15W
Roscrea	**35**	52 58N	7 50W
Roseau	**180**	15 20N	61 24W
Roseburg	**171**	43 10N	123 20W
Rosenberg	**168**	29 30N	95 48W
Rosendaël	**38**	51 3N	2 24E

Rosetown	**152**	51 35N	107 59W
Roseville	**172**	38 46N	121 17W
Rosewood	**116**	27 38S	152 36 E
Roskilde	**61**	55 38N	12 3 E
Ross on Wye	**24**	51 55N	2 34W
Ross Sea	**15**	74 0S	178 0 E
Rossan Pt.	**34**	54 42N	8 47W
Rossland	**155**	49 6N	117 50W
Rosslare	**35**	52 17N	6 23W
Røssvatnet	**65**	65 45N	14 5 E
Rosthern	**152**	52 40N	106 20W
Rostock	**43**	54 4N	12 9 E
Rostov	**68**	47 15N	39 45 E
Roswell	**161**	33 26N	104 32W
Rosyth	**31**	56 2N	3 26W
Rother →	**25**	50 59N	0 40 E
Rotherham	**29**	53 26N	1 21W
Rothesay	**30**	55 50N	5 3W
Roto	**117**	33 0S	145 30 E
Rotorua	**122**	38 9S	176 16 E
Rotorua, L.	**122**	38 5S	176 18 E
Rotterdam	**40**	51 55N	4 30 E
Rotuma	**122**	12 25S	177 5 E
Roubaix	**37**	50 40N	3 10 E
Rouen	**38**	49 27N	1 4 E
Round Mt.	**116**	30 26S	152 16 E
Roussillon	**37**	42 30N	2 35 E
Rouyn	**151**	48 20N	79 0W
Rovaniemi	**67**	66 29N	25 41 E
Rovno	**68**	50 40N	26 10 E
Ruahine Ra.	**122**	39 55S	176 2 E
Ruapehu	**122**	39 17S	175 35 E
Rub' al Khali	**83**	18 0N	48 0 E
Rubh a' Mhail	**30**	55 55N	6 10W
Rubio	**184**	7 43N	72 22W
Rubtsovsk	**71**	51 30N	81 10 E
Rudnyy	**71**	52 57N	63 7 E
Rudolf, Ostrov	**69**	81 45N	58 30 E
Rufiji →	**135**	7 50S	39 15 E
Rufino	**190**	34 20S	62 50W
Rugby	**25**	52 23N	1 16W
Rügen	**43**	54 22N	13 25 E
Ruhr →	**42**	51 25N	6 44 E
Rukwa L.	**135**	8 0S	32 20 E
Rumania = Romania ■	**57**	46 0N	25 0 E
Rumford	**148**	44 30N	70 30W
Rumoi	**103**	43 56N	141 39W
Runcorn	**28**	53 20N	2 44W
Rupat	**111**	1 45N	101 40 E
Rupert →	**140**	51 29N	78 45W
Rupert House = Fort Rupert	**140**	51 30N	78 40W
Ruschuk = Ruse	**53**	43 48N	25 59 E
Ruse	**53**	43 48N	25 59 E
Russell	**152**	50 50N	101 20W
Russellville, Ala., U.S.A.	**169**	34 30N	87 44W
Russellville, Ark., U.S.A.	**168**	35 15N	93 8W
Ruston	**168**	32 30N	92 58W
Rutherglen	**31**	55 50N	4 11W
Rutland I.	**94**	11 25N	92 40 E
Ruwenzori	**132**	0 30N	29 55 E
Rwanda ■	**135**	2 0S	30 0 E
Ryan, L.	**30**	55 0N	5 2W
Ryazan	**68**	54 40N	39 40 E
Rybache	**71**	46 40N	81 20 E
Rybinsk = Andropov	**68**	58 5N	38 50 E
Ryde	**25**	50 44N	1 9W
Rye	**25**	50 57N	0 46 E
Rylstone	**117**	32 46S	149 58 E
Ryōhaku-Sanchi	**106**	36 9N	136 49 E
Ryūgasaki	**107**	35 54N	140 11 E
Rzeszów	**58**	50 5N	21 58 E
Sa Dec	**95**	10 20N	105 46 E
Saar →	**42**	49 41N	6 32 E
Saarbrücken	**42**	49 15N	6 58 E
Saaremaa	**68**	58 30N	22 30 E
Saarland □	**42**	49 15N	7 0 E
Sabadell	**51**	41 28N	2 7 E
Sabae	**106**	35 57N	136 11 E
Sabah □	**112**	6 0N	117 0 E
Sábana de la Mar	**180**	19 7N	69 24W
Sabhah	**127**	27 9N	14 29 E
Sabi →	**137**	18 50S	31 40 E
Sabinas	**174**	27 51N	101 7W
Sabinas Hidalgo, R. →	**176**	26 50N	99 35W
Sabine →	**158**	30 0N	93 35W
Sable, C., Canada	**148**	43 29N	65 38W
Sable, C., U.S.A.	**159**	25 13N	81 0W
Sable I.	**149**	44 0N	60 0W
Sabrina Coast	**15**	68 0S	120 0 E
Sabzevār	**86**	36 15N	57 40 E
Saco	**148**	43 30N	70 27W
Sacramento	**172**	38 33N	121 30 E
Sacramento →	**172**	38 3N	121 56W
Sacramento Mts.	**161**	32 30N	105 30W
Sado, Shima	**103**	38 15N	138 30 E
Safed Koh	**87**	34 0N	70 0 E
Saffron Walden	**25**	52 2N	0 15 E
Safi	**126**	32 18N	9 20W
Saga	**108**	33 15N	130 16 E
Sagami-Nada	**107**	34 58N	139 30 E
Sagami-Wan	**107**	35 15N	139 25 E
Sagamihara	**107**	35 33N	139 25 E
Sagar	**91**	14 14N	75 6 E
Sagara	**107**	34 41N	138 12 E
Saginaw	**167**	43 26N	83 55W
Saginaw B.	**167**	43 50N	83 40W
Saglouc	**146**	62 14N	75 38W
Sagres	**50**	37 0N	8 58W
Sagua la Grande	**178**	22 50N	80 10W
Saguenay →	**148**	48 22N	71 0W
Sahara	**126**	23 0N	5 0 E
Saharanpur	**89**	29 58N	77 33 E
Saharien, Atlas	**127**	33 30N	1 0 E
Sahiwal	**89**	30 45N	73 8 E
Sahuaripa	**174**	29 3N	109 14W
Saigō	**109**	36 12N	133 20 E
Saigon = Thanh Pho Ho Chi Minh	**95**	10 58N	106 40 E
Saijō, Ehime, Japan	**109**	33 55N	133 11 E
Saijō, Hiroshima, Japan	**109**	34 25N	132 45 E
Saikhoa Ghat	**93**	27 50N	95 40 E
Saiki	**108**	32 58N	131 51 E
Saimaa	**67**	61 15N	28 15 E
Şa'in Dezh	**81**	36 40N	46 25 E
St. Abb's Head	**31**	55 55N	2 10W
St. Albans, U.K.	**25**	51 44N	0 19W
St. Albans, U.S.A.	**151**	44 49N	73 7W
St. Alban's Head	**24**	50 34N	2 3W
St. Albert	**155**	53 37N	113 32W
St. Andrews	**31**	56 20N	2 48W
St. Arnaud	**119**	36 40S	143 16 E
St. Asaph	**26**	53 15N	3 27W
St-Augustin-Saguenay	**141**	51 13N	58 38W
St. Augustine	**170**	29 52N	81 20W
St. Austell	**27**	50 20N	4 48W
St. Bee's Hd.	**28**	54 30N	3 38 E
St. Boniface	**153**	49 53N	97 5W
St. Bride's B.	**26**	51 48N	5 15W
St-Brieuc	**36**	48 30N	2 46W
St. Catharines	**151**	43 10N	79 15W
St. Charles	**166**	38 46N	90 30W
St. Christopher-Nevis ■	**180**	17 20N	62 40W
St. Cloud	**156**	45 30N	94 11W
St. Croix	**180**	17 45N	64 45W
St. David's	**26**	51 54N	5 16W
St. David's Head	**26**	51 55N	5 16W
St-Denis	**39**	48 56N	2 22 E
St-Dizier	**37**	48 40N	5 0 E
St. Elias, Mt.	**144**	60 14N	140 50W
St. Elias Mts.	**144**	60 33N	139 28W
St-Étienne	**37**	45 27N	4 22 E
St-Félicien	**151**	48 40N	72 25W
St. Gallen	**44**	47 25N	9 20 E
St. George, Australia	**116**	28 1S	148 30 E
St. George, Bermuda	**180**	32 24N	64 42W
St. Georges, Fr. Gui.	**185**	4 0N	52 0W
St. Georges, Grenada	**180**	12 5N	61 43W
St. George's Channel	**20**	52 0N	6 0W

St. Gotthard P. = San Gottardo, Paso del	**44**	46 33N	8 33 E
St. Helena	**125**	15 55S	5 44W
St. Helena B.	**136**	32 40S	18 10 E
St. Helens, Australia	**119**	41 20S	148 15 E
St. Helens, U.K.	**28**	53 28N	2 44W
St. Helens, U.S.A.	**171**	45 55N	122 50W
St. Helier	**36**	49 11N	2 6W
St-Hyacinthe	**151**	45 40N	72 58W
St. Ives, Cambs., U.K.	**25**	52 20N	0 5W
St. Ives, Cornwall, U.K.	**27**	50 13N	5 29W
St-Jean	**151**	45 20N	73 20W
St-Jérôme	**151**	45 47N	74 0W
St. John	**148**	45 20N	66 8W
St. John's	**149**	47 35N	52 40W
St. John's →	**170**	30 20N	81 30W
St. Johnsbury	**148**	44 25N	72 1W
St. Joseph, Mich., U.S.A.	**167**	42 5N	86 30W
St. Joseph, Mo., U.S.A.	**166**	39 46N	94 50W
St. Kilda, N.Z.	**123**	45 53S	170 31 E
St. Kilda, U.K.	**22**	57 9N	8 34W
St. Lawrence	**149**	46 54N	55 23W
St. Lawrence →	**148**	49 30N	66 0W
St. Lawrence, Gulf of	**149**	48 25N	62 0W
St. Lawrence I.	**142**	63 0N	170 0W
St. Leonard	**148**	47 12N	67 58W
St-Louis	**130**	16 8N	16 27W
St. Louis	**166**	38 40N	90 12W
St. Lucia ■	**180**	14 0N	60 50W
St. Maarten	**180**	18 0N	63 5W
St-Malo	**36**	48 39N	2 1W
St-Marc	**180**	19 10N	72 41W
St-Martin, I.	**180**	18 0N	63 0W
St. Mary Pk.	**118**	31 32S	138 34 E
St. Marys	**164**	41 27N	78 33W
St. Matthews, I. = Zadetkyi Kyun	**94**	10 0N	98 25 E
St. Michael's Mt.	**27**	50 7N	5 30W
St. Moritz	**44**	46 30N	9 51 E
St-Nazaire	**36**	47 17N	2 12W
St. Neots	**25**	52 14N	0 16W
St-Omer	**38**	50 45N	2 15 E
St. Pascal	**148**	47 32N	69 48W
St. Paul	**166**	44 54N	93 5W
St. Paul, I.	**149**	47 12N	60 9W
St. Petersburg	**170**	27 45N	82 40W
St-Pierre et Miquelon □	**149**	46 55N	56 10W
St-Quentin	**38**	49 50N	3 16 E
St-Raphaël	**37**	43 25N	6 46 E
St-Servan-sur-Mer	**36**	48 38N	2 0W
St. Thomas, Canada	**151**	42 45N	81 10W
St. Thomas, W. Indies	**180**	18 21N	64 55W
St-Tropez	**37**	43 17N	6 38 E
St. Vincent and the Grenadines ■	**180**	13 0N	61 10W
Ste-Adresse	**38**	49 31N	0 5 E
Ste Anne de Beaupré	**148**	47 2N	70 58W
Ste Marie	**180**	14 48N	61 1W
Ste-Rose	**180**	16 20N	61 45W
Ste. Rose du lac	**153**	51 4N	99 30W
Saintes	**36**	45 45N	0 37W
Saintonge	**36**	45 40N	0 50W
Saito	**108**	32 3N	131 24 E
Sajama	**187**	18 7S	69 0W
Sakai	**106**	34 30N	135 30 E
Sakaide	**109**	34 15N	133 50 E
Sakaiminato	**109**	35 38N	133 11 E
Sakakawea, L.	**163**	47 30N	102 0W
Sakata	**103**	38 55N	139 50 E
Sakhalin	**79**	51 0N	143 0 E
Sakhalinskiy Zaliv	**75**	54 0N	141 0 E
Saku	**107**	36 17N	138 31 E
Sakura	**107**	35 43N	140 14 E
Sakurai	**106**	34 30N	135 51 E
Salaberry-de-Valleyfield	**151**	45 15N	74 8W
Salado →	**190**	31 40S	60 41W
Salado, R. →	**176**	26 52N	99 19W
Salamanca, Spain	**50**	40 58N	5 39W
Salamanca, U.S.A.	**164**	42 10N	78 42W
Salamis	**55**	37 56N	23 30 E
Salcombe	**27**	50 14N	3 47W
Sale	**117**	38 6S	147 6 E
Salem, India	**90**	11 40N	78 11 E
Salem, Mass., U.S.A.	**164**	42 29N	70 53W
Salem, Oreg., U.S.A.	**171**	45 0N	123 0W
Salem, Va., U.S.A.	**165**	37 19N	80 8W
Salerno	**49**	40 40N	14 44 E
Salford	**28**	53 30N	2 17W
Salida	**163**	38 35N	106 0W
Salina, Italy	**49**	38 35N	14 50 E
Salina, U.S.A.	**161**	38 50N	97 40W
Salina Cruz	**177**	16 10N	95 12W
Salinas, Ecuador	**184**	2 10S	80 58W
Salinas, U.S.A.	**173**	36 40N	121 41W
Salinas →	**173**	36 45N	121 48W
Salinas Grandes	**190**	30 0S	65 0W
Salisbury = Harare	**137**	17 43S	31 2 E
Salisbury, U.K.	**24**	51 4N	1 48W
Salisbury, Md., U.S.A.	**165**	38 20N	75 38W
Salisbury, N.C., U.S.A.	**165**	35 20N	80 29W
Salisbury Plain	**24**	51 13N	1 50W
Salle, La	**166**	41 20N	89 6W
Salmon	**162**	45 12N	113 56W
Salmon →	**171**	45 51N	116 46W
Salmon Arm	**155**	50 40N	119 15W
Salmon River Mts.	**162**	45 0N	114 30W
Salon-de-Provence	**37**	43 39N	5 6 E
Salonica = Thessaloníki	**54**	40 38N	22 58 E
Salop = Shropshire □	**24**	52 36N	2 45W
Salt Fork →	**161**	36 37N	97 7W
Salt Lake City	**163**	40 45N	111 58W
Salta	**190**	24 57S	65 25W
Saltcoats	**30**	55 38N	4 47W
Saltillo	**174**	25 25N	101 0W
Salto	**191**	31 27S	57 50W
Salton Sea	**173**	33 20N	115 50W
Salûm	**128**	31 31N	25 7 E
Salvador	**189**	13 0S	38 30W
Salween →	**93**	16 31N	97 37 E
Salzburg	**45**	47 48N	13 2 E
Salzburg □	**45**	47 15N	13 0 E
Salzgitter	**43**	52 13N	10 22 E
Sam Neua	**95**	20 29N	104 0 E
Sama	**69**	60 12N	60 22 E
Samangán □	**87**	36 15N	68 3 E
Samar	**112**	12 0N	125 0 E
Samarkand	**70**	39 40N	66 55 E
Sāmarrā	**81**	34 12N	43 52 E
Sambalpur	**92**	21 28N	84 4 E
Sambhal	**89**	28 35N	78 37 E
Sámos	**55**	37 45N	26 50 E
Samothráki	**55**	40 28N	25 28 E
Samsun	**80**	41 15N	36 22 E
Samut Prakan	**95**	13 32N	100 40 E
Samut Sakhon	**94**	13 31N	100 13 E
Samut Songkhram →	**94**	13 24N	100 1 E
San Andreas	**172**	38 0N	120 39W
San Andres Mts.	**161**	33 0N	106 45W
San Andrés Tuxtla	**177**	18 27N	95 13W
San Angelo	**161**	31 30N	100 30W
San Antonio, Chile	**190**	33 40S	71 40W
San Antonio, U.S.A.	**161**	29 30N	98 30W
San Antonio, C., Argentina	**191**	36 15S	56 40W
San Antonio, C., Cuba	**178**	21 50N	84 57W
San Antonio de los Baños	**178**	22 54N	82 31W
San Antônio Falls	**182**	9 30S	65 0W
San Antonio Oeste	**192**	40 40S	65 0W
San Bernardino	**173**	34 7N	117 18W
San Bernardino Str.	**112**	13 0N	125 0 E
San Bernardo	**190**	33 40S	70 50W
San Blas, C.	**169**	29 40N	85 12W
San Carlos, Chile	**190**	36 10S	72 0W
San Carlos, Mexico	**174**	29 1N	100 51W
San Carlos, Nic.	**179**	11 12N	84 50W
San Carlos de Bariloche	**192**	41 10S	71 25W
San Clemente I.	**173**	32 53N	118 30W
San Cristóbal, Argentina	**190**	30 20S	61 10W
San Cristóbal, Dom. Rep.	**180**	18 25N	70 6W
San Cristóbal, Venezuela	**184**	16 50N	92 40W
San Cristóbal de las Casas	**177**	16 45N	92 38W
San Diego	**173**	32 43N	117 10W
San Felipe, Chile	**190**	32 43S	70 42W

Place	Page	Lat.	Long.
San Felipe, Colombia	**184**	1 55N	67 6W
San Fernando, Chile	**190**	34 30S	71 0W
San Fernando, Mexico	**174**	30 0N	115 10W
San Fernando, Trin. & Tob.	**180**	10 20N	61 30W
San Fernando, U.S.A.	**173**	34 15N	118 29W
San Fernando de Apure	**184**	7 54N	67 15W
San Francisco	**172**	37 47N	122 30W
San Francisco de Macorís	**180**	19 19N	70 15W
San Francisco del Oro	**174**	26 52N	105 51W
San Gabriel	**191**	0 36N	77 49W
San Gottardo, Paso del	**44**	46 33N	8 33 E
San Ignacio	**187**	16 20S	60 55W
San Joaquin →	**172**	37 4N	121 51W
San Jorge, Golfo	**192**	46 0S	66 0W
San Jorge, G. de	**51**	40 50N	0 55W
San José, Bolivia	**187**	17 53S	60 50W
San José, C. Rica	**179**	10 0N	84 2W
San José, U.S.A.	**172**	37 20N	121 53W
San José de Mayo	**191**	34 27S	56 40W
San José del Cabo	**175**	23 3N	109 41W
San José del Guaviare	**184**	2 35N	72 38W
San Juan, Argentina	**190**	31 30S	68 30W
San Juan, Dom. Rep.	**180**	18 49N	71 12W
San Juan, Puerto Rico	**180**	18 28N	66 8W
San Juan →	**179**	10 56N	83 42W
San Juan de los Morros	**184**	9 55N	67 21W
San Juan Mts.	**163**	38 30N	108 30W
San Julián	**192**	49 15S	67 45W
San Leandro	**172**	37 40N	122 6W
San Lorenzo	**184**	1 15N	78 50W
San Lucas, C. de	**175**	22 50N	110 0W
San Luis	**190**	33 20S	66 20W
San Luis de la Paz	**177**	21 18N	100 31W
San Luis Obispo	**173**	35 21N	120 38W
San Luis Potosí	**177**	22 9N	100 59W
San Luis Potosí □	**177**	22 30N	100 30W
San Marcos	**177**	14 59N	91 52W
San Marino ■	**47**	43 56N	12 25 E
San Mateo	**172**	37 32N	122 19W
San Matías	**187**	16 25S	58 20W
San Matías, Golfo	**192**	41 30S	64 0W
San Miguel	**177**	13 30N	88 12W
San Miguel de Tucumán	**190**	26 50S	65 20W
San Pedro →	**175**	21 45N	105 30W
San Pedro de las Colonias	**174**	25 45N	102 59W
San Pedro de Macorís	**180**	18 30N	69 18W
San Pedro Sula	**177**	15 30N	88 0W
San Rafael, Argentina	**190**	34 40S	68 21W
San Rafael, U.S.A.	**172**	37 59N	122 32W
San Roque	**190**	28 25S	58 45W
San Salvador, Bahamas	**178**	24 0N	74 40W
San Salvador, El Salv.	**177**	13 40N	89 10W
San Salvador de Jujuy	**190**	24 10S	64 48W
San Sebastián	**51**	43 17N	1 58W
San Valentin, Mte.	**192**	46 30S	73 30W
Sana'	**82**	15 27N	44 12 E
Sanandaj	**81**	35 18N	47 1 E
Sancti-Spíritus	**178**	21 52N	79 33W
Sanda	**106**	34 53N	135 14 E
Sandgate	**116**	27 18S	153 3 E
Sandomierz	**58**	50 40N	21 43 E
Sandpoint	**171**	48 20N	116 34W
Sandringham	**29**	52 50N	0 30 E
Sandstone	**120**	27 59S	119 16 E
Sandusky	**167**	41 25N	82 40W
Sandwip Chan.	**93**	22 35N	91 35 E
Sandy C.	**119**	41 25S	144 45 E
Sandy Lake	**153**	53 0N	93 15W
Sanford, Fla., U.S.A.	**170**	28 45N	81 20W
Sanford, Maine, U.S.A.	**148**	43 28N	70 47W
Sanford, N.C., U.S.A.	**165**	35 30N	79 10W
Sangay	**184**	2 0S	78 20W
Sangihe, P.	**113**	3 45N	125 30 E
Sangli	**91**	16 55N	74 33 E
Sangre de Cristo Mts.	**161**	37 0N	105 0W
Sankuru →	**134**	4 17S	20 25 E
Sano	**107**	36 19N	139 35 E
Sanok	**59**	49 35N	22 10 E
Sanquhar	**31**	55 21N	3 56W
Sanshui	**99**	23 10N	112 56 E
Santa Ana, Bolivia	**187**	13 50S	65 40W
Santa Ana, Mexico	**174**	30 33N	111 7W
Santa Ana, U.S.A.	**173**	33 48N	117 55W
Santa Bárbara, Mexico	**174**	26 48N	105 49W
Santa Bárbara, U.S.A.	**173**	34 25N	119 40W
Santa Barbara I.	**160**	33 29N	119 2W
Santa Catarina □	**191**	27 25S	48 30W
Santa Clara, Cuba	**178**	22 20N	80 0W
Santa Clara, U.S.A.	**162**	37 21N	122 0W
Santa Clotilde	**186**	2 33S	73 45W
Santa Cruz, Bolivia	**187**	17 43S	63 10W
Santa Cruz, U.S.A.	**172**	36 55N	122 1W
Santa Cruz, Is.	**122**	10 30S	166 0 E
Sta. Cruz de Tenerife	**126**	28 28N	16 15W
Santa Cruz del Sur	**178**	20 44N	78 0W
Santa Cruz do Sul	**191**	29 42S	52 25W
Santa Fe, Argentina	**190**	31 35S	60 41W
Santa Fe, U.S.A.	**161**	35 40N	106 0W
Santa Inés, I.	**192**	54 0S	73 0W
Santa Isabel = Rey Malabo	**131**	3 45N	8 50 E
Santa Lucia Range	**173**	36 0N	121 20W
Santa Maria, Brazil	**191**	29 40S	53 48W
Santa Maria, U.S.A.	**173**	34 58N	120 29W
Santa Maria da Vitória	**188**	13 24S	44 12W
Santa Maria di Leuca, C.	**49**	39 48N	18 20 E
Santa Marta	**184**	11 15N	74 13W
Santa Maura = Levkás	**54**	38 40N	20 43 E
Santa Monica	**173**	34 0N	118 30W
Santa Rosa, Argentina	**190**	36 40S	64 17W
Santa Rosa, U.S.A.	**172**	38 26N	122 43W
Santa Rosa I., Calif., U.S.A.	**173**	34 0N	120 6W
Santa Rosa I., Fla., U.S.A.	**169**	30 23N	87 0W
Santa Rosalía	**174**	27 19N	112 17W
Santana do Livramento	**191**	30 55S	55 30W
Santander	**50**	43 27N	3 51W
Santander Jiménez	**176**	24 13N	98 28W
Santarém, Brazil	**185**	2 25S	54 42W
Santarém, Portugal	**50**	39 12N	8 42W
Santiago, Brazil	**191**	29 11S	54 52W
Santiago, Chile	**190**	33 24S	70 40W
Santiago, Panama	**179**	8 0N	81 0W
Santiago de Compostela	**50**	42 52N	8 37W
Santiago de Cuba	**178**	20 0N	75 49W
Santiago de los Cabelleros	**180**	19 30N	70 40W
Santiago del Estero	**190**	27 50S	64 15W
Santiago Ixcuintla	**175**	21 50N	105 11W
Santo Amaro	**189**	12 30S	38 43W
Santo Ângelo	**191**	28 15S	54 15W
Santo Domingo	**180**	18 30N	64 54W
Santo Tomé	**191**	28 40S	56 5W
Santoña	**50**	43 29N	3 27W
Santos	**191**	24 0S	46 20W
São Borja	**191**	28 39S	56 0W
São Carlos	**188**	22 0S	47 50W
São Francisco →	**189**	10 30S	36 24W
São Francisco do Sul	**191**	26 15S	48 36W
São João del Rei	**188**	21 8S	44 15W
São José do Rio Prêto	**188**	20 50S	49 20W
São Leopoldo	**191**	29 50S	51 10W
São Lourenço	**188**	22 7S	45 3W
São Luís	**188**	2 39S	44 15W
São Paulo	**191**	23 32S	46 37W
São Paulo □	**188**	22 0S	49 0W
São Paulo de Olivença	**184**	3 27S	68 48W
São Roque, C. de	**189**	5 30S	35 16W
São Tomé	**131**	0 10N	6 39 E
São Tomé & Principe ■	**131**	0 12N	6 39 E
São Vicente, Cabo de	**50**	37 0N	9 0W
Saône →	**37**	45 44N	4 50 E
Sapporo	**103**	43 0N	141 21 E
Sapulpa	**168**	36 0N	96 0W
Saqqez	**81**	36 15N	46 20 E
Sar Planina	**52**	42 10N	21 0 E
Saragossa = Zaragoza	**51**	41 39N	0 53W
Sarajevo	**52**	43 52N	18 26 E
Saranac Lake	**151**	44 20N	74 10W
Sarangani B.	**112**	6 0N	125 13 E
Saransk	**68**	54 10N	45 10 E
Sarapul	**69**	56 28N	53 48 E
Sarasota	**165**	27 20N	82 30W
Saratoga Springs	**164**	43 5N	73 47W
Saratov	**68**	51 30N	46 2 E

Sarawak □ 111 2 0N 113 0 E
Sardegna 48 39 57N 9 0 E
Sardinia = Sardegna 48 39 57N 9 0 E
Sargodha 89 32 10N 72 40 E
Sarh 131 9 5N 18 23 E
Sārī 86 36 30N 53 4 E
Sarina 121 21 22S 149 13 E
Sarmiento 192 45 35S 69 5W
Sarnia 150 42 58N 82 23W
Saronikós Kólpos 55 37 45N 23 45 E
Sarre = Saar → 42 49 41N 6 32 E
Sarre, La 151 48 45N 79 15W
Sarthe → 36 47 33N 0 31W
Sasaram 92 24 57N 84 5 E
Sasebo 108 33 10N 129 43 E
Saskatchewan □ 152 54 40N 106 0W
Saskatchewan → 152 53 37N 100 40W
Saskatoon 152 52 10N 106 38W
Sassandra 130 5 0N 6 8W
Sássari 48 40 44N 8 33 E
Sata-Misaki 108 30 59N 130 40 E
Satara 91 17 44N 73 58 E
Satmala Hills 91 20 15N 74 40 E
Satna 92 24 35N 80 50 E
Satpura Ra. 91 21 25N 76 10 E
Sattahip 95 12 41N 100 54 E
Satu Mare 56 47 46N 22 55 E
Sauðarkrókur 64 65 45N 19 40W
Saudi Arabia ■ 82 26 0N 44 0 E
Sault Ste. Marie, Canada 150 46 30N 84 20W
Sault Ste. Marie, U.S.A. 150 46 27N 84 22W
Saumur 36 47 15N 0 5W
Sava → 52 44 50N 20 26 E
Savanna la Mar 180 18 10N 78 10W
Savannah 170 32 4N 81 4W
Savannah → 170 32 2N 80 53W
Savannakhet 95 16 30N 104 49 E
Savoie □ 37 45 26N 6 35 E
Savona 46 44 19N 8 29 E
Sawankhalok 94 17 19N 99 50 E
Sawara 107 35 55N 140 30 E
Sawatch Mts. 163 38 30N 106 30W
Sawu, I. 113 10 35S 121 50 E
Sawu Sea 113 9 30S 121 50 E
Saxony, Lower = Niedersachsen □ 42 52 45N 9 0 E
Sayan, Zapadnyy 77 52 30N 94 0 E
Saydā 80 33 35N 35 25 E
Sayḩut 83 15 12N 51 10 E
Sayula 175 19 52N 103 36W
Sazan 52 40 30N 19 20 E
Scafell Pikes 28 54 26N 3 14W
Scalloway 30 60 9N 1 16W
Scandinavia 16 64 0N 12 0 E
Scapa Flow 33 58 52N 3 6W
Scarborough 29 54 17N 0 24W
Schaffhausen 44 47 42N 8 39 E
Schefferville 146 54 48N 66 50W
Schelde → 42 51 15N 4 16 E
Schenectady 164 42 50N 73 58W
Scheveningen 40 52 6N 4 16 E
Schiedam 40 51 55N 4 25 E
Schiermonnikoog 41 53 30N 6 15 E
Schleswig-Holstein □ 42 54 10N 9 40 E
Schouten I. 119 42 20S 148 20 E
Schouten Is. 113 1 0S 136 0 E
Schouwen 40 51 43N 3 45 E
Schreiber 150 48 45N 87 20W
Schwäbische Alb 42 48 30N 9 30 E
Schwarzwald 42 48 0N 8 0 E
Schwerin 43 53 37N 11 22 E
Schwyz 44 47 2N 8 39 E
Scilly, Isles of 20 49 55N 6 15W
Scone, Australia 116 32 5S 150 52 E
Scone, U.K. 31 56 25N 3 26W
Scoresbysund 13 70 20N 23 0W
Scotia Sea 14 56 5S 56 0W
Scotland □ 23 57 0N 4 0W
Scottsbluff 163 41 55N 103 35W
Scottsdale 119 41 9S 147 31 E
Scranton 164 41 22N 75 41W
Scunthorpe 29 53 35N 0 38W
Scutari = Üsküdar 80 41 0N 29 5 E
Seaforth 150 43 35N 81 25W
Searcy 168 35 15N 91 45W
Seascale 28 54 24N 3 29W
Seattle 171 47 41N 122 15W
Sebastián Vizcaíno, B. 174 28 0N 114 30W
Sebastopol = Sevastopol 68 44 35N 33 30 E
Sebring 170 27 30N 81 26W
Sebta = Ceuta 126 35 52N 5 18W
Sebuku, Teluk 111 4 0N 118 10 E
Sechura, Desierto de 186 6 0S 80 30W
Seclin 38 50 33N 3 2 E
Sedalia 166 38 40N 93 18W
Segamat 96 2 30N 102 50 E
Ségou 130 13 30N 6 16W
Segovia = Coco → 179 15 0N 83 8W
Segovia 50 40 57N 4 10W
Séguéla 130 7 55N 6 40W
Segura → 51 38 6N 0 54W
Seine → 38 49 26N 0 26 E
Seistan 85 30 50N 61 0 E
Seki 106 35 29N 136 55 E
Sekondi-Takoradi 130 4 58N 1 45W
Selangor □ 96 3 10N 101 30 E
Selby 29 53 47N 1 5W
Sélibabi 130 15 10N 12 15W
Selkirk, Canada 153 50 10N 96 55W
Selkirk, U.K. 31 55 33N 2 50W
Selkirk Mts. 155 51 15N 117 40W
Selma, Ala., U.S.A. 169 32 30N 87 0W
Selma, Calif., U.S.A. 173 36 39N 119 39W
Selsey Bill 24 50 44N 0 47W
Selvas 187 6 30S 67 0W
Semarang 111 7 0S 110 26 E
Seminole 168 35 15N 96 45W
Semipalatinsk 71 50 30N 80 10 E
Semnān 86 35 55N 53 25 E
Semnān □ 86 36 0N 54 0 E
Sendai, Kagoshima, Japan 108 31 50N 130 20 E
Sendai, Miyagi, Japan 103 38 15N 140 53 E
Senegal ■ 130 14 30N 14 30W
Senegal → 126 15 48N 16 32W
Senge Khambab = Indus → 88 24 20N 67 47 E
Senhor-do-Bonfim 189 10 30S 40 10W
Senja I. 64 69 15N 17 30 E
Senlis 39 49 13N 2 35 E
Sennâr 129 13 30N 33 35 E
Senneterre 151 48 25N 77 15W
Sens 39 48 11N 3 15 E
Senta 52 45 55N 20 3 E
Seoul = Sŏul 98 37 31N 126 58 E
Sept-Îles 148 50 13N 66 22W
Seram 113 3 10S 129 0 E
Seram Sea 113 2 30S 128 30 E
Seremban 96 2 43N 101 53 E
Serena, La 190 29 55S 71 10W
Sereth = Siret → 57 47 58N 26 5 E
Sergipe □ 189 10 30S 37 30W
Sérifos 55 37 9N 24 30 E
Serny Zavod 70 39 59N 58 50 E
Serov 69 59 29N 60 35 E
Serowe 137 22 25S 26 43 E
Serpukhov 68 54 55N 37 28 E
Serra do Navio 185 0 59N 52 3W
Sérrai 55 41 5N 23 31 E
Sesheke 134 17 29S 24 13 E
Setana 103 42 26N 139 51 E
Sète 37 43 25N 3 42 E
Sétif 127 36 9N 5 26 E
Seto 106 35 14N 137 6 E
Setonaikai 109 34 20N 133 30 E
Settle 28 54 5N 2 18W
Setúbal 50 38 30N 8 58W
Sevastopol 68 44 35N 33 30 E
Seven Sisters 154 54 56N 128 10W
Severn →, Canada 140 56 2N 87 36W
Severn →, U.K. 24 51 35N 2 38W
Severnaya Zemlya 72 79 0N 100 0 E
Severodinsk 69 64 27N 39 58 E

Sevilla **50** 37 23N 6 0W
Seville = Sevilla **50** 37 23N 6 0W
Seward **142** 60 6N 149 26W
Seward Pen. **142** 65 0N 164 0W
Seychelles ■ **78** 5 0S 56 0E
Seyðisfjörður **64** 65 16N 14 0W
Seymour **117** 37 0S 145 10E
Seyne-sur-Mer, La **37** 43 7N 5 52E
Sézanne **39** 48 40N 3 40E
Sfax **127** 34 49N 10 48E
Sfîntu Gheorghe **57** 45 52N 25 48E
Shaanxi □ **99** 35 0N 109 0E
Shaba □ **135** 8 0S 25 0E
Shache **100** 38 20N 77 10E
Shaftesbury **24** 51 0N 2 12W
Shahdād **85** 30 30N 57 40E
Shakhty **68** 47 40N 40 16E
Shamo = Gobi **98** 44 0N 111 0E
Shamokin **164** 40 47N 76 33W
Shan □ **93** 21 30N 98 30E
Shandong □ **99** 36 0N 118 0E
Shanghai **99** 31 15N 121 26E
Shangqiu **99** 34 26N 115 36E
Shangrao **99** 28 25N 117 59E
Shangshui **99** 33 42N 114 35E
Shannon → **35** 52 35N 9 30W
Shansi = Shanxi □ **98** 37 0N 112 0E
Shantou **99** 23 18N 116 40E
Shantung = Shandong □ **99** 36 0N 118 0E
Shanxi □ **98** 37 0N 112 0E
Shaoguan **99** 24 48N 113 35E
Shaoxing **99** 30 0N 120 35E
Shaoyang **99** 27 14N 111 25E
Shap **28** 54 32N 2 40W
Sharjah = Ash Shāriqah **85** 25 23N 55 26E
Shark B. **120** 25 55S 113 32E
Sharon **164** 41 18N 80 30W
Shashi **99** 30 25N 112 14E
Shasta, Mt. **172** 41 30N 122 12W
Shasta L. **172** 40 50N 122 15W
Shaunavon **152** 49 35N 108 25W
Shawano **167** 44 45N 88 38W
Shawinigan **151** 46 35N 72 50W
Shawnee **168** 35 15N 97 0W
Shcherbakov = Andropov **68** 58 5N 38 50E
Shebele, Wabi → **133** 2 0N 44 0E
Sheboygan **167** 43 46N 87 45W
Sheerness **24** 51 26N 0 47E
Sheffield **28** 53 23N 1 28W
Shekhupura **89** 31 42N 73 58E
Shelburne **148** 43 47N 65 20W
Shelby, Mont., U.S.A. **163** 48 30N 111 52W
Shelby, N.C., U.S.A. **165** 35 18N 81 34W
Shelbyville, Ind., U.S.A. **167** 39 30N 85 42W
Shelbyville, Tenn., U.S.A. **169** 35 30N 86 25W
Shelikhova, Zaliv **73** 59 30N 157 0E
Shellharbour **117** 34 31S 150 51E
Shelton **171** 47 15N 123 6W
Shenandoah **166** 40 50N 95 25W
Shensi = Shaanxi □ **99** 35 0N 109 0E
Shenyang **98** 41 50N 123 25E
Shepparton **117** 36 23S 145 26E
Sheppey, I. of **24** 51 23N 0 50E
Sherborne **27** 50 56N 2 31W
Sherbrooke **148** 45 28N 71 57W
Sheridan **163** 44 50N 107 0W
Sherman **168** 33 40N 96 35W
Sherridon **152** 55 8N 101 5W
Sherwood Forest **29** 53 5N 1 5W
Shetland Is. **30** 60 30N 1 30W
Shibām **83** 16 0N 48 36E
Shibata **103** 37 57N 139 20E
Shibetsu **103** 44 10N 142 23E
Shibukawa **107** 36 29N 139 0E
Shibushi-Wan **108** 31 24N 131 8E
Shiel, L. **32** 56 48N 5 32W
Shihchiachuangi = Shijiazhuang **98** 38 2N 114 28E
Shijiazhuang **98** 38 2N 114 28E
Shikarpur **88** 27 57N 68 39E
Shikine-Jima **107** 34 19N 139 13E
Shikoku **109** 33 30N 133 30E
Shikoku □ **109** 33 30N 133 30E
Shikoku-Sanchi **109** 33 30N 133 30E
Shillong **93** 25 35N 91 53E
Shimabara **108** 32 48N 130 20E
Shimada **107** 34 49N 138 10E
Shimizu **107** 35 0N 138 30E
Shimo-Jima **108** 32 15N 130 7E
Shimo-Koshiki-Jima **108** 31 40N 129 43E
Shimoda **107** 34 40N 138 57E
Shimodate **107** 36 20N 139 55E
Shimoga **90** 13 57N 75 32E
Shimonoseki **108** 33 58N 131 0E
Shin, L. **33** 58 7N 4 30W
Shin-Tone → **107** 35 44N 140 51E
Shinano → **105** 36 50N 138 30E
Shingū **106** 33 40N 135 55E
Shinji Ko **109** 35 26N 132 57E
Shinjō **103** 38 46N 140 18E
Shinminato **106** 36 47N 137 4E
Shinshiro **106** 34 54N 137 30E
Shio-no-Misaki **106** 33 25N 135 45E
Shiogama **103** 38 19N 141 1E
Shiojiri **107** 36 6N 137 58E
Shipka **53** 42 46N 25 33E
Shirane-San, Gumma, Japan **107** 36 48N 139 22E
Shirane-San, Yamanashi, Japan **107** 35 42N 138 9E
Shīrāz **85** 29 42N 52 30E
Shire → **137** 17 42S 35 19E
Shiriya-Zaki **103** 41 25N 141 30E
Shivpuri **91** 25 26N 77 42E
Shizuoka **107** 35 0N 138 24E
Shkoder = Shkodra **52** 42 6N 19 20E
Shkodra **52** 42 6N 19 20E
Shkumbini → **52** 41 5N 19 50E
Shō-Gawa → **106** 36 47N 137 4E
Shōbara **109** 34 51N 133 1E
Shoeburyness **24** 51 31N 0 49E
Sholapur = Solapur **91** 17 43N 75 56E
Shoshone **172** 43 0N 114 27W
Shreveport **168** 32 30N 93 50W
Shrewsbury **28** 52 42N 2 45W
Shrirampur **92** 22 44N 88 21E
Shropshire □ **24** 52 36N 2 45W
Shuangyashan **98** 46 37N 131 22E
Siahan Range **88** 27 30N 64 40E
Sialkot **89** 32 32N 74 30E
Siam = Thailand ■ **95** 16 0N 102 0E
Sian = Xi'an **99** 34 15N 109 0E
Siberia **77** 60 0N 100 0E
Siberut **111** 1 30S 99 0E
Sibi **88** 29 30N 67 54E
Sibiu **57** 45 45N 24 9E
Sichuan □ **99** 31 0N 104 0E
Sicilia **49** 37 30N 14 30E
Sicily = Sicilia **49** 37 30N 14 30E
Sicuani **187** 14 21S 71 10W
Sidi-bel-Abbès **127** 35 13N 0 39W
Sidlaw Hills **31** 56 32N 3 10W
Sidley, Mt. **15** 77 2S 126 2W
Sidmouth **27** 50 40N 3 13W
Sidney **154** 48 39N 123 24W
Sidon = Saydā **80** 33 35N 35 25E
Sidra, G. of = Surt, Khalīj **127** 31 40N 18 30E
Siedlce **58** 52 10N 22 20E
Siena **46** 43 20N 11 20E
Sierra Blanca Pk. **161** 33 20N 105 54W
Sierra Leone ■ **130** 9 0N 12 0W
Sífnos **55** 37 0N 24 45E
Siglufjörður **64** 66 12N 18 55W
Sihanoukville = Kompong Som **95** 10 38N 103 30E
Siirt **81** 37 57N 41 55E
Sikar **89** 27 33N 75 10E
Sikeston **169** 36 52N 89 35W
Sikhote Alin, Khrebet **75** 46 0N 136 0E
Síkinos **55** 36 40N 25 8E
Sikkim □ **92** 27 50N 88 30E
Silchar **93** 24 49N 92 48E
Silesia = Slask **58** 51 0N 16 30E

Siling Co	**101**	31 50N	89 20 E
Silloth	**28**	54 53N	3 25W
Simcoe	**151**	42 50N	80 20W
Simenga	**74**	62 42N	108 25 E
Simeulue	**111**	2 45N	95 45 E
Simferopol	**68**	44 55N	34 3 E
Simi Valley	**173**	34 16N	118 47W
Simla	**89**	31 2N	77 9 E
Simplon Pass	**44**	46 15N	8 0 E
Simushir, Ostrov	**75**	46 50N	152 30 E
Sinai = Es Sînâ'	**128**	29 0N	34 0 E
Sinaloa	**174**	25 50N	108 20W
Sinaloa □	**174**	25 0N	107 30W
Sincelejo	**184**	9 18N	75 24W
Sinclair Mills	**155**	54 5N	121 40W
Sind □	**88**	26 0N	69 0 E
Sind Sagar Doab	**89**	32 0N	71 30 E
Singa	**129**	13 10N	33 57 E
Singapore ■	**96**	1 17N	103 51 E
Singapore, Straits of	**96**	1 15N	104 0 E
Singkaling Hkamti	**92**	26 0N	95 39 E
Singleton	**117**	32 33S	151 0 E
Singora = Songkhla	**97**	7 13N	100 37 E
Sinkiang Uighur = Xinjiang Uygur Zizhiqu □	**100**	42 0N	86 0 E
Sioux City	**166**	42 32N	96 25W
Sioux Falls	**166**	43 35N	96 40W
Sioux Lookout	**153**	50 10N	91 50W
Siping	**98**	43 8N	124 21 E
Sipora	**111**	2 18S	99 40 E
Siracusa	**49**	37 4N	15 17 E
Sirajganj	**92**	24 25N	89 47 E
Siret ⟶	**57**	47 58N	26 5 E
Síros	**55**	37 28N	24 57 E
Sitapur	**92**	27 38N	80 45 E
Sitka	**143**	57 9N	135 20W
Sittard	**41**	51 0N	5 52 E
Sivas	**80**	39 43N	36 58 E
Siverek	**81**	37 50N	39 19 E
Sivrihisar	**80**	39 30N	31 35 E
Sîwa	**128**	29 11N	25 31 E
Siwalik Range	**92**	28 0N	83 0 E
Sizewell	**24**	52 13N	1 38 E
Sjumen = Kolarovgrad	**53**	43 18N	26 55 E
Skadarsko Jezero	**52**	42 10N	19 20 E
Skagerrak	**60**	57 30N	9 0 E
Skagway	**143**	59 23N	135 20W
Skaraborgs län □	**60**	58 20N	13 30 E
Skeena ⟶	**154**	54 9N	130 5W
Skegness	**29**	53 9N	0 20 E
Skellefte ⟶	**66**	65 30N	18 30 E
Skellefteå	**67**	64 45N	20 58 E
Skerries, The	**26**	53 27N	4 40W
Skiddaw	**28**	54 39N	3 9W
Skien	**60**	59 12N	9 35 E
Skierniewice	**58**	51 58N	20 10 E
Skikda	**127**	36 50N	6 58 E
Skipton	**28**	53 57N	2 1W
Skíros	**55**	38 55N	24 34 E
Skopje	**52**	42 1N	21 32 E
Skowhegan	**148**	44 49N	69 40W
Skull	**35**	51 32N	9 40W
Skye	**32**	57 15N	6 10W
Skyros = Skíros	**55**	38 55N	24 34 E
Slaney ⟶	**35**	52 52N	6 45W
Slask	**58**	51 0N	16 30 E
Slave ⟶	**145**	61 18N	113 39W
Slave Coast	**124**	6 0N	2 30 E
Sleaford	**29**	53 0N	0 22W
Sliedrecht	**40**	51 50N	4 45 E
Slieve Aughty	**35**	53 4N	8 30W
Slieve Bloom	**35**	53 4N	7 40W
Slieve Donard	**34**	54 10N	5 57W
Slieve Mish	**35**	52 12N	9 50W
Slievenamon	**35**	52 25N	7 37W
Sligo	**34**	54 17N	8 28W
Sligo □	**34**	54 10N	8 35W
Sliven	**53**	42 42N	26 19 E
Slovakian Ore Mts. = Slovenské Rudohorie	**59**	48 45N	20 0 E
Slovenia = Slovenija □	**52**	45 58N	14 30 E
Slovenija □	**52**	45 58N	14 30 E
Slovenské Rudohorie	**59**	48 45N	20 0 E
Słupsk	**58**	54 30N	17 3 E
Slyne Hd.	**34**	53 25N	10 10W
Smara	**126**	32 9N	8 16W
Smithers	**154**	54 45N	127 10W
Smithfield	**165**	35 31N	78 16W
Smiths Falls	**151**	44 55N	76 0W
Smithton	**119**	40 53S	145 6 E
Smolensk	**68**	54 45N	32 0 E
Smolikas, Óros	**54**	40 9N	20 58 E
Smyrna = İzmir	**80**	38 25N	27 8 E
Snœfell, Iceland	**64**	64 48N	15 34W
Snœfell, U.K.	**28**	54 18N	4 26W
Snœfellsjökull	**64**	64 49N	23 46W
Snake ⟶	**171**	46 12N	119 2W
Sneek	**41**	53 2N	5 40 E
Snowdon	**26**	53 4N	4 8W
Snowdrift	**145**	62 24N	110 44W
Snowy Mts.	**117**	36 30S	148 20 E
Sobat ⟶	**129**	8 32N	32 40 E
Sobral	**177**	3 50S	40 20W
Soch'e = Shache	**100**	38 20N	77 10 E
Sochi	**70**	43 35N	39 40 E
Société, Is. de la	**123**	17 0S	151 0W
Society Is. = Société, Is. de la	**123**	17 0S	151 0W
Socorro	**161**	34 4N	106 54W
Socotra	**78**	12 30N	54 0 E
Söderhamn	**60**	61 18N	17 10 E
Södermanlands län □	**60**	59 10N	16 30 E
Södertälje	**60**	59 12N	17 39 E
Sodo	**132**	7 0N	37 41 E
Sofala	**137**	33 4S	149 43 E
Sofia = Sofiya	**53**	42 45N	23 20 E
Sofiya	**53**	42 45N	23 20 E
Sogn og Fjordane fylke □	**60**	61 40N	6 0 E
Soissons	**39**	49 25N	3 19 E
Sōja	**109**	34 40N	133 45 E
Söke	**80**	37 48N	27 28 E
Sol Iletsk	**70**	51 10N	55 0 E
Solapur	**91**	17 43N	75 56 E
Soledad, Colombia	**184**	10 55N	74 46W
Soledad, Venezuela	**185**	8 10N	63 34W
Solent, The	**24**	50 45N	1 25W
Solesmes	**38**	50 10N	3 30 E
Solikamsk	**69**	59 38N	56 50 E
Solimões ⟶ = Amazonas ⟶	**185**	0 5S	50 0W
Sóller	**51**	39 46N	2 43 E
Sololá	**177**	14 49N	91 10 E
Solomon Is. ■	**122**	6 0S	155 0 E
Solţānābād	**86**	36 29N	58 5 E
Solway Firth	**31**	54 45N	3 38W
Somali Rep. ■	**133**	7 0N	47 0 E
Sombor	**52**	45 46N	19 9 E
Sombrerete	**175**	23 38N	103 39W
Somerset, Bermuda	**180**	32 16N	64 55W
Somerset, U.S.A.	**169**	37 5N	84 40W
Somerset □	**27**	51 9N	3 0W
Somerset I.	**145**	73 30N	93 0W
Somme □	**36**	50 0N	2 20 E
Somport, Puerto de	**51**	42 48N	0 31W
Søndre Strømfjord	**147**	66 59N	50 40W
Songkhla	**97**	7 13N	100 37 E
Sonora □	**174**	29 20N	110 40W
Soochow = Suzhou	**99**	31 19N	120 38 E
Sop's Arm	**149**	49 46N	56 56W
Sør-Rondane	**14**	72 0S	25 0 E
Sør-Trøndelag fylke □	**65**	63 0N	10 0 E
Sorata	**187**	15 50S	68 40W
Sorel	**151**	46 0N	73 10W
Soria	**51**	41 43N	2 32W
Sorocaba	**191**	23 31S	47 27W
Sørøya	**67**	70 40N	22 30 E
Sorsogon	**112**	13 0N	124 0 E
Sosnowiec	**58**	50 20N	19 10 E
Sotteville-lès-Rouen	**38**	49 24N	1 5 E
Sŏul	**98**	37 31N	126 58 E
Souris, Man., Canada	**153**	49 40N	100 20W
Souris, P.E.I., Canada	**149**	46 21N	62 15W

South Africa, Rep. of ■	**136**	32 0S	17 0E
South Auckland & Bay of Plenty □	**122**	38 30S	177 0E
South Australia □	**118**	32 0S	139 0E
South Bend	**167**	41 38N	86 20W
South Carolina □	**165**	33 45N	81 0W
South Charleston	**165**	38 20N	81 40W
South China Sea	**77**	10 0N	113 0E
South Dakota □	**163**	45 0N	100 0W
South Downs	**25**	50 53N	0 10W
South Georgia	**183**	54 30S	37 0W
South Glamorgan □	**27**	51 30N	3 20W
South Haven	**167**	42 22N	86 20W
South Island	**123**	44 0S	170 0E
South Korea ■	**98**	36 0N	128 0E
South Orkney Is.	**14**	63 0S	45 0W
South Platte →	**163**	41 7N	100 42W
South Pole	**14**	90 0S	0 0E
South Porcupine	**151**	48 30N	81 12W
South Ronaldsay	**33**	58 46N	2 58W
South Sandwich Is.	**14**	57 0S	27 0W
South Sentinel I.	**94**	11 1N	92 16E
South Shetland Is.	**14**	62 0S	59 0W
South Shields	**28**	54 59N	1 26W
South Taranaki Bight	**122**	39 40S	174 5E
South Uist	**32**	57 20N	7 15W
South West Africa = Namibia ■	**136**	22 0S	18 9E
South West Cape	**123**	47 16S	167 31E
South Yemen ■	**83**	15 0N	48 0E
South Yorkshire □	**29**	53 30N	1 20W
Southampton	**25**	50 54N	1 23W
Southampton I.	**146**	64 30N	84 0W
Southend-on-Sea	**25**	51 32N	0 42E
Southern Alps	**123**	43 41S	170 11E
Southern Cross	**120**	31 12S	119 15E
Southern Indian L.	**143**	57 10N	98 30W
Southern Uplands	**31**	55 30N	3 3W
Southland □	**123**	45 51S	168 13E
Southport, Australia	**116**	27 58S	153 25E
Southport, U.K.	**28**	53 38N	3 1W
Southwold	**25**	52 19N	1 41E
Sovetskaya Gavan	**75**	48 50N	140 0E
Soviet Union ■ = Union of Soviet Socialist Republics ■	**79**	60 0N	100 0E
Sōya-Kaikyō = Perouse Str., La	**77**	45 40N	142 0E
Spain ■	**50**	40 0N	5 0W
Spalding	**29**	52 47N	0 9W
Spandau	**43**	52 35N	13 7E
Spanish Fork	**163**	40 10N	111 37W
Spanish Town	**180**	18 0N	76 57W
Sparks	**172**	39 30N	119 45W
Sparta = Spárti	**54**	37 5N	22 25E
Sparta	**166**	43 55N	90 47W
Spartanburg	**165**	35 0N	82 0W
Spárti	**54**	37 5N	22 25E
Spartivento, C., Calabria, Italy	**49**	37 56N	16 4E
Spartivento, C., Sard., Italy	**48**	38 52N	8 50E
Spassk-Dalniy	**75**	44 40N	132 48E
Speightstown	**180**	13 15N	59 39W
Spence Bay	**145**	69 32N	93 32W
Spencer	**166**	43 5N	95 19W
Spencer G.	**119**	34 0S	137 20E
Spenser Mts.	**123**	42 15S	172 45E
Sperrin Mts.	**34**	54 50N	7 0W
Spessart	**42**	50 10N	9 20E
Spey →	**33**	57 26N	3 25W
Spézia, La	**46**	44 8N	9 50E
Spinazzola	**49**	40 58N	16 5E
Spithead	**25**	50 43N	1 5W
Spitzbergen = Svalbard	**13**	78 0N	17 0E
Split	**52**	43 31N	16 26E
Splügenpass	**44**	46 30N	9 20E
Spokane	**171**	47 45N	117 25W
Sporyy Navolok, Mys	**69**	75 50N	68 40E
Spratly, I.	**112**	8 20N	112 0E
Spring Mts.	**173**	36 20N	115 43W
Springfield, Ill., U.S.A.	**166**	39 48N	89 40W
Springfield, Mass., U.S.A.	**164**	42 8N	72 37W
Springfield, Mo., U.S.A.	**168**	37 15N	93 20W
Springfield, Ohio, U.S.A.	**167**	39 58N	83 48W
Springfield, Oreg., U.S.A.	**171**	44 2N	123 0W
Springfield, Tenn., U.S.A.	**169**	36 35N	86 55W
Springfield, Vt., U.S.A.	**164**	43 20N	72 30W
Springhill	**148**	45 40N	64 4W
Springs	**137**	26 13S	28 25E
Springwood	**117**	33 41S	150 33E
Spurn Hd.	**29**	53 34N	0 8E
Squamish	**154**	49 45N	123 10W
Sredinnyy Khrebet	**73**	57 0N	160 0E
Srednekolymsk	**73**	67 27N	153 40E
Sremska Mitrovica	**52**	44 59N	19 33E
Srepok →	**95**	13 33N	106 16E
Sretensk	**74**	52 10N	117 40E
Sri Lanka ■	**90**	7 30N	80 50E
Srinagar	**89**	34 5N	74 50E
Stadskanaal	**41**	53 4N	6 55E
Staffa	**30**	56 26N	6 21W
Stafford	**28**	52 49N	2 9W
Stafford □	**28**	52 53N	2 10W
Staines	**25**	51 26N	0 30W
Stalingrad = Volgograd	**68**	48 40N	44 25E
Stalino = Donetsk	**68**	48 0N	37 45E
Stalinogorsk = Novomoskovsk	**68**	54 5N	38 15E
Stalybridge	**28**	53 29N	2 4W
Stamford, U.K.	**25**	52 39N	0 29W
Stamford, U.S.A.	**164**	41 5N	73 30W
Stanislav = Ivano-Frankovsk	**68**	48 40N	24 40E
Stanley, Canada	**152**	55 24N	104 22W
Stanley, Falk. Is.	**192**	51 40S	59 51W
Stanovoy Khrebet	**75**	55 0N	130 0E
Stanthorpe	**116**	28 36S	151 59E
Stara Planina	**53**	43 15N	23 0E
Stara Zagora	**53**	42 26N	25 39E
Starkville	**169**	33 26N	88 48W
Start Pt.	**27**	50 13N	3 38W
State College	**164**	40 47N	77 49W
Staten, I. = Estados, I. de los	**192**	54 40S	64 30W
Statesboro	**170**	32 26N	81 46W
Statesville	**165**	35 48N	80 51W
Staunton	**165**	38 7N	79 4W
Stavanger	**60**	58 57N	5 40E
Staveren	**40**	52 53N	5 22E
Stavropol	**70**	45 5N	42 0E
Stawell	**119**	37 5S	142 47E
Steenwijk	**41**	52 47N	6 7E
Stefanie L. = Chew Bahir	**132**	4 40N	36 50E
Steiermark □	**45**	47 26N	15 0E
Steinbach	**153**	49 32N	96 40W
Steinkjer	**65**	63 59N	11 31E
Stellarton	**149**	45 32N	62 30W
Stephenville	**149**	48 31N	58 35W
Stereá Ellas □	**54**	38 50N	22 0E
Sterling, Colo., U.S.A.	**163**	40 40N	103 15W
Sterling, Ill., U.S.A.	**166**	41 45N	89 45W
Sterlitamak	**71**	53 40N	56 0E
Stettin = Szczecin	**58**	53 27N	14 27E
Stettler	**155**	52 19N	112 40W
Steubenville	**164**	40 21N	80 39W
Stevens Port	**166**	44 32N	89 34W
Stewart	**144**	63 19N	139 26W
Stewart I.	**123**	46 58S	167 54E
Stikine →	**144**	56 40N	132 30W
Stillwater, Minn., U.S.A.	**166**	45 3N	92 47W
Stillwater, Okla., U.S.A.	**168**	36 5N	97 3W
Stillwater Ra.	**172**	39 45N	118 6W
Stip	**53**	41 42N	22 10E
Stirling	**31**	56 7N	3 57W
Stirling Ra.	**120**	34 23S	118 0E
Stockholm	**60**	59 20N	18 3E
Stockholms län □	**60**	59 30N	18 20E
Stockport	**28**	53 25N	2 11W
Stockton	**172**	38 0N	121 20W
Stockton-on-Tees	**29**	54 34N	1 20W
Stoke-on-Trent	**28**	53 1N	2 11W
Stonehaven	**33**	56 58N	2 11W
Stonehenge	**24**	51 9N	1 45W
Stonewall	**153**	50 10N	97 19W
Stora Lulevatten	**66**	67 10N	19 30E

Place	Page	Lat.	Long.
Storavan	**66**	65 45N	18 10 E
Store Bælt	**61**	55 20N	11 0 E
Storm B.	**119**	43 10S	147 30 E
Storm Lake	**166**	42 35N	95 11W
Stornoway	**32**	58 12N	6 23W
Storsjön	**66**	63 12N	14 18 E
Storuman	**66**	65 5N	17 10 E
Stour →, Hereford & Worcs., U.K.	**24**	52 25N	2 13W
Stour →, Kent, U.K.	**25**	51 15N	1 20 E
Stour →, Suffolk, U.K.	**25**	51 55N	1 5 E
Stourbridge	**24**	52 28N	2 8W
Stowmarket	**25**	52 11N	1 0 E
Strabane	**34**	54 50N	7 28W
Stralsund	**43**	54 17N	13 5 E
Strangford, L.	**34**	54 30N	5 37W
Stranraer	**30**	54 54N	5 0W
Strasbourg	**37**	48 35N	7 42 E
Stratford, Canada	**151**	43 23N	81 0W
Stratford, N.Z.	**122**	39 20S	174 19 E
Stratford-on-Avon	**24**	52 12N	1 42W
Strath Spey	**33**	57 15N	3 40W
Strathalbyn	**119**	35 13S	138 53 E
Strathclyde □	**30**	56 0N	4 50W
Strathmore	**33**	56 40N	3 4W
Strathy Pt.	**33**	58 35N	4 0W
Streaky B.	**118**	32 51S	134 18 E
Streator	**167**	41 9N	88 52W
Strómboli	**49**	38 48N	15 12 E
Stromeferry	**32**	57 20N	5 33W
Stromness	**33**	58 58N	3 18W
Stronsay	**33**	59 8N	2 38W
Stroud	**24**	51 44N	2 12W
Strumica	**53**	41 28N	22 41 E
Stuart L.	**154**	54 30N	124 30W
Stung Treng	**95**	13 31N	105 58 E
Sturgeon Bay	**167**	44 52N	87 20W
Sturgeon Falls	**151**	46 25N	79 57W
Stuttgart, Germany	**42**	48 46N	9 10 E
Stuttgart, U.S.A.	**168**	34 30N	91 33W
Styria = Steiermark □	**45**	47 26N	15 0 E
Suakin	**129**	19 8N	37 20 E
Subotica	**52**	46 6N	19 49 E
Suchitoto	**177**	13 56N	89 0W
Suchou = Suzhou	**99**	31 19N	120 38 E
Süchow = Xuzhou	**99**	34 18N	117 10 E
Sucre	**187**	19 0S	65 15W
Sudan ■	**129**	15 0N	30 0 E
Sudbury, Canada	**151**	46 30N	81 0W
Sudbury, U.K.	**25**	52 2N	0 44 E
Sudetan Mts. = Sudety	**58**	50 20N	16 45 E
Sudety	**58**	50 20N	16 45 E
Suez = El Suweis	**128**	29 58N	32 31 E
Suez Canal = Suweis, Qanâl es	**128**	31 0N	32 20 E
Suffolk	**165**	36 47N	76 33W
Suffolk □	**25**	52 16N	1 0 E
Sugluk = Saglouc	**146**	62 14N	75 38W
Suhbaatar	**98**	50 17N	106 10 E
Suir →	**35**	52 15N	7 10W
Suita	**106**	34 45N	135 32 E
Sukhona →	**68**	60 30N	45 0 E
Sukhumi	**70**	43 0N	41 0 E
Sukkertoppen	**147**	65 26N	52 55W
Sukkur	**88**	27 42N	68 54 E
Sukkur Barrage	**88**	27 40N	68 50 E
Sukumo	**109**	32 56N	132 44 E
Sulaiman Range	**89**	30 30N	69 50 E
Sulawesi □	**113**	2 0S	120 0 E
Sulina	**57**	45 10N	29 40 E
Sulitjelma	**66**	67 9N	16 3 E
Sullana	**186**	4 52S	80 39W
Sullivan	**167**	39 5N	87 26W
Sullivan I. = Lambi Kyun	**96**	10 50N	98 20 E
Sulphur Springs	**168**	33 5N	95 36W
Sulu Arch.	**112**	6 0N	121 0 E
Sulu Sea	**112**	8 0N	120 0 E
Suluq	**128**	31 44N	20 14 E
Sumatera □	**111**	0 40N	100 20 E
Sumatra = Sumatera □	**111**	0 40N	100 20 E
Sumba	**113**	9 45S	119 35 E
Sumbawa	**113**	8 26S	117 30 E
Sumburgh Hd.	**30**	59 52N	1 17W
Summerland	**155**	49 32N	119 41W
Summerside	**148**	46 24N	63 47W
Sumoto	**109**	34 21N	134 54 E
Sumter	**165**	33 55N	80 22W
Sumy	**68**	50 57N	34 50 E
Sunbury, Australia	**117**	37 35S	144 44 E
Sunbury, U.S.A.	**164**	40 50N	76 46W
Sunda, Selat	**111**	6 20S	105 30 E
Sundarbans, The	**92**	22 0N	89 0 E
Sunderland	**28**	54 54N	1 22W
Sundsvall	**66**	62 23N	17 17 E
Sungei Patani	**96**	5 38N	100 29 E
Sungei Siput	**96**	4 51N	101 6 E
Sungurlu	**80**	40 12N	34 21 E
Sunnyside	**171**	46 24N	120 2W
Sunnyvale	**172**	37 23N	122 2W
Suntar	**74**	62 15N	117 30 E
Suō-Nada	**108**	33 50N	131 30 E
Superior	**150**	46 45N	92 5W
Superior, L.	**150**	47 40N	87 0W
Suphan Dağı	**81**	38 54N	42 48 E
Sūr	**80**	22 34N	59 32 E
Surabaja = Surabaya	**111**	7 17S	112 45 E
Surabaya	**111**	7 17S	112 45 E
Surakarta	**111**	7 35S	110 48 E
Surat	**91**	21 12N	72 55 E
Surat Thani	**96**	9 6N	99 20 E
Suratgarh	**89**	29 18N	73 55 E
Surgut	**69**	61 14N	73 20 E
Surin	**95**	14 50N	103 34 E
Surinam ■	**185**	4 0N	56 0W
Surrey □	**25**	51 16N	0 30W
Surt	**127**	31 11N	16 39 E
Surt, Khalīj	**127**	31 40N	18 30 E
Suruga-Wan	**107**	34 45N	138 30 E
Susaki	**109**	33 22N	133 17 E
Susanville	**172**	40 28N	120 40W
Susquehanna →	**164**	39 33N	76 5W
Sutherland Falls	**123**	44 48S	167 46 E
Sutlej →	**89**	29 23N	71 3 E
Sutton-in-Ashfield	**29**	53 7N	1 20W
Suva	**122**	18 6S	178 30 E
Suwa	**107**	36 2N	138 8 E
Suwa-Ko	**107**	36 3N	138 5 E
Suwannee →	**170**	29 18N	83 9W
Suwanose-Jima	**104**	29 38N	129 43 E
Suweis, Qanâl es	**128**	31 0N	32 20 E
Suzaka	**107**	36 39N	138 19 E
Suzhou	**99**	31 19N	120 38 E
Suzu-Misaki	**105**	37 31N	137 21 E
Svalbard	**13**	78 0N	17 0 E
Svartenhuk Halvø	**146**	71 50N	54 30W
Svendborg	**61**	55 4N	10 35 E
Sverdlovsk	**69**	56 50N	60 30 E
Sverdrup Is.	**12**	79 0N	97 0W
Svishtov	**53**	43 36N	25 23 E
Svobodnyy	**75**	51 20N	128 0 E
Swabian Alps = Schwäbische Alb	**42**	48 30N	9 30 E
Swakopmund	**136**	22 37S	14 30 E
Swale →	**28**	54 5N	1 20W
Swan Hill	**117**	35 20S	143 33 E
Swan Hills	**155**	54 42N	115 24W
Swan Islands	**178**	17 22N	83 57W
Swan River	**152**	52 10N	101 16W
Swanage	**24**	50 36N	1 59W
Swansea	**27**	51 37N	3 57W
Swartberge	**136**	33 20S	22 0 E
Swatow = Shantou	**99**	23 18N	116 40 E
Swaziland ■	**137**	26 30S	31 30 E
Sweden ■	**66**	57 0N	15 0 E
Sweetwater	**161**	32 30N	100 28W
Swift Current	**152**	50 20N	107 45W
Swindon	**24**	51 33N	1 47W
Switzerland ■	**44**	46 30N	8 0 E
Swords	**34**	53 27N	6 15W
Sydney, Australia	**117**	33 53S	151 10 E
Sydney, Canada	**149**	46 7N	60 7W
Sydney Mines	**149**	46 18N	60 15W

Sydprøven	**147**	60 30N	45 35W
Sydra G. of = Surt, Khalīj	**127**	31 40N	18 30 E
Syktyvkar	**69**	61 45N	50 40 E
Sylacauga	**169**	33 10N	86 15W
Sylhet	**92**	24 54N	91 52 E
Sylvan Lake	**155**	52 20N	114 3W
Syracuse	**164**	43 4N	76 11W
Syrdarya →	**71**	46 3N	61 0 E
Syria ■	**80**	35 0N	38 0 E
Syrian Desert	**76**	31 0N	40 0 E
Syzran	**68**	53 12N	48 30 E
Szczecin	**58**	53 27N	14 27 E
Szechwan = Sichuan □	**99**	31 0N	104 0 E
Szeged	**59**	46 16N	20 10 E
Székesfehérvár	**59**	47 15N	18 25 E
Szolnok	**59**	47 10N	20 15 E
Szombathely	**59**	47 14N	16 38 E
Tabacal	**190**	23 15S	64 15W
Ţābah	**82**	26 55N	42 38 E
Tabasco □	**177**	18 0N	92 40W
Taber	**155**	49 47N	112 8W
Tablas	**112**	12 25N	122 2 E
Table Mt.	**136**	34 0S	18 22 E
Table Top, Mt.	**121**	23 24S	147 11 E
Tabora	**135**	5 2S	32 50 E
Tabrīz	**81**	38 7N	46 20 E
Tabūk	**82**	28 23N	36 36 E
Tachibana-Wan	**108**	32 45N	130 7 E
Tachikawa	**107**	35 42N	139 25 E
Tacna	**187**	18 0S	70 20W
Tacoma	**171**	47 15N	122 30W
Tacuarembó	**191**	31 45S	56 0W
Tademaït, Plateau du	**127**	28 30N	2 30 E
Tadoussac	**148**	48 11N	69 42W
Tadzhik S.S.R. □	**71**	35 30N	70 0 E
Taegu	**98**	35 50N	128 37 E
Taejŏn	**98**	36 20N	127 28 E
Taganrog	**68**	47 12N	38 50 E
Tagish	**144**	60 19N	134 16W
Tagua, La	**184**	0 3N	74 40W
Tagus = Tajo →	**50**	38 40N	9 24W
Tahiti	**123**	17 37S	149 27W
Tahoua	**131**	14 57N	5 16 E
Taibei	**99**	25 4N	121 29 E
T'aichung = Taizhong	**99**	24 12N	120 35 E
Taidong	**99**	22 43N	121 9 E
Taihape	**122**	39 41S	175 48 E
Tailem Bend	**119**	35 12S	139 29 E
Taimyr = Taymyr, Poluostrov	**72**	75 0N	100 0 E
Tain	**33**	57 49N	4 4W
Tainan	**99**	23 17N	120 18 E
Taínaron, Ákra	**54**	36 22N	22 27 E
T'aipei = Taibei	**99**	25 4N	121 29 E
Taiping	**96**	4 51N	100 44 E
Taisha	**109**	35 24N	132 40 E
Taitao, Pen. de	**192**	46 30S	75 0W
Taiwan ■	**99**	23 30N	121 0 E
Taiyuan	**98**	37 52N	112 33 E
Taizhong	**99**	24 12N	120 35 E
Ta'izz	**83**	13 35N	44 2 E
Tajimi	**106**	35 19N	137 8 E
Tajo →	**50**	38 40N	9 24W
Tak	**94**	16 52N	99 8 E
Takachiho	**108**	32 42N	131 18 E
Takada	**105**	37 7N	138 15 E
Takahashi	**109**	34 51N	133 39 E
Takamatsu	**109**	34 20N	134 5 E
Takaoka	**106**	36 47N	137 0 E
Takapuna	**122**	36 47S	174 47 E
Takasago	**109**	34 45N	134 48 E
Takasaki	**107**	36 20N	139 0 E
Takatsuki	**106**	34 51N	135 37 E
Takawa	**108**	33 38N	130 51 E
Takayama	**106**	36 18N	137 11 E
Takayama-Bonchi	**106**	36 0N	137 18 E
Takefu	**106**	35 50N	136 10 E
Takehara	**109**	34 21N	132 55 E
Taketa	**108**	32 58N	131 24 E
Takhār □	**87**	36 40N	70 0 E
Takla Landing	**154**	55 30N	125 50W
Takla Makan	**76**	39 0N	83 0 E
Taku	**108**	33 18N	130 3 E
Talara	**186**	4 38S	81 18 E
Talaud, Kepulauan	**113**	4 30N	127 10 E
Talca	**190**	35 28S	71 40W
Talcahuano	**190**	36 40S	73 10W
Ţālesh, Kūhhā-ye	**81**	39 0N	48 30 E
Talguppa	**90**	14 10N	74 45 E
Taliabu	**113**	1 45S	125 0 E
Talkeetna	**142**	62 20N	150 9W
Tall 'Afar	**81**	36 22N	42 27 E
Talladega	**169**	33 28N	86 2W
Tallahassee	**170**	30 25N	84 15W
Tallangatta	**117**	36 15S	147 19 E
Tallinn	**68**	59 22N	24 48 E
Tallulah	**168**	32 25N	91 12W
Tamale	**130**	9 22N	0 50W
Tamana	**108**	32 58N	130 32 E
Tamano	**109**	34 29N	133 59 E
Tamanrasset	**127**	22 50N	5 30 E
Tamar →	**27**	50 33N	4 15W
Tamaulipas □	**176**	24 0N	98 45W
Tambellup	**120**	34 4S	117 37 E
Tambov	**68**	52 45N	41 28 E
Tamgak, Mts.	**127**	19 12N	8 35 E
Tamil Nadu □	**90**	11 0N	77 0 E
Tammerfors = Tampere	**67**	61 30N	23 50 E
Tamo Abu, Pegunungan	**111**	3 10N	115 0 E
Tampa	**170**	27 57N	82 38W
Tampa B.	**170**	27 40N	82 40W
Tampere	**67**	61 30N	23 50 E
Tampico	**177**	22 20N	97 50W
Tamrah	**83**	20 24N	45 25 E
Tamsagbulag	**98**	47 14N	117 21 E
Tamworth, Australia	**116**	31 7S	150 58 E
Tamworth, U.K.	**24**	52 38N	1 41W
Tana →, Kenya	**133**	2 32S	40 31 E
Tana →, Norway	**67**	70 30N	28 23 E
Tana, L.	**132**	13 5N	37 30 E
Tanabe	**106**	33 44N	135 22 E
Tanana	**142**	65 10N	152 15W
Tananarive = Antananarivo	**137**	18 55S	47 31 E
Tanba-Sanchi	**106**	35 7N	135 48 E
Tandil	**190**	37 15S	59 6W
Tando Adam	**88**	25 45N	68 40 E
Tane-ga-Shima	**104**	30 30N	131 0 E
Tanen Tong Dan	**93**	16 30N	98 30 E
Tanezrouft	**127**	23 9N	0 11 E
Tanga	**135**	5 5S	39 2 E
Tanganyika, L.	**135**	6 40S	30 0 E
Tanger	**126**	35 50N	5 49W
Tanggula Shan	**101**	32 40N	92 10 E
Tangier = Tanger	**126**	35 50N	5 49W
Tangshan	**98**	39 38N	118 10 E
Tanimbar, Kepulauan	**113**	7 30S	131 30 E
Taniyama	**108**	31 31N	130 31 E
Tanjore = Thanjavur	**90**	10 48N	79 12 E
Tannu Ola	**74**	51 0N	94 0 E
Tanout	**131**	14 50N	8 55 E
Tanta	**128**	30 45N	30 57 E
Tantung = Dandong	**98**	40 10N	124 20 E
Tanunda	**119**	34 30S	139 0 E
Tanzania ■	**135**	6 40S	34 0 E
Tapa Shan = Daba Shan	**99**	32 0N	109 0 E
Tapachula	**177**	14 54N	92 17W
Tapajós →	**185**	2 24S	54 41W
Tapanui	**123**	45 56S	169 18 E
Tapi →	**91**	21 8N	72 41 E
Tara →	**71**	56 42N	74 36 E
Tarabagatay, Khrebet	**71**	48 0N	83 0 E
Tarābulus, Lebanon	**80**	34 31N	35 50 E
Tarābulus, Libya	**127**	32 49N	13 7 E
Taranaki □	**122**	39 5S	174 51 E
Táranto	**49**	40 30N	17 11 E
Táranto, G. di	**49**	40 0N	17 15 E
Tarapoto	**186**	6 30S	76 20W
Tarare	**37**	45 54N	4 26 E
Tararua Range	**123**	40 45S	175 25 E
Tarauacá	**187**	8 6S	70 48W

Tarbela Dam	**89**	34 8N	72 52 E
Tarbert	**32**	57 54N	6 49W
Tarbes	**36**	43 15N	0 3 E
Tarcoola	**118**	30 44S	134 36 E
Taree	**116**	31 50S	152 30 E
Tarfaya	**126**	27 55N	12 55W
Tarifa	**50**	36 1N	5 36W
Tarija	**187**	21 30S	64 40W
Tarim →	**100**	41 5N	86 40 E
Tarim Pendi	**100**	40 0N	84 0 E
Tarko Sale	**69**	64 55N	77 50 E
Tarn →	**36**	44 5N	1 6 E
Tarnobrzeg	**58**	50 35N	21 41 E
Tarnów	**58**	50 3N	21 0 E
Tarragona	**51**	41 5N	1 17 E
Tarrasa	**51**	41 34N	2 1 E
Tarsus	**80**	36 58N	34 55 E
Tartagal	**190**	22 30S	63 50W
Tarţūs	**80**	34 55N	35 55 E
Tarumizu	**108**	31 29N	130 42 E
Tarutao, Ko	**96**	6 33N	99 40 E
Taschereau	**151**	48 40N	78 40W
Tashi Chho Dzong = Thimphu	**92**	27 31N	89 45 E
Tashkent	**71**	41 20N	69 10 E
Tasman B.	**123**	40 59S	173 25 E
Tasman Mts.	**123**	41 3S	172 25 E
Tasman Sea	**122**	36 0S	160 0 E
Tasmania □	**119**	42 0S	146 30 E
Tatabánya	**59**	47 32N	18 25 E
Tatarsk	**71**	55 14N	76 0 E
Tateshina-Yama	**107**	36 8N	138 11 E
Tateyama	**107**	35 0N	139 50 E
Tatra = Tatry	**59**	49 20N	20 0 E
Tatry	**59**	49 20N	20 0 E
Tatsuno	**109**	34 52N	134 33 E
Tat'ung = Datong	**98**	40 6N	113 18 E
Taubaté	**191**	23 0S	45 36W
Tauern	**45**	47 15N	12 40 E
Taumarunui	**122**	38 53S	175 15 E
Taunggyi	**93**	20 50N	97 0 E
Taungup Taunggya	**93**	18 20N	93 40 E
Taunton, U.K.	**27**	51 1N	3 7W
Taunton, U.S.A.	**164**	41 54N	71 6W
Taunus	**42**	50 15N	8 20 E
Taupo	**122**	38 41S	176 7 E
Taupo, L.	**122**	38 46S	175 55 E
Tauranga	**122**	37 42S	176 11 E
Taurus Mts. = Toros Dağlari	**80**	37 0N	35 0 E
Taverny	**39**	49 2N	2 13 E
Tavistock	**27**	50 33N	4 9W
Tavoy	**94**	14 2N	98 12 E
Tawas City	**167**	44 16N	83 31W
Tay →	**33**	56 37N	3 38W
Tayabamba	**186**	8 15S	77 16W
Taylor Mt.	**161**	35 16N	107 36W
Taymā	**82**	27 35N	38 45 E
Taymyr, Poluostrov	**72**	75 0N	100 0 E
Tayshet	**74**	55 58N	98 1 E
Tayside □	**31**	56 25N	3 30W
Taz →	**69**	67 32N	78 40 E
Tbilisi	**70**	41 43N	44 50 E
Tchad ■ = Chad ■	**131**	15 0N	17 15 E
Tchad, L.	**131**	13 30N	14 30 E
Tch'eng-tou = Chengdu	**99**	30 38N	104 2 E
Tch'ong-k'ing = Chongqing	**99**	29 35N	106 25 E
Te Anau, L.	**123**	45 15S	167 45 E
Te Kuiti	**122**	38 20S	175 11 E
Tecuala	**175**	22 23N	105 27W
Tefé	**185**	3 25S	64 50W
Tegal	**111**	6 52S	109 8 E
Tegucigalpa	**179**	14 5N	87 14W
Tehachapi Mts.	**173**	35 0N	118 40W
Tehrān	**86**	35 44N	51 30 E
Tehuacán	**177**	18 27N	97 23W
Tehuantepec	**177**	16 21N	95 13W
Tehuantepec, G. de	**177**	16 0N	94 50W
Tehuantepec, Istmo de	**177**	17 0N	94 30W
Teifi →	**26**	52 4N	4 14W
Teignmouth	**27**	50 33N	3 30W
Tejo →	**50**	38 40N	9 24W

Tekax	**177**	20 12N	89 17W
Tekeli	**71**	44 50N	79 0 E
Tekirdağ	**80**	40 58N	27 30 E
Tel Aviv-Yafo	**80**	32 4N	34 48 E
Tela	**179**	15 40N	87 28W
Telanaipura = Jambi	**111**	1 38S	103 30 E
Telegraph Cr. →	**144**	58 0N	131 10W
Telemark fylke □	**60**	59 25N	8 30 E
Teles Pires →	**187**	7 21S	58 3W
Telford	**28**	52 42N	2 31W
Tell City	**167**	38 0N	86 44W
Teme →	**24**	52 23N	2 15W
Temerloh	**96**	3 27N	102 25 E
Temirtau	**71**	50 5N	72 56 E
Temora	**117**	34 30S	147 30 E
Temosachic	**174**	28 57N	107 51W
Temple	**158**	31 5N	97 22W
Temuco	**190**	38 45S	72 40W
Temuka	**123**	44 14S	171 17 E
Tenali	**91**	16 15N	80 35 E
Tenancingo	**177**	19 0N	99 33W
Tenango	**177**	19 7N	99 33W
Tenby	**27**	51 40N	4 42W
Tenerife	**126**	28 15N	16 35W
Teng Xian	**99**	35 5N	117 10 E
Tennessee □	**169**	36 0N	86 30W
Tennessee →	**169**	37 4N	88 34W
Tenri	**106**	34 39N	135 49 E
Tenryū	**107**	34 52N	137 49 E
Tenryū-Gawa →	**107**	35 39N	137 48 E
Tenterfield	**116**	29 0S	152 0 E
Teófilo Otoni	**189**	17 50S	41 30W
Tepic	**175**	21 30N	104 54W
Terang	**119**	38 15S	142 55 E
Terek →	**70**	44 0N	47 30 E
Terengganu □	**96**	4 55N	103 0 E
Teresina	**188**	5 9S	42 45W
Terewah, L.	**116**	29 52S	147 35 E
Termez	**70**	37 15N	67 15 E
Términos, L. de	**177**	18 37N	91 33W
Terneuzen	**40**	51 20N	3 50 E
Terni	**46**	42 34N	12 38 E
Terrace	**154**	54 30N	128 35W
Terre Haute	**167**	39 28N	87 24W
Terrell	**168**	32 44N	96 19W
Terschelling	**40**	53 25N	5 20 E
Teruel	**51**	40 22N	1 8W
Teshio	**103**	44 53N	141 44 E
Teslin	**144**	60 10N	132 43W
Test →	**24**	51 7N	1 30W
Tete	**137**	16 13S	33 33 E
Teteven	**53**	42 58N	24 17 E
Tétouan	**126**	35 35N	5 21W
Tetuán = Tétouan	**126**	35 35N	5 21W
Teuco →	**190**	25 35S	60 11W
Teutoburger Wald	**42**	52 5N	8 20 E
Tevere →	**46**	41 44N	12 14 E
Tewkesbury	**24**	51 59N	2 8W
Texarkana, Ark., U.S.A.	**168**	33 25N	94 0W
Texarkana, Tex., U.S.A.	**168**	33 25N	94 3W
Texas □	**161**	31 40N	98 30W
Texel	**40**	53 5N	4 50 E
Teziutlán	**177**	19 49N	97 21W
Tezpur	**93**	26 40N	92 45 E
Thabana Ntlenyana	**137**	29 30S	29 16 E
Thailand ■	**95**	16 0N	102 0 E
Thailand, G. of	**95**	11 30N	101 0 E
Thal Desert	**89**	31 10N	71 30 E
Thame →	**24**	51 35N	1 8W
Thames	**122**	37 7S	175 34 E
Thames →	**25**	51 30N	0 35 E
Thane	**91**	19 12N	72 59 E
Thanh Hoa	**95**	19 48N	105 46 E
Thanh Pho Ho Chi Minh	**95**	10 58N	106 40 E
Thanjavur	**90**	10 48N	79 12 E
Thar Desert	**89**	28 0N	72 0 E
Thásos	**55**	40 40N	24 40 E
Thaungdut	**93**	24 30N	94 40 E
Thazi	**93**	21 0N	96 5 E
The Dalles	**171**	45 40N	121 11W
The Grenadines, Is.	**180**	12 40N	61 20W

The Hague = 's-Gravenhage	**40**	52 7N	4 17 E
The Macumba →	**118**	27 52S	137 12 E
The Neales →	**118**	28 8S	136 47 E
The Pas	**152**	53 45N	101 15W
The Rock	**117**	35 15S	147 2 E
The Warburton →	**118**	28 4S	137 28 E
Thebes = Thívai	**55**	38 19N	23 19 E
Thermaïkos Kólpos	**54**	40 15N	22 45 E
Thermopolis	**163**	43 35N	108 10W
Thessalía □	**54**	39 30N	22 0 E
Thessalon	**150**	46 20N	83 30W
Thessaloníki	**54**	40 38N	22 58 E
Thessaly = Thessalía □	**54**	39 30N	22 0 E
Thetford Mines	**148**	46 8N	71 18W
Thicket Portage	**153**	55 19N	97 42W
Thies	**130**	14 50N	16 51W
Thimphu	**92**	27 31N	89 45 E
Thionville	**37**	49 20N	6 10 E
Thíra	**55**	36 23N	25 27 E
Thirsk	**29**	54 15N	1 20W
Thisted	**61**	56 58N	8 40 E
Thívai	**55**	38 19N	23 19 E
Thomaston	**170**	32 54N	84 20W
Thomasville, Ga., U.S.A.	**170**	30 50N	84 0W
Thomasville, N.C., U.S.A.	**165**	35 55N	80 4W
Thon Buri	**94**	13 43N	100 29 E
Thornaby on Tees	**29**	54 36N	1 19W
Thrace = Thráki □	**55**	41 9N	25 30 E
Thráki □	**55**	41 9N	25 30 E
Three Hills	**155**	51 43N	113 15W
Three Hummock I.	**119**	40 25S	144 55 E
Thule	**13**	77 40N	69 0W
Thundelarra	**120**	28 53S	117 7 E
Thunder B.	**150**	45 0N	83 20W
Thunder Bay	**150**	48 20N	89 15W
Thüringer Wald	**43**	50 35N	11 0 E
Thurles	**35**	52 40N	7 53W
Thursday I.	**115**	10 30S	142 3 E
Thurso	**33**	58 34N	3 31W
Tian Shan	**100**	43 0N	84 0 E
Tianjin	**98**	39 8N	117 10 E
Tianshui	**99**	34 32N	105 40 E
Tiber = Tevere →	**46**	41 44N	12 14 E
Tibesti	**127**	21 0N	17 30 E
Tibet = Xizang □	**101**	32 0N	88 0 E
Tibooburra	**118**	29 26S	142 1 E
Ticul	**177**	20 24N	89 32W
Tiel	**40**	51 53N	5 26 E
Tien Shan	**76**	42 0N	80 0 E
Tien-tsin = Tianjin	**98**	39 8N	117 10 E
T'iench'ing = Tianjin	**98**	39 8N	117 10 E
Tientsin = Tianjin	**98**	39 8N	117 10 E
Tierra de Campos	**50**	42 10N	4 50W
Tierra del Fuego □	**192**	54 0S	67 45W
Tiffin	**167**	41 8N	83 10W
Tiflis = Tbilisi	**70**	41 43N	44 50 E
Tifton	**170**	31 28N	83 32W
Tignish	**148**	46 58N	64 2W
Tigris = Dijlah, Nahr →	**81**	31 0N	47 25 E
Tijuana	**174**	32 32N	117 1W
Tiksi	**72**	71 40N	128 45 E
Tilburg	**40**	51 31N	5 6 E
Tilbury	**25**	51 27N	0 24 E
Tillsonburg	**151**	42 53N	80 44W
Tílos	**55**	36 27N	27 27 E
Timaru	**123**	44 23S	171 14 E
Timbuktu = Tombouctou	**130**	16 50N	3 0W
Timişoara	**56**	45 43N	21 15 E
Timmins	**151**	48 28N	81 25W
Timor	**113**	9 0S	125 0 E
Timor Sea	**113**	10 0S	127 0 E
Tinaca Pt.	**112**	5 30N	125 25 E
Tindouf	**126**	27 42N	8 10W
Tinnevelly = Tirunelveli	**90**	8 45N	77 45 E
Tinogasta	**190**	28 5S	67 32W
Tínos	**55**	37 33N	25 8 E
Tioman, Pulau	**96**	2 50N	104 10 E
Tipperary	**35**	52 28N	8 10W
Tipperary □	**35**	52 37N	7 55W
Tipton	**24**	52 32N	2 4W
Tirana	**52**	41 18N	19 49 E
Tiraspol	**68**	46 55N	29 35 E
Tire	**80**	38 5N	27 50 E
Tirebolu	**81**	40 58N	38 45 E
Tiree	**30**	56 31N	6 55W
Tîrgu Mureş	**57**	46 31N	24 38 E
Tirol □	**45**	47 3N	10 43 E
Tiruchchirappalli	**90**	10 45N	78 45 E
Tirunelveli	**90**	8 45N	77 45 E
Tisa →	**59**	45 15N	20 17 E
Tisdale	**152**	52 50N	104 0W
Titicaca, L.	**187**	15 30S	69 30W
Titograd	**52**	42 30N	19 19 E
Titov Veles	**53**	41 46N	21 47 E
Titovo Užice	**52**	43 55N	19 50 E
Tiverton	**27**	50 54N	3 30W
Tívoli	**46**	41 58N	12 45 E
Tizimín	**177**	21 9N	88 9W
Tjirebon = Cirebon	**111**	6 45S	108 32 E
Tlaxcala □	**177**	19 25N	98 10W
Tlaxiaco	**177**	17 18N	97 40W
Tlemcen	**127**	34 52N	1 21W
To-Shima	**107**	34 31N	139 17 E
Toamasina	**137**	18 10S	49 25 E
Toba Kakar	**88**	31 30N	69 0 E
Tobago	**180**	11 10N	60 30W
Tobermory	**30**	56 37N	6 4W
Tobolsk	**69**	58 15N	68 10 E
Tobruk = Tubruq	**128**	32 7N	23 55 E
Tocantins →	**188**	1 45S	49 10W
Toccoa	**165**	34 32N	83 17W
Tochigi	**107**	36 25N	139 45 E
Tocopilla	**190**	22 5S	70 10W
Todos Santos	**175**	23 27N	110 13W
Tōgane	**107**	35 33N	140 22 E
Togliatti	**68**	53 32N	49 24 E
Togo ■	**130**	6 15N	1 35 E
Tōhoku □	**103**	39 50N	141 45 E
Tōjō	**109**	34 53N	133 16 E
Tokai	**106**	35 2N	136 55 E
Tokaj	**58**	48 8N	21 27 E
Tokara Kaikyō	**104**	30 0N	130 0 E
Tokat	**80**	40 22N	36 35 E
Tokelau Is.	**123**	9 0S	171 45W
Toki	**106**	35 18N	137 8 E
Tokoname	**106**	34 53N	136 51 E
Tokorozawa	**107**	35 47N	139 28 E
Tokushima	**109**	34 4N	134 34 E
Tokuyama	**108**	34 3N	131 50 E
Tōkyō	**107**	35 45N	139 45 E
Tōkyō-Wan	**107**	35 25N	139 47 E
Tolbukhin	**53**	43 37N	27 49 E
Toledo, Spain	**50**	39 50N	4 2W
Toledo, U.S.A.	**167**	41 37N	83 33W
Tolga	**127**	34 40N	5 22 E
Tolima, Vol.	**184**	4 40N	75 19W
Toluca	**177**	19 20N	99 40W
Tomakomai	**103**	42 38N	141 36 E
Tombigbee →	**169**	31 4N	87 58W
Tombouctou	**130**	16 50N	3 0W
Tomini, Teluk	**113**	0 10S	122 0 E
Tomsk	**71**	56 30N	85 5 E
Tonalá	**177**	16 4N	93 45W
Tonantins	**184**	2 45S	67 45W
Tonbridge	**25**	51 12N	0 18 E
Tong Xian	**98**	39 55N	116 35 E
Tonga ■	**123**	19 50S	174 30W
Tongchuan	**99**	35 6N	109 3 E
Tonghua	**98**	41 42N	125 58 E
Tongking, G. of	**95**	20 0N	108 0 E
Tongue	**33**	58 29N	4 25W
Tonk	**91**	26 6N	75 54 E
Tonkin = Bac Phan	**95**	22 0N	105 0 E
Tonlé Sap	**95**	13 0N	104 0 E
Tonopah	**172**	38 4N	117 12W
Tonoshō	**109**	34 29N	134 11 E
Tooele	**162**	40 30N	112 20W
Toowoomba	**116**	27 32S	151 56 E
Topeka	**166**	39 3N	95 40W
Toppenish	**171**	46 27N	120 16W
Torbay	**27**	50 26N	3 31W
Torino	**46**	45 4N	7 40 E

Tormes →	**50**	41 18N	6 29W
Torne älv →	**67**	65 50N	24 12 E
Torneå = Tornio	**67**	65 50N	24 12 E
Torneträsk	**66**	68 24N	19 15 E
Tornio	**67**	65 50N	24 12 E
Toro, Cerro del	**190**	29 10S	69 50W
Toronto, Australia	**117**	33 0S	151 30 E
Toronto, Canada	**151**	43 39N	79 20W
Toros Daglari	**80**	37 0N	35 0 E
Torquay	**27**	50 27N	3 31W
Torre Annunziata	**49**	40 45N	14 26 E
Tôrre de Moncorvo	**50**	41 12N	7 8W
Torremolinos	**50**	36 38N	4 30W
Torrens, L.	**119**	31 0S	137 50 E
Torreón	**174**	25 33N	103 26W
Torres Vedras	**50**	39 5N	9 15W
Torridge →	**27**	50 51N	4 10W
Torrington	**164**	41 50N	73 9W
Tortosa	**51**	40 49N	0 31 E
Tortosa, C.	**51**	40 41N	0 52 E
Toruń	**58**	53 0N	18 39 E
Tory I.	**34**	55 17N	8 12W
Tosa-Shimizu	**109**	32 52N	132 58 E
Tosa-Wan	**109**	33 15N	133 30 E
Toscana	**46**	43 30N	11 5 E
Tostado	**190**	29 15S	61 50W
Tosu	**109**	33 22N	130 31 E
Totnes	**27**	50 26N	3 41W
Totonicapán	**177**	14 58N	91 12W
Tottori	**109**	35 30N	134 15 E
Toubkal, Djebel	**126**	31 0N	8 0W
Touggourt	**127**	33 6N	6 4 E
Toulon	**37**	43 10N	5 55 E
Toulouse	**36**	43 37N	1 27 E
Toungoo	**93**	19 0N	96 30 E
Touraine	**36**	47 20N	0 30 E
Tourane = Da Nang	**95**	16 4N	108 13 E
Tourcoing	**38**	50 42N	3 10 E
Tournai	**42**	50 35N	3 25 E
Tours	**36**	47 22N	0 40 E
Townsville	**121**	19 15S	146 45 E
Towson	**164**	39 26N	76 34W
Toyama	**106**	36 40N	137 15 E
Toyama-Wan	**105**	37 0N	137 30 E
Toyohashi	**106**	34 45N	137 25 E
Toyokawa	**106**	34 48N	137 27 E
Toyonaka	**106**	34 50N	135 28 E
Toyooka	**109**	35 35N	134 48 E
Toyota	**106**	35 3N	137 7 E
Tozeur	**127**	33 56N	8 8 E
Trabzon	**81**	41 0N	39 45 E
Tracy	**172**	37 46N	121 27W
Trafalgar, C.	**50**	36 10N	6 2W
Trail	**155**	49 5N	117 40W
Tralee	**35**	52 16N	9 42W
Tralee B.	**35**	52 17N	9 55W
Tran Ninh, Cao Nguyen	**95**	19 30N	103 10 E
Trangan	**113**	6 40S	134 20 E
Trangie	**116**	32 4S	148 0 E
Transantarctic Mts.	**15**	85 0S	170 0W
Transcona	**153**	49 55N	97 0W
Transilvania	**57**	46 19N	25 0 E
Transkei	**137**	32 15S	28 15 E
Transvaal □	**137**	25 0S	29 0 E
Transylvania = Transilvania	**57**	46 19N	25 0 E
Transylvanian Alps	**17**	45 30N	25 0 E
Trápani	**48**	38 1N	12 30 E
Traralgon	**117**	38 12S	146 34 E
Trasimeno, L.	**46**	43 10N	12 5 E
Travers, Mt.	**123**	42 1S	172 45 E
Traverse City	**167**	44 45N	85 39W
Travnik	**52**	44 17N	17 39 E
Tredegar	**27**	51 47N	3 16W
Tregaron	**26**	52 14N	3 56W
Treinta y Tres	**191**	33 16S	54 17W
Trelew	**192**	43 10S	65 20W
Trenque Lauquen	**190**	36 5S	62 45W
Trent →	**29**	53 33N	0 44W
Trentino-Alto Adige □	**47**	46 30N	11 0 E
Trento	**47**	46 5N	11 8 E
Trenton, Canada	**151**	44 10N	77 34W
Trenton, Mo., U.S.A.	**166**	40 5N	93 37W
Trenton, N.J., U.S.A.	**164**	40 15N	74 41W
Tréport, Le	**38**	50 3N	1 20 E
Tres Arroyos	**190**	38 26S	60 20W
Três Lagoas	**188**	20 50S	51 43W
Tres Montes, C.	**192**	46 50S	75 30W
Tres Puntas, C.	**192**	47 0S	66 0W
Treviso	**47**	45 40N	12 15 E
Trichinopoly = Tiruchchirappalli	**90**	10 45N	78 45 E
Trichur	**90**	10 30N	76 18 E
Trier	**42**	49 45N	6 37 E
Trieste	**47**	45 39N	13 45 E
Tríkkala	**54**	39 34N	21 47 E
Trincomalee	**90**	8 38N	81 15 E
Trinidad, Bolivia	**187**	14 46S	64 50W
Trinidad, Colombia	**184**	5 25N	71 40W
Trinidad, Cuba	**178**	21 48N	80 0W
Trinidad, Uruguay	**191**	33 30S	56 50W
Trinidad, U.S.A.	**163**	37 15N	104 30W
Trinidad & Tobago ■	**180**	10 30N	61 20W
Trinity →	**168**	30 30N	95 0W
Trinity Mts.	**172**	40 20N	118 50W
Tripoli = Tarābulus, Lebanon	**80**	34 31N	35 50 E
Tripoli = Tarābulus, Libya	**127**	32 49N	13 7 E
Trípolis	**54**	37 31N	22 25 E
Tripura □	**93**	24 0N	92 0 E
Trivandrum	**90**	8 41N	77 0 E
Trois-Riviéres	**151**	46 25N	72 34W
Troitsk	**71**	54 10N	61 35 E
Trollhättan	**60**	58 17N	12 20 E
Tromsø	**66**	69 40N	18 56 E
Trondheim	**65**	63 36N	10 25 E
Trossachs, The	**31**	56 14N	4 24W
Trotternish	**32**	57 32N	6 15W
Trouville	**38**	49 21N	0 5 E
Trowbridge	**24**	51 18N	2 12W
Troy, Ala., U.S.A.	**169**	31 50N	85 58W
Troy, N.Y., U.S.A.	**164**	42 45N	73 39W
Troyes	**39**	48 19N	4 3 E
Trucial States = United Arab Emirates ■	**85**	23 50N	54 0 E
Trujillo, Hond.	**179**	16 0N	86 0W
Trujillo, Peru	**186**	8 6S	79 0W
Trujillo, Venezuela	**184**	9 22N	70 38W
Trundle	**117**	32 53S	147 35 E
Trung-Phan	**95**	16 0N	108 0 E
Truro, Canada	**149**	45 21N	63 14W
Truro, U.K.	**27**	50 17N	5 2W
Tselinograd	**71**	51 10N	71 30 E
Tsinan = Jinan	**98**	36 38N	117 1 E
Tsinghai = Qinghai □	**101**	36 0N	98 0 E
Tsingtao = Qingdao	**98**	36 5N	120 20 E
Tsu	**106**	34 45N	136 25 E
Tsuchiura	**107**	36 5N	140 15 E
Tsugaru-Kaikyō	**103**	41 35N	141 0 E
Tsukumi	**108**	33 4N	131 52 E
Tsukushi-Sanchi	**108**	33 25N	130 30 E
Tsuruga	**106**	35 45N	136 2 E
Tsurugi-San	**109**	33 51N	134 6 E
Tsuruoka	**103**	38 44N	139 50 E
Tsushima, Gifu, Japan	**106**	35 10N	136 43 E
Tsushima, Nagasaki, Japan	**104**	34 20N	129 20 E
Tuamotu Arch.	**123**	17 0S	144 0W
Tubarão	**191**	28 30S	49 0W
Tubruq	**128**	32 7N	23 55 E
Tubuai Is.	**123**	25 0S	150 0W
Tucacas	**184**	10 48N	68 19W
Tucson	**160**	32 14N	110 59W
Tucumcari	**161**	35 12N	103 45W
Tucupita	**185**	9 2N	62 3W
Tucuruí	**188**	3 42S	49 44W
Tudmur	**80**	34 36N	38 15 E
Tuktoyaktuk	**144**	69 27N	133 2W
Tula, Mexico	**177**	23 0N	99 43W
Tula, U.S.S.R.	**68**	54 13N	37 38 E
Tulare	**173**	36 15N	119 26W
Tulcán	**184**	0 48N	77 43W
Tullahoma	**169**	35 23N	86 12W
Tullamore	**35**	53 17N	7 30W
Tully	**121**	17 56S	145 55 E

Tulsa 168 36 10N 96 0W
Tulua 184 4 6N 76 11W
Tuma → 179 13 6N 84 35W
Tumaco 184 1 50N 78 45W
Tumatumari 185 5 20N 58 55W
Tumbarumba 117 35 44S 148 0E
Túmbes 186 3 37S 80 27W
Tumkur 90 13 18N 77 6E
Tummel, L. 33 56 43N 3 55W
Tummo 127 22 45N 14 8E
Tump 88 26 7N 62 16E
Tumucumaque, Serra 188 2 0N 55 0W
Tumut 117 35 16S 148 13E
Tunbridge Wells 25 51 7N 0 16E
Tundzha → 53 41 40N 26 35E
Tunis 127 36 50N 10 11E
Tunisia ■ 127 33 30N 9 10E
Tunja 184 5 33N 73 25W
Tunxi 99 29 42N 118 25E
Tupelo 169 34 15N 88 42W
Tupiza 187 21 30S 65 40W
Tupper L. 151 44 18N 74 30W
Tuque, La 151 47 30N 72 50W
Túquerres 184 1 5N 77 37W
Tura 92 25 30N 90 16E
Turayf 82 31 41N 38 39E
Turfan = Turpan 100 43 58N 89 10E
Turfan Depression = Turpan Hami 100 42 40N 89 25E
Tŭrgovishte 53 43 17N 26 38E
Turgutlu 80 38 30N 27 48E
Turin = Torino 46 45 4N 7 40E
Turkana, L. 132 3 30N 36 5E
Turkestan 71 43 17N 68 16E
Turkey ■ 80 39 0N 36 0E
Turkmen S.S.R. □ 70 39 0N 59 0E
Turks Is. 180 21 20N 71 20W
Turku 67 60 30N 22 19E
Turlock 172 37 30N 120 55W
Turnagain, C. 122 40 28S 176 38E
Turnhout 42 51 19N 4 57E
Tŭrnovo 53 43 5N 25 41E
Turnu Rosu Pasul 57 45 33N 24 17E
Turnu-Severin 56 44 39N 22 41E
Turpan 100 43 58N 89 10E
Turpan Hami 100 42 40N 89 25E
Turukhansk 74 65 21N 88 5E
Tuscaloosa 169 33 13N 87 31W
Tuscany = Toscana 46 43 30N 11 5E
Tuskegee 169 32 24N 85 39W
Tutrakan 53 44 2N 26 40E
Tuvalu ■ 122 8 0S 178 0E
Tuxpan 177 20 57N 97 24W
Tuxtla Gutiérrez 177 16 45N 93 7W
Tuy Hoa 95 13 5N 109 10E
Tuyen Hoa 95 17 50N 106 10E
Tuz Gölü 80 38 45N 33 30E
Ṭūz Khurmātū 81 34 56N 44 38E
Tuzla 52 44 34N 18 41E
Tweed → 31 55 42N 2 10W
Tweed Heads 116 28 10S 153 31E
Twin Falls 172 42 30N 114 30W
Two Harbors 156 47 1N 91 40W
Tyler 168 32 18N 95 18W
Tyne → 28 54 58N 1 28W
Tyne & Wear □ 28 54 55N 1 35W
Tynemouth 28 55 1N 1 27W
Tyrol = Tirol □ 45 47 3N 10 43E
Tyrrhenian Sea 48 40 0N 12 30E
Tyumen 69 57 11N 65 29E
Tzukong = Zigong 99 29 15N 104 48E

Uaupés 184 0 8S 67 5W
Ubangi = Oubangi → 131 1 0N 17 50E
Ube 108 33 56N 131 15E
Uberaba 188 19 50S 47 55W
Uberlândia 188 19 0S 48 20W
Ubon Ratchathani 95 15 15N 104 50E
Ucayali → 186 4 30S 73 30W
Uchi Lake 153 51 5N 92 35W
Uchiura-Wan 103 42 25N 140 40E
Uchur → 75 58 48N 130 35E
Udaipur 91 24 36N 73 44E
Uddevalla 60 58 21N 11 55E
Údine 47 46 5N 13 10E
Udmurt A.S.S.R. □ 69 57 30N 52 30E
Udon Thani 95 17 29N 102 46E
Ueda 107 36 24N 138 16E
Uelen 73 66 10N 170 0W
Uelzen 43 53 0N 10 33E
Ueno 106 34 45N 136 8E
Ufa 69 54 45N 55 55E
Uganda ■ 132 2 0N 32 0E
Uinta Mts. 163 40 45N 110 30W
Uithuizen 41 53 24N 6 41E
Uji 106 34 53N 135 48E
Ujjain 91 23 9N 75 43E
Újpest 59 47 32N 19 6E
Ujung Pandang 113 5 10S 119 20E
Ukiah 172 39 10N 123 9W
Ukrainian S.S.R. □ 68 49 0N 32 0E
Ulaanbaatar 98 47 55N 106 53E
Ulan Bator = Ulaanbaatar 98 47 55N 106 53E
Ulan Ude 74 51 45N 107 40E
Ulcinj 52 41 58N 19 10E
Ulhasnagar 91 19 15N 73 10E
Ulladulla 117 35 21S 150 29E
Ullapool 32 57 54N 5 10W
Ullswater 28 54 35N 2 52W
Ulm 42 48 23N 10 0E
Ulster □ 34 54 35N 6 30W
Ulverston 28 54 13N 3 7W
Ulverstone 119 41 11S 146 11E
Ulyanovsk 68 54 20N 48 25E
Ulyasutay 100 47 56N 97 28E
Umbrella Mts 123 45 35S 169 5E
Umbria □ 46 42 53N 12 30E
Ume älv → 66 63 45N 20 20E
Umeå 66 63 45N 20 20E
Umm al Qaywayn 85 25 30N 55 35E
Umm Lajj 82 25 0N 37 23E
Umnak 142 53 20N 168 20W
Umpang 94 16 3N 98 54E
Umtata 137 31 36S 28 49E
Unalaska 142 53 40N 166 40W
Ungava B. 146 59 30N 67 30W
Ungava Pen. 146 60 0N 74 0W
União da Vitória 191 26 13S 51 5W
Unimak 142 55 0N 164 0W
Union City 169 36 25N 89 0W
Union of Soviet Socialist Republics ■ 79 60 0N 100 0E
Uniontown 164 39 54N 79 45W
United Arab Emirates ■ 85 23 50N 54 0E
United Kingdom ■ 18 55 0N 3 0W
United States of America ■ 139 37 0N 96 0W
Unity 152 52 30N 109 5W
Unnao 92 26 35N 80 30E
Unst 30 60 50N 0 55W
Uozu 106 36 48N 137 24E
Upata 185 8 1N 62 24W
Upper Austria = Oberösterreich □ 45 48 10N 14 0E
Upper Hutt 123 41 8S 175 5E
Upper Taimyr → 72 74 15N 99 48E
Upper Volta ■ = Burkina Faso ■ 130 12 0N 1 0W
Uppsala 60 59 53N 17 38E
Uppsala län □ 60 60 0N 17 30E
Ur 84 30 55N 46 25E
Uracara 185 2 20S 57 50W
Urakawa 103 42 9N 142 47E
Ural → 70 47 0N 51 48E
Ural Mts. = Uralskie Gory 69 60 0N 59 0E
Uralsk 70 51 20N 51 20E
Uralskie Gory 69 60 0N 59 0E
Uranium City 145 59 34N 108 37W
Urawa 107 35 50N 139 40E
Urbana, Ill., U.S.A. 167 40 7N 88 12W
Urbana, Ohio, U.S.A. 167 40 9N 83 44W

Urbana, La	**184**	7 8N	66 56W
Urcos	**187**	13 40S	71 38W
Ures	**174**	29 26N	110 24W
Urfa	**81**	37 12N	38 50 E
Urgench	**70**	41 40N	60 41 E
Uribia	**184**	11 43N	72 16W
Urk	**41**	52 39N	5 36 E
Urmia = Orūmīyeh	**81**	37 40N	45 0 E
Urmia, L. = Orūmīyeh, Daryācheh-ye	**81**	37 50N	45 30 E
Uruapan	**175**	19 30N	102 0W
Uruçuí	**188**	7 20S	44 28W
Uruguaiana	**191**	29 50S	57 0W
Uruguay ■	**191**	32 30S	56 30W
Uruguay →	**191**	34 12S	58 18W
Urumchi = Ürümqi	**100**	43 45N	87 45 E
Ürümqi	**100**	43 45N	87 45 E
Urup, Os.	**75**	46 0N	151 0 E
Usa	**108**	33 31N	131 21 E
Uşak	**80**	38 43N	29 28 E
Usfan	**82**	21 58N	39 27 E
Ushant = Ouessant, Île d'	**36**	48 28N	5 6W
Ushibuka	**108**	32 11N	130 1 E
Ushuaia	**192**	54 50S	68 23W
Usk →	**26**	51 37N	2 56W
Üsküdar	**80**	41 0N	29 5 E
Usolye Sibirskoye	**74**	52 48N	103 40 E
Uspenskiy	**71**	48 41N	72 43 E
Ussuriysk	**75**	43 48N	131 59 E
Ust-Aldan = Batamay	**74**	63 30N	129 15 E
Ust-Ilimsk	**74**	58 3N	102 39 E
Ust-Kamchatsk	**73**	56 10N	162 28 E
Ust-Kamenogorsk	**71**	50 0N	82 36 E
Ust Maya	**75**	60 30N	134 28 E
Ust Olenek	**72**	73 0N	119 48 E
Ust Port	**69**	69 40N	84 26 E
Ust Urt = Ustyurt, Plato	**70**	44 0N	55 0 E
Ust Vorkuta	**69**	67 24N	64 0 E
Ústí nad Labem	**58**	50 41N	14 3 E
Ustica	**48**	38 42N	13 10 E
Ustinov	**69**	56 51N	53 14 E
Ustyurt, Plato	**70**	44 0N	55 0 E
Usu	**100**	44 27N	84 40 E
Usuki	**108**	33 8N	131 49 E
Usumbura = Bujumbura	**135**	3 16S	29 18 E
Utah □	**163**	39 30N	111 30W
Utah, L.	**163**	40 10N	111 58W
Uthai Thani	**94**	15 22N	100 3 E
Utica	**164**	43 5N	75 18W
Uto	**108**	32 41N	130 40 E
Utrecht	**40**	52 5N	5 8 E
Utrecht □	**40**	52 6N	5 7 E
Utrera	**50**	37 12N	5 48W
Utsunomiya	**107**	36 30N	139 50 E
Uttar Pradesh □	**92**	27 0N	80 0 E
Uttoxeter	**28**	52 53N	1 50W
Uusikaupunki	**66**	60 47N	21 25 E
Uvalde	**161**	29 15N	99 48W
Uvs Nuur	**74**	50 20N	92 30 E
Uwajima	**109**	33 10N	132 35 E
Uzbek S.S.R. □	**70**	41 30N	65 0 E
Vaal →	**137**	29 4S	23 38 E
Vaals	**41**	50 46N	6 1 E
Vaasa	**67**	63 6N	21 38 E
Vác	**58**	47 49N	19 10 E
Vach →	**69**	60 45N	76 45 E
Vadodara	**91**	22 20N	73 10 E
Vadsø	**67**	70 3N	29 50 E
Váh →	**59**	47 55N	18 0 E
Vaigach	**69**	70 10N	59 0 E
Val d'Or	**151**	48 7N	77 47W
Valahia	**57**	44 35N	25 0 E
Valcheta	**192**	40 40S	66 8W
Valdés, Pen.	**192**	42 30S	63 45W
Valdez	**142**	61 14N	146 17W
Valdivia	**190**	39 50S	73 14W
Valdosta	**170**	30 50N	83 20W
Valence	**37**	44 57N	4 54 E
Valencia, Spain	**51**	39 27N	0 23W
Valencia, Venezuela	**184**	10 11N	68 0W
Valencia □	**51**	39 20N	0 40W
Valencia, Albufera de	**51**	39 20N	0 27W
Valencia, G. de	**51**	39 30N	0 20 E
Valencia de Alcántara	**50**	39 25N	7 14W
Valenciennes	**38**	50 20N	3 34 E
Valentia I.	**35**	51 54N	10 22W
Valera	**184**	9 19N	70 37W
Valkenswaard	**41**	51 21N	5 29 E
Valladolid, Mexico	**177**	20 41N	88 12W
Valladolid, Spain	**50**	41 38N	4 43W
Valle d'Aosta □	**46**	45 45N	7 22 E
Valle de la Pascua	**184**	9 13N	66 0W
Valle de Santiago	**177**	20 23N	101 12W
Vallecas	**50**	40 23N	3 41W
Vallejo	**172**	38 12N	122 15W
Valletta	**49**	35 54N	14 30 E
Valley City	**163**	46 57N	98 0W
Valley View	**155**	40 39N	76 33W
Valona = Vlóra	**52**	40 32N	19 28 E
Valparaíso, Chile	**190**	33 2S	71 40W
Valparaíso, Mexico	**175**	22 46N	103 34W
Valsad	**91**	20 40N	72 58 E
Van	**81**	38 30N	43 20 E
Van, L. = Van Gölü	**81**	38 30N	43 0 E
Van Buren, Canada	**148**	47 10N	67 55W
Van Buren, U.S.A.	**168**	35 28N	94 18W
Van Gölü	**81**	38 30N	43 0 E
Van Wert	**167**	40 52N	84 31W
Vancouver, Canada	**154**	49 15N	123 10W
Vancouver, U.S.A.	**171**	45 44N	122 41W
Vancouver I.	**154**	49 50N	126 0W
Vandalia	**166**	38 57N	89 4W
Vanderhoof	**154**	54 0N	124 0W
Vänern	**60**	58 47N	13 30 E
Vanier	**151**	45 27N	75 40W
Vankarem	**73**	67 51N	175 50 E
Vännäs	**66**	63 58N	19 48 E
Vannes	**36**	47 40N	2 47W
Vanua Levu	**122**	16 33S	179 15 E
Vanuatu ■	**122**	15 0S	168 0 E
Varanasi	**92**	25 22N	83 0 E
Varangerfjorden	**67**	70 3N	29 25 E
Varaždin	**52**	46 20N	16 20 E
Vardak □	**87**	34 0N	68 0 E
Vardø	**67**	70 23N	31 5 E
Värmland	**60**	60 0N	13 30 E
Varna	**53**	43 13N	27 56 E
Vascongadas	**50**	42 50N	2 45W
Västerås	**60**	59 37N	16 38 E
Västmanlands län □	**60**	59 45N	16 20 E
Vatnajökull	**64**	64 30N	16 48W
Vatra-Dornei	**57**	47 22N	25 22 E
Vättern	**60**	58 25N	14 30 E
Vaygach, Ostrov	**69**	70 0N	60 0 E
Veendam	**41**	53 5N	6 52 E
Vega, La	**180**	19 20N	70 30W
Veghel	**41**	51 37N	5 32 E
Vegreville	**155**	53 30N	112 5W
Vela, La	**184**	11 27N	69 34W
Vellore	**90**	12 57N	79 10 E
Venado Tuerto	**190**	33 50S	62 0W
Vendôme	**39**	47 47N	1 3 E
Véneto □	**47**	45 40N	12 0 E
Venézia	**47**	45 27N	12 20 E
Venézia, Golfo di	**47**	45 20N	13 0 E
Venezuela ■	**184**	8 0N	65 0W
Venezuela, Golfo de	**184**	11 30N	71 0W
Vengurla	**91**	15 53N	73 45 E
Venice = Venézia	**47**	45 27N	12 20 E
Venlo	**41**	51 22N	6 11 E
Venraij	**41**	51 31N	6 0 E
Ventnor	**24**	50 35N	1 12W
Ventoux	**37**	44 10N	5 17 E
Ventura	**173**	34 16N	119 18W
Veracruz	**177**	19 10N	96 10W
Veracruz □	**177**	19 20N	96 40W
Verde, R. →	**175**	15 59N	97 50W
Verdun	**37**	49 12N	5 24 E
Vereeniging	**137**	26 38S	27 57 E

Verkhoyansk	**72**	67 35N	133 25 E
Verkhoyanskiy Khrebet	**72**	66 0N	129 0 E
Vermilion	**152**	53 20N	110 50W
Vermont □	**164**	43 40N	72 50W
Verneuil-sur-Avre	**39**	48 45N	0 55 E
Vernon, Canada	**155**	50 20N	119 15W
Vernon, France	**39**	49 5N	1 30 E
Vernon, U.S.A.	**161**	34 10N	99 20W
Verona	**46**	45 27N	11 0 E
Versailles	**39**	48 48N	2 8 E
Vert, C.	**130**	14 45N	17 30W
Verviers	**42**	50 37N	5 52 E
Vest-Agder fylke □	**60**	58 30N	7 15 E
Vesterålen	**64**	68 45N	15 0 E
Vestfjorden	**64**	67 55N	14 0 E
Vestfold fylke □	**60**	59 15N	10 0 E
Vestspitsbergen	**13**	78 40N	17 0 E
Vesuvio	**49**	40 50N	14 22 E
Vesuvius, Mt. = Vesuvio	**49**	40 50N	14 22 E
Viacha	**187**	16 39S	68 18W
Viborg	**61**	56 27N	9 23 E
Vicenza	**47**	45 32N	11 31 E
Vichy	**37**	46 9N	3 26 E
Vicksburg	**169**	32 22N	90 56W
Victor Harbor	**119**	35 30S	138 37 E
Victoria, Canada	**154**	48 30N	123 25W
Victoria, Chile	**190**	38 13S	72 20W
Victoria, U.S.A.	**158**	28 50N	97 0W
Victoria □	**117**	37 0S	144 0 E
Victoria, L.	**132**	1 0S	33 0 E
Victoria de las Tunas	**178**	20 58N	76 59W
Victoria Falls	**137**	17 58S	25 52 E
Victoria I.	**145**	71 0N	111 0W
Victoria Ld.	**15**	75 0S	160 0 E
Victoriaville	**148**	46 4N	71 56W
Vidalia	**170**	32 13N	82 25W
Vidin	**53**	43 59N	22 50 E
Viedma	**192**	40 50S	63 0W
Vienna = Wien	**45**	48 12N	16 22 E
Vienne	**37**	45 31N	4 53 E
Vienne →	**36**	47 13N	0 5 E
Vientiane	**95**	17 58N	102 36 E
Vientos, Paso de los	**180**	20 0N	74 0W
Vietnam ■	**95**	19 0N	106 0 E
Vigo	**50**	42 12N	8 41W
Vijayawada	**92**	16 31N	80 39 E
Vila Real de Santo António	**50**	37 10N	7 28W
Vilhelmina	**66**	64 35N	16 39 E
Vilhena	**187**	12 40S	60 5W
Villa Bella	**187**	10 25S	65 22W
Villa Bens = Tarfaya	**126**	27 55N	12 55W
Villa Cisneros = Dakhla	**126**	23 50N	15 53W
Villa Dolores	**190**	31 58S	65 15W
Villa María	**190**	32 20S	63 10W
Villa Montes	**187**	21 10S	63 30W
Villaguay	**190**	32 0S	59 0W
Villahermosa	**177**	17 59N	92 55W
Villanueva de la Serena	**50**	38 59N	5 50W
Villarreal	**51**	39 55N	0 3W
Villarrica	**191**	39 15S	72 15W
Villazón	**187**	22 0S	65 35W
Ville Platte	**168**	30 45N	92 17W
Villefranche-sur-Saône	**37**	45 59N	4 43 E
Villers-Cotterêts	**39**	49 15N	3 4 E
Vilnius	**68**	54 38N	25 19 E
Vilskutskogo, Proliv	**72**	78 0N	103 0 E
Vilyuy →	**74**	64 24N	126 26 E
Vilyuysk	**74**	63 40N	121 35 E
Viña del Mar	**190**	33 0S	71 30W
Vincennes	**167**	38 42N	87 29W
Vindhya Ra.	**91**	22 50N	77 0 E
Vinh	**95**	18 45N	105 38 E
Vinita	**168**	36 40N	95 12W
Vinkovci	**52**	45 19N	18 48 E
Vinnitsa	**68**	49 15N	28 30 E
Viramgam	**91**	23 5N	72 0 E
Virden	**153**	49 50N	100 56W
Vire	**36**	48 50N	0 53W
Vírgenes, C.	**192**	52 19S	68 21W
Virgin →	**173**	36 50N	114 10W
Virgin Is.	**180**	18 40N	64 30W
Virginia	**156**	47 30N	92 32W
Virginia □	**165**	37 45N	78 0W
Virginia Beach	**165**	36 54N	75 58W
Visalia	**173**	36 25N	119 18W
Visby	**60**	57 37N	18 18 E
Viscount Melville Sd.	**145**	74 10N	108 0W
Višegrad	**52**	43 47N	19 17 E
Vishakhapatnam	**92**	17 45N	83 20 E
Vistula = Wisła →	**58**	54 22N	18 55 E
Vitebsk	**68**	55 10N	30 15 E
Viti Levu	**122**	17 30S	177 30 E
Vitim →	**74**	59 26N	112 34 E
Vitória, Brazil	**189**	20 20S	40 22W
Vitória, Spain	**50**	42 50N	2 41W
Vitória da Conquista	**189**	14 51S	40 51W
Vizianagaram	**92**	18 6N	83 30 E
Vlaardingen	**40**	51 55N	4 21 E
Vladimir	**68**	56 15N	40 30 E
Vladivostok	**75**	43 10N	131 53 E
Vlieland	**40**	53 16N	4 55 E
Vlissingen	**40**	51 26N	3 34 E
Vlóra	**52**	40 32N	19 28 E
Vltava →	**59**	50 21N	14 30 E
Vogelkop	**113**	1 25S	133 0 E
Vogels Berg, mt.	**42**	50 37N	9 30 E
Vohimena, Tanjon' i	**137**	25 36S	45 8 E
Voi	**133**	3 25S	38 32 E
Volendam	**40**	52 30N	5 4 E
Volga →	**68**	48 30N	46 0 E
Volga Hts. = Privolzhskaya Vozvyshennost	**17**	51 0N	46 0 E
Volgograd	**68**	48 40N	44 25 E
Vollenhove	**41**	52 40N	5 58 E
Vologda	**68**	59 10N	40 0 E
Vólos	**54**	39 24N	22 59 E
Volsk	**68**	52 5N	47 22 E
Volta →	**130**	5 46N	0 41 E
Volta, L.	**130**	7 30N	0 15 E
Volta Redonda	**188**	22 31S	44 5W
Voorburg	**40**	52 5N	4 24 E
Vopnafjörður	**64**	65 45N	14 40W
Voríai Sporádhes	**55**	39 15N	23 30 E
Voronezh	**68**	51 40N	39 10 E
Voroshilovgrad	**68**	48 38N	39 15 E
Vosges	**37**	48 20N	7 10 E
Vostochnyy Sayan	**74**	54 0N	96 0 E
Vrangelya, Ostrov	**73**	71 0N	180 0 E
Vranje	**53**	42 34N	21 54 E
Vratsa	**53**	43 13N	23 30 E
Vršac	**52**	45 8N	21 18 E
Vught	**40**	51 38N	5 20 E
Vulcan	**155**	50 25N	113 15W
Vyborg	**68**	60 43N	28 47 E
Vychegda →	**69**	61 18N	46 36 E
Vychodné Beskydy	**59**	49 30N	22 0 E
Wa	**130**	10 7N	2 25W
Waal →	**41**	51 59N	4 30 E
Waalwijk	**40**	51 42N	5 4 E
Wabash	**167**	40 48N	85 46W
Wabash →	**167**	37 46N	88 2W
Wąbrzeźno	**58**	53 16N	18 57 E
Waco	**168**	31 33N	97 5W
Wâd Medanî	**129**	14 28N	33 30 E
Waddenzee	**40**	53 6N	5 10 E
Waddington, Mt.	**154**	51 23N	125 15W
Waddinxveen	**40**	52 2N	4 40 E
Wadena	**152**	51 57N	103 47W
Wadi Halfa	**129**	21 53N	31 19 E
Wageningen	**41**	51 58N	5 40 E
Wager Bay	**146**	65 56N	90 49W
Wagga Wagga	**117**	35 7S	147 24 E
Wagin	**120**	33 17S	117 25 E
Waigeo	**113**	0 20S	130 40 E
Waihi	**122**	37 23S	175 52 E
Waikerie	**119**	34 9S	140 0 E
Waikokopu	**122**	39 3S	177 52 E
Waimate	**123**	44 45S	171 3 E
Wainwright, Canada	**152**	52 50N	110 50W

Wainwright, U.S.A.	**142**	70 39N	160 1W
Waipara	**123**	43 3S	172 46 E
Waipu	**122**	35 59S	174 29 E
Waipukurau	**122**	40 1S	176 33 E
Wairoa	**122**	39 3S	177 25 E
Waitara	**122**	38 59S	174 15 E
Wajima	**105**	37 30N	137 0 E
Wajir	**133**	1 42N	40 5 E
Wakasa-Wan	**106**	35 40N	135 30 E
Wakatipu, L.	**123**	45 5S	168 33 E
Wakayama	**106**	34 15N	135 15 E
Wakefield, N.Z.	**123**	41 24S	173 5 E
Wakefield, U.K.	**28**	53 41N	1 31W
Wakkanai	**103**	45 28N	141 35 E
Wałbrzych	**58**	50 45N	16 18 E
Walcha	**116**	30 55S	151 31 E
Walcheren	**40**	51 30N	3 35 E
Wales □	**26**	52 30N	3 30W
Walgett	**116**	30 0S	148 5 E
Walkerton	**151**	44 10N	81 10W
Walla Walla	**171**	46 3N	118 25W
Wallaceburg	**150**	42 34N	82 23W
Wallachia = Valahia	**57**	44 35N	25 0 E
Wallangarra	**116**	28 56S	151 58 E
Wallaroo	**119**	33 56S	137 39 E
Wallasey	**28**	53 26N	3 2W
Wallerawang	**117**	33 25S	150 4 E
Wallis & Futuna	**122**	13 18S	176 10W
Wallowa, Mts.	**171**	45 20N	117 30W
Wallsend, Australia	**117**	32 55S	151 40 E
Wallsend, U.K.	**28**	54 59N	1 30W
Walney, Isle of	**28**	54 5N	3 15W
Walpole	**120**	34 58S	116 44 E
Walsall	**24**	52 36N	1 59W
Walvis Bay	**136**	23 0S	14 28 E
Wana	**88**	32 20N	69 32 E
Wanaka L.	**123**	44 33S	169 7 E
Wang Saphung	**95**	17 18N	101 46 E
Wanganui	**122**	39 56S	175 3 E
Wangaratta	**117**	36 21S	146 19 E
Wanxian	**99**	30 42N	108 20 E
Warabi	**107**	35 49N	139 41 E
Warangal	**91**	17 58N	79 35 E
Warburton	**117**	37 47S	145 42 E
Wardha	**91**	20 45N	78 39 E
Wardha →	**91**	19 57N	79 11 E
Warialda	**116**	29 29S	150 33 E
Warley	**24**	52 30N	2 0W
Warner Mts.	**172**	41 30N	120 20W
Waroona	**120**	32 50S	115 58 E
Warracknabeal	**119**	36 9S	142 26 E
Warragul	**117**	38 10S	145 58 E
Warrego →	**116**	30 24S	145 21 E
Warrego Ra.	**121**	24 58S	146 0 E
Warren, Australia	**116**	31 42S	147 51 E
Warren, Ark., U.S.A.	**168**	33 35N	92 3W
Warren, Mich., U.S.A.	**167**	42 31N	83 2W
Warren, Ohio, U.S.A.	**164**	41 18N	80 52W
Warren, Pa., U.S.A.	**164**	41 52N	79 10W
Warrenpoint	**34**	54 7N	6 15W
Warrensburg	**166**	38 45N	93 45W
Warrington, U.K.	**28**	53 25N	2 38W
Warrington, U.S.A.	**169**	30 22N	87 16W
Warrnambool	**119**	38 25S	142 30 E
Warsaw = Warszawa	**58**	52 13N	21 0 E
Warszawa	**58**	52 13N	21 0 E
Warta →	**58**	52 35N	14 39 E
Warthe = Warta →	**58**	52 35N	14 39 E
Warwick, Australia	**116**	28 10S	152 1 E
Warwick, U.K.	**24**	52 17N	1 36W
Warwick, U.S.A.	**164**	41 43N	71 25W
Warwick □	**24**	52 20N	1 30W
Wasatch Ra.	**163**	40 30N	111 15W
Wasco	**173**	35 37N	119 16W
Wash, The	**29**	52 58N	0 20 E
Washim	**91**	20 3N	77 0 E
Washington, D.C., U.S.A.	**165**	38 52N	77 0W
Washington, Ind., U.S.A.	**167**	38 40N	87 8W
Washington, Mo., U.S.A.	**166**	38 35N	91 1W
Washington, Pa., U.S.A.	**164**	40 10N	80 20W
Washington □	**171**	47 45N	120 30W
Wassenaar	**40**	52 8N	4 24 E
Waterbury	**164**	41 32N	73 0W
Waterford	**35**	52 16N	7 8W
Waterford □	**35**	52 10N	7 40W
Waterloo, Canada	**151**	43 30N	80 32W
Waterloo, U.S.A.	**166**	42 27N	92 20W
Watertown, N.Y., U.S.A.	**151**	43 58N	75 57W
Watertown, Wis., U.S.A.	**167**	43 15N	88 45W
Waterville	**148**	44 35N	69 40W
Watling I. = San Salvador	**178**	24 0N	74 40W
Watrous	**152**	51 40N	105 25W
Watson Lake	**144**	60 6N	128 49W
Watsonville	**173**	36 55N	121 49W
Watubela, Kepulauan	**113**	4 28S	131 35 E
Wauchope	**116**	31 28S	152 45 E
Waukegan	**167**	42 22N	87 54W
Waukesha	**167**	43 0N	88 15W
Wausau	**166**	44 57N	89 40W
Wauwatosa	**167**	43 6N	87 59W
Waveney →	**25**	52 24N	1 20 E
Wâw	**129**	7 45N	28 1 E
Waxahachie	**168**	32 22N	96 53W
Waycross	**170**	31 12N	82 25W
Waynesboro, Pa., U.S.A.	**164**	39 46N	77 32W
Waynesboro, Va., U.S.A.	**165**	38 4N	78 57W
Waynesville	**165**	35 31N	83 0W
Wazirabad	**89**	32 30N	74 8 E
Weald, The	**25**	51 7N	0 9 E
Webo = Nyaake	**130**	4 52N	7 37W
Weddell Sea	**14**	72 30S	40 0W
Wedderburn	**117**	36 26S	143 33 E
Wee Waa	**116**	30 11S	149 26 E
Weert	**41**	51 15N	5 43 E
Weesp	**40**	52 18N	5 2 E
Weifang	**98**	36 47N	119 10 E
Weiser	**171**	44 10N	117 0W
Welbourn Hill	**118**	27 21S	134 6 E
Welch	**165**	37 29N	81 36W
Welland	**151**	43 0N	79 15W
Welland →	**29**	52 43N	0 10W
Wellingborough	**25**	52 18N	0 41W
Wellington, Australia	**116**	32 35S	148 59 E
Wellington, N.Z.	**123**	41 19S	174 46 E
Wellington, Salop, U.K.	**28**	52 42N	2 31W
Wellington, Somerset, U.K.	**27**	50 58N	3 13W
Wellington □	**123**	40 8S	175 36 E
Wellington, I.	**192**	49 30S	75 0W
Wells, Norfolk, U.K.	**29**	52 57N	0 51 E
Wells, Somerset, U.K.	**27**	51 12N	2 39W
Wells, U.S.A.	**172**	41 8N	115 0W
Wellsville, N.Y., U.S.A.	**164**	42 9N	77 53W
Wellsville, Ohio, U.S.A.	**164**	40 36N	80 40W
Welshpool	**26**	52 40N	3 9W
Wem	**28**	52 52N	2 45W
Wenatchee	**171**	47 30N	120 17W
Wenchow = Wenzhou	**99**	28 0N	120 38 E
Wensleydale	**28**	54 18N	2 0W
Wentworth	**119**	34 2S	141 54 E
Wenzhou	**99**	28 0N	120 38 E
Werribee	**117**	37 54S	144 40 E
Werris Creek	**116**	31 18S	150 38 E
Weser →	**42**	53 33N	8 30 E
West Bengal □	**92**	23 0N	88 0 E
West Bromwich	**24**	52 32N	2 1W
West Falkland	**192**	51 40S	60 0W
West Frankfort	**166**	37 56N	89 0W
West Germany ■	**42**	52 0N	9 0 E
West Glamorgan □	**27**	51 40N	3 55W
West Memphis	**169**	35 5N	90 11W
West Midlands □	**24**	52 30N	1 55W
West Palm Beach	**170**	26 44N	80 3W
West Schelde → = Westerschelde →	**40**	51 25N	3 25 E
West Siberian Plain	**76**	62 0N	75 0 E
West Sussex □	**25**	50 55N	0 30W
West Virginia □	**165**	39 0N	81 0W
West Yorkshire □	**28**	53 45N	1 40W
Western Australia □	**114**	25 0S	118 0 E
Western Ghats	**90**	14 0N	75 0 E
Western Isles □	**32**	57 30N	7 10W
Western Sahara ■	**126**	25 0N	13 0W

Western Samoa ■ **123** 14 0S 172 0W
Westerschelde → **40** 51 25N 3 25 E
Westerwald **42** 50 39N 8 0 E
Westfriesche Eilanden **40** 53 20N 5 10 E
Westland □ **123** 43 33S 169 59 E
Westland Bight **123** 42 55S 170 5 E
Westlock **155** 54 9N 113 55W
Westmeath □ **34** 53 30N 7 30W
Westminster **164** 39 34N 77 1W
Weston **165** 39 3N 80 29W
Weston-super-Mare **27** 51 20N 2 59W
Westport **123** 41 46S 171 37 E
Westray **33** 59 18N 3 0W
Wetar **113** 7 30S 126 30 E
Wetaskiwin **155** 52 55N 113 24W
Wewaka **168** 35 10N 96 35W
Wexford **35** 52 20N 6 28W
Wexford □ **35** 52 20N 6 25W
Weyburn **152** 49 40N 103 50W
Weymouth **27** 50 36N 2 28W
Whakatane **122** 37 57S 177 1 E
Whale Cove **145** 62 11N 92 36W
Whalsay **30** 60 22N 1 0W
Whangamomona **122** 39 8S 174 44 E
Whangarei **122** 35 43S 174 21 E
Wharfe → **29** 53 55N 1 30W
Wheeler Pk. **172** 38 57N 114 15W
Wheeling **164** 40 2N 80 41W
Whernside **28** 54 14N 2 24W
Whitby **29** 54 29N 0 37W
Whitchurch **28** 52 58N 2 42W
White →, Ark., U.S.A. **168** 33 53N 91 3W
White →, Ind., U.S.A. **167** 38 25N 87 45W
White →, S. Dak., U.S.A. **163** 43 45N 99 30W
White Cliffs **118** 30 50S 143 10 E
White Mts. **157** 44 15N 71 15W
White Nile = Nîl el Abyad → **129** 15 38N 32 31 E
White Russia = Byelorussian S.S.R. □ **68** 53 30N 27 0 E
White Sea = Beloye More **69** 66 30N 38 0 E
Whitecliffs **123** 43 26S 171 55 E
Whitehaven **28** 54 33N 3 35W
Whitehorse **144** 60 43N 135 3W
Whitney, Mt. **173** 36 35N 118 14W
Whitstable **25** 51 21N 1 2 E
Whitsunday I. **121** 20 15S 149 4 E
Whittier **142** 60 46N 148 48W
Whyalla **118** 33 2S 137 30 E
Wichita **158** 37 40N 97 20W
Wichita Falls **161** 33 57N 98 30W
Wick **33** 58 26N 3 5W
Wickepin **120** 32 50S 117 30 E
Wicklow **35** 53 0N 6 2W
Wicklow □ **35** 52 59N 6 25W
Wicklow Mts. **35** 53 0N 6 30W
Widnes **28** 53 22N 2 44W
Wieluń **58** 51 15N 18 34 E
Wien **45** 48 12N 16 22 E
Wiesbaden **42** 50 7N 8 17 E
Wigan **28** 53 33N 2 38W
Wight, I. of **25** 50 40N 1 20W
Wigtown **31** 54 52N 4 27W
Wigtown B. **31** 54 46N 4 15W
Wilcannia **118** 31 30S 143 26 E
Wildwood **164** 38 59N 74 46W
Wilhelmshaven **42** 53 30N 8 9 E
Wilkes Barre **164** 41 15N 75 52W
Wilkes Sub-Glacial Basin **15** 75 0S 130 0 E
Wilkie **152** 52 27N 108 42W
Willamina **171** 45 9N 123 32W
Willemstad **181** 12 5N 69 0W
Williams L. **154** 51 48N 90 45W
Williamsburg **165** 37 17N 76 44W
Williamson **165** 37 46N 82 17W
Williamsport **164** 41 18N 77 1W
Williamstown **117** 37 51S 144 52 E
Williston **163** 48 10N 103 35W
Willits **172** 39 28N 123 17W
Willmar **156** 45 5N 95 0W
Wilmette **167** 42 6N 87 44W
Wilmington, Del., U.S.A. **164** 39 45N 75 32W
Wilmington, N.C., U.S.A. **165** 34 14N 77 54W
Wilson **165** 35 44N 77 54W
Wilsons Promontory **117** 38 55S 146 25 E
Wilton **24** 51 5N 1 52W
Wiltshire □ **24** 51 20N 2 0W
Wiluna **120** 26 36S 120 14 E
Wimereux **38** 50 45N 1 37 E
Winchester, U.K. **25** 51 4N 1 19W
Winchester, Ind., U.S.A. **167** 40 10N 84 56W
Winchester, Ky., U.S.A. **165** 38 0N 84 8W
Winchester, Va., U.S.A. **164** 39 14N 78 8W
Wind River Range **163** 43 0N 109 30W
Windermere **28** 54 24N 2 56W
Windermere, L. **28** 54 20N 2 57W
Windhoek **136** 22 35S 17 4 E
Windsor, Australia **117** 33 37S 150 50 E
Windsor, Nfld., Canada **149** 48 57N 55 40W
Windsor, Ont., Canada **150** 42 18N 83 0W
Windsor, U.K. **25** 51 28N 0 36W
Windward Is. **181** 13 0N 63 0W
Windward Passage = Vientos, Paso de los **180** 20 0N 74 0W
Winisk → **140** 55 17N 85 5W
Winkler **153** 49 10N 97 56W
Winnemucca **172** 41 0N 117 45W
Winnfield **168** 31 57N 92 38W
Winnipeg **153** 49 54N 97 9W
Winnipeg, L. **153** 52 0N 97 0W
Winnipegosis L. **153** 52 30N 100 0W
Winona **166** 44 2N 91 39W
Winooski **151** 44 31N 73 11W
Winschoten **41** 53 9N 7 3 E
Winslow **161** 35 2N 110 41W
Winston-Salem **165** 36 7N 80 15W
Winter Haven **170** 28 0N 81 42W
Winter Park **170** 28 34N 81 19W
Winterswijk **41** 51 58N 6 43 E
Winterthur **44** 47 30N 8 44 E
Wirral **28** 53 25N 3 0W
Wisbech **29** 52 39N 0 10 E
Wisconsin □ **166** 44 30N 90 0W
Wisconsin → **166** 43 0N 91 15W
Wisconsin Rapids **166** 44 25N 89 50W
Wishaw **31** 55 46N 3 55W
Wisła → **58** 54 22N 18 55 E
Witham → **29** 53 3N 0 8W
Withernsea **29** 53 43N 0 2 E
Witney **24** 51 47N 1 29W
Włocławek **58** 52 40N 19 3 E
Wodonga **117** 36 5S 146 50 E
Wokam **113** 5 45S 134 28 E
Woking **25** 51 18N 0 33W
Wolin **58** 53 50N 14 37 E
Wollaston L. **145** 58 7N 103 10W
Wollaston Pen. **145** 69 30N 115 0W
Wollongong **117** 34 25S 150 54 E
Wolverhampton **24** 52 35N 2 6W
Wondai **116** 26 20S 151 49 E
Wŏnsan **98** 39 11N 127 27 E
Wonthaggi **117** 38 37S 145 37 E
Woodburn **116** 29 6S 153 23 E
Woodenbong **116** 28 24S 152 39 E
Woodend **117** 37 20S 144 33 E
Woodland **172** 38 40N 121 50W
Woods, L. of the **153** 49 15N 94 45W
Woodstock, N.B., Canada **148** 46 11N 67 37W
Woodstock, Ont., Canada **151** 43 10N 80 45W
Woolgoolga **116** 30 6S 153 11 E
Woomera **118** 31 30S 137 10 E
Woonsocket **164** 42 0N 71 30W
Wooroloo **120** 31 48S 116 18 E
Worcester, U.K. **24** 52 12N 2 12W
Worcester, U.S.A. **164** 42 14N 71 49W
Workington **28** 54 39N 3 34W
Worksop **29** 53 19N 1 9W
Wormerveer **40** 52 30N 4 46 E
Worms **42** 49 37N 8 21 E
Worthing **25** 50 49N 0 21W
Worthington **166** 43 35N 95 36W
Wou-han = Wuhan **99** 30 31N 114 18 E

Woy Woy 117 33 30S 151 19 E
Wrangel I. 138 71 0N 180 0 E
Wrangell 143 56 30N 132 25W
Wrangell Mts. 142 61 40N 143 30W
Wrath, C. 32 58 38N 5 0W
Wrekin, The 28 52 41N 2 35W
Wrexham 26 53 5N 3 0W
Wrigley 144 63 16N 123 37W
Wrocław 58 51 5N 17 5 E
Września 58 52 21N 17 36 E
Wu Jiang → 99 29 40N 107 20 E
Wubin 120 30 6S 116 37 E
Wuhan 99 30 31N 114 18 E
Wuhsi = Wuxi 99 31 33N 120 18 E
Wuhu 99 31 22N 118 21 E
Wulumuchi = Ürümqi 100 43 45N 87 45 E
Wuppertal 42 51 15N 7 8 E
Würzburg 42 49 46N 9 55 E
Wutongqiao 99 29 22N 103 50 E
Wuxi 99 31 33N 120 18 E
Wuzhong 98 38 2N 106 12 E
Wuzhou 99 23 30N 111 18 E
Wyalkatchem 120 31 8S 117 22 E
Wyandotte 167 42 14N 83 13W
Wycheproof 119 36 0S 143 17 E
Wye → 27 51 36N 2 40W
Wyndham 114 15 33S 128 3 E
Wynnum 116 27 27S 153 9 E
Wynyard 152 51 45N 104 10W
Wyoming □ 163 42 48N 109 0W
Wytheville 165 37 0N 81 3W

Xánthi 55 41 10N 24 58 E
Xapuri 187 10 35S 68 35W
Xenia 167 39 42N 83 57W
Xiamen 99 24 25N 118 4 E
Xi'an 99 34 15N 109 0 E
Xiangfan 99 32 2N 112 8 E
Xiangtan 99 27 51N 112 54 E
Xiao Hinggan Ling 98 49 0N 127 0 E
Xigazê 101 29 5N 88 45 E
Xingtai 98 37 3N 114 32 E
Xingu → 188 1 30S 51 53W
Xining 98 36 34N 101 40 E
Xinjiang Uygur Zizhiqu □ 100 42 0N 86 0 E
Xinxiang 99 35 18N 113 50 E
Xinyang 99 32 6N 114 3 E
Xinzhu 99 24 49N 120 57 E
Xique-Xique 188 10 50S 42 40W
Xizang □ 101 32 0N 88 0 E
Xuanhua 98 40 40N 115 2 E
Xuchang 99 34 2N 113 48 E
Xuzhou 99 34 18N 117 10 E

Ya'an 99 29 58N 103 5 E
Yablonovy Khrebet 74 53 0N 114 0 E
Yablonovy Ra. = Yablonovy Khrebet 74 53 0N 114 0 E
Yacuiba 187 22 0S 63 43W
Yaizu 107 34 52N 138 20 E
Yakima 171 46 42N 120 30W
Yaku-Jima 104 30 20N 130 30 E
Yakut A.S.S.R. □ 72 62 0N 130 0 E
Yakutat 143 59 29N 139 44W
Yakutsk 75 62 5N 129 50 E
Yalgoo 120 28 16S 116 39 E
Yalinga 129 6 33N 23 10 E
Yamaga 108 33 1N 130 41 E
Yamagata 103 38 15N 140 15 E
Yamaguchi 108 34 10N 131 32 E
Yamal, Poluostrov 69 71 0N 70 0 E
Yamato 107 35 27N 139 25 E
Yamatotakada 106 34 31N 135 45 E
Yamazaki 109 35 0N 134 32 E
Yamba 116 29 26S 153 23 E
Yambol 53 42 30N 26 36 E
Yamdena 113 7 45S 131 20 E
Yame 108 33 13N 130 35 E
Yamma-Yamma, L. 118 26 16S 141 20 E
Yampa → 163 40 37N 108 59W
Yamuna → 92 25 30N 81 53 E
Yamzho Yumco 101 28 48N 90 35 E
Yana → 72 71 30N 136 0 E
Yanagawa 108 33 10N 130 24 E
Yanai 109 33 58N 132 7 E
Yanco 117 34 38S 146 27 E
Yangch'ü = Taiyuan 98 37 52N 112 33 E
Yangquan 98 37 58N 113 31 E
Yangtze Kiang = Chang Jiang → 99 31 48N 121 10 E
Yanji 98 42 59N 129 30 E
Yantai 98 37 34N 121 22 E
Yao 106 34 32N 135 36 E
Yaoundé 131 3 50N 11 35 E
Yaqui → 174 27 37N 110 39W
Yare → 25 52 36N 1 28 E
Yarensk 69 61 10N 49 8 E
Yarkand = Shache 100 38 20N 77 10 E
Yarmouth 148 43 50N 66 7W
Yaroslavl 68 57 35N 39 55 E
Yarram 117 38 29S 146 9 E
Yashiro-Jima 109 33 55N 132 15 E
Yass 117 34 49S 148 54 E
Yasugi 109 35 26N 133 15 E
Yatsushiro 108 32 30N 130 40 E
Yavari → 186 4 21S 70 2W
Yavatmal 91 20 20N 78 15 E
Yawatahama 109 33 27N 132 24 E
Yazd 85 31 55N 54 27 E
Yazoo → 169 32 35N 90 50W
Yazoo City 169 32 48N 90 28W
Ye Xian 98 37 8N 119 57 E
Yegros 191 26 20S 56 25W
Yell 30 60 35N 1 5W
Yellow Sea 99 35 0N 123 0 E
Yellowhead P. 155 52 53N 118 25W
Yellowknife 145 62 27N 114 29W
Yellowstone → 163 47 58N 103 59W
Yellowstone National Park 163 44 35N 110 0W
Yemen ■ 82 15 0N 44 0 E
Yenisey → 69 71 50N 82 40 E
Yeniseyskiy Zaliv 69 72 20N 81 0 E
Yeo → 27 51 10N 3 0W
Yeola 91 20 0N 74 30 E
Yeovil 27 50 57N 2 38W
Yeppoon 121 23 5S 150 47 E
Yerevan 70 40 10N 44 31 E
Yes Tor 27 50 41N 3 59W
Yetman 116 28 56S 150 48 E
Yezd = Yazd 85 31 55N 54 27 E
Yiannitsa 54 40 46N 22 24 E
Yibin 99 28 45N 104 32 E
Yichang 99 30 40N 111 20 E
Yichun 98 47 44N 128 52 E
Yilan 99 24 51N 121 44 E
Yinchuan 98 38 30N 106 15 E
Yingkou 98 40 37N 122 18 E
Yingtan 99 28 12N 117 0 E
Yining 100 43 58N 81 10 E
Yíthion 54 36 46N 22 34 E
Yiyang 99 28 45N 112 16 E
Yogyakarta 111 7 49S 110 22 E
Yōkaichiba 107 35 42N 140 33 E
Yokkaichi 106 35 0N 136 38 E
Yokohama 107 35 27N 139 28 E
Yokosuka 107 35 20N 139 40 E
Yokote 103 39 20N 140 30 E
Yonago 109 35 25N 133 19 E
Yoneshiro → 103 40 15N 140 15 E
Yonezawa 103 37 57N 140 4 E
Yongji 99 34 52N 110 28 E
Yonkers 164 40 57N 73 51W
York, Australia 120 31 52S 116 47 E
York, U.K. 29 53 58N 1 7W
York, U.S.A. 164 39 57N 76 43W
Yorke Pen. 119 34 50S 137 40 E
Yorkshire Wolds 29 54 0N 0 30W
Yorkton 152 51 11N 102 28W

Yosemite National Park **172** 38 0N 119 30W
Youghal **35** 51 58N 7 51W
Young **117** 34 19S 148 18 E
Younghusband Pen. **119** 36 0S 139 25 E
Youngstown **164** 41 7N 80 41W
Yuba City **172** 39 12N 121 37W
Yūbari **103** 43 4N 141 59 E
Yūbetsu **103** 43 13N 144 5 E
Yucatán □ **177** 20 50N 89 0W
Yucatán, Canal de **178** 22 0N 86 30W
Yucatan Str. = Yucatán, Canal de **178** 22 0N 86 30W
Yuci **98** 37 42N 112 46 E
Yugoslavia ■ **52** 44 0N 20 0 E
Yukon → **142** 65 30N 150 0W
Yukon Territory □ **144** 63 0N 135 0W
Yuma **173** 32 45N 114 37W
Yunnan □ **101** 25 0N 102 30 E
Yuribei **69** 71 8N 76 58 E
Yurimaguas **186** 5 55S 76 7W
Yushu **101** 33 5N 96 55 E
Yuzhno-Sakhalinsk **75** 46 58N 142 45 E
Yvetot **38** 49 37N 0 44 E

Zaandam **40** 52 26N 4 49 E
Zabaykalskiy **74** 49 40N 117 25 E
Zabid **82** 14 0N 43 10 E
Zābol **85** 31 0N 61 32 E
Zābol □ **87** 32 0N 67 0 E
Zabrze **58** 50 18N 18 50 E
Zacapa **177** 14 59N 89 31W
Zacatecas **175** 22 47N 102 35W
Zacatecas □ **175** 23 0N 103 0W
Zacatecoluca **177** 13 29N 88 51W
Zadar **52** 44 8N 15 14 E
Zadetkyi Kyun **94** 10 0N 98 25 E
Zagreb **52** 45 50N 16 0 E
Zāhedān **86** 29 30N 60 50 E
Zahlah **80** 33 52N 35 50 E
Zaïre ■ **134** 3 0S 23 0 E
Zaïre → **134** 6 4S 12 24 E
Zákinthos **54** 37 47N 20 57 E
Zambeze → **135** 18 55S 36 4 E
Zambezi = Zambeze → **135** 18 55S 36 4 E
Zambia ■ **135** 15 0S 28 0 E
Zamboanga **112** 6 59N 122 3 E
Zamora, Mexico **175** 20 0N 102 21W
Zamora, Spain **50** 41 30N 5 45W
Zandvoort **40** 52 22N 4 32 E
Zanesville **167** 39 56N 82 2W
Zanjan **81** 36 40N 48 35 E
Zante = Zákinthos **54** 37 47N 20 57 E
Zanzibar **135** 6 12S 39 12 E
Zaouiet El-Kala = Bordj Omar Driss **127** 28 10N 6 40 E
Zaouiet Reggane **127** 26 32N 0 3 E
Zapadnaya Dvina → **68** 57 4N 24 3 E
Západné Beskydy **59** 49 30N 19 0 E
Zapala **190** 39 0S 70 5W
Zaporozhye **68** 47 50N 35 10 E
Zaragoza, Mexico **174** 28 29N 100 55W
Zaragoza, Spain **51** 41 39N 0 53W
Zaranj **87** 30 55N 61 55 E
Zaria **131** 11 0N 7 40 E
Zaruma **184** 3 40S 79 38W
Zaskar Mountains **89** 33 15N 77 30 E
Zavitinsk **75** 50 10N 129 20 E
Zaysan, Oz. **71** 48 0N 83 0 E
Zayü **101** 28 48N 97 27 E
Zduńska Wola **58** 51 37N 18 59 E
Zeebrugge **42** 51 19N 3 12 E
Zeeland □ **40** 51 30N 3 50 E
Zeila **133** 11 21N 43 30 E
Zeist **40** 52 5N 5 15 E
Zemlya Frantsa Iosifa **13** 81 0N 55 0 E
Zentsūji **109** 34 14N 133 47 E
Zeya **75** 53 48N 127 14 E
Zêzere → **50** 39 28N 8 20W
Zhanghua **99** 24 6N 120 29 E
Zhangjiakou **98** 40 48N 114 55 E
Zhangzhou **99** 24 30N 117 35 E
Zhanjiang **99** 21 15N 110 20 E
Zhdanov **68** 47 5N 37 31 E
Zhejiang □ **99** 29 0N 120 0 E
Zhengzhou **99** 34 45N 113 34 E
Zhenjiang **99** 32 11N 119 26 E
Zhenyuan **99** 27 4N 108 21 E
Zhijiang **99** 27 27N 109 42 E
Zhitomir **68** 50 20N 28 40 E
Zhumadian **99** 32 59N 114 2 E
Zhupanovo **73** 53 40N 159 52 E
Zhuzhou **99** 27 49N 113 12 E
Zibo **98** 36 47N 118 3 E
Zielona Góra **58** 51 57N 15 31 E
Zierikzee **40** 51 40N 3 55 E
Zigong **99** 29 15N 104 48 E
Zile **80** 40 15N 35 52 E
Žilina **59** 49 12N 18 42 E
Zimbabwe **137** 20 16S 30 54 E
Zimbabwe ■ **137** 20 0S 30 0 E
Zinder **131** 13 48N 9 0 E
Zipaquirá **184** 5 0N 74 0W
Zitácuaro **175** 19 24N 100 22W
Zlatograd **53** 41 22N 25 7 E
Zlatoust **69** 55 10N 59 40 E
Zlin = Gottwaldov **59** 49 14N 17 40 E
Zomba **137** 15 22S 35 19 E
Zonguldak **80** 41 28N 31 50 E
Zorritos **186** 3 43S 80 40W
Zoutkamp **41** 53 20N 6 18 E
Zrenjanin **52** 45 22N 20 23 E
Zufar **83** 17 40N 54 0 E
Zug **44** 47 10N 8 31 E
Zuid-Holland □ **40** 52 0N 4 35 E
Zuidhorn **41** 53 15N 6 23 E
Zungeru **131** 9 48N 6 8 E
Zunyi **99** 27 42N 106 53 E
Zürich **44** 47 22N 8 32 E
Zutphen **41** 52 9N 6 12 E
Zuwārah **127** 32 58N 12 1 E
Zvolen **59** 48 33N 19 10 E
Zwickau **43** 50 43N 12 30 E
Zwolle **41** 52 31N 6 6 E
Zyryanovsk **71** 49 43N 84 20 E